S0-BIU-653

3DS MAX 4 MAGIC

By Sean Bonney

With contributions from Laurent M. Abecassis, Sue Blackman, Peter Draper, Richard Katz, Randy M. Kreitzman, Daniel Manahan, Michael Reiser, and Marcus Richardson

201 West 103rd Street, Indianapolis, Indiana 46290

3ds max 4 Magic

Copyright © 2001 by New Riders Publishing

All rights reserved. No part of this book shall be reproduced, stored in a retrieval system, or transmitted by any means—electronic, mechanical, photocopying, recording, or otherwise—without written permission from the publisher. No patent liability is assumed with respect to the use of the information contained herein. Although every precaution has been taken in the preparation of this book, the publisher and author(s) assume no responsibility for errors or omissions. Neither is any liability assumed for damages resulting from the use of the information contained herein.

International Standard Book Number: 0-7357-1093-7

Library of Congress Catalog Card Number: 00-111146

Printed in the United States of America

First Printing: May 2001

05 04 03 02 01 7 6 5 4 3 2 1

Interpretation of the printing code: The rightmost double-digit number is the year of the book's printing; the rightmost single-digit number is the number of the book's printing. For example, the printing code 01-1 shows that the first printing of the book occurred in 2001.

Trademarks

All terms mentioned in this book that are known to be trademarks or service marks have been appropriately capitalized. New Riders Publishing cannot attest to the accuracy of this information. Use of a term in this book should not be regarded as affecting the validity of any trademark or service mark.

Warning and Disclaimer

Every effort has been made to make this book as complete and as accurate as possible, but no warranty of fitness is implied. The information provided is on an "as is" basis. The authors and the publisher shall have neither liability nor responsibility to any person or entity with respect to any loss or damages arising from the information contained in this book or from the use of the CD or programs accompanying it.

Publisher
David Dwyer

Associate Publisher
Al Valvano

Executive Editor
Steve Weiss

Product Marketing Manager
Kathy Malmloff

Managing Editor
Sarah Kearns

Acquisitions Editors
Linda Anne Bump
Theresa Gheen

Development Editor
Katherine Pendergast

Project Editor
Jake McFarland

Copy Editors
Amy Lepore
Audra McFarland

Technical Editors
Sean Bonney
Richard Lapidus
Eric Schuck
Jeff Solenberg

Cover Designer and Project Opener Images
Aren Howell

Interior Designer
Steve Gifford

Compositor
Wil Cruz

Proofreader
Debra Neel

Indexer
Lisa Stumpf

Software Development Specialists
Jay Payne
Jason Haines

Contents at a Glance

About the Authors

Sean Bonney is a 3D animator, fine artist, and game designer who lives in historic Fredericksburg, Virginia. Sean graduated from Virginia Commonwealth University in Richmond, Virginia, in 1991 with a BFA in illustration and design. He has been employed as Graphic Designer for the Central Rappahannock Regional Library system for nine years. He has worked for Rainbow Studios in Phoenix, Arizona, on a variety of game and broadcast projects. Sean has written for two previous New Riders books, *3D Studio MAX 3 Magic* and *3D Studio MAX 3 Professional Animation*. Sean is currently the principal of Anvil Studio and specializes in freelance animation and game design. For more information about Sean Bonney or Anvil Studio, visit the Web site at **www.anvil-studio.com** or email **sbonney@anvil-studio.com**.

Laurent M. Abecassis comes from a traditional animation background and has worked with 3ds max since the release of 3D Studio R3 for DOS. His projects have included character projects for video games, TV series, special effects, motion capture performances, and other outlets. Prompted by his desire to spend more energy on enhancing his expertise in 3ds max, Laurent left his position as the research and development lead for KliK Animation in 1999 to pursue freelance opportunities. He has since found numerous ways to share his knowledge with the 3D community. Laurent is now a discreet Training Specialist based in Montreal, Canada. He teaches all class levels of 3ds max, character studio, mental ray, combustion, and Lightscape, as well as how to incorporate plug-ins from various developers. All his courses are devoted to bringing 3D characters to life. Laurent is also president/product manager of Di-O-Matic, a company that produces plug-ins and training CDs for 3ds max. For more information, visit **www.di-o-matic.com**.

Sue Blackman is a freelance artist from Temecula, California, who in the early 1990s was delighted to find a common use for all her interests as a 3D artist. Horse training, exhibiting and judging, fine furniture design and creation, landscaping and horticulture, house construction, and of course, several of the more traditional fine art media have come together to provide a solid base for the 3D environments and animation she produces for Radish Works, a Southern California game developer. She also finds time to teach 3ds max at two Southland community colleges and is in the process of finishing a long-forgotten degree at UC Riverside. She admits to being a "max junkie" and a compulsive tutorial writer, and she has always been fascinated by widgets and all things mechanical. If she can ever find enough time to create her Web page, it will be found at **www.3dxxzone.com**. That is, XX as in the female chromosome, not X-rated (sorry guys)!

Pete Draper had a passion for 3D from an early age. Pete originally started out as a fine artist and graphic designer before and during university, where he studied for an Engineering IT degree. After discovering 3D Studio MAX 3 in one of the uni's CAD labs, he decided to channel his love for art into this new medium. Now a die-hard max nut, he spends his days as Head of Media for Orchard Creative Design Group, based in the southwest of England, and he moonlights by night as an artist and tutorial and Q&A writer for *3D World* magazine. If you've got nothing else better to do, his Web page can be viewed at **www.xenomorphic.co.uk**.

Richard Katz is an artist and animator living in the San Francisco Bay area. Originally from New Jersey, he received his BFA from Trenton State College before heading west to make games. He is currently the Lead Artist on the Playstation 2 title *Warriors of Might and Magic* at the 3DO company. He has been working in the games industry for four years and has been using 3ds max on a daily basis on several titles for 3DO and Sierra On-Line. He can be contacted by email at **katz@katz3d.com** or through his Web site **www.katz3d.com**.

Randy M. Kreitzman is a senior Quality Engineer at discreet (a division of Autodesk, Inc.), working exclusively with 3ds max. His career in computer graphics began in 1991, producing fully animated shorts for a Southern California cable affiliate using Autodesk Animator and 3D Studio R1 for DOS. In 1994, he relocated to Northern California in search of high-end 3D-production work. He joined FTI Communications (San Francisco) in 1995 to create 3D forensic animation for a variety of corporate clients including AT&T, Boeing, Chyron, Chevron, and DSC, using Alias/Wavefront software. In 1996, he joined Autodesk, Inc.'s Multimedia Division as a Quality Analyst to test 3D Studio MAX in real-world production scenarios. Randy now resides in Central California with his lovely wife, Kimberlie, four sled dogs, and three horses. He wishes to thank Kimberlie and the critters for their never-ending love and support. He can be reached via email at **randy.kreitzman@autodesk.com**.

Daniel Manahan is more than just an artist, musician, singer, dancer, chess and Go expert, swimmer, water polo goalie, wrestler, husband, and father. He is a passionate teacher who is on a mission to make life simpler for eager learners. He currently teaches max at five colleges in Southern California and has helped develop curriculum for 12 schools in the last four years. When not busy helping develop artists for employment, he is in his studio performing animations for film, forensics, and commercial visualization. For information on his Southern California beginning and advanced classes, contact **3DMan@Charter.net**.

Michael Reiser, MD is currently a radiology resident in Pittsburgh, Pennsylvania. He began working with 3D graphics five years ago and has been addicted ever since. He has written multiple magazine articles and numerous online tutorials. Michael enjoys 3D medical illustration and its applications in radiology. However, his real love lies in creature development. "I am playing doctor until someone wants to hire me to model dinosaurs all day." Contact Michael at **MikeReiser@aol.com**.

Marcus Richardson has always been a fine artist at heart. He started his CG pilgrimage back in 1994 when he created his first 3D world in Rend 386. Since then, he has endeavored to pursue a serious career in 3D graphics and film by forming IonAmation Studios. A graduate from the Art Institute of Colorado, Marcus has produced numerous professional animations for many clients, including Qwest Communications. Currently he is settled in Aspen, Colorado, where he is living out his dream of living in the mountains and creating television and film animations for Versatile Productions, Inc. For more information on IonAmation Studios, please visit **www.ionamation.com**. For Versatile Productions, Inc., visit **www.versatileproductions.com** or email **crazymoose@ionamation.com**.

Dedication

*To my father, Richard Scott Bonney, who wouldn't have understood this technical stuff but would have proudly told every coffee shop clerk in the Boulder area about his son, the author/artist.—**Sean Bonney***

*To my Nanna, Marie Fletcher; hope you got the card! —**Pete Draper***

*To my loving wife, Lourdes, whose patience gives me the sincerity to conquer life's challenges. —**Daniel Manahan***

*To Asher, Lauren, and Emma. They helped me see the world as a child again! —**Marcus Richardson***

Acknowledgments

Thanks go to Earl Simpson and Chad Carter for researching appropriate quotes. I would also like to thank my editors at New Riders, particularly Linda Bump, for their patience and encouragement throughout the development of this book. And, most importantly, my wife of 10 years, Sydney, for her love and support, without which I would never have completed this work. —**Sean Bonney**

Thanks to Ben and Garrick at Future Publishing for giving me a shot in the first place; my family, whom I think about although we're so far away; Carol, Mark, and Jenny Baker for putting up with us; and to Marlon—cheers for the help, mate! Finally, to my better half, Laura, for putting up with me when I'm spending way too much of our quality time on this blasted computer! —**Pete Draper**

My "Underwater Scene" tutorial was carefully developed from the years I spent answering questions from my artists. Thanks to those who fought, struggled, and had the courage to ask "Why?" In your quests to becoming great 3D artists, you've taught me how a new learner perceives this complicated interface. —**Daniel Manahan**

I'd like to thank my parents for their unfailing support and belief in me; my teacher and mentor Todd Debreceni, who helped me see the world in a different way; Charles Sutherland, who brought me back to reality; and Mike Canu of TTCE Online, who constantly pushed me to do better. —**Marcus Richardson**

A Message from New Riders

As the reader of this book, you are our most important critic and commentator. We value your opinion and want to know what we're doing right, what we could do better, in what areas you'd like to see us publish, and any other words of wisdom you're willing to pass our way.

As Executive Editor at New Riders, I welcome your comments. You can fax, email, or write me directly to let me know what you did or didn't like about this book—as well as what we can do to make our books better. When you write, please be sure to include this book's title, ISBN, and author, as well as your name and phone or fax number. I will carefully review your comments and share them with the authors and editors who worked on the book.

Please note that I cannot help you with technical problems related to the topic of this book, and that due to the high volume of email I receive, I might not be able to reply to every message. Thanks.

Email: steve.weiss@newriders.com

Mail: Steve Weiss
Executive Editor
New Riders Publishing
201 West 103rd Street
Indianapolis, IN 46290 USA

Visit Our Web Site: www.newriders.com

On our Web site, you'll find information about our other books, the authors we partner with, book updates and file downloads, promotions, discussion boards for online interaction with other users and with technology experts, and a calendar of trade shows and other professional events with which we'll be involved. We hope to see you around.

Email Us from Our Web Site

Go to www.newriders.com and click on the Contact link if you

- Have comments or questions about this book.
- Want to report errors that you have found in this book.
- Have a book proposal or are interested in writing for New Riders.
- Would like us to send you one of our author kits.
- Are an expert in a computer topic or technology and are interested in being a reviewer or technical editor.
- Want to find a distributor for our titles in your area.
- Are an educator/instructor who wants to preview New Riders books for classroom use. In the body/comments area, include your name, school, department, address, phone number, office days/hours, text currently in use, and enrollment in your department, along with your request for either desk/examination copies or additional information.

Call Us or Fax Us

You can reach us toll-free at 1-800-571-5840 + 9 + 3567 (ask for New Riders). If outside the U.S., please call 1-317-581-3500 and ask for New Riders. If you prefer, you can fax us at 1-317-581-4663, Attention: New Riders.

Technical Support for This Book Although we encourage entry-level users to get as much as they can out of our books, keep in mind that our books are written assuming a non-beginner level of user-knowledge of the technology. This assumption is reflected in the brevity and shorthand nature of some of the tutorials.

New Riders will continually work to create clearly written, thoroughly tested and reviewed technology books of the highest educational caliber and creative design. We value our customers more than anything—that's why we're in this business—but we cannot guarantee to each of the thousands of you who buy and use our books that we will be able to work individually with you through tutorials or content with which you may have questions. We urge readers who need help in working through exercises or other material in our books—and who need this assistance immediately—to use as many of the resources that our technology and technical communities can provide, especially the many online user groups and list servers available.

INTRODUCTION

3ds max is a powerful force in modern computer graphics. Since the early '90s, max has grown more popular and more powerful, and it is now a full-featured graphics medium with virtually limitless possibilities. *3ds max 4 Magic* helps you explore some of these possibilities.

WHO WE ARE

The authors of this book are among the top 3D artists in the industry today. Some work as special effects artists, producing effects used in major Hollywood feature films. Others apply their skills to create effects for regular television and commercials. Still others make their living helping create many of the most popular video games sold today.

None of the authors who contributed to this book makes a living solely as a writer—and that's a good thing. Although these folks do write and contribute to many of the top-selling books and magazines on 3ds max and CG in general, their focus and their time is spent on their art. This book does not rehash the product manual or feature sets; it's a source of great inspiration and technical savvy brought to you by the people who actually live in and are connected to the CG industry.

WHO YOU ARE

This book is intended for intermediate to advanced users of 3ds max 4. We have striven to provide you all the instruction you will need to work through a project to achieve a spectacular effect, without spoon-feeding you every detail of every step. Every effort has been made to strike a balance between clarity and functionality.

We assume you are familiar with the fundamentals of 3ds max 4. We assume you either have or have access to 3ds max 4, that you've read the documentation that comes with the program, and that you've worked through the tutorials. In other words, we assume you have a basic understanding of how to use features like the Modify Command panel, the Material Editor, space warps, NURBS, particle systems, Video Post, and so on. This doesn't mean that a beginner can't use this book. On the contrary, if you're the type of person who likes to learn by diving in head first, this book will accelerate your understanding of 3ds max 4 and quickly bring you up to speed.

What's in This Book

Every chapter in *3ds max 4 Magic* is a step-by-step project explaining how to create eye-popping effects ranging from planet-shattering explosions using particles and advanced materials to a heaving, stormy sea using displacement, environmental effects, and particle clouds. These effects are achieved by exploiting the powerful tools that ship with max. In this book, you will find invaluable tips and tricks to get the most out of max.

The Companion CD

Included on the CD that comes with this book you will find all the necessary files and textures you need to complete the exercises in each chapter. In addition to the starting max files necessary for each tutorial, you'll find a finished version of each effect with which you can compare your results. You will also find the plug-ins necessary to complete some of the chapters. Most of the projects in this book are intended to finish in a rendered animation, in which case you will find an AVI animation in the project folder. With the AVI file, you can either preview the final results or view the completed project (in case you don't want to render the animation yourself). You'll also find five bonus projects to help you continue learning and improving even after you've finished this book. Be sure to check out the appendix, "What's on the CD-ROM" at the back of this book for more information.

Our Assumptions as We Wrote the Book

We had five assumptions when we wrote this book. These assumptions are based on our collective experience in learning and working with software.

- You don't have time to spend forever learning one effect.

  Don't you hate working through a tutorial that seems to go on and on forever? The steps in these chapters have been designed to help you quickly achieve the final effect without unnecessary fluff. You won't find any pointless humor or rambling. Each chapter begins with a short paragraph explaining what you will be doing, as well as a brief summary of the steps you will take to achieve the effect.

- You don't want to sit down and read the book from start to finish.

  This book wasn't intended to be read in a linear fashion. Each chapter is unique unto itself. Everything you will need for any chapter is contained within those pages. Find the effect that most fascinates you and start with that chapter.

- You want to be able to reproduce the effects demonstrated in this book.

  One of the common complaints about tutorial-style books is that often, after setting this parameter and tweaking that transform according to the instructions, you may have a nice effect, but you do not understand exactly how you accomplished it or why you ended up with the result you did. One of the goals of this book is to not only take you through the necessary steps toward the end result, but to make sure you understand why it's necessary to set a given parameter to a certain value. You will find that most steps and parameters include a brief explanation about why you're changing it to this value. Sometimes, for example, you might see a note to let you know that you will change it later on when it's animated.

- You want additional ideas to enable variations on the effect.

  When you're learning new effects, the best way to solidify your knowledge is through repetition. At the end of each chapter, you will find suggestions for variations on each of the effects. One characteristic top computer graphic experts share is that when they learn something new, they will work with many different variations until they have thoroughly mastered it. Try the variations suggested with these effects and then come up with some of your own. This is the best way to really gain an understanding of how all the different parameters work.

- You like to learn visually.

  A picture is worth a thousand words. That is doubly true when you're speaking of computer tutorials. Nothing is more frustrating than working through step after step in a tutorial and being unsure if you're following the instructions correctly because you have no visual clue. We've added a figure adjacent to as many steps as necessary to make sure it is easy to stay on track.

Conventions Used in This Book

Every computer book has its own style of presenting information. In this book, you'll notice that we have an unusual layout. Because we know that most of our readers wouldn't be reading this book if they weren't into graphics, the project openers are cool-looking eye candy. The real meat of the project starts on the next page.

In the left column, you'll find step-by-step instructions for completing the project, as well as succinct but extremely valuable explanations. In the corresponding column to the right, you'll find screen captures illustrating these steps. We want to say it one more time: If you get lost at any time in the completion of a project, just refer to the completed project file on the CD, and you'll find the answer to your quandary.

Join the Revolution

The world of computer graphics and animation is an exciting and rapidly expanding field. Every day it becomes more pervasive in the world around us. Computer graphics are used for education and entertainment in the movies, television shows, documentaries, commercials, games, and more. Graphics also exist outside the world of entertainment in architectural renderings and walkthroughs, courtroom forensic animations, technical training programs, and prototype product visualizations. As Internet bandwidth increases, it is even becoming a way to make World Wide Web sites more exciting and appealing. There doesn't seem to be any end to the possible uses of computer enhanced effects.

3ds max is rapidly becoming one of the most dominant forces in this computer graphics revolution. From its humble beginnings as 3D Studio for DOS in the early 1990s, it sought to fill a need in the market as an affordable alternative to the high-end and outrageously expensive 3D graphics packages of the time. In fewer than 10 years, it has become arguably the most versatile and powerful professional modeling and animation program available. The introduction of 3D Studio Max 3 in mid-1999 removed any doubt that this program is capable of producing effects just as eye-catching and spectacular—if not more so—than even the most powerful and expensive of the 3D programs available.

3ds max 4 Magic is a valuable tool that will help further your understanding of 3ds max 4 and the potential it offers you as an artist. This book was designed to help you take your skills to the next level by demonstrating the techniques used by the top innovative professionals in the industry.

IMPACT!

"It's what we call a global killer. Nothing would survive, not even bacteria."

—FROM THE FILM *ARMAGEDDON*

Blowing Up a Planet

One of the first things many artists do when they start out in 3D is model a planet and blow it up. In this chapter, you will simulate the effect of an object hitting the earth with enough force to generate a nuclear explosion and a shockwave ring that encompasses the earth, showering the planet with debris, scorching and illuminating the surface, and displacing the sea as it passes.

Project 1

Impact!

by Pete Draper

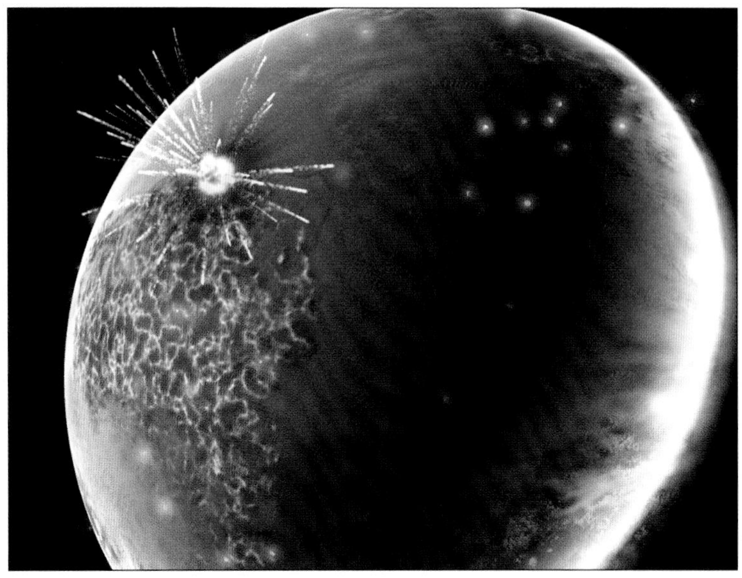

How It Works

In this chapter, you will re-create the age-old story of "asteroid meets planet." You will create not only an initial explosion, but also cloud displacement, fiery debris trails, small debris impacts, and a shockwave that scorches the foliage on the planet and displaces the sea. Not a simple task to animate, you might think, and it's not … if you manually keyframe everything. But in this particular example, we have set up the entire scene so that all you have to do is animate a few spinner settings, scale an object or two, and move a few UVW maps.

To lessen the confusion of animating and setting up the entire scene, the scene is divided into several sections. The overall shockwave, cloud displacement, and earth-scorching effects will be material based, so these can be set up as separate tasks and overlaid to generate the final effect. The impact explosion will be material, geometry, and particle based, and the debris impacts will be a simple particle and multiple space warp setup. Finally, you will add a post effect or two to brighten up some elements and to fake impact explosions.

Getting Started

Start with a basic scene, impact.max. The only things you will use that have been previously prepared are several maps to control the effect: a custom Earth Diffuse map (earth diffuse.jpg), a Specular map (earth map reflection.jpg), a Sea map (earth map sea bump mask.jpg), a Burn mask (earth map burn mask.jpg), a Cloud map that comes with max (CloudMap.jpg, located in 3ds max 4's Maps/Space folder), and an Impact Mark mask (impact mark.jpg). These can all be found on the accompanying CD-ROM in this project's folder.

An Earth material consisting of the earth diffuse.jpg, earth map reflection.jpg, and CloudMap.jpg images with self-illumination falloff has already been created. This material has been applied to a Nurbs sphere with adaptive detail in the center of the scene and is the subject of a collision with an asteroid (animated for you) that will hit the sphere at frame 200; this gives you a few frames for dramatic build-up! If necessary, you can replace the Nurbs sphere with a sphere geometry primitive. Tesselation is set to Medium by default. Also included in the scene is an Explosion Glow Omni light, created to generate an initial glow blast, with an animated Attenuation and Multiplier. Because none of the lights are set to cast shadows, don't worry about turning off relevant cast/receive shadows in the properties of any of the items in this chapter.

Note: The custom earth bitmaps were created in Photoshop by masking all colors apart from the green foliage for the burn mask. For the sea bump mask, all colors apart from blue were masked out. These custom bitmaps will be used to overlay maps on existing maps assigned to the Earth object to generate the desired effect.

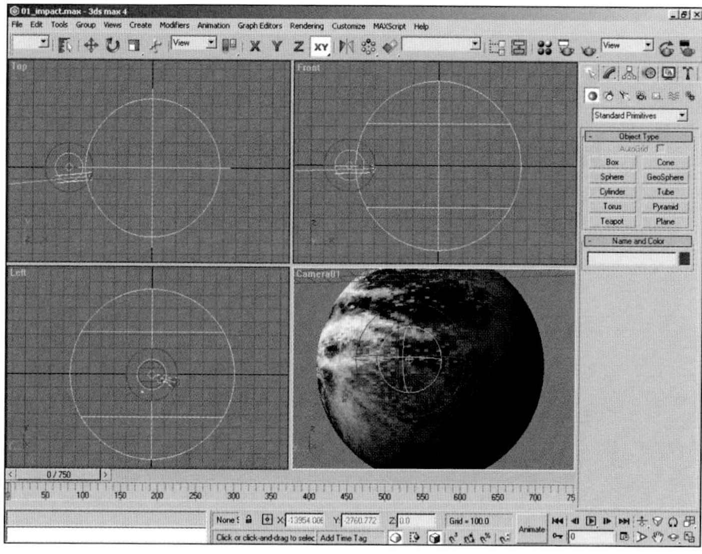

Load the basic max scene file.

Creating the Displaced Clouds Texture

To simulate the initial force of the impact, you will create a cloud displacement/evaporation effect using a gradient opacity that is controlled by a UVW map.

1 Open the Material Editor and click the Earth material in slot one.

2 Navigate to the Diffuse Color, click the Mix Amount slot, and in this Clouds Bitmap map, click the Bitmap button next to the Clouds Bitmap text and add a new Mask map. Check Keep Old Map as Sub-map and click OK. Name this Mask map **Clouds & Nuclear Opacity**.

Using this method, you are creating a new map but are including the existing map as one of its components.

3 Click the Mask slot and add a Gradient Ramp map. Name this **Cloud Displacement Gradient Mask**. Set up the gradient as illustrated.

There should be one point at position 99 and one at position 0, both set to white, and the one at position 100 should be set to black.

4 Increase the Map Channel spinner to **4** and turn off U and V tiling. Expand the Output rollout and turn on Invert.

5 Click the Go to Parent button twice to go back to the earth and clouds mix level, and instance copy the Mix slot into the Color #2 slot. This gradient will be used to mask out a section of the cloud layer when the asteroid hits the planet and will be controlled by a UVW map. The gradient is inverted because it is not tiled; any area outside the UVW Map gizmo is normally set to black. Inverting it makes it white, therefore displaying the cloud layer when the UVW gizmo is positioned off the sphere. Inverting the gradient is necessary because you will use it and invert it in another map later on without disturbing any settings.

6 Return to the Earth top-level material and click the Specular Level slot.

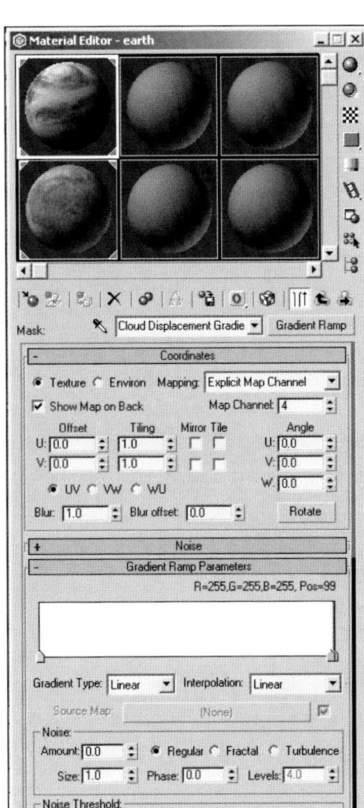

Set up the gradient parameters as shown.

You will notice that the Clouds & Nuclear Opacity Mask map is already here. This is because the original material was an instanced copy of the one you previously changed and therefore changed this one also.

7 In this earth minus clouds ref Mix map, add a new Mask map in the Color #2 slot (name this new Mask map **Inverted Clouds**) and keep old map as sub-map. Instance copy the Cloud Displacement Gradient Mask into the Inverted Clouds Mask slot.

The Earth material, by default, has an inverted Cloud map mixed with an Earth Reflection map so that their specular highlights do not smudge together. Therefore, when the cloud is displaced, the Cloud Specular map also needs to be masked out, hence using the same gradient to mask out the same section but on an inverted Cloud map (the Color #2 slot).

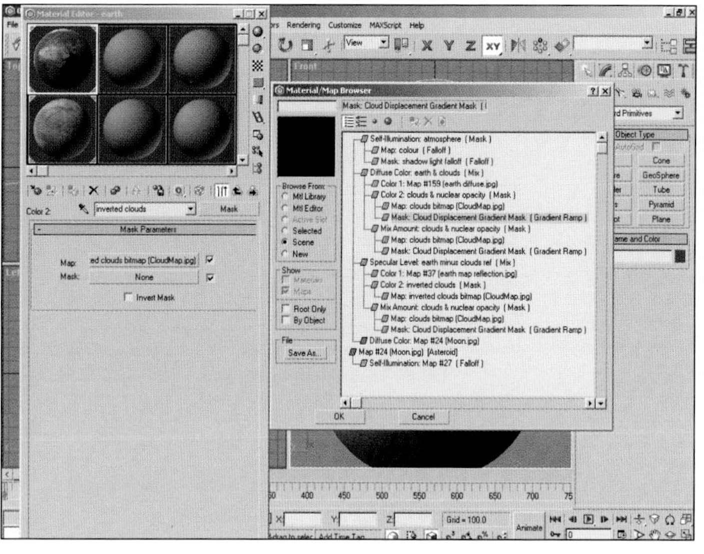

Instance copy the Gradient Mask by selecting Browse From Scene and select the Cloud Displacement Gradient Mask map.

8 Select the Earth Nurbs sphere. Add another UVW Map modifier and set it to Planar with a Map Channel of **4**. Name this **UVW Cloud Displacement**. In the Top viewport, select the modifier's gizmo and move it left along the X-axis so that it is just in front of the sphere.

It is worthwhile to turn on Show Map in Viewport in the Cloud Displacement Gradient Mask Gradient Ramp map to position it correctly.

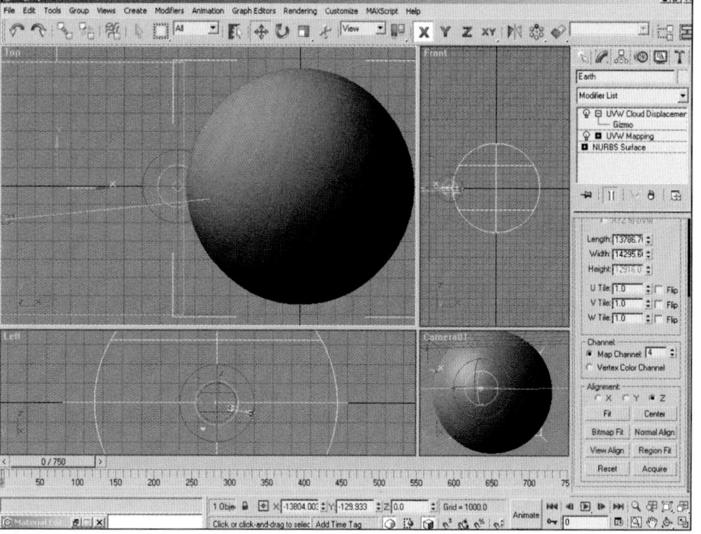

In the Top viewport, create a UVW map as illustrated and offset the gizmo.

9 To check the displacement, position the UVW gizmo so that it intersects the sphere. Activate ActiveShade in the Camera viewport by right-clicking the Camera text and navigate to Views/ActiveShade.

The Camera viewport should now show the cloud layer being masked out by the Gradient Ramp map. Right-click the ActiveShade viewport and select Close in the Quad menu to return to the Camera view. In the Top viewport, move the gizmo back so that it doesn't intersect the sphere. This is the UVW gizmo that controls the gradients and masks you have just set up; it is assigned to control the displacement of the clouds when the asteroid hits the planet. By offsetting the gizmo beyond the sphere, the entirety of the sphere's Cloud map is, as yet, unaffected.

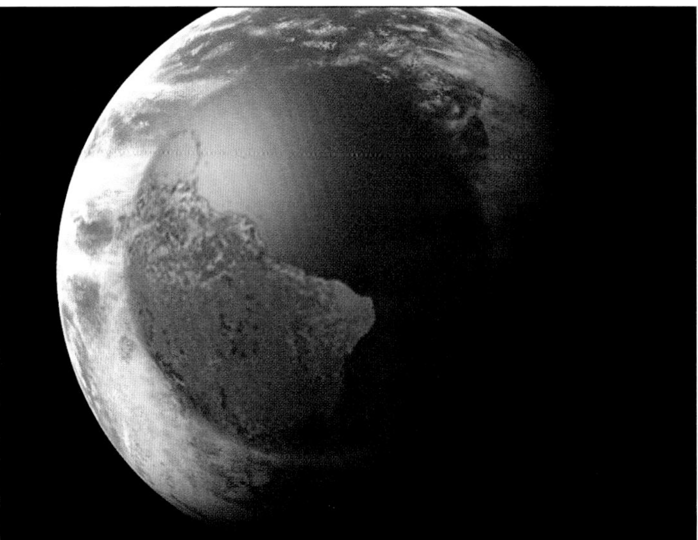

The intersection of the UVW gizmo should result in the cloud layer being displaced.

Creating the Scorched Earth and Displaced Sea Texture

Because you are mainly concentrating on the impact explosion effect, the animation of the asteroid has already been set up, along with its Visibility Track to hide the geometry from the renderer after the impact. Using multiple-layered procedural textures and gradient opacities, you will then set up and animate the scorched earth and sea displacement textures and blend them with the original Earth map.

1 Copy the Earth material you have been working on and name it **Earth Scorched**.

2 In the Diffuse slot, rename this **Earth & Foam & Clouds**. Click the Color #1 slot and add a new Mix map. Keep the old map as a sub-map. Name this **Earth & Sea Foam**. In the Mix Amount slot, create a Bitmap map and select the earth map sea bump mask.jpg file. Go up one level to the Mix map.

This mask mixes the Earth bitmap with a procedural map that you will use as foamy water.

3 With the Earth Diffuse bitmap in the Color #1 slot, create a new Mask map in the Color #2 slot. Name this **Waves Overlay**.

4 Create a Noise map in the Mask slot; set it to **Turbulence** with a High of **0.5**. Name this **Wave Foam Mask**.

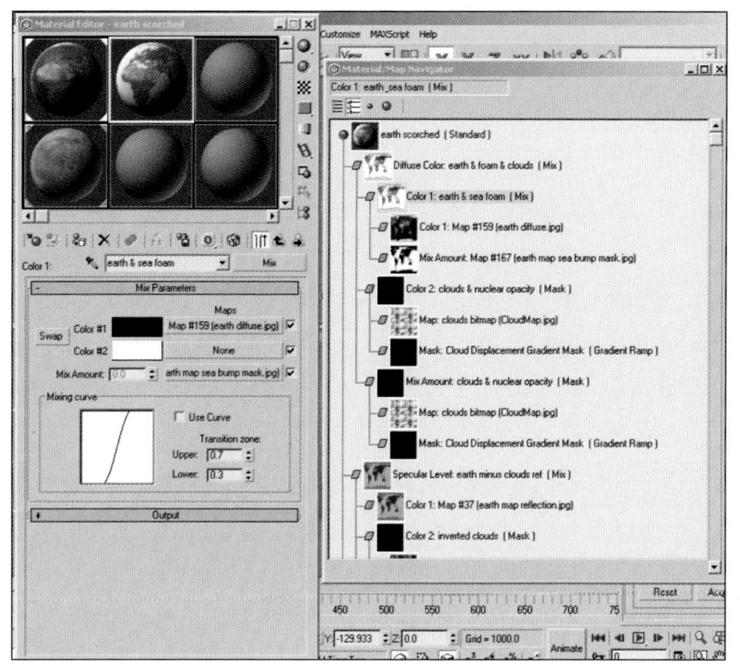

Add the bitmap file to the Mix slot of the new mix material.

5 Go up one level to the Waves Overlay Mask map and create a new Gradient Ramp map in the Map slot. Name this **Waves**. Set the Map Channel to **2**, turn off U and V tiling, and create a gradient of waves using a fading white and a dark blue with an RGB of 11, 21, 48 as illustrated.

This time, the gradient is used as a map and not as a mask, but it will be controlled in the same way as before, with the use of UVW Map gizmos. This gradient is masked out by a procedural Noise map and is mixed in with the earth bitmap only where there is water, using the earth map sea bump mask.jpg bitmap.

6 In the Earth Modifier stack, right-click the UVW Cloud Displacement modifier, copy it, right-click again, and paste. Rename the new UVW Modifier **UVW Transition** and set the Map Channel spinner value to **2**.

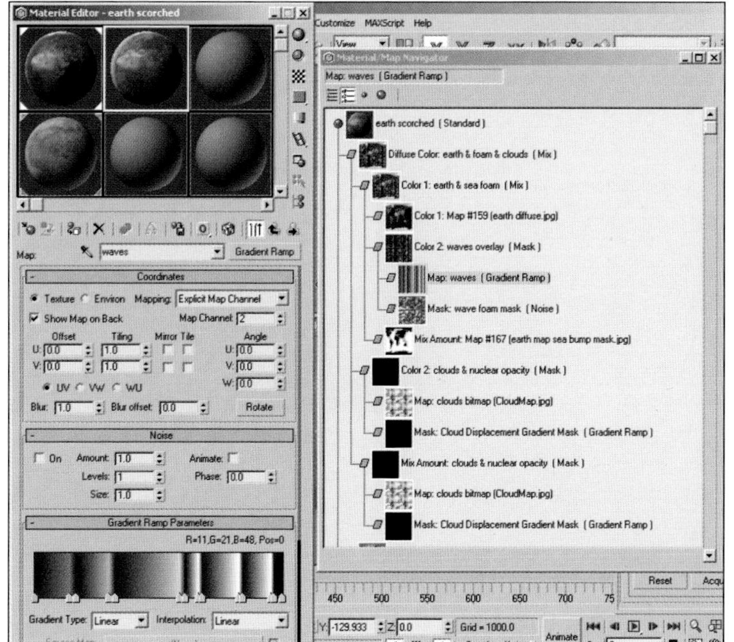

The Gradient Ramp wave design.

This ensures that both maps start their animation in the same place. Now you will create the Scorched Earth texture.

7 At the top level, add a new composite map to the Self-Illumination slot. Keep old map as sub-map. Name this **Atmosphere & Fire**.

8 In the Map 2 slot, add a new Mask map and name it **Scorch**. In the Scorch Mask slot, add the earth map burn mask.jpg bitmap.

9 In the Map slot, add a new Noise map set to **Turbulence** with a Size of **200**, a High of **0.5**, and **10** Levels. Click the Swap button to flip the white and black colors. Name this new Noise map **Fire Noise Patches**.

10 In the Noise Parameters Color #1 slot, add another new Noise map and name it **Red Fire**. Set it to **Turbulence** with a Size of **200**, a High of **0.3**, and **10** Levels. Set the Color #2 for this new Noise map to red (R 255, G 0, B 0).

11 Again, in the Color #1 slot of the Red Fire map, add another Noise map and name it **Yellow & White Fire**. Set it to **Turbulence** with a Size of **200**, a High of **0.2**, and **10** Levels. Set Color #1 to white and Color #2 to yellow (R 255, G 225, B 0).

Note: You have created a multilayered map to generate a fire effect using multiple Noise maps layered on top of each other to generate the required result because the fire effect requires more than two colors and different sizes. This effect has been masked out by the earth map burn mask.jpg bitmap and composited with the atmosphere map in the Self-Illumination slot.

You can test the Earth Scorched map by assigning it to the Earth sphere.

CREATING THE IMPACT MARK

Using the gradient opacity created for the displaced clouds, you will now add an impact mark on the earth's texture.

1. In a new material slot, create an Oren-Nayar-Blinn material with Specular Level and Glossiness set to **0**. Name it **Impact Mark**.
2. In the Diffuse slot, create a Gradient Ramp map and name it **Impact Fire**. Set the Map Channel to **3** and turn off U and V tiling. Change the Gradient Type to Radial.
3. Create a gradient like the one illustrated by using colors from white at positions 0 and 5, to yellow (R 255, G 255, B 0) at position 10, to orange (R 255, G 100, B 0) at position 16, to dark red (R 130, G 0, B 0) at position 33, and finally to black at positions 60 and 100. In the Gradient Ramp Parameters, increase the Noise Amount to **0.1**, Fractal, and **0.1** Size.
4. Go up to the top-level material and instance copy the Impact Fire Gradient Ramp into the Self-Illumination slot.
5. In the Opacity slot, create a Mask map and name it **Impact Mark & Mask**. In the Map slot, add a new Bitmap map and add the impact mark.jpg bitmap. Turn off U and V tiling and set the Map Channel spinner to **3**.

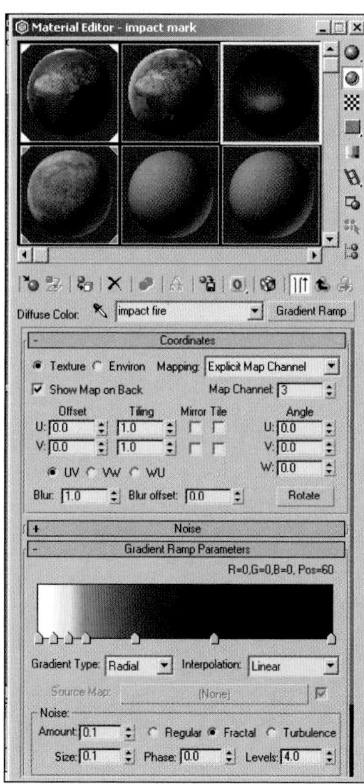

Design the gradient using the settings illustrated.

6 In the Impact Mark & Mask mask slot (the parent map), instance copy the Cloud Displacement Gradient Mask previously created.

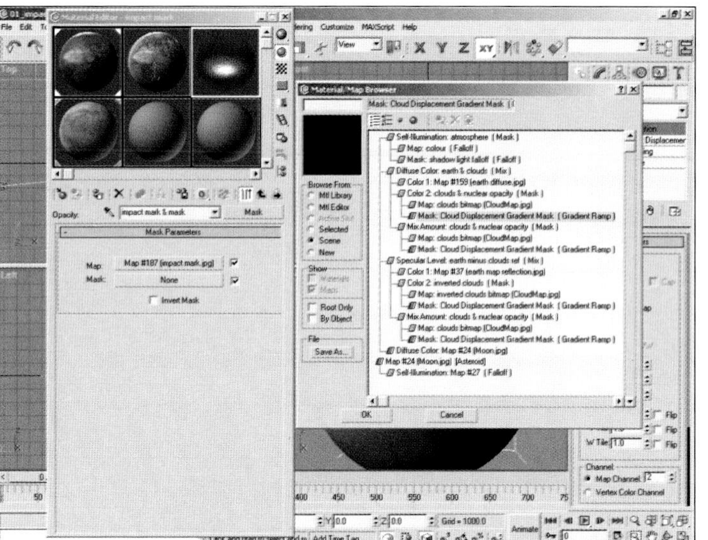

Instance copy the Gradient Ramp map by browsing from the scene.

7 In the Impact Mark & Mask mask map, check Invert Mask.

Inverting the gradient occludes the impact mark until the cloud displacement UVW map intersects the sphere. The inverted gradient is inverted again; because it is not tiled, any area outside the UVW Map gizmo is set to white (normally black, but the gradient is inverted). Hence, you now invert it back to black to occlude the impact mark without affecting the instance.

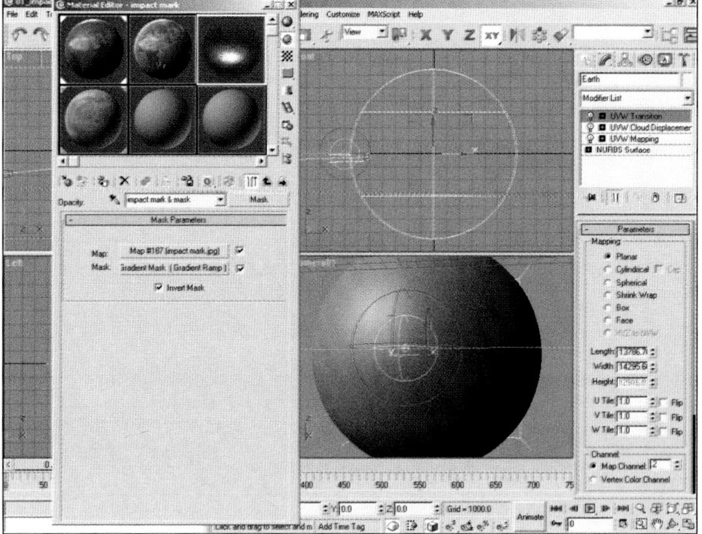

The Mask map's mask is inverted here, not inside the Gradient Ramp map.

8 In the Top viewport, add a new UVW Map modifier to the earth's stack, name it **UVW Impact Mark**, and set the Map Channel spinner to **3**. Select the Gizmo sub-object, select Rotate, and enter **–90** in the Y transformation spinner so that it is facing from inside the sphere out to the impact site.

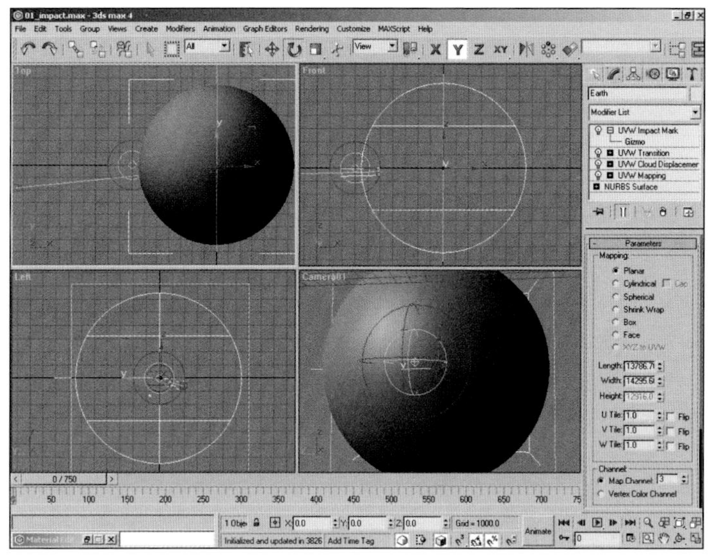

The resulting rotation.

9 Select Uniform Scale and turn on the Absolute Transform Type-In button at the bottom of the screen. Enter **20** in the X entry box.

Scaling the gizmo, not tiling the Impact Opacity map, and using the same map channel and gradient as the Cloud map will properly display the impact mark at the same time as the Cloud layer is masked out.

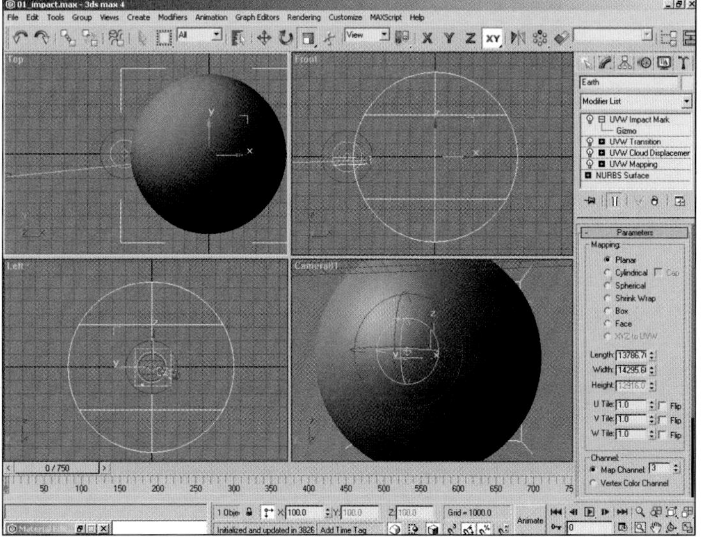

The resulting uniform scale.

Creating the Shockwave

Finally, you will create the shockwave blast that will illuminate the Earth texture in front of and behind its wake.

1. Create a new Oren-Nayar-Blinn material and name it **Shockwave Gradient**. Set the Ambient, Diffuse, and Specular colors to white, set Self-Illumination to **100**, and set Specular Level and Glossiness to **0**.

   For an overlay like this (and the impact mark), it is always best to use custom or no specular and glossiness settings because they will also be overlaid.

2. In the Opacity slot, create a new Gradient Ramp map and name it **Shockwave**. Turn off U and V tiling and set the Map Channel spinner to **2**. Design the gradient as illustrated: black at positions 0, 93, 99, and 100 and white at position 98.

   This is the band of white that will pass over the sphere, controlled by the same UVW gizmo that controls the cloud displacement and impact mark opacities. You will now get the shockwave to illuminate the earth's surface.

3. In the Earth material, add a new Mix map to the Self-Illumination slot and keep old map as sub-map. Name this **Atmosphere & Shockwave Illumination**.

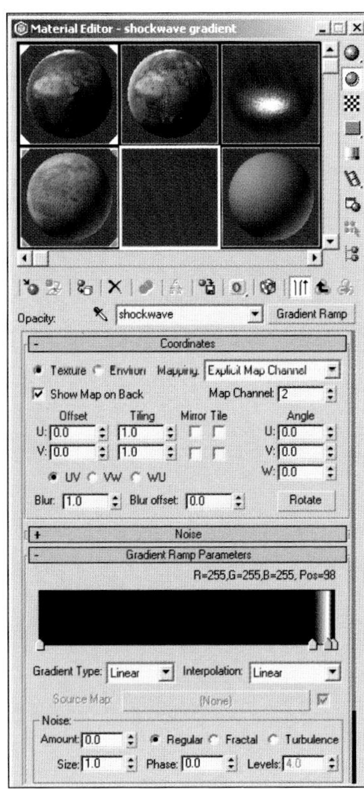

The Shockwave Gradient Ramp map settings.

4 In the Color #2 slot, instance copy the Earth & Clouds Mix map previously created.

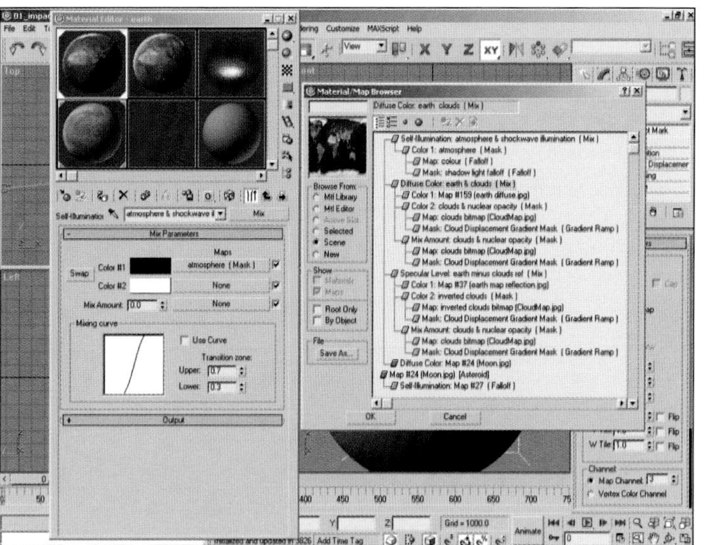

Instancing the Earth & Clouds Mix map.

5 In the Mix Amount slot of the Atmosphere & Shockwave Illumination Mix map, copy (not instance) the Shockwave Gradient Ramp to create a new map. Name this new gradient **Shockwave Glow**.

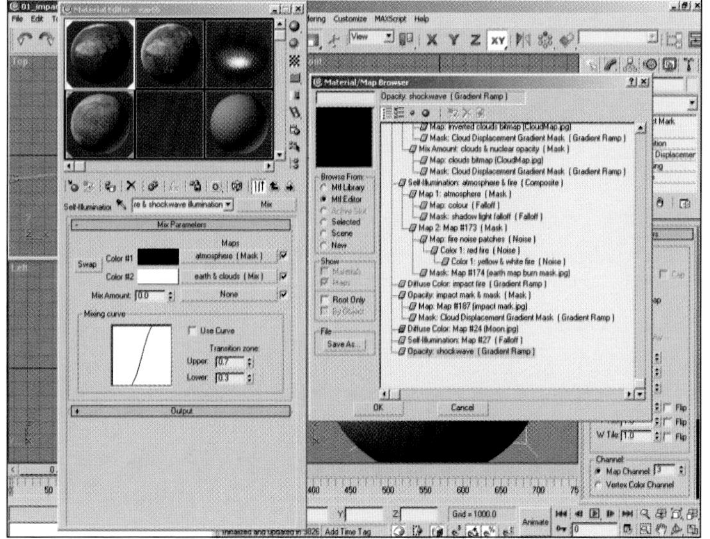

Copy the Shockwave Gradient Ramp map by selecting Browse From Material Editor and selecting the Shockwave Gradient Ramp map.

6 Delete the black flag at position 99 and move the black flag at position 93 to 87.

This enables you to slightly modify the gradient to illuminate the Earth map in front of and behind the Shockwave gradient, with the intensity building up to the front of the shockwave and fading out behind it.

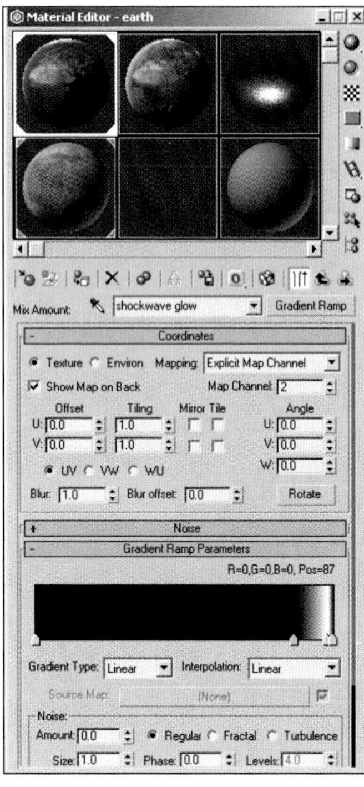

Amend the Gradient Ramp settings to those illustrated.

Putting the Materials Together

By using Blend and composite materials, you will overlay each material to generate one fully animated composite material that will be applied to our Earth object.

1 Create a new Blend material and name it **Earth Blend**. Instance copy the Earth material to the Material 1 slot and the Earth Scorched material to the Material 2 slot by dragging them to the Blend material's slots.

2 Copy the Shockwave Gradient Ramp to the Mask slot. Name the new gradient **Earths Gradient** and amend the gradient flag positions so there are black flags at positions 87 and 100 and white ones at positions 0 and 69.

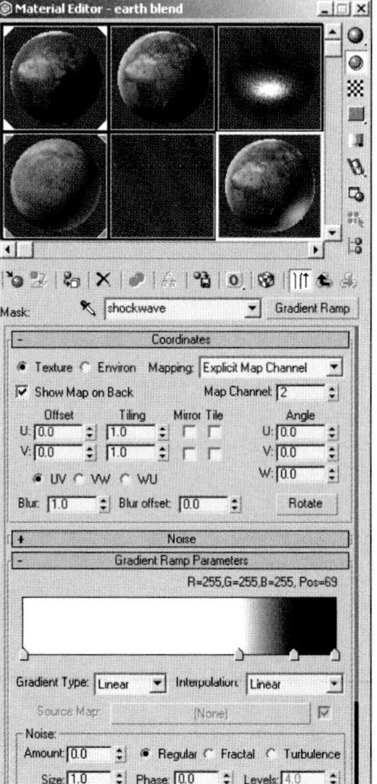

Amend the copied Gradient Ramp to the illustrated settings.

This is the transition gradient from the normal Earth material to the scorched copy. You are using Blend for this material because the composite material you will use to assemble the complete material overlays materials that can produce undesired results such as brightening or additive compositing. This is acceptable for the other materials because they are designed to do so.

3 Create a new composite material and name it **Earth Composite**. Instance copy the Earth Blend material to the Base Material slot, instance the Impact Mark material to the Material 1 slot, and instance the Shockwave Gradient material to the Material 2 slot. Uncheck every other material in the composite material. Assign the composite material to the Earth Nurbs sphere.

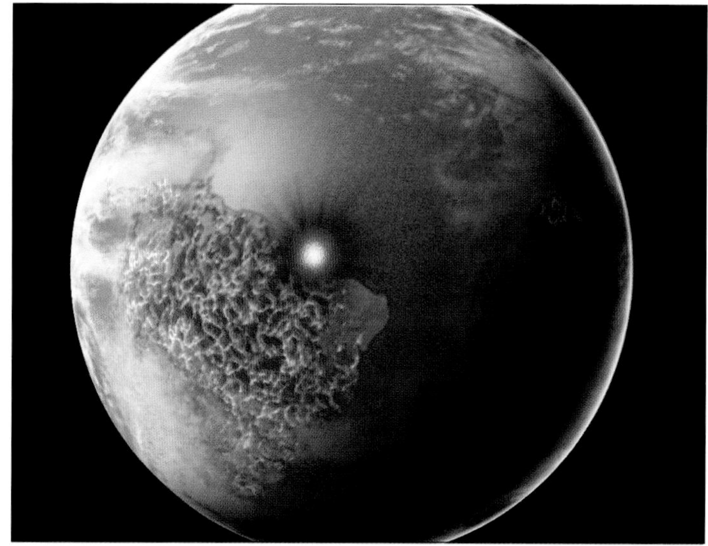

A test render with the composite material applied to the Earth sphere and the UVW gizmos offset. The Impact mark is revealed, the clouds are displaced, and the scorched surface can be viewed.

Animating the Materials

Now that all that hard work has been done, all you need to do now is animate the UVW Cloud Displacement and UVW Transition gizmos.

1 Scrub the time bar across to frame 750 and turn on Animate. Turn on Smooth + Highlights in the Top and Left viewports (if they are not on already), and turn on Show Map in Viewport in the Shockwave Gradient Ramp.

2 In the Top viewport, move the UVW Transition gizmo along the X-axis to the right of the sphere so that it passes over it, roughly up to about 3/4 of the way across.

This animates the position of the shockwave, controls the self-illumination of the planet's surface, and controls the transition from the Earth material to the Scorched Earth material including the sea foam waves.

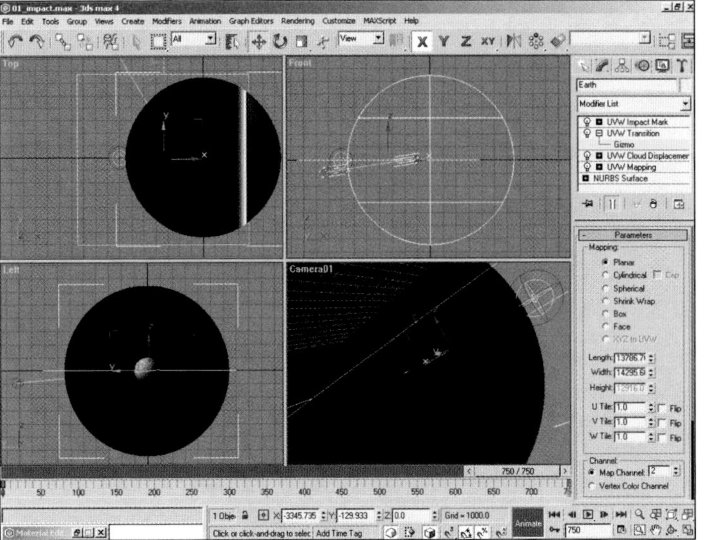

Moving the UVW Transition gizmo across the Nurbs sphere.

3 Scrub back to frame 225. Turn on Show Map in Viewport in the Cloud Displacement Gradient Mask Gradient Ramp. Select the UVW Cloud Displacement gizmo and move it slightly to the right in the Top viewport so that it just intersects the sphere.

The resulting map will be just slightly larger than the Moon Nurbs sphere when viewed in the Left viewport.

4 Turn off Animate. In the timeline, drag-select the key(s) at frame 0 and drag them to frame 200.

This offsets the start time of the impact effects to frame 200, when the asteroid intersects the Nurbs sphere.

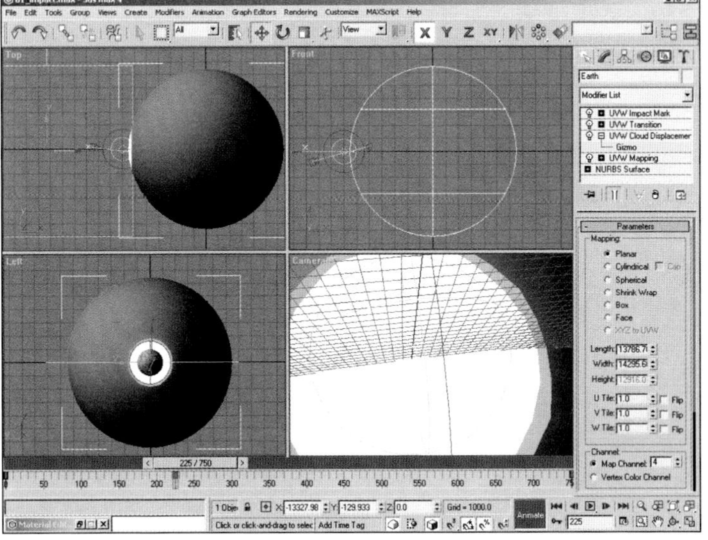

Moving the UVW Cloud Displacement gizmo in the Top viewport while viewing it in the Left viewport.

Creating the Impact Explosion and Initial Impact Glow

Now that the Earth Impact material is set up, you will add a few pyrotechnics to the scene. The impact fireball will be created using a Scatter compound object with an animated emitter, allowing the fireball to grow. We will then add a subtle glow to the Scatter object to give the impression of intense illumination.

1 Create a geosphere primitive in the Left viewport with a radius of **50** and **3** segments; make it a Tetra Base Type and name it **Explosion Fireball**.

2 Create another geosphere primitive in the Left viewport at X = 0, Y = 0, Z = 0 with a radius of **100** and **10** segments; name this **Scatter Explosion Emitter** and make it a Tetra Base Type. Check Base to Pivot and select Move. Enter **–6500** in the X Transformation Type-In box at the bottom of the screen so that the geosphere sits just on the surface of the Nurbs sphere.

3 Scrub the timeline to 750 and turn on Animate. Increase the Radius value to **300** and move the radius key generated at frame 0 in the timeline to frame 200. Turn off Animate.

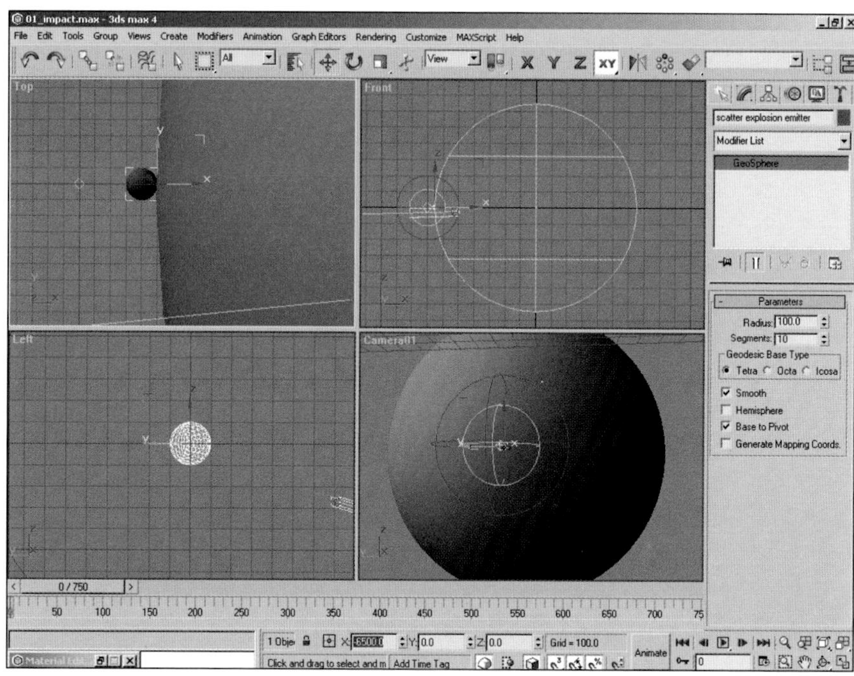

Create the geosphere in the Left viewport and move it by entering the transformation value in the X Transformation Type-In box.

4 Select the Explosion Fireball geosphere and create a Scatter compound object; select the Scatter Explosion Emitter geosphere as the Distribution Object. Increase the amount of duplicates to **100**, check Use Maximum Range and Lock Aspect Ratio in the Scaling section in the Transforms rollout, and enter a value of **100** in the X percentage spinner. Check Hide Distribution Object in the Display rollout.

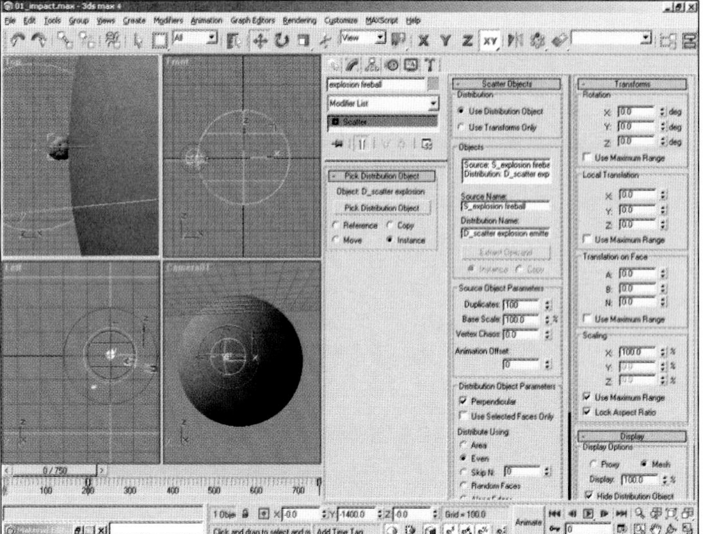

Create the Scatter compound object with these settings.

5 Select the Explosion Fireball Scatter object and the Scatter Explosion Emitter and open Track View. Add a Visibility Track to both the Scatter Explosion Emitter and the Explosion Fireball. Create keys in the visibility track of the Scatter Explosion Emitter at frames 199 and 200 with values of **0** and **1**, respectively.

6 Select the Visibility Track with the created keys and click the Copy icon in Track View. Select the Visibility Track for the Explosion Fireball and instance paste by clicking the Paste icon in Track View.

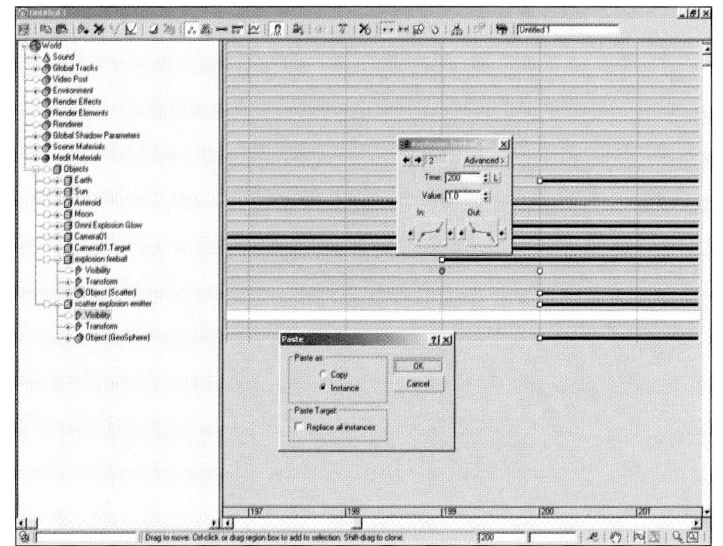

Instance-copying the Visibility Track.

Because you do not want to see the explosion before frame 200 (when the asteroid hits), using Visibility Tracks enables you to hide the Scatter and Emitter objects before frame 200 and then display them on and after frame 200.

7 Create a new Blinn material and name it **Explosion Fireball**. Give it a Material ID of **1**, check 2-Sided, and set Specular and Glossiness to **0**. Check the Color box in the Self-Illumination box and leave the color as black.

8 Create a Towards/Away Falloff map in the Diffuse slot; name this **Fire Falloff**. Swap the black and white colors. In the Towards (top) slot, add a Noise map and name this **Fire Noise**. Use Turbulence with a Size of **200**, a High of **0.75**, and **10** Levels. Click the Swap button.

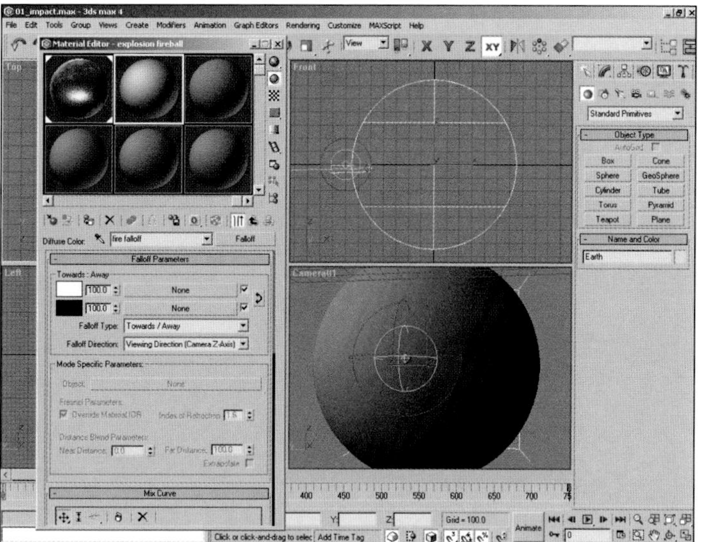

The Towards/Away Falloff map.

9 Add another Noise map in the Fire Noise Color #1 slot and name this **Red Fireball Fire**. Give the Color #2 slot value of R 255, G 0, B 0. Change the noise type to **Turbulence** with a Size of **200**, a High of **0.3**, and **10** Levels.

10 Add another Noise map in the Red Fireball Fire Color #1 slot and name this **White & Yellow Fireball Fire**. Make the Color #1 slot white and the Color #2 slot R 255, G 225, B 0. Change the noise type to **Turbulence** with a Size of **200**, a High of **0.2**, and **10** Levels.

11 Back at the top level of the material, instance copy the Fire Falloff map to the Self-Illumination and Opacity slots. In Extended Parameters, change the Advanced Transparency Type to Additive. Assign this material to the Explosion Fireball Scatter object.

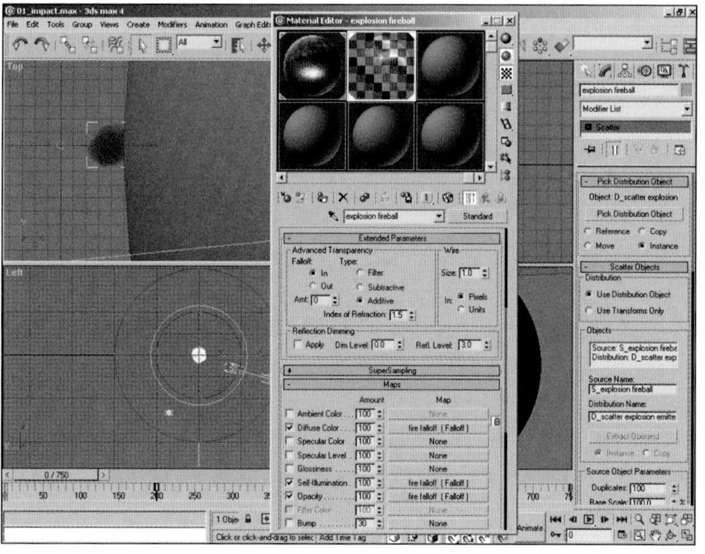

Instance copy the Fire Falloff into the Self-Illumination and Opacity slots and amend the Advanced Transparency settings.

12 Copy the material and name the new one **Explosion Emitter**. Uncheck the Opacity Map. Change the Advanced Transparency Type back to Filter, change the Falloff to Out, and increase the Amount spinner to **100**. Uncheck 2-Sided. Assign this material to the Scatter Explosion Emitter geosphere.

13 In the Rendering Effects window, add a Lens Effects effect and name it **Lens Effects Explosion**. Add a Glow Element to the right pane of the Lens Effects Parameters. Click the new Glow Element.

14 In the Glow Element's rollout, amend the Size spinner to **0.02**. The Intensity, Occlusion, and Use Source Color spinners should each be set to **100**. Turn off Glow Behind.

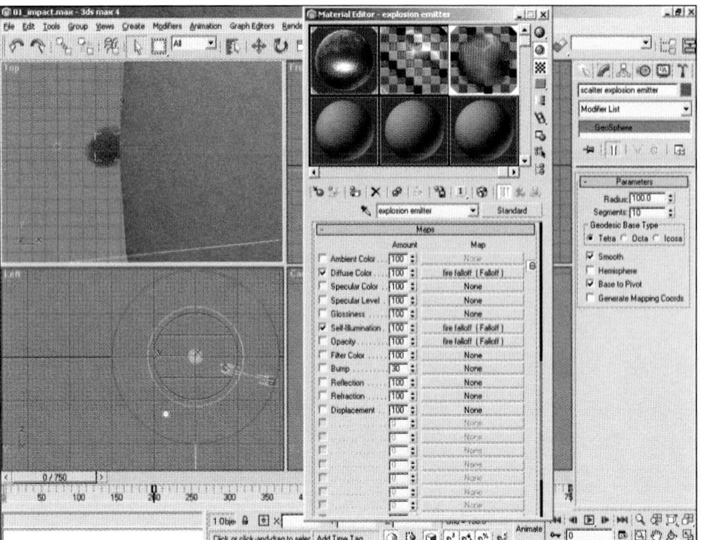

The amended Material settings.

15 In the Glow Element's Options tab, turn off Lights and turn on Effects ID. Make sure the Effects ID spinner is set to **1**.

Because the explosion effect uses additive transparency on the Scatter object, the glow effect need not be too intense as there is already an initial glow. The glow breaks up any harsh edges and adds a sense of intense illumination in the scene.

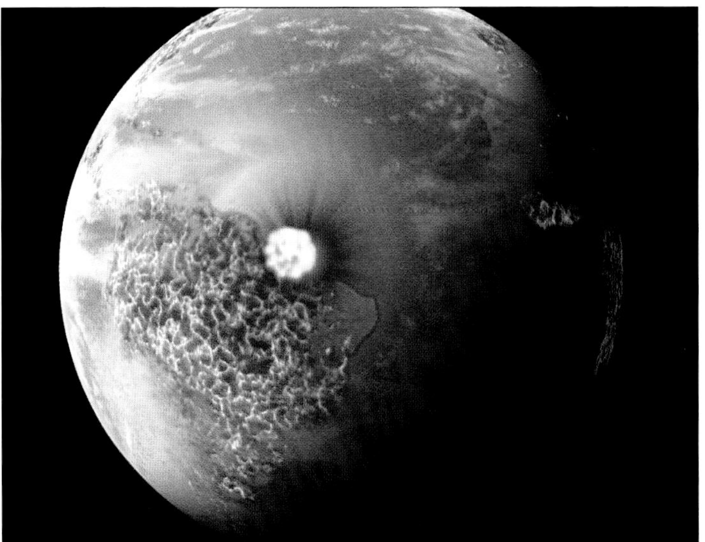

The resulting Scatter object combined with the Scatter emitter at frame 750.

Creating the Impact Fire Debris

To add emphasis to the dramatic scene, you will now add large fiery debris trails emanating from the impact site using additive materials and Particle Spawn.

1. In the Top viewport, at X = –6500, Y = 0, Z = 0, create a Super Spray particle system and name it **Fire Trails**. Rotate it –90 along the Y-axis so that it is facing back out, away from the earth.

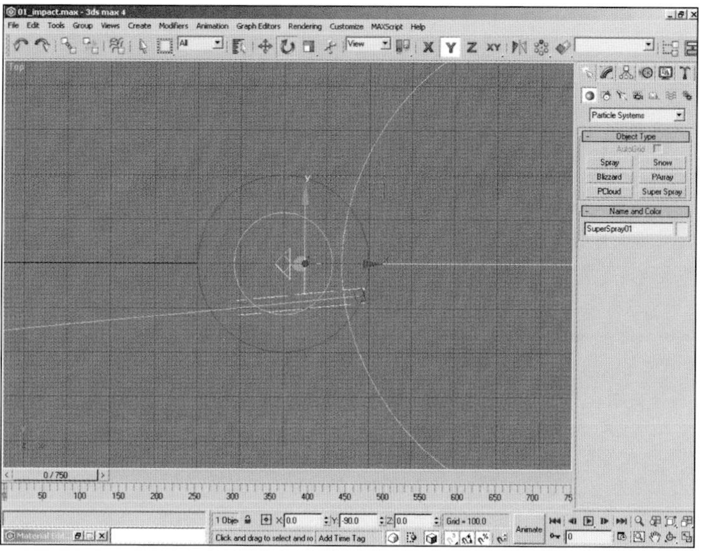

Create and position the Super Spray particle system.

2. Give an Off Axis Spread of **100** degrees and an Off Plane Spread of **90** degrees. By default, the Viewport Display type should be set to Ticks. Set Percentage of Particles to view to **5%**.

3. In the Particle Generation rollout, click Use Total and change the spinner value to a value between 10 and 60. Set Particle Motion Speed to **8** and Variation to **30%**.

Note: Vary your setting from 10 to 60 in the Use Total spinner; if your computer is not very powerful, you might want to drop the setting down further because a lot of particles will be created later on using Particle Spawn, which will dramatically increase render times. The more particles, however, the better the impact effect.

4. Change the Particle Timing Emit Start and Emit Stop spinners to **200** and the Display Until and Life spinners to **1000**.

5. In the Particle Size section, change the Size spinner to **15** with **50%** Variation. Set the Grow and Fade For spinners to **0**. In the Particle Type Rollout, use Standard Particles set to Facing.

6 In the Particle Spawn Rollout, toggle on Spawn Trails. Change the Direction Chaos spinner to **1%**, the Speed Chaos Factor spinner to **100%**, and toggle on Both. Turn on Inherit Parent Velocity. In the Lifespan Value Queue, enter **500** in the Lifespan spinner and click the Add button.

This is the lifespan for the spawned particle trails, not the emitter particles.

7 Create a new Blinn material and name it **Fire Trails**. Turn on 2-sided and Face Map in the Basic Parameters rollout. Amend the Specular Level and Glossiness spinners to **0** and increase the Self-Illumination spinner to **100**.

8 Under the Extended Parameters rollout, change the Advanced Transparency Type to Additive.

Using additive transparency means you don't have to create a glow effect for the particles.

9 In the Diffuse slot, add a Particle Age map and name it **Trails**. Make Color #3 black and set the Age #2 spinner to **5**. Add a Noise map in the Color #1 slot. Name this **Yellow & Orange**. Set the Low to **0.25**. Set Color #1 to R 255, G 255, B 0 and Color #2 to R 255, G 148, B 0.

10 Go up one level to the Trails map, copy the Yellow & Orange Noise map to the Particle Age's Color #2 slot, and name the new map **Orange & Red**. Amend this Noise map's Color #1 slot to R 255, G 148, B 0 and Color #2 to R 255, G 0, B 0.

11 Back at the top, create a Mask map in the Opacity slot and name it **Masked Fire Trails.** Instance copy the Trails Particle Age to the Map slot.

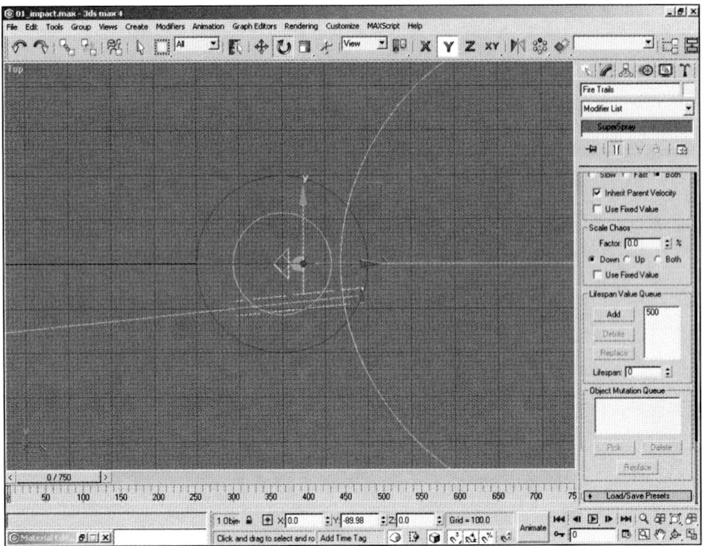

Amend the Super Spray settings to those illustrated.

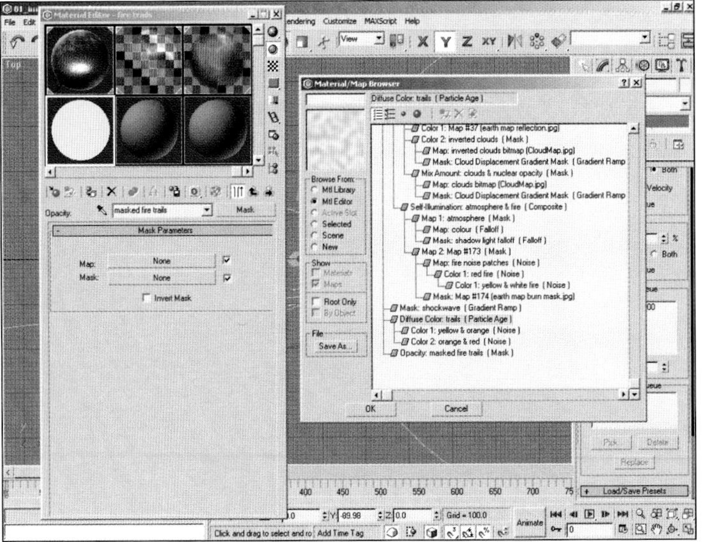

Selecting the Particle Age map to instance into the Map slot.

12 Go up one level to the Masked Fire Trails map, add a Gradient map to the Mask slot, and name it **Gradient Circular Mask**. Change the Gradient Type to Radial. Assign the material to the Fire Trails particle system.

Using a Particle Age map enables you to design exactly how you would like the particle colors to change over a particle's life. Using it in conjunction with the circular gradient also enables you to control its density over its life.

13 Create a Gravity space warp set to Spherical Force at X = 0, Y = 0, Z = 0. Set the Strength spinner to **0.01**. Name it **Gravity Fire Trails**.

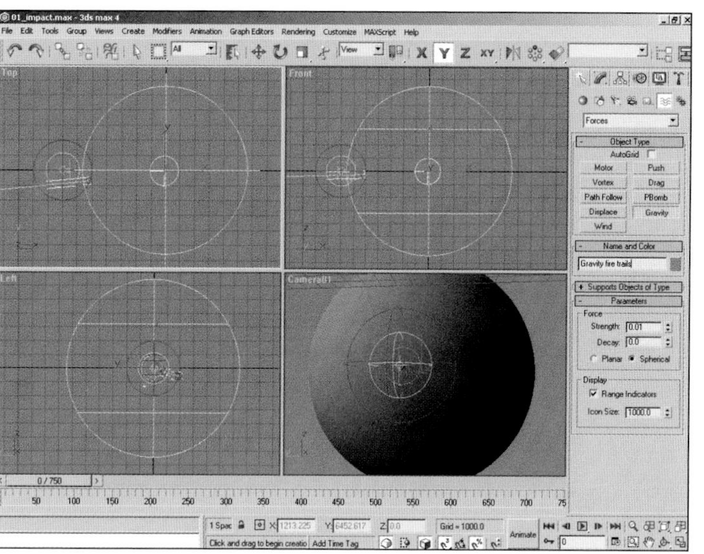

Creating the Gravity Fire Trails space warp.

14 Create a SOmniFlect space warp at X = 0, Y = 0, Z = 0 with a radius of **6470** and name it **SOmniFlect Fire Trails**. Under Parameters, increase the Time Off spinner to **750** and set the Reflection Bounce to **0** and Friction to **5**.

15 Bind the Fire Trails particle system to the Gravity Fire Trails and SOmniFlect Fire Trails space warps.

The Gravity space warp pulls the particles back down to the Earth sphere, but the SOmniFlect space warp prevents them from intersecting the sphere, enabling them to skid across the atmosphere.

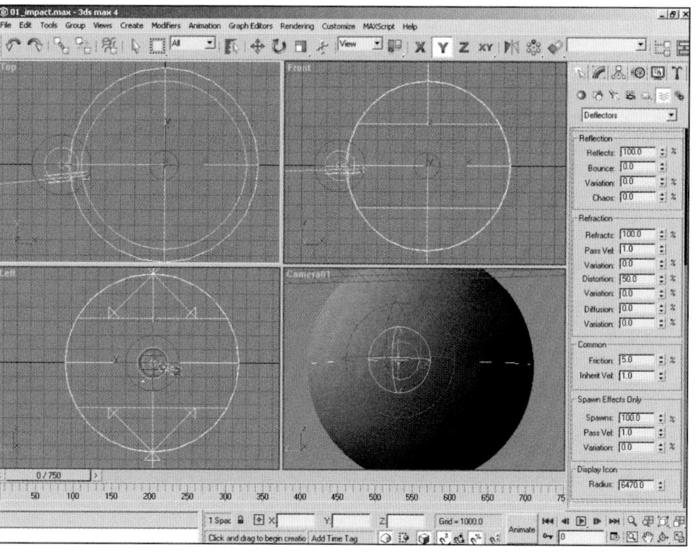

Create the SOmniFlect space warp with the illustrated settings.

Creating the Impact Small Debris Shower

You will now create the small shower of debris that has been kicked up by the blast and is re-entering the Earth's atmosphere and impacting with the surface, using a Super Spray particle system, two space warps, and two low poly instanced spheres with different materials. You will also add an additional impact effect using the Glow effect to slightly illuminate the Earth's surface.

1. Create two sphere primitives, one named **Small Debris Instance** with a Radius of **10** and **4** segments and the other named **Small Debris Impact** with a Radius of **40** and **6** segments.

2. In the Top viewport, create another Super Spray particle system at X = –7000, Y = 0, Z = 0. Name it **Small Debris**. Rotate it –90 along the Y-axis so that it is facing back out, away from the earth.

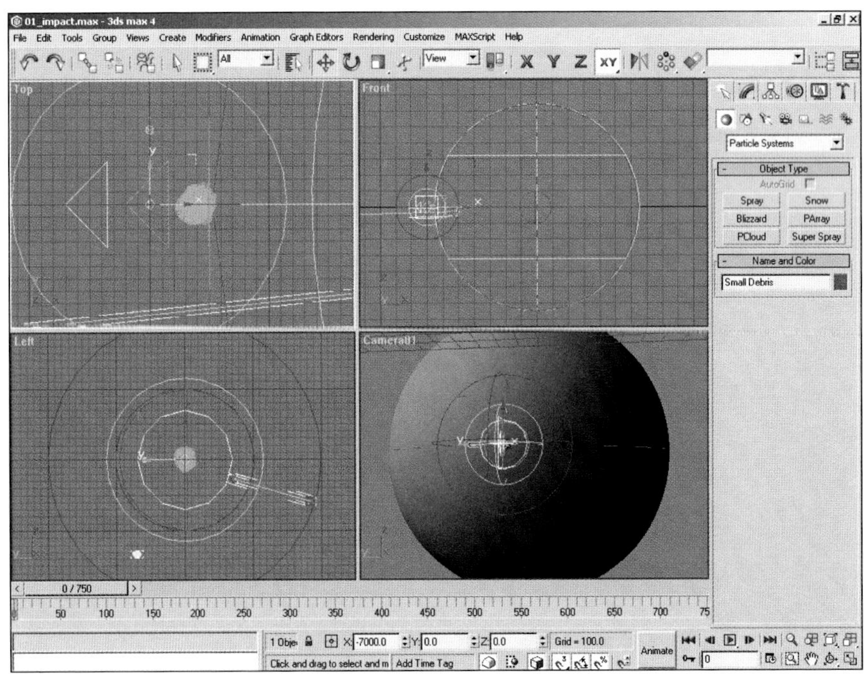

Position the new particle system just in front of the Fire Trails particle system.

3 Set the Off Axis Spread and the Off Plane Spread spinners both to **90** degrees. Amend the Percentage of Particles spinner to **5%**.

4 Under the Particle Generation rollout, increase the Use Rate spinner to **300**. Set the Particle Motion Speed spinner to **100** and the Variation spinner to **50%**. Set the Particle timing Emit Start and Stop spinners to **200** and the Display Until and Life spinners to **1000**. Set the Grow For and Fade For spinners to **0**.

5 Under the Particle Type rollout, change the Particle Types to Instanced Geometry, click the Pick Object button under Instancing Parameters, and select the Small Debris Instance sphere.

6 Under the Particle Spawn rollout, check Spawn on Collision. Add **1000** to the Lifespan Value Queue. Under the Object Mutation Queue section, click the Pick button and select the Small Debris Impact sphere.

7 Create a new Blinn material and set the Glossiness and Opacity to **0**. Name this **Small Debris Instance** and assign it to the Small Debris Instance sphere.

8 Copy the Explosion Fireball material, rename the copy **Small Debris Impact Explosion,** and amend its Material ID from 1 to **2**. Assign this to the Small Debris Impact sphere. Hide the Small Debris Instance and Small Debris Impact spheres.

9 In the Small Debris particle system, click the Get Material From button in the Mat'l Mapping and Source section of the Particle Type rollout.

10 Copy the Gravity Fire Trails space warp and name the new space warp **Gravity Small Debris**. Amend the Strength spinner to **0.5**.

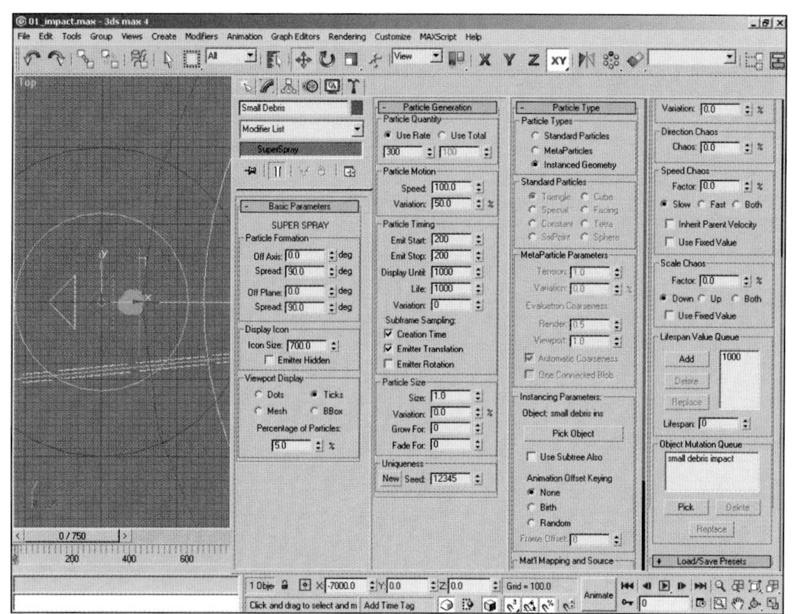

Amend the particle system's settings to those illustrated.

Note: Due to the way Particle Spawn works, particles can only change their color with spawn on collision if Instanced Geometry is the main particle type. Therefore, you will use a transparent material for the main particles to hide them from the scene and another material and object for the spawned particles. At a later date, you might want to see the initial particles emit from the explosion, in which case you can amend the Small Debris Instance material properties.

11 Create a SOmniFlect space warp at X = 0, Y = 0, Z = 0 with a Radius of **6470** and name it **SOmniFlect Small Debris**. Under Parameters, increase the Time Off spinner to **750**, set the Reflection Bounce to **0**, and Friction to **100**.

12 Bind the Small Debris particle system to the Gravity Small Debris and SOmniFlect Small Debris space warps.

By using Particle Spawn, the initial particles are pulled back to the Earth sphere and are replaced with the larger self-illuminating particles when they hit the SOmniFlect Small Debris space warp, which holds them in place due to the high Friction value.

13 In the Rendering Effects window, add a Lens Effects effect and name it **Lens Effects Small Debris Impacts**. Add a Glow Element to the right pane of the Lens Effects Parameters. Click the new Glow Element.

14 In the Glow Element's rollout, amend the Size spinner to **0.1**, Intensity to **120**, and the Occlusion and Use Source Color spinners to **100**. Turn off Glow Behind. In the Glow Element's Options tab, turn off Lights, turn on Effects ID, and set the Spinner to **2**.

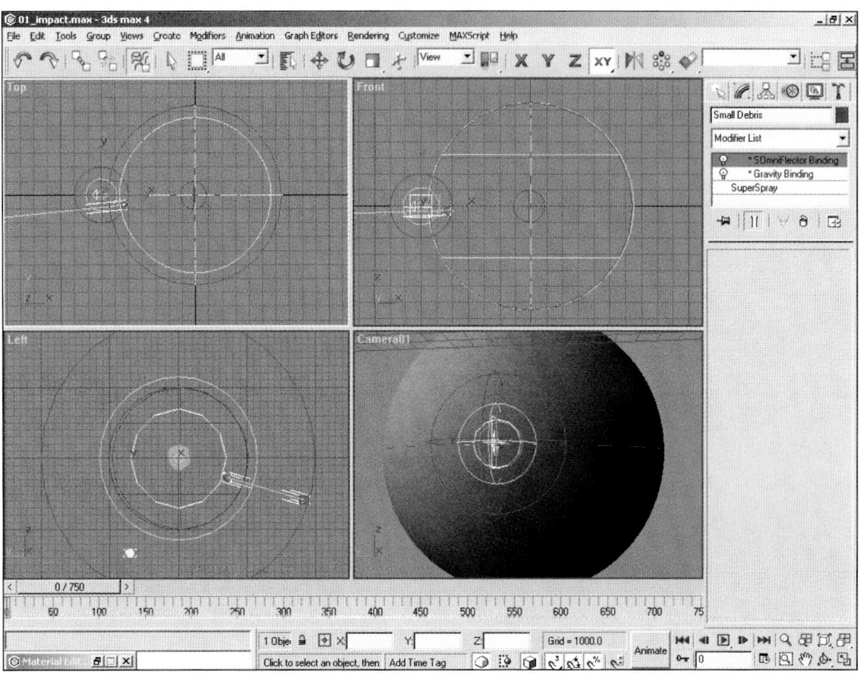

The resulting particle systems' modifier stack.

FINAL ANIMATION

Now it is time to put the entire scene together. It will become apparent why an additional UVW map for the Earth map and the Cloud Layer map was included, even if you used a sphere primitive with Generate Mapping turned on. You can simply rotate the Spherical UVW map so that the asteroid hits any place on the planet without disturbing or having to amend the position of the other UVW maps and the other elements of the scene.

1 Pick a continent that has a large amount of green in it (such as the Americas, Europe, or Asia) and target the impact on the continent's coastline to view both the sea's wave and the scorched earth effect at frame 200. Scrub the time bar back to frame 0.

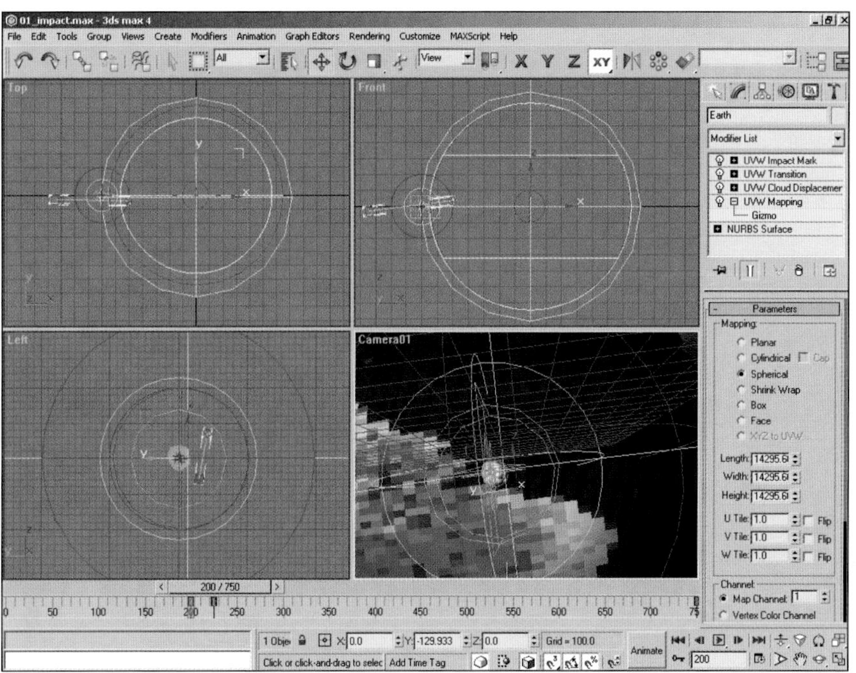

Amend the UVW Mapping modifier's gizmo to rotate the Earth texture map without affecting the other maps you have set up.

2 Go to Video Post, add a Camera event and a Starfield Image filter event (with the Scene camera as the selected camera, about 30,000 stars, and the default Motion Blur settings), and add an Image Output event. Render the animation.

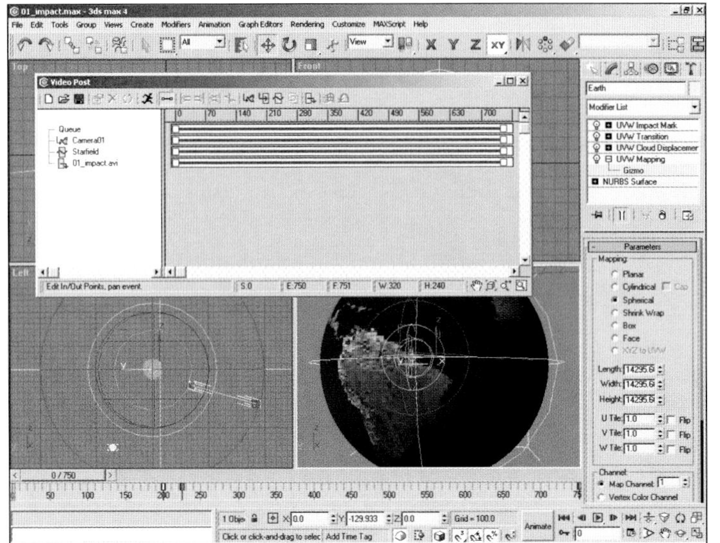

The Video Post sequence.

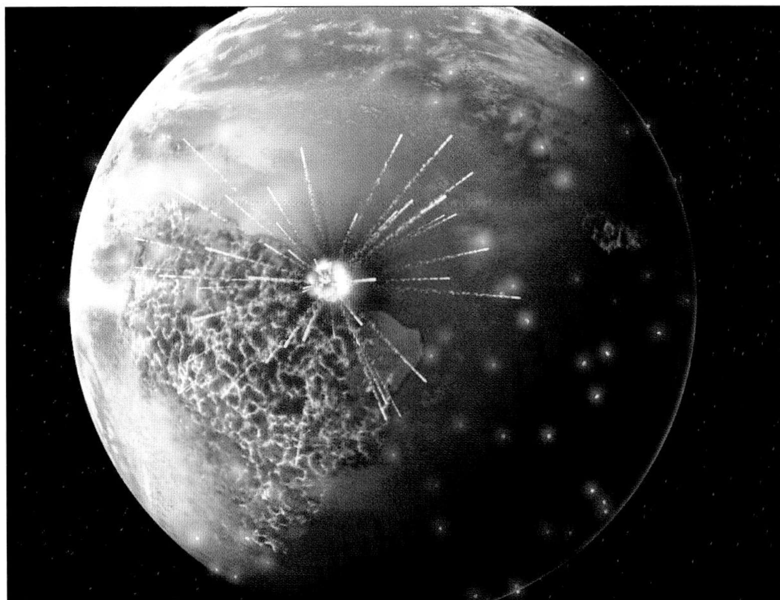

The final animation at frame 500.

MODIFICATIONS

There are, of course, any number of enhancements you could make to this scene. Additional elements could be added, such as binding the large debris particle trails to the Earth object deflector and increasing the gravity on the particle system's Gravity space warp. This will then pull the trails closer to the earth and, upon impact, remain stationary until they die. This gives a very nice effect, although it is a very CPU-intensive operation. Also, you could add different starfield backgrounds and other galactic phenomenon such as the Milky Way or nebulae.

You could also change the asteroid to a comet or even multiple smaller meteors using particles and generate impacts as illustrated in this chapter. You could add elements of civilization, such as satellites, space junk, and pinpoint lights, to represent cities on the dark side of the planet. There are numerous plug-ins that could enhance your scene, namely Cebas Pro Optics Suite, Ultrashock, Outburst, Phoenix, or Afterburn; there are also a few freeware ones around, such as FreePyro.

The overall effect mainly depends on which disaster movie you are basing your animation on! For this particular one, I mainly concentrated on the blockbuster *Armageddon*, but you might not altogether agree with the global (pardon the pun) effect of the impact. Look at other disaster movies such as *Deep Impact*, *Mission to Mars* (although the Mars impact is rather short), and *Dinosaur*, and you will get a different artist's representation of pretty much the same event. You could also incorporate additional cut scenes such as the asteroid entering the atmosphere and passing through a cloud layer (displacing clouds) and another for the sea or land impact before cutting back to outer space.

FLOWING WATER

"Five miles meandering with a mazy motion
Through wood and dale the sacred river ran."

—T.S. ELIOT, *"THE LOVE SONG OF J. ALFRED PRUFROCK"*

Creating a Flowing, Splashing Volume of Water

There are as many ways to approach the challenge of simulating water as there are artists interested in taking on that challenge. Given the wide variety of surface properties, mass characteristics, and viscosity changes a body of water can go through, an approach that incorporates several different techniques will probably meet with the greatest success.

In this tutorial, you will create a discrete volume of water that will flow from a tap, splash against a barrier, swirl into a funnel, and collect in a spherical jar. The water will be created using a combination of particles and solid geometry and will be controlled by space warps, deflectors, and some modifier trickery.

Project 2

Flowing Water

by Sean Bonney

Getting Started

Start 3ds max 4 and open the file **FlowingWater.max** from this project's folder on the accompanying CD-ROM. To preview the final result of this tutorial, view the rendered animation **FlowingWater.avi**.

The background objects for this scene have been provided for you on the accompanying CD-ROM. If you scrub the time slider, you will note that some props have been preanimated. There are two cameras: Camera01 is a static camera that covers the entire set, and Camera02 is a moving target camera that will follow the action more closely.

Viewing the scene from either of these cameras, follow the planned course of the water:

Frame	Action
9	The main faucet handle opens, triggering a stream of water.
13–44	The stream of water issues from the faucet.
30–57	The stream passes through the hole in the glass shelf, impacting on its surface.
35	The faucet handle closes.
40–65	The water is captured by the funnel and directed into the spherical jar.
85–105	The water collects in the jar.

SETTING UP THE INITIAL STREAM OF WATER

In this section, you will create a particle system to generate the stream of water and a Gravity space warp to direct the stream.

1 Go to the Top viewport and create a Super Spray particle system at X = –22, Y = 0, Z = 93. Go to the Camera01 viewport and rotate the gizmo 140 degrees on the View Y-axis.

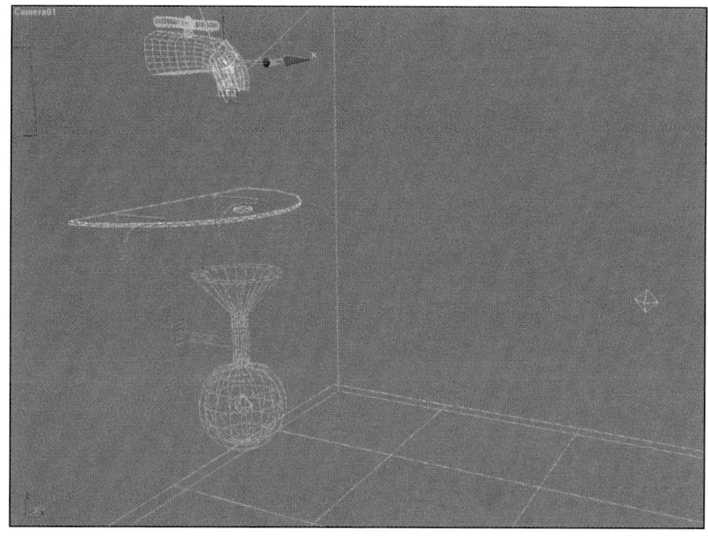

Create a Super Spray particle system for the main stream of water.

Note: The new Transform Type-In boxes on the status bar facilitate precise positioning of scene objects.

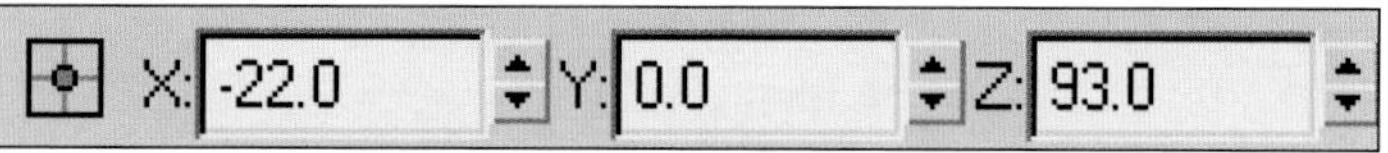

The Transform Type-In boxes make precise positioning of scene objects very easy.

2 Name this particle system **SuperSpray_Stream** and set the following values:

Basic Parameters

Particle Formation

Off Axis Spread: **15**

Off Plane Spread: **15**

Viewport Display

Percentage of Particles: **50%**

This will cause the particle dispersion to spread over a conic area 30 degrees wide. Larger spread values would result in a wider cone.

Note: You will most likely want to reduce the displayed percentage of particles as the scene complexity increases in order to speed up screen refresh.

3 To set the speed, quantity, and size of particles to closely match the desired look of water, set the following values:

Particle Generation

Particle Quantity

Use Rate: **10**

Particle Motion

Speed: **3**

Particle Timing

Display Until: **200**

Life: **70**

Particle Size

Size: **20**

Variation: **50%**

4 Scrub the time slider to see the water particles issue from the faucet while the handle is turned to the open position.

5 Go to the Top viewport and create a Gravity space warp. Set Strength to **0.5**.

Adding the gravity effect will give the falling water a more natural look. The positioning of the Gravity space warp is not important because this space warp will not vary with distance. It will be universally applied throughout World space.

6 Use the Bind to Space Warp tool to bind the gravity effect to the particle system. Go to the Camera01 viewport.

Note how the water now arcs naturally toward the floor.

Note: To change the dispersion of your generated particles, feel free to click the New button under Uniqueness to generate a new seed number.

Note: The Particle Timing settings should be given special attention because they are often a source of confusion for animators. In the event that particles seem to disappear prematurely or die out before striking a target, check these settings to ensure that the particles have been given an adequate lifespan.

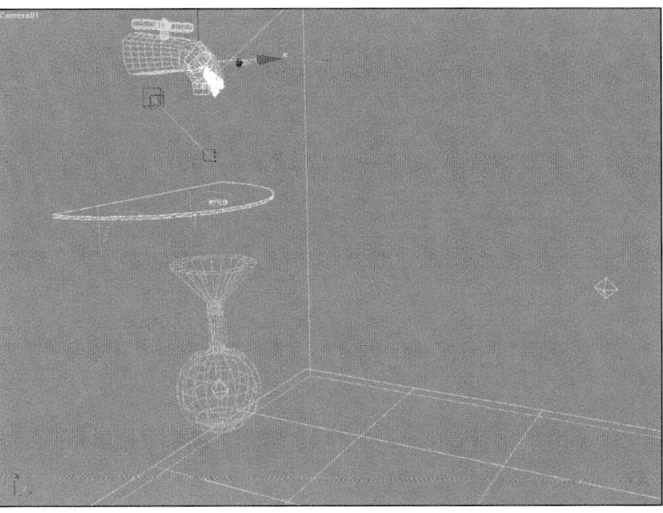

A stream of particles issues from the generator within the faucet.

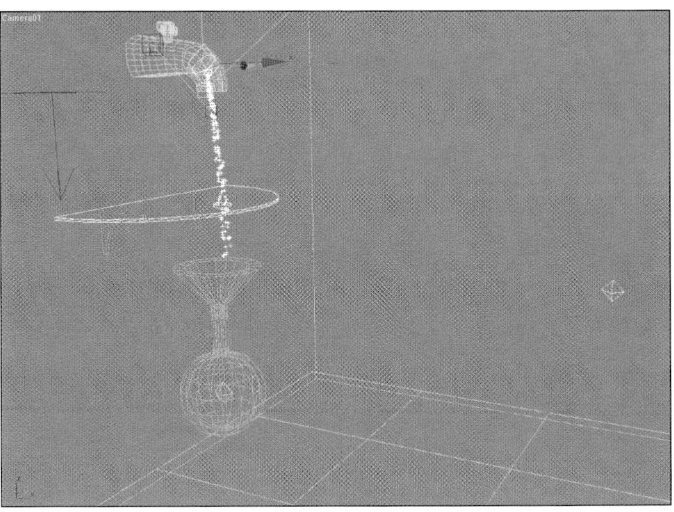

The Gravity space warp now sends the particles arcing toward the floor, shown at frame 37.

Controlling the Water with Deflectors

In some instances, you might want to create deflectors to keep the water from passing through the faucet head or the body of the glass shelf. Of course, the CPU overhead entailed by deflecting particles with highly detailed meshes might not always be worth the added accuracy. In this case, careful aiming of the water stream keeps it from obviously violating "solid" scene geometry, and the speed and blur of the stream should cover up any small errors.

To add a little swirl to the water as it is captured by the funnel, you will use a Motor space warp at the funnel mouth.

After the stream has passed through the glass shelf, it approaches the funnel where it will be collected and directed down into the spherical container. Although you could use the funnel/container object as a deflector to accomplish this task, it wouldn't be the most efficient choice. Instead you will use a proxy object.

1. Go to the Top viewport and create a Motor space warp at X = 0, Y = 5, Z = –645. Set the following values:

   Timing
   - On Time: **35**
   - Off Time: **95**

   Strength Control
   - Basic Torque: **50**
   - (Leave Type set to **N-m**)

   Particle Effect Range
   - Enable: **On**
   - Range: **175**

   The Display icon size has no bearing on the space warp's functioning, but to match the figure, set Icon Size to **100**.

2. Go to the Camera01 viewport and rotate the gizmo –20 degrees on the View Y-axis.

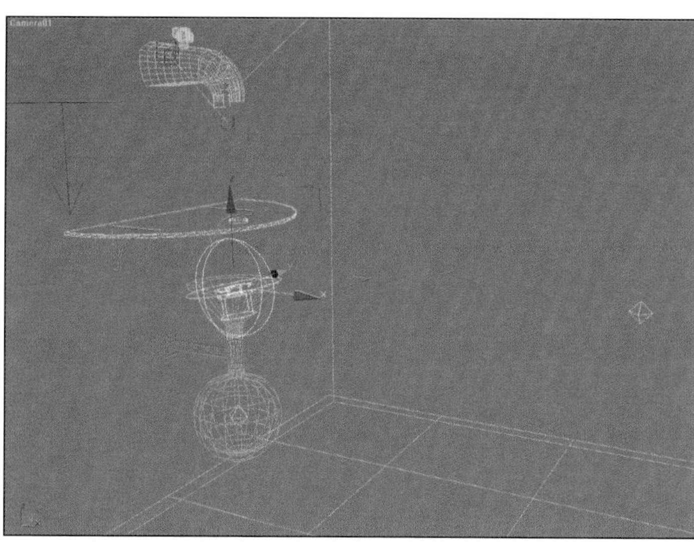

Create a Motor space warp to control the swirling of the particles as they enter the funnel mouth.

Note: Unlike the Gravity space warp, the placement of Motor gizmos is crucial to controlling their effect because the force is centered on the gizmo.

3 Use the Bind to Space Warp tool to bind the space warp to the particle system.

Until you have forced the water into the funnel, it will be hard to detect how the water is being subtly swirled by the Motor space warp.

4 Unhide the Funnel/Container_Proxy object.

This simple mesh object was modeled to approximate the shape of the funnel/container but with fewer polygons and, of course, only the interior faces. Notice that the upper edge of the funnel has been extended to catch stray particles. Moreover, the proxy's face normals point inward to catch particles inside the object.

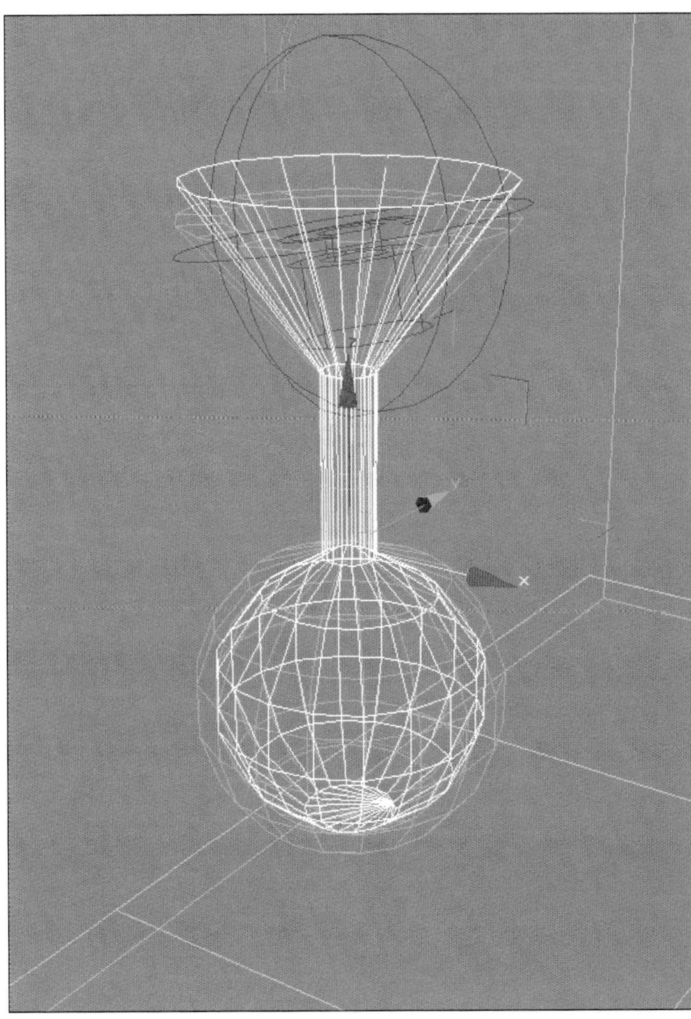

This stand-in mesh will deflect particles more efficiently than the renderable version.

5 Go to the Top viewport and create a UDynaFlect space warp. Name it **UDynaFlect_Funnel**. Set the following values:

Timing

Time Off: **200**

Particle Bounce

Bounce: **0.15**

Friction: **35**

The Time Off value serves a function similar to that of the Particle Timing settings in that it determines how long the deflector solution will function in the scene. The Particle Bounce settings determine the "stickiness" of the surface. In this case, deflected particles will rebound from the surface with a low amount (15%) of reflected energy and will have approximately one-third of their momentum impeded by friction.

6 Click the Pick Object button in the Modifier panel and select the Funnel/Container_Proxy object.

7 Use the Bind to Space Warp tool to bind the deflector to the particle system. Go to the Camera01 viewport and note how the water is being deflected by the funnel.

Note: If you find that some particles are escaping the funnel, try editing the proxy object to enlarge it where the hole is. Alternatively, you could try generating a new seed value for the original particle generation. If all else fails, copy the proxy, apply a Push modifier with a small negative value such as –5, and make this a second deflector to catch strays.

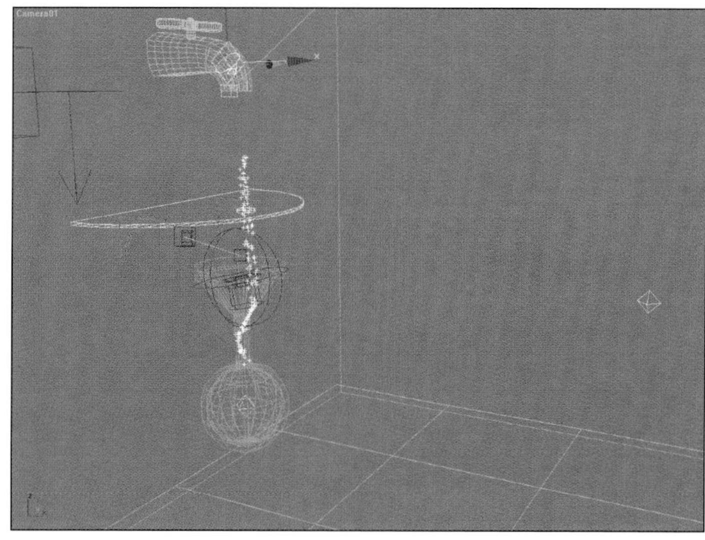

The proxy funnel mesh is now being used to deflect the particles into the funnel.

A Little Splash

The final effect to add is a splash of water where the stream passes through the hole in the glass shelf.

1 Go to the Top viewport and create a Super Spray particle system at X = 30, Y = 0, Z = –395. Name this particle system **SuperSpray_Splash01** and set the following values:

Basic Parameters

Particle Formation

Off Axis Spread: **90**

Off Plane Spread: **90**

Viewport Display

Percentage of Particles: **100%**

These settings will result in a wide dispersion of particles. The high display percentage will aid in visualizing how this particle system will function and shouldn't be a heavy burden on screen refresh due to the low number of total emitted particles.

2 Set the following values to control the quantity, speed, and lifespan of the spawned water droplets.

Particle Generation

Particle Quantity

Use Rate: **1**

Particle Motion

Speed: **15**

Particle Timing

Emit Start: **30**

Emit Stop: **60**

Display Until: **200**

Life: **200**

Particle Size

Size: **20**

Variation: **25%**

In this case, the Particle Timing settings are set to spawn particles during the time the original water spray is impacting with the shelf.

3 Use the Bind to Space Warp tool to bind the particle system to the Gravity space warp.

4 Go to the Top viewport and create a UDynaFlect space warp. Name it **UDynaFlect_Shelf**. Set the following values:

Timing

Time On: **0**

Time Off: **200**

Particle Bounce

Bounce: **0.2**

Friction: **50**

Using an Object deflector and a Planar deflector keeps the droplets from passing through the shelf and floor.

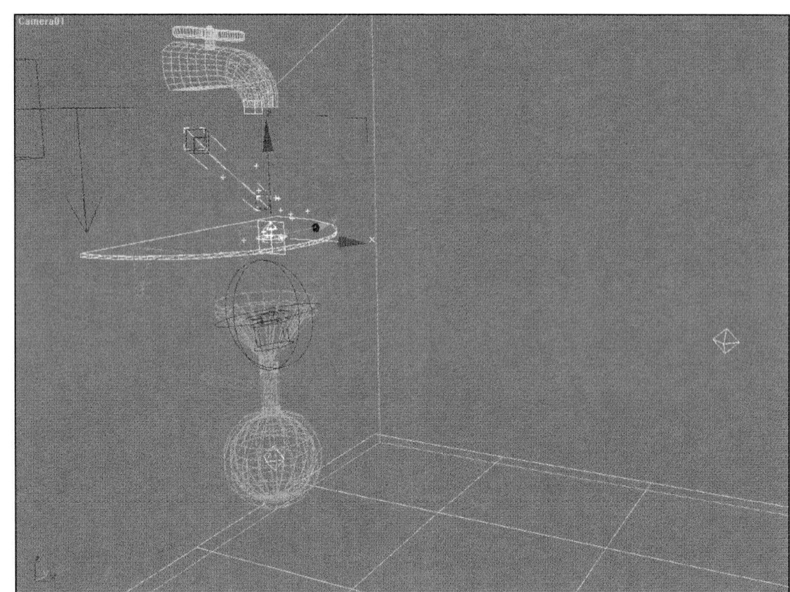

Create a Super Spray particle system to generate a small splash as the main stream goes through the hole in the shelf.

5 Click the Pick Object button and select the Shelf object.

6 Use the Bind to Space Warp tool to bind the deflector to the SuperSpray_Splash particle system. Still in the Top viewport, create a PDynaFlect space warp at X = 1000, Y = 0, Z = –1515.0. Name it **PDynaFlect_Floor**. Set the following values:

Timing

Time Off: **200**

Particle Bounce

Bounce: **0.2**

Friction: **50**

7 Set the following values to ensure that the deflector covers the entire floor area:

Display Icon

Width: **2800**

Height: **2800**

8 Use the Bind to Space Warp tool to bind the deflector to the SuperSpray_Splash01 particle system.

If you scrub the time slider (particularly in a Front viewport), you will notice that most of the splashed particles land on the shelf, and those that don't are stopped by the floor.

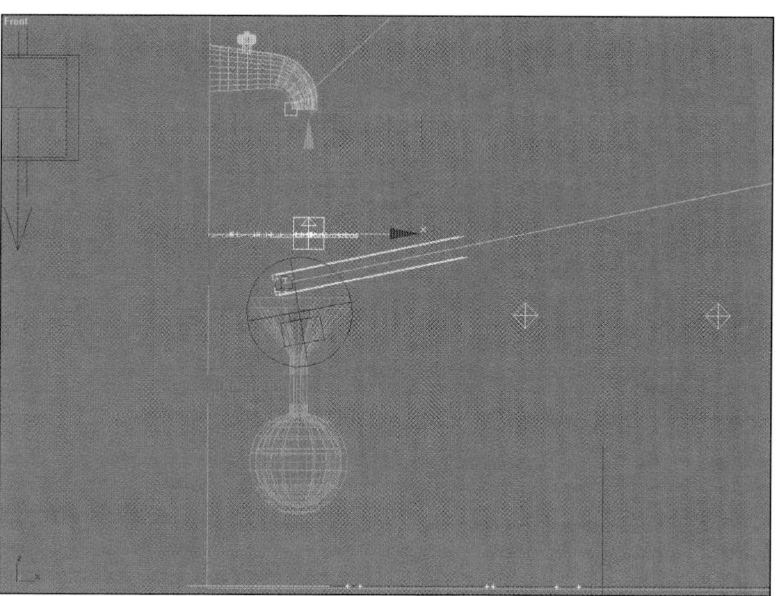

The Splash particle system is now being stopped by the shelf and the floor, shown at frame 200.

Give the Water Some Body

Up to this point, the water has been represented only by particle ticks. To successfully convey the illusion of streaming and splashing water, metablob particles will be used.

1 Select the SuperSpray_Stream system and go to the root SuperSpray object in the Modifier List. Set the Percentage of Particles displayed to **100%**.

   You will be able to see all of the particles in the viewports and get a more accurate view of the overall metablob shape.

2 Go to the Camera viewport around frame 30. In the Particle Type rollout, set the following values:

   Particle Types
      MetaParticles: **On**

   MetaParticle Parameters
      Tension: **0.1**

3 Go up to the Viewport Display area and select **Mesh**.

   Notice how the particle ticks are replaced with a blobby mesh simulating cascading water. To speed up screen refresh, set Viewport Display back to **Ticks** and reduce Percentage of Particles.

4 Select the SuperSpray_Splash system and go to the root SuperSpray object in the Modifier List. Set the Particle Type to **MetaParticles**. Set Tension to **0.5**.

   This will add volume to the splashed droplets.

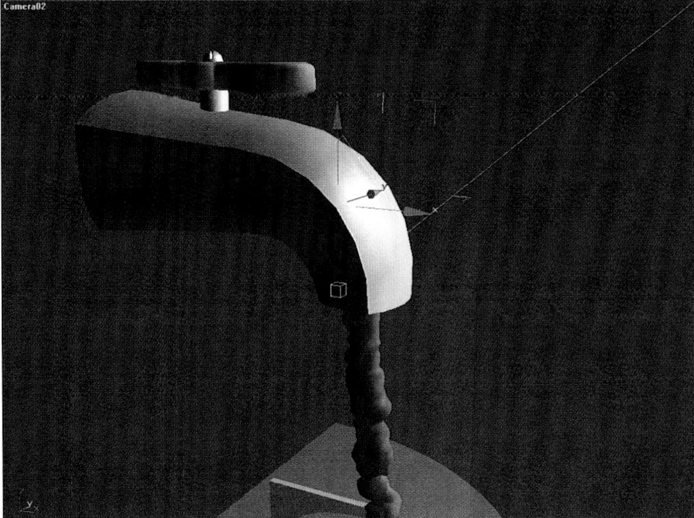

The blobby water mesh created with MetaParticles.

Collecting the Water

If all has gone well, the main stream of water will pass through the shelf, be collected by the funnel, and be directed into the spherical jar. The particles should die out as they approach the bottom of the jar. Feel free to adjust the Life value of the particle system, if necessary, to prevent particles from bouncing around at the bottom of the jar.

The actual volume of water collecting in the jar will be created using an animated Boolean compound object.

1. Go to the Top viewport and create a Box object at X = 0, Y = 0, Z = –1225. Name this object **Box_Boolean**. Set the following values:

   Length: **400**
   Width: **400**
   Height: **400**

   This box will be subtracted as part of a Boolean object to determine the level of the rising water.

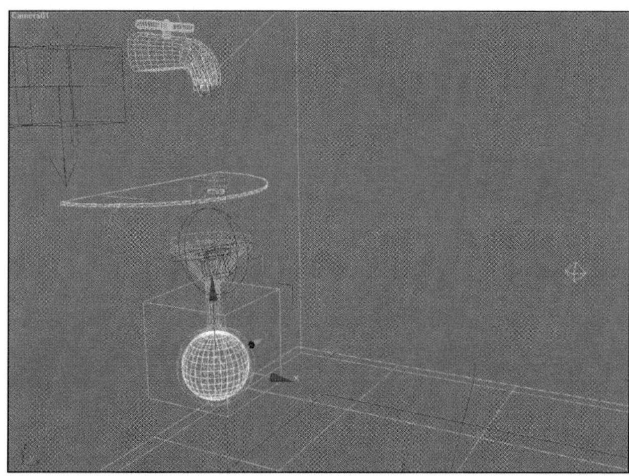

The Box and Sphere objects used to create the animated Boolean compound object.

2. Right-click on the box, go to Properties, and uncheck Renderable.

   You could simply hide this object before rendering, but this extra step ensures that it will not be accidentally rendered.

3. Create a Sphere object at X = 0, Y = 0, Z = –1120. Name this object **Sphere_Water**. Set the following values:

   Radius: **140**
   Segments: **32**

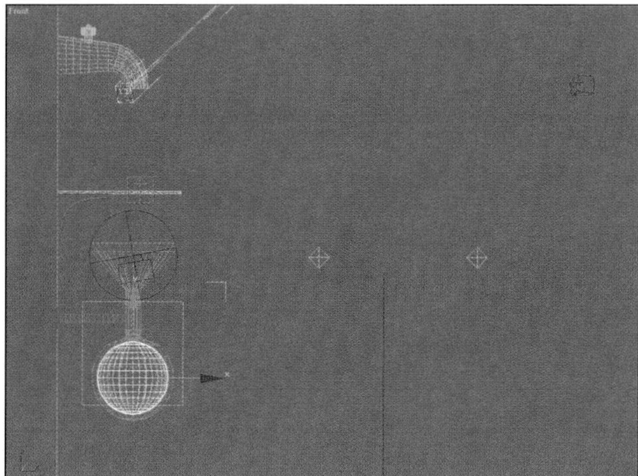

The Box_Boolean object will be animated to follow the rising water level as the stream collects.

4 Select the Box_Boolean object and turn Animate on. Go to frame 75 and set a Position key. Go to frame 105 and move the box 145 units on the View Z-axis to Z = −1080. Turn Animate off.

Note: Boolean operations can sometimes be a bit unpredictable, so it is advisable to either save your file or perform a Hold prior to creating the Boolean.

5 Select the sphere and create a Boolean compound object. Click the Pick Operand B button and select Box Boolean.

Scrub the time slider to see how the water level rises as the streaming particles enter the jar.

The animated Boolean object creates a rising level of water in the jar.

6 Go to frame 200 and apply a UVW modifier. Select Box as the mapping type and click the Fit button.

By fitting the Mapping gizmo when the object is at its largest, you avoid undesired UV tiling if the object should at some point exceed the gizmo's boundaries.

7 Apply an Edit Mesh modifier, go to Face, Sub-Object mode, and select all faces. Go to the Surface Properties rollout and set Material ID to **1**.

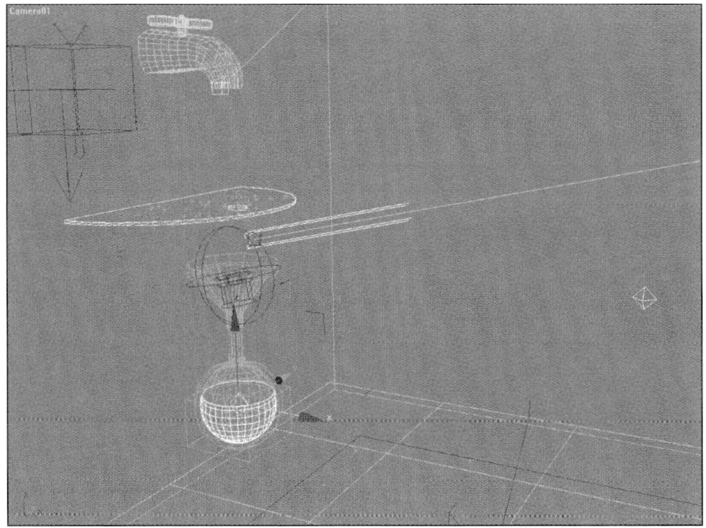

Apply a UVW modifier fit to the largest size the Boolean will attain.

The "Look" of Water

Arguably, the most important aspect of creating convincing water is the material. Given how quickly and chaotically water can move, slightly unorthodox movement or volume can be overlooked, but the most perfectly flowing body of water will not read as water without the appropriate look.

1 Go to the Camera02 viewport at frame 35.

If you render a still, you will see that the default material looks more like gooey plastic than water.

Even with a nice shape, the water does not look convincing without an appropriate material.

2 Open the Material Editor and select an unused material. Name this material **Water**. Set the following values:

Diffuse Color: **R 110, G 130, B 140**
Opacity: **75**
Specular Highlights
    Specular Level: **20**
    Glossiness: **60**

This shiny, subtly transparent material will be expanded with maps to look more like water.

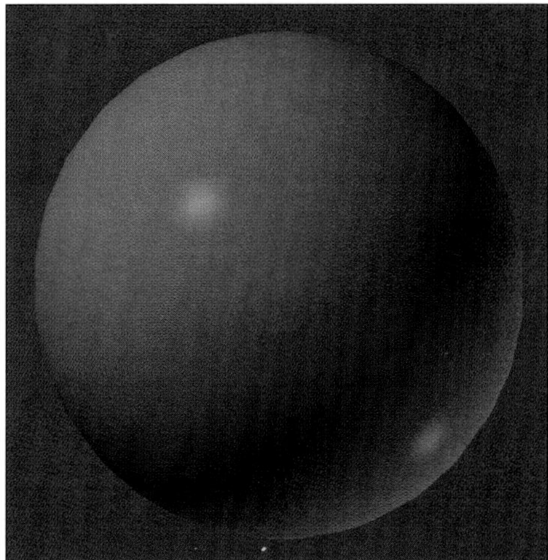

Create a shiny blue-green material as the basis for the water material.

3 Under Extended Parameters, set the following values:

Advanced Transparency

Falloff: **Out**

Index of Refraction: **1.3**

Reflection Dimming

Apply: **On**

Dim Level: **0.25**

The Advanced Transparency values determine that the material will become more transparent toward the outside of the object. Reflection Dimming serves to diminish the impact of reflection maps in shadowed areas of the object.

Note: It's a good idea to give each map/material a unique and significant name to facilitate moving through the material hierarchy. This is particularly useful for complex materials.

4 Go to the Diffuse Color channel and apply a Noise material. Under Noise Parameters, set the following values:

Noise Type: **Fractal**

Size: **5**

Noise Threshold

High: **0.85**

Low: **0.25**

Color #1: **R 95, G 165, B 140**

Color #2: **R 115, G 140, B 160**

This Noise map will serve as the main coloring for the water material.

5 Go up to the root Water material and set the Diffuse Color to **75%**.

This enables you to mix the Diffuse color set in step 2 with the Diffuse color channel.

6 Set the Reflection channel's amount to **35%**. Apply a Reflect/Refract material to the Reflection channel.

You will use this material to apply reflection mapping to the water based on the surrounding scene objects. When applying automatic reflection mapping, the object's pivot point is used to generate the maps. Because the pivot point of the SuperSpray_Stream particle system is within the faucet and not in a good position to generate Reflection maps, you will create a set of bitmaps based on a temporary object.

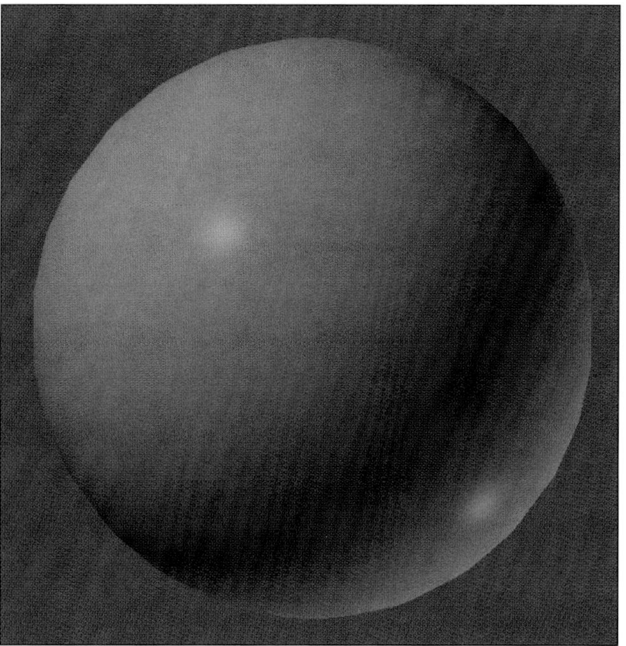

Mix the Diffuse color with the Diffuse channel by reducing the Diffuse color amount from 100%.

7 Set the Reflect/Refract map's Source to **From File**. Go to the Top viewport and create a Sphere at X = 300, Y = 0, Z = –200. Set Radius to **20**.

8 Under the Render Cubic Map Files section of the Reflect/Refract map, click the To File button. Enter **Water** in the File Name box, set Save as Type to **BMP**, and accept **RGB 24bit** as the BMP Configuration.

Using 24-bit files, as opposed to 8-bit, preserves more color depth information and results in a richer image.

9 Hide the following objects: SuperSpray_Stream, SuperSpray_Splash, and Sphere_Boolean.

This will prevent unwanted objects from showing up in the reflection maps.

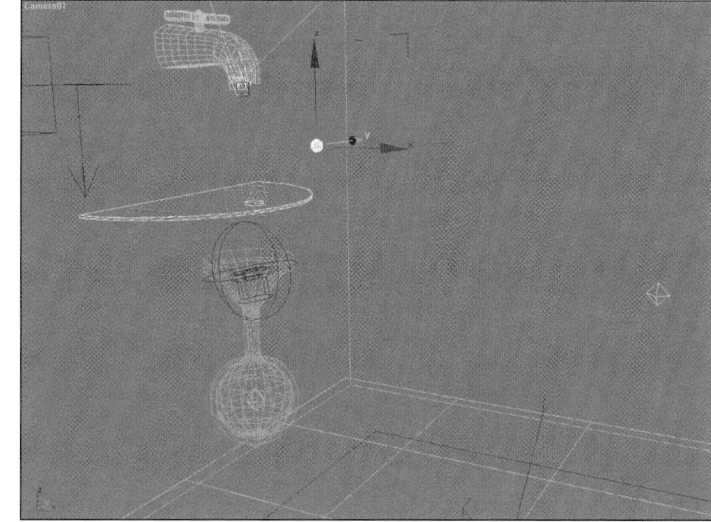

The temporary sphere used to create Reflection maps for the water material.

10 Click the Pick Object and Render Maps button and choose the sphere you created in step 8 to render six orthogonal views from the point of view of the temporary object.

3ds max 4 should now render six 100×100 bitmaps and assign them to the Up, Down, Left, Right, Front, and Back slots. Because this set is not a complete room and consists of only two walls and a floor, several of these maps will be flat black. You can change the slot assignments so that all slots have some texture to them.

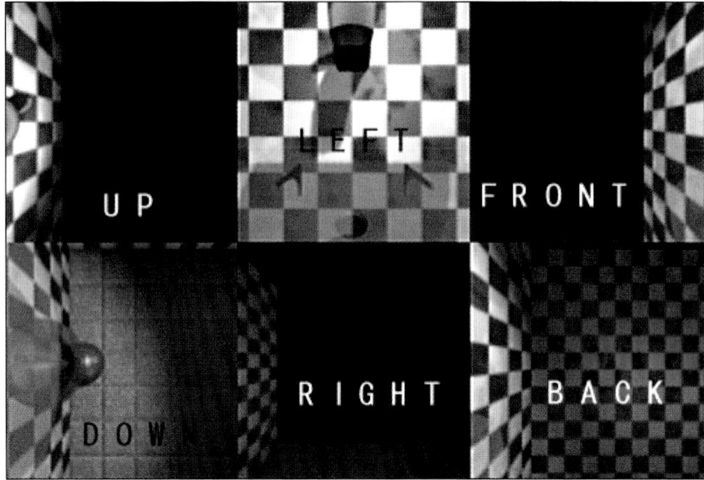

The six orthogonal views that are automatically rendered using the Render Cubic Maps function.

11 Click the Up slot and choose **water_DN.bmp**. Click the Right slot and choose **water_LF.bmp**. Click the Front slot and choose **water_BK.bmp**. Delete the sphere.

12 Unhide SuperSpray_Stream, SuperSpray_Splash, and Sphere_Water. Assign the Water material to the SuperSpray_Stream particle system.

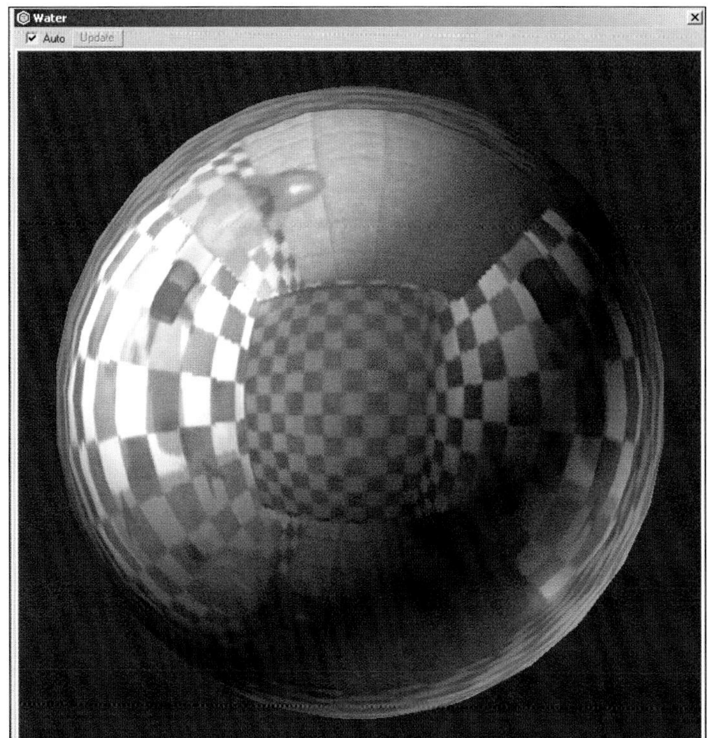

The finished material as seen in a magnified Material Editor window.

13 Go to the Camera02 viewport, still at frame 35. If you render another still, you will see that the water looks quite a bit more realistic.

14 Assign this material to the SuperSpray_Splash particle system as well.

The final material, applied to the water stream, shown at frame 35.

Material for the Rising Water

The animated Boolean object used for the rising water requires an extra level of materials to separate the rippling top surface from the main body of water.

1 Select an unused material, name it **Rising_Water**, and change the material type to **Top/Bottom**. Set Blend to **15**. Assign this material to the Sphere_Water object.

The Top/Bottom material assigns one of two materials to object faces, depending on whether the face normals are pointing above or below the horizon.

2 Drag the Water material to the Material button for the Bottom material. Choose **Instance** as the method of copying. Rename this material **Water#2**.

3 Drag the Water material to the Material button for the Top material. Be sure to choose **Copy** as the method. Click the Material button for the Top material and rename this material **Water_Surface**.

4 Set the Top material's Bump channel amount to **150** and assign a Mask material to the Bump channel.

5 Assign a Gradient map to the Mask channel, with the following values:

Gradient Parameters
  Color #2: **R 0, G 0, B 0**
  Color 2 Position: **0**
  Gradient Type: **Radial**
  Noise
    Amount: **0.2**
    Size: **2**

At this point, the map should appear completely black if you deactivate Show End Result in the Material Editor.

6 Go to frame 200, turn Animate on, and set Phase to **15**.

You will animate this Gradient map to open like a shutter as the water stream hits the surface, adding a ripple bump effect to the water's material.

7 Go to frame 70 and set a key locking the current Color #2 value. The most straightforward way to accomplish this is to open the Color Selector, change an RGB value, and then return to R 0, G 0, B 0.

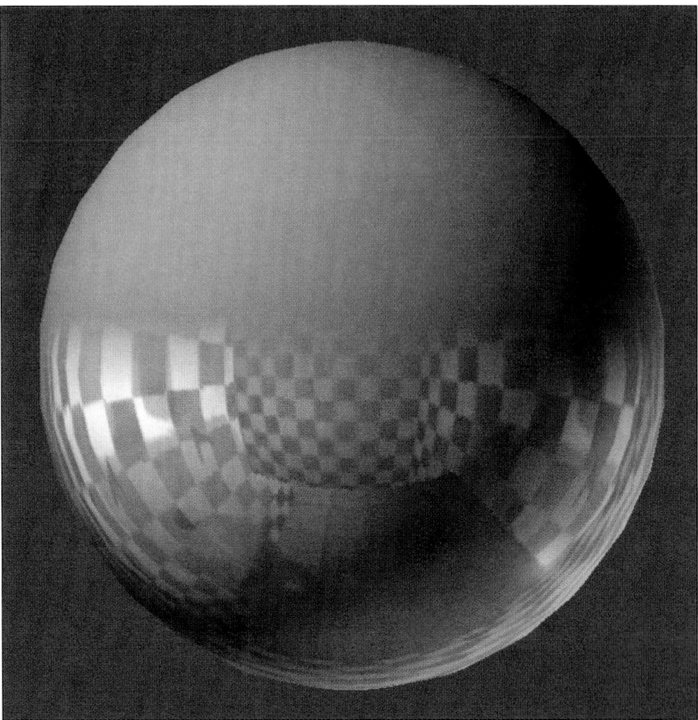

Assign the Water material to the Bottom channel of the Top/Bottom material.

8 Set the following keys to animate the opening of the shutter:

Frame	Color #2
80	R 200, G 200, B 200
105	R 85, G 85, B 85
130	R 0, G 0, B 0

9 Turn Animate off. Go up to the Bump material and assign a Cellular map to the Map slot. Set Source to **Explicit Mapping Channel**.

Note: The Source setting determines how the map is applied to scene objects. The default of Object XYZ applies the map according to the shape of the object in reference to its pivot point. By changing this setting to Explicit Mapping Channel, you apply the map according to whatever UVW channels have been applied either in a UVW Mapping modifier or in an object's creation parameters.

10 Go to the Cellular Parameters rollout and drag the second Division Color onto the first, choosing **Copy**. Under Cell Characteristics, set Size to **0.25**.

You will animate the Cell Color to provide the appearance of rippling water.

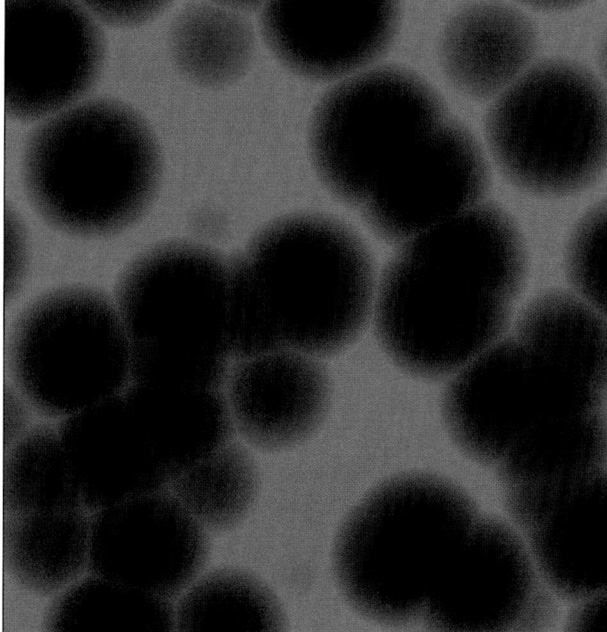

Create a Cellular map to provide the look of a rippling water surface.

11 Open Track View and expand the Sphere_Water object to reveal the Rising_Water material track. Continue expanding levels to reveal, in turn, Top: Water_Surface, Bump, Map, and Cell Color. Select the Cell Color track.

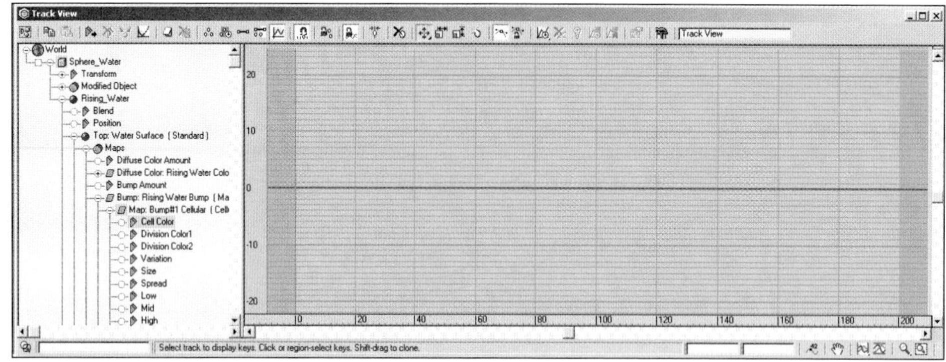

Select the Cell Color track, which will determine the height of the water ripples.

12 Assign a Noise Point3 controller to the Cell Color track. Set the following values in the Properties dialog:

X Strength: **256**

>0: **On**

Y Strength: **512**

>0: **On**

Z Strength: **512**

>0: **On**

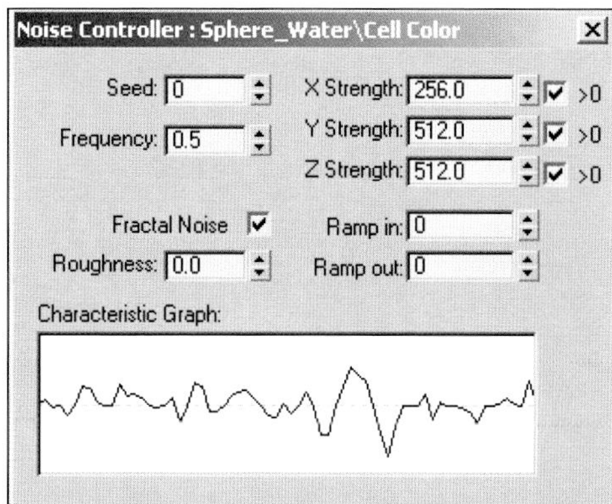

The Noise Controller dialog.

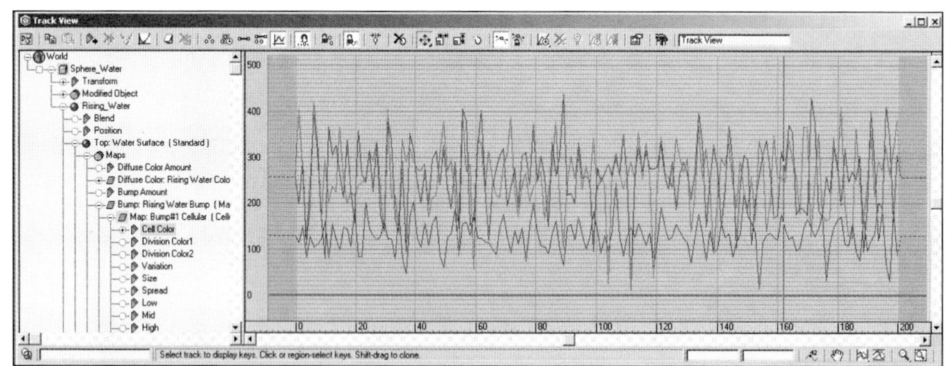

Set the Noise controller's properties to create a consistent degree of variation.

13 Expand Cell Color and choose the Noise Strength track. Go to Edit Keys mode and add keys at frames 75, 110, and 140. Set the following values for these keys:

Frame 75

X Value: **0**

Y Value: **0**

Z Value: **0**

Frame 110

X Value: **1**

Y Value: **3**

Z Value: **3**

Frame 140

X Value: **0**

Y Value: **0**

Z Value: **0**

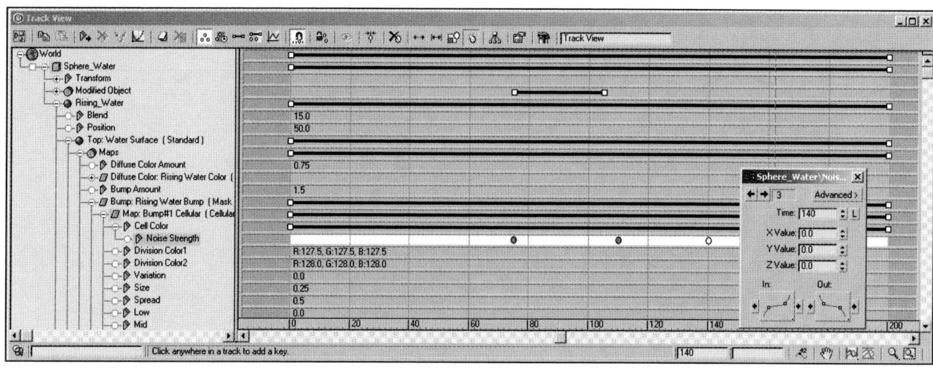

Add keys to the Noise Strength track to vary the agitation of the water ripples.

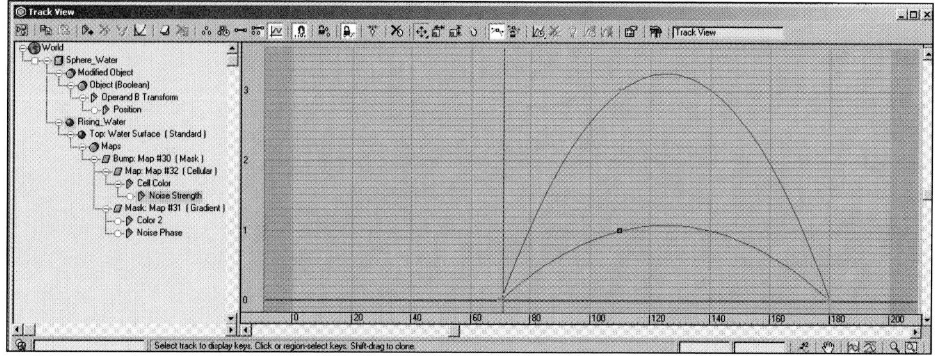

The Noise Strength track shows how the intensity increases as the water level rises and then settles down.

Note: If the Noise Strength track does not show up, go to the Track View Filters dialog and uncheck Show Animated Tracks Only.

Note: Click the left and right arrows in the Key Properties dialog to advance to the preceding or next key.

14 Go to Function Curves mode and select the Cell Color track to see how the curve will ramp up and then down as the surface of the water is agitated by the falling stream.

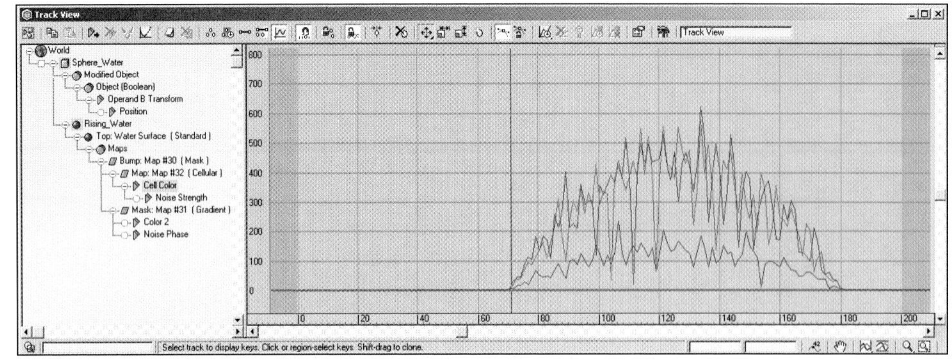

The Cell Color track as determined by the Noise controller.

Rendering

The final tweak to add before rendering this sequence is a motion blur. The blur will add to the liquid feel of the water and will smooth out the boundaries between MetaParticles.

1 Select the SuperSpray_Stream and SuperSpray_Splash particle systems, right-click one, and go to the Properties dialog.

2 Ensure that Enabled is on in the Motion Blur section. Select the Object radio button.

This will activate object-based motion blur, which blurs the object according to its motion over time. This is in contrast to image-based motion blur, which blurs the entire image and is more useful for very fast camera moves.

3 Open the Render Scene dialog, open the MAX Default Scanline A-Buffer rollout, and go to the Object Motion Blur panel. Set the following values:

Apply: **On**
Duration (frames): **0.5**
Samples: **5**
Duration Subdivisions: **5**

These settings will blur objects according to their movements over half of a frame, rendering five samples to blend together.

Note: Keeping the Object Motion Blur Samples and Duration Subdivisions settings the same means that all samples will be evenly spaced, avoiding a choppy, random effect that can result when Samples is set to a value less than Duration Subdivisions.

The effect of Object Motion Blur on the water, shown without blur (left) and with blur (right) at frame 36.

Modifications

There are many ways in which you could enhance this animation. Additional splash emitters could be placed in the faucet, at the funnel's mouth, or inside the jar itself. Additionally, a particle system emitting bubbles could be used inside the jar. The animated Boolean technique could be used to fill a variety of containers and tubes or to empty them.

The water could be changed to almost any fluid by varying the materials, particularly the Opacity and Diffuse channels. By changing the distribution of the particles, the fluid could be made to spray wildly, trickle slowly, or flow in chunks. The Friction, Bounce, and Chaos settings of the various emitters control how the viscosity of individual droplets is perceived. Increasing Friction will make them appear to be stickier, while increasing the Bounce value will give them a stiff, rubbery feel.

UNDERWATER SCENE

"I do."

—LOURDES PEGUERO MANAHAN, MY WIFE

(NOVEMBER 5, 2000)

Underwater Environment

The atmosphere sets the mood. We'll work with camera animation, depth of field, light, and texture to create a vibrant, realistic underwater atmosphere. The sunlight will beam through the rippling waves and illuminate a spider web caustic pattern on the spiky ocean ground. As the camera travels through the underwater archway, you will see blurry bubbles coming out of thin spikes in the ground.

Project 3

Underwater Scene

by Daniel Manahan

GETTING STARTED

This underwater environment starts you off with most of the objects logically named and placed. You will learn how to set parameters, modifiers, color, texture, atmosphere, and animation and how to have the freedom to make creative changes along the way.

Note: Pressing Shift+Q will create a quick rendering of the active view. Use this when you want to observe and understand the changes. On slow computers, don't use the Depth of Field and disable the bubbles by changing the Use Total to 0.

Note: By pressing F1, new users can review the help files containing information on how to create and move objects and can learn the locations of the menus and buttons listed in the tutorial.

There are several helpful files on the accompanying CD-ROM. You'll need the file Underwater_Environment_Start.max to start the project. You will also find a file called Underwater_Environment_Finished.max that you can use to compare any parameters you might have missed. Finally, you can run Underwater_Environment 0_300.avi to see the final rendering. Also included on the accompanying CD-ROM is a bonus section that contains more in-depth instructions for deleting and modeling a new ground.

Pay close attention to the explanations, notes, warnings, and suggestions for creative variations.

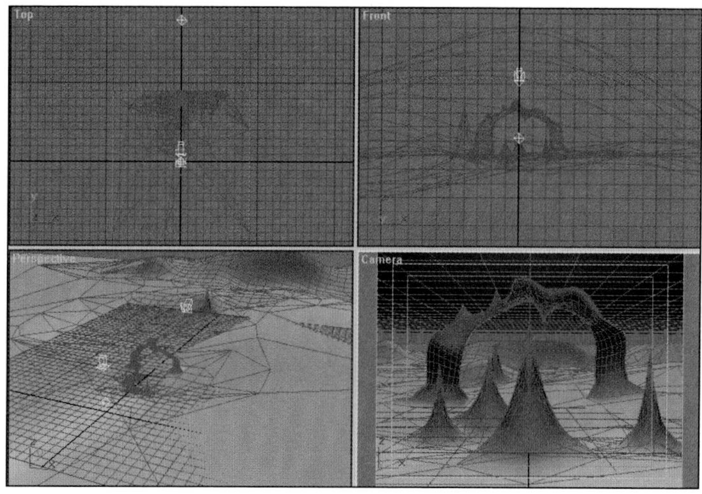

This is Underwater_Environment_start.max as it opens.

Set Up the Camera's Depth of Field

The ocean has a very thick atmosphere. The details should fade on objects in the background, and only objects close to you will be clear.

1 Open the file **Underwater_Environment_Start.max** from the accompanying CD-ROM.

2 Go to the Camera view, press "H" to select by name, select Camera from the list, and click Select to exit.

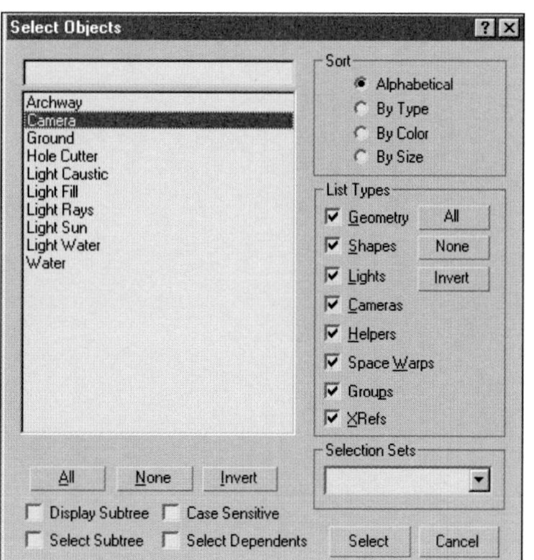

From now on, you will be using the keyboard shortcut "H" to select objects by name. Having the wrong object selected will be the most common error among new users.

3 From the Modify panel within the Camera's Parameters rollout, set Lens to **35mm**.

Setting the Lens to a lower number increases the field of view and enables you to see the environment distorted as if seen through a fish-eye lens. The Lens can be animated for a special effect.

4 In Environment Ranges, set the Near Range to **0'** and the Far Range to **1300'**.

Lower Far values make the fog thicker. You will be able to see this when fog is added to the Environment effect.

5 In Clipping Planes, check Clip Manually, set Near Clip to **0'** and Far Clip to **1300'**.

The Near Clip distance will cause foreground objects within this range to disappear. By setting this to 0, you prevent portions of the ground from becoming invisible if the camera passes too close.

6 Under Multi-Pass Effect, check Enable for Depth of Field and set the Target Distance to **250**.

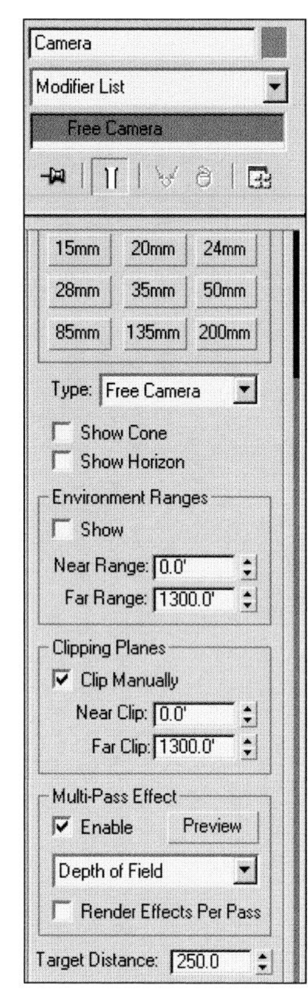

Set the Camera modifiers.

7 Within the Depth of Field Parameters rollout, under Sampling, set Total Passes to **5**.

The Target Distance can be animated to create the illusion that you are focusing a camera lens. After the ground is modeled, use the Preview button to help decide what distance you want in focus.

Warning: On slow computers, skip step 6. On fast computers, disable Depth of Field when making test renderings.

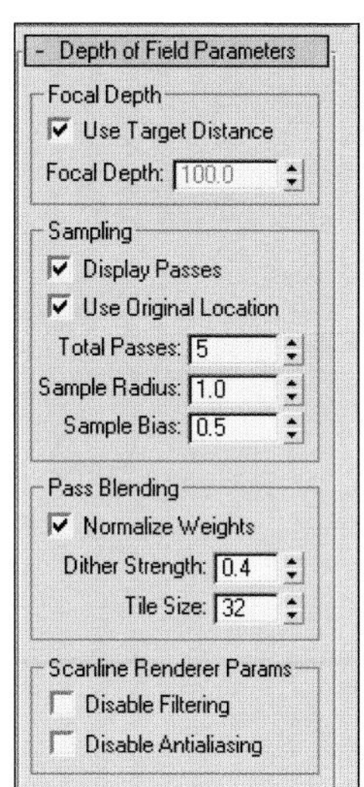

The number of passes will multiply the time it takes to render. A value of 5 might take five times as long to render, but it is worth it to create this very important illusion of murky water.

Animate Large Waves

You will use noise to animate the large waves. Noise is a modifier that will deform and animate the water to appear as large, rolling waves. You will set the size, the amount they fall over on themselves, and the speed realistic to an ocean surface.

1 Go to the Camera view, press "H" to select by name, and choose Water.

Warning: Often, typing in a keyboard shortcut will happen right after typing a parameter. Keyboard shortcuts will not work if there is a flashing cursor in a value box. Press Esc prior to typing a keyboard shortcut to clear the flashing cursor.

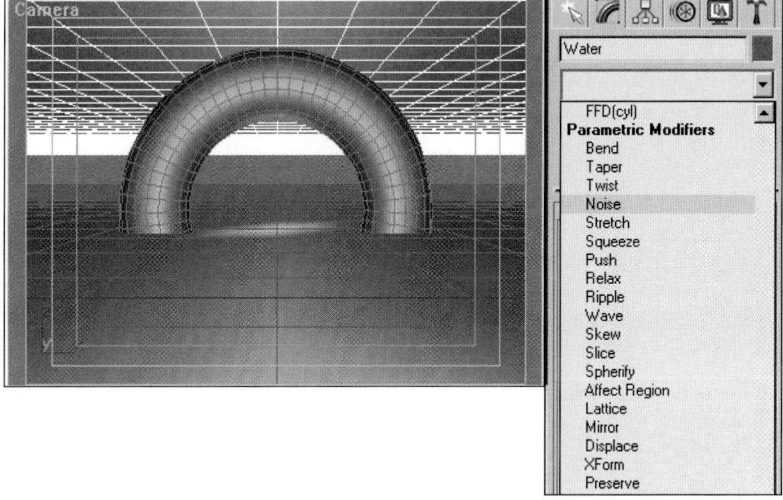

Click on the Modifiers List and drop way down to find the Parametric Modifiers section.

2 Click on the Modifier List and, under Parametric Modifiers, choose Noise. Within the Noise Parameters rollout, set Scale to **1000** and Strength to **X = 90'**, **Y = 90'**, and **Z = 15'**. Check Animate Noise and set the Frequency to **0.075**.

3 Click the Play button and, from the Camera view, watch the motion of the large slow waves. Adjust the Frequency to change the speed.

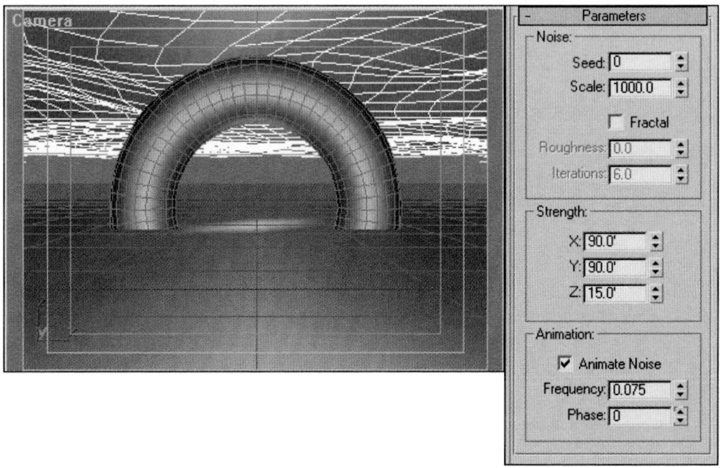

The Z Strength parameter determines the height of the waves, whereas the X and Y settings will adjust how far the waves will roll and fold over on themselves. The Frequency determines the speed of the waves.

Animate the Bubbles

The bubbles need to come out of the ground and interact with each other as they fight their way to the surface from the force of an upward current. Start by creating the Wind space warp and particle array. Then, choose polygons on the spikes to be the emitter that will send the bubbles out of the ground and toward the surface. Finally, use Motion Blur to soften the bubbles as they travel.

1 From the Create panel, click the Space Warps button, and within the Object Type rollout, click the Wind button.

This will make the bubbles rise.

2 In the Camera view, click and drag out a Wind space warp and name it **Wind**. Activate the Move tool and place the Wind in front of the archway.

The Wind arrow should point up in the Camera view. This will be the direction of the Wind's strength. The icon size and position won't matter.

3 From the Create panel, click the Geometry button and change the listing to Particle Systems.

4 Within the Object Type rollout, click PArray. In the Camera view, drag out a PArray in front of the archway and name it **Bubbles**. Activate the Move tool and place the Bubbles in front of the archway.

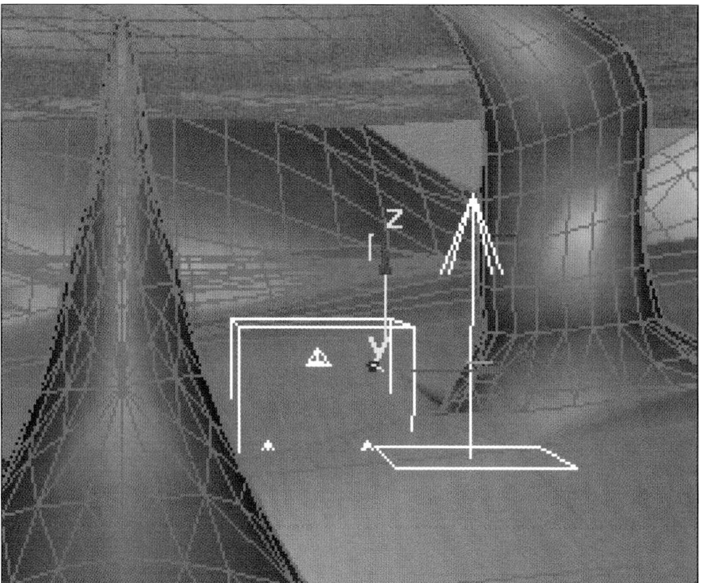

A cube displays the position of the Bubbles PArray. Since you will be choosing polygons from the ground to emit the bubbles, it won't matter where the Bubbles PArray is positioned or its icon size.

5 Activate the Select Object tool, select the ground, go to the Modify panel, and edit Sub-objects Polygon. Hold down Ctrl and multiple select polygons at the tips of some thin spikes.

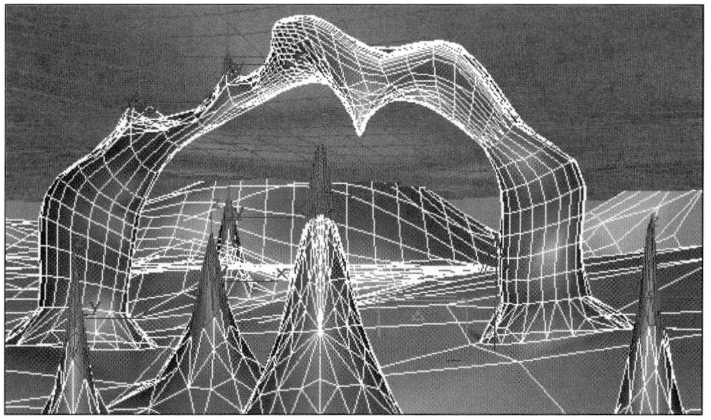

Don't select polygons in the background. You can hold Alt to deselect polygons if you selected too many. Try working from all views to get just the tips of the spikes.

6 Get off Sub-objects, select the bubbles, right-click, and choose Properties. Under Motion Blur, select Image and set Multiplier to **2**.

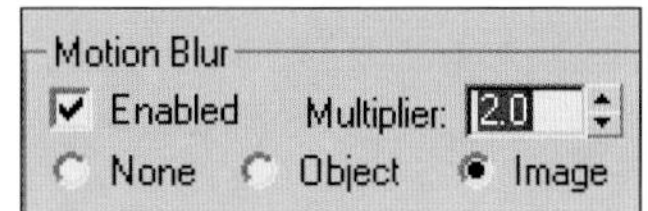

Higher Multiplier values will make a larger smear of the rendered bubbles.

Pick the Emitter Object

Now you will specify which object in the scene will emit the bubbles and limit them to emit only from the selected polygons.

1 Within the Basic Parameters rollout, click the Pick Object button, press "H", and choose Ground. Under Particle Formation, check Use Selected Sub-Objects.

You won't see much until most of the parameters are set. Bubbles will come out of spikes in the ground where you selected the polygons.

2 Under Viewport Display select Mesh.

Selecting Mesh will change the displayed bubbles from white tick marks to blobby spheres. The Percentage of Particles amount will display in the Camera view a percentage of what will render.

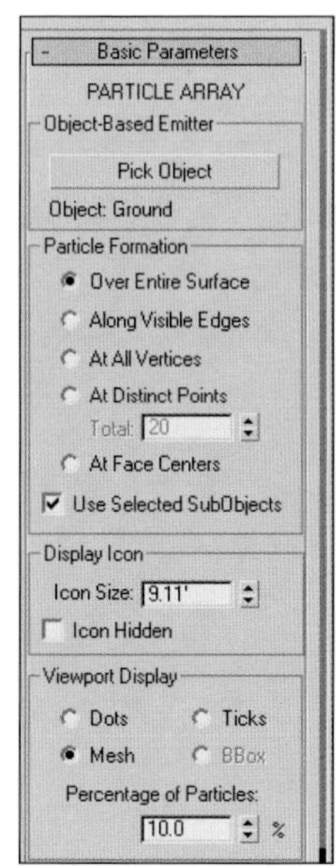

The Basic Parameters rollout of the Particle Array.

Note: Only the specified Percentage of Particles will be visible in the Camera view, though all the bubbles will render. However, if you were to render a preview of the bubbles, you would need to increase this percentage temporarily to 100 percent to preview the full effect.

Set the Bubbles' Timing and Size

You need enough large bubbles to be slowly spit out as they undulate up, break apart, and create realistic collisions.

1 Within the Particle Generation rollout, under Quantity, select Use Total and set it to **700**.

   There will be 700 bubbles used from the time when the emitter starts to when it ends.

2 Under Particle Motion, set Speed to **0.01'** and Variation to **50%**.

   To create randomness, below many of the parameters is a Variation amount. Use the Variation to make each bubble vary from its parameter an amount equal to the specified percentage.

3 Under Particle Timing, set the Emit Start to **–300**, and the Emit Stop to **300**.

   Bubbles have already been in motion 300 frames before the scene starts its rendering at frame 0. Half of the 700 bubbles will already have traveled up by frame 0. In the following steps, you will set the Life of the bubbles to **600** frames so that a bubble that was emitted at frame –300 will still be alive on frame 300.

4 For the timing, set the Display Until to **300** and the Life to **600**. Under Particle Size, set the Size to **2'**, Variation to **150%**, Grow For to **5**, and Fade For to **0**.

   The bubbles will take 5 frames to grow to approximately 2 feet. You don't have to worry about how long they will fade because their life has been set to 600 frames, thus dying after the scene is finished rendering.

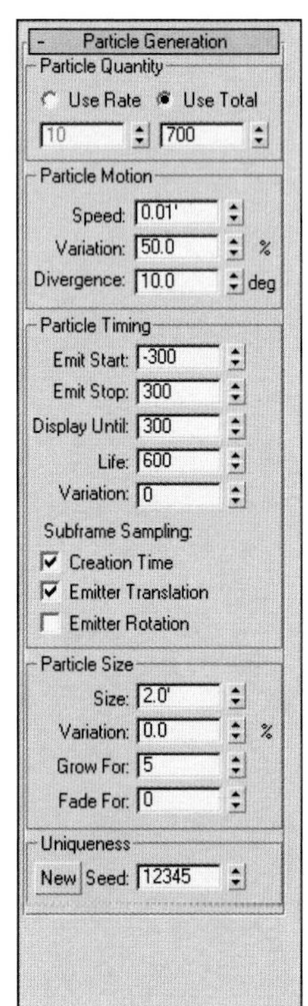

The Particle Generation rollout.

Note: On slow computers, you can disable bubbles by setting the Use Total to **0**.

Animate the Bubbles' Interaction and Upward Motion

The bubbles shouldn't look like stiff ping-pong balls, so you will use MetaParticles to make the bubble geometry blend together during collisions.

1 Within the Particle Types rollout, select MetaParticles. Under MetaParticle Parameters, set the Tension to **1.5**.

Setting a higher tension will make the blobby bubbles harder to blend and will maintain more of their roundness. Depending on the space between your bubbles, you might need to adjust this value. You can change this value without significantly affecting the rendering times.

If Particle Types is set to Standard Particles, they will not blend. Use this only if MetaParticles takes too long to calculate on a slower computer.

Warning: As you make changes to the bubbles, adjustments in the Evaluation Coarseness might be necessary to maintain the shape you want. The Evaluation Coarseness specifies the accuracy of the bubbles. If the coarseness is set too low, both screen refresh and render times will increase.

Warning: Even on fast computers, make only moderate changes to any of the bubble parameters so rendering and screen refresh time won't slow your production.

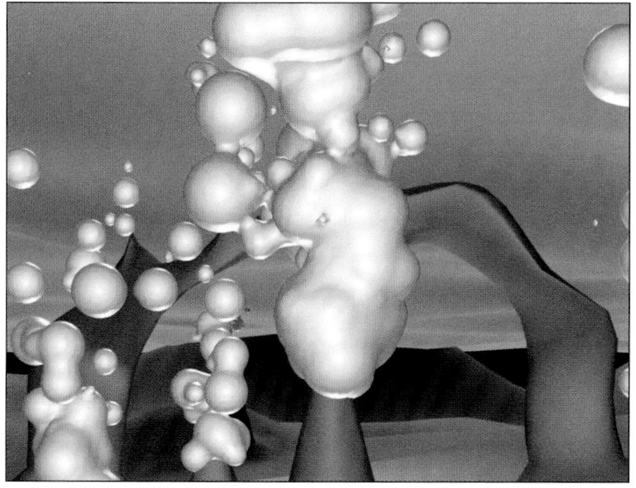

With Tension set to 0.5, the bubbles blend too much and don't create as many contours.

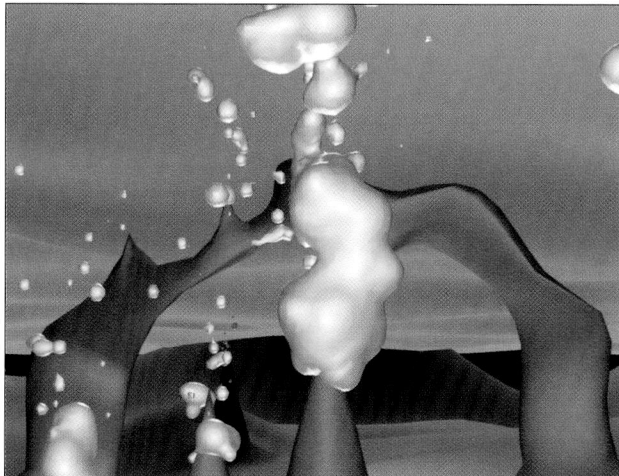

With the Tension set to a higher 1.5, the bubbles will maintain more of their roundness. Your test rendering might vary.

2 Select the Wind object. Within the Parameters rollout, under Force set the Strength to **0.003** and under Wind set Turbulence to **0.01**. Select the Bubbles object and, from the toolbar, activate the Bind to Space Warp tool.

The Bind to Space Warp tool will associate an object with the bound space warp. The bubbles will be pushed up by the wind.

3 Press "H" to bind by name and choose Wind. Right-click to activate the Move tool.

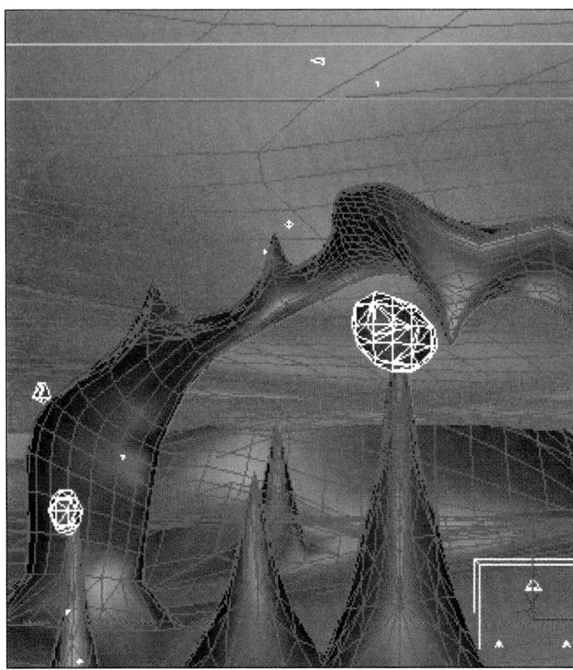

The Wind space warp pushes the bubbles up. The bubbles are bound to the parameters of the wind, and they will slowly undulate up with a slight turbulence. The speed of the bubbles along with the strength of the wind will affect how fast the bubbles travel up.

Note: Once the bubbles are bound to the wind, any changes to either object will take longer for the screen to update. Make sure you are no longer on the Bind to Space Warp tool; otherwise, selecting objects by name will instead bind objects by name.

Note: Instead of the popular RGB format, to maintain a consistent blue color palette, you will set a color's Hue, Saturation, and Value. Whenever blue is used, it will always be a Hue of 150 with a variety of Saturations and Values. Variations with a lower hue between 120 and 150 will give a greener and warmer look to the color. It won't matter what Hue is used for blue, as long as it is consistent throughout all the blue colors.

Texture the Glossy Water

The water should have sunlight beaming through it. Later, when the camera animates, the bright light on the water surface will follow the camera's motion.

1 Select the Water object. Press "M" to open the Material Editor, right-click any material slot, and check 3×2 Sample Windows.

Within the Material Editor, six slots can be edited and assigned to objects in the scene by dragging and dropping.

2 Activate an available material slot and name it **Water**. Drag and drop from the Water material slot to the Water object in the Camera view.

Four corner triangles appear on the material slot, telling you it is assigned. The Water object will reflect some of the changes to the Water material.

3 Within the Blinn Basic Parameters rollout, for Self-Illumination check Color.

A black color swatch should appear, and you can click it to change the color's Hue, Saturation, and Value.

4 Click the color swatch and set the following values:

Self-Illumination

- Hue: **150**
- Sat: **255**
- Value: **100**

Diffuse

- Hue: **150**
- Sat: **200**
- Value: **255**

Specular

- Hue: **150**
- Sat: **20**
- Value: **255**

Specular Highlights

- Specular Level: **200**
- Glossiness: **30**

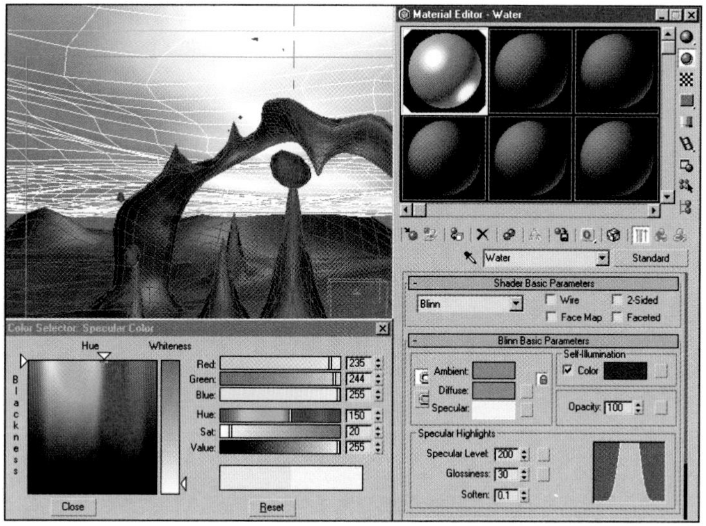

Blinn Basic Parameters.

All the colors use a blue Hue at 150. Lightening the Self-Illumination color will avoid any black areas in the shadows of the water ripples. The Diffuse color is the basic blue color of the water, and the Specular color is a bright blue highlight hitting the ripples of the water surface. The Specular Level controls the brightness, and Glossiness controls the size of the highlight. Watch the graph and visualize how you want a highlight to appear on the water ripples.

5 Within the Maps rollout, set the Bump amount to **40** and click its None button. Choose Noise from the list and name it **Ripples**.

Noise is a type of map that produces a chaotic fractal pattern. The light and dark areas of this pattern will roughen the water texture, and highlights will bounce off the ripples. Noise will animate smaller ripples within the larger animated waves on the surface of the water.

6 Within the Noise Parameters rollout, under Noise Type select Fractal, and set the Size to **80**. Press the End key to go to frame 300 and press "N" to turn on the Animate button. Set the Phase to **300**, press "N" to exit animation mode, and press Home to go to frame 0.

A Size of 80 makes larger ripples. You need to animate the Phase number to make the ripples churn.

Warning: When Animate is on, the borders of the Material and Camera view turn red, and any changes will create a range of animation from frame 0 to frame 300. Only animate the Phase of the ripples and then turn off the Animate button when finished.

Note: By opening the Material/Map Navigator, you can quickly navigate from the material levels. Use this if you want to go back and edit the Blinn Basic Parameters or the Maps rollout.

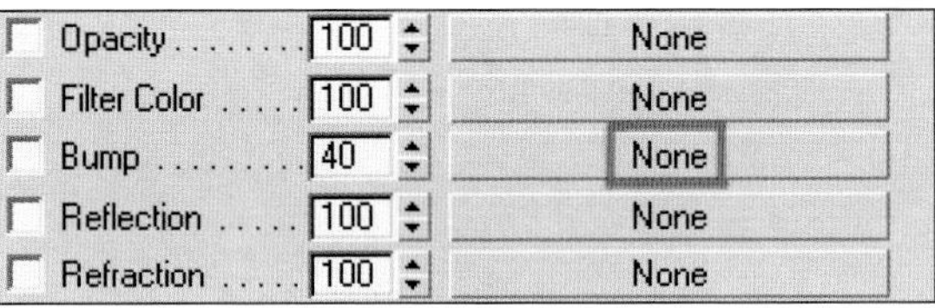

The Material/Map Browser will appear with a listing of the available map types.

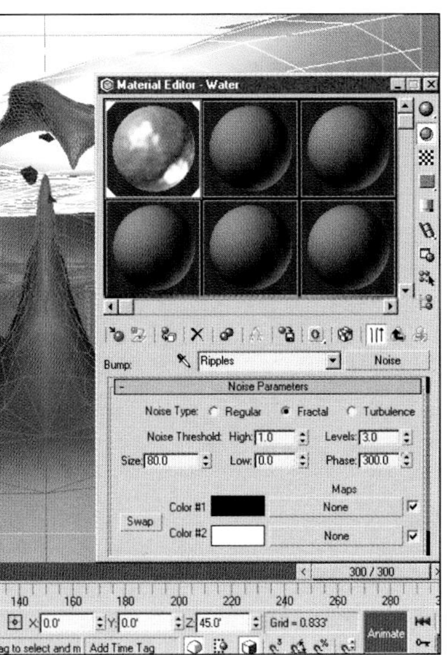

As the Phase of the noise in the Bump map changes, the ripples will appear to boil, and the textured highlights will flicker on the water from frame 0 to 300.

Texture the Rocky Ground

The ground should have a rocky and mossy texture that is more clear and detailed in the foreground, and that fades to blue in the background. If you've ever opened your eyes underwater, you've noticed that underwater objects aren't visible at a distance.

1 Select the Ground object and leave the Material Editor open. Activate a different material slot and name it **Ground**. Drag and drop the Ground material onto the Ground object. Click the Color for Diffuse and set Hue to **150**, Sat to **255**, and Value to **255**.

Note: The Ground's blue Diffuse color will later be blended with another set of maps that use warm red, yellow, and green colors.

2 Set the Specular Level to **50** and Glossiness to **50**.

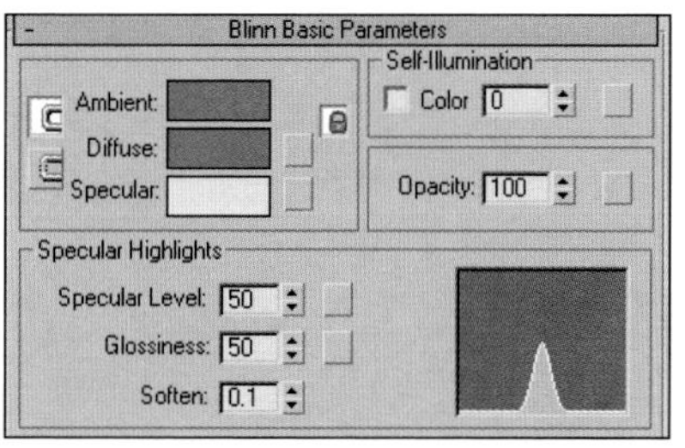

The ground will not need to be as glossy as the water.

3 Within the Maps rollout, set the Diffuse Amount to **90** and click its None button. Choose Falloff and name this map **Distance Blend**.

By setting the Diffuse Amount to 90%, only 10% of the Diffuse color will blend with 80% of the Distance Blend Falloff map. The Falloff map will enable us to blend two new maps together.

4 Within the Falloff Parameters rollout, change the Falloff Type to **Distance Blend** and the Falloff Direction to **Viewing Direction (Camera Z-Axis)**.

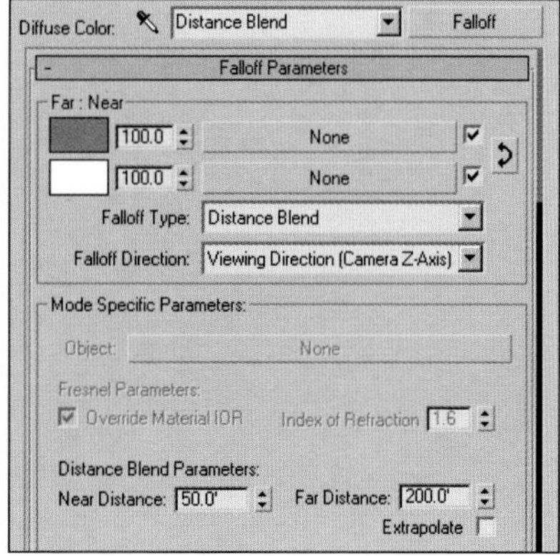

This blue is the Far color and is the same as the blue made in the Diffuse color.

The distance from the camera will determine how much to blend the two Map slots. Near and Far Distance amounts will determine how the blending will start and end.

5 Under Mode Specific Parameters, set Near Distance to **50'** and Far Distance to **200'**. Under Far:Near, click the top color and set Hue to **150**, Sat to **255**, and Value to **255**.

6 Click the bottom color's None button, Assign Cellular, and name this **Mossy Rocks**.

These will be the Near textures for rocks and moss in the foreground, which is blended with the Diffuse color.

7 Within the Cellular Parameters rollout, set the following:

Cell Color
- Hue: **35**
- Sat: **35**
- Value: **255**

Top Division Color
- Hue: **10**
- Sat: **130**
- Value: **200**

Bottom Division Color
- Hue: **80**
- Sat: **200**
- Value: **130**

For the Mossy Rocks, three warm colors—yellow, brown, and green—will blend with the cool blue Diffuse color.

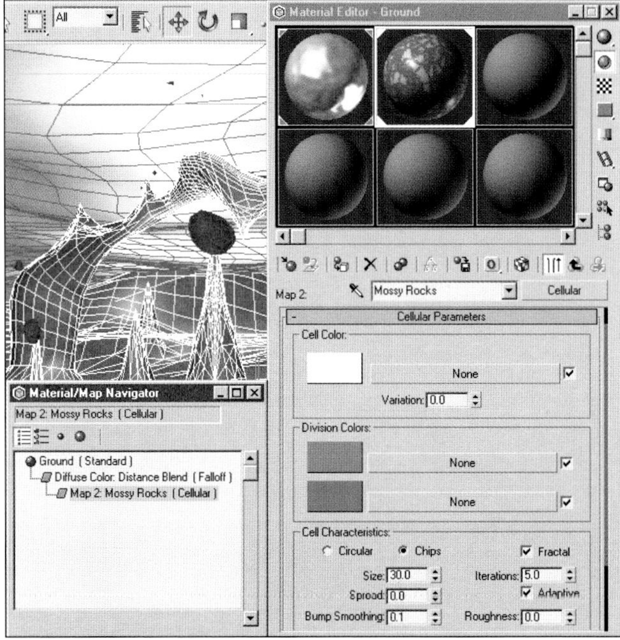

Cellular Parameters.

8 Under Cell Characteristics, select Chips and check Fractal. Set Size to **30**, Spread to **0.8**, and Iterations to **5**.

The Spread value determines the distance between the chips.

9 Use the Material/Map Navigator to get back to the Ground material. Within the Maps rollout, drag and drop the Distance Blend map from Diffuse down to the Bump's None slot and select Instance from the pop-up window. Set the Bump Amount to **200**.

Higher Bump Amount numbers make the rocks deeper.

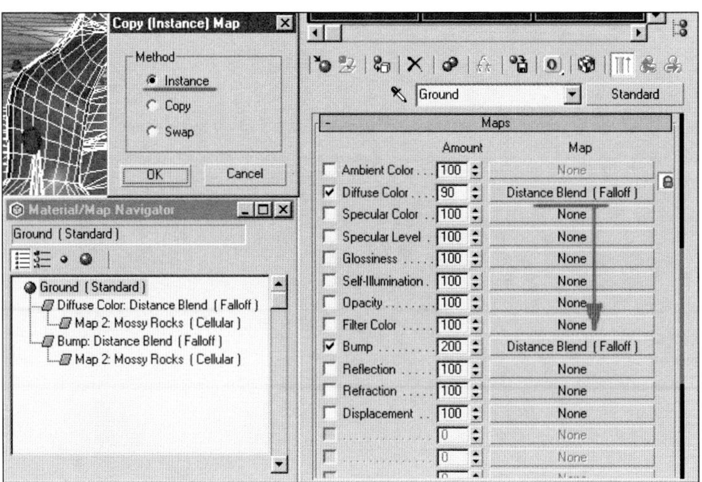

Instance uses the same map for both Diffuse and Bump. This keeps both of them consistent so that changes made to the Distance Blend in the Diffuse map will also change the Distance Blend in the Bump map.

Texture the Transparency of the Bubbles

The perimeter edges of the bubbles should be opaque and the centers should be transparent.

1 Select the Bubbles object and leave the Material Editor open. Activate a different material slot and name it **Bubbles**. Drag and drop the Bubbles material onto the Bubbles object.

Note: You can also click the Assign Material to Selection button if the Bubbles icon is too hard to get.

2 Set the following:

Diffuse Color
- Hue: **150**
- Sat: **100**
- Value: **255**

Self-Illumination Color
- Hue: **150**
- Sat: **255**
- Value: **150**

Specular Color
- Hue: **150**
- Sat: **30**
- Value: **255**

Specular Level: **250**
Glossiness: **20**

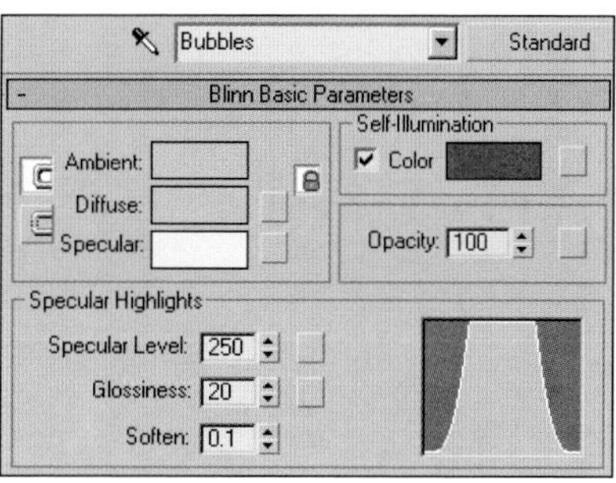

The bubbles should not have any black in their shadows.

3 Within the Extended Parameters rollout, under Advanced Transparency, select In under Falloff and set Amt to **100**.

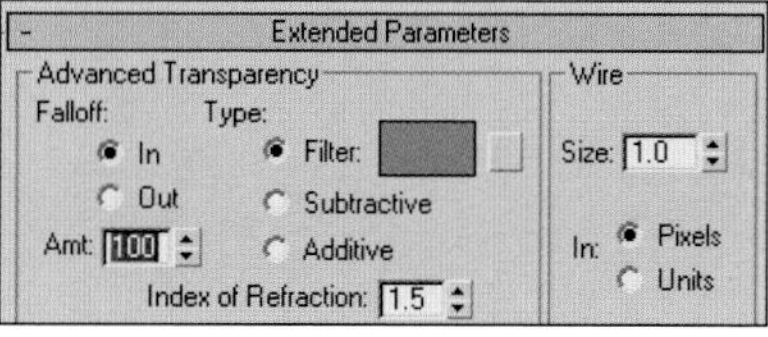

Where the surface of the bubbles is parallel to the camera, the material will be transparent. This should make the inside of the bubbles clear.

Animate Simulated Caustics

Sunlight beams through the waves and refracts to light an animated caustic spider web pattern on the ground.

1 Select by Name, choose the Light Caustic object, and keep the Material Editor open. From the Modify panel, within the General Parameters rollout, click the color and set Hue to **150**, Sat to **100**, and Value to **255**.

This sets the color that the light emits.

2 Select Exclude and, under Scene Objects, double-click Water. Check Cast Shadows and set the Multiplier to **3**.

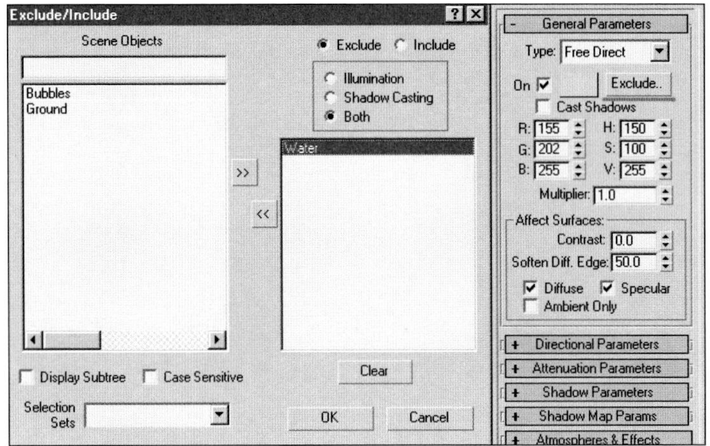

The Water object will be sent to the listing on the right and will not be lit or create shadows from this light. The Multiplier will intensify the brightness of the light's color. Objects that block the light will cast their shadow on the ground.

3 Within the Directional Parameters rollout, set the Hotspot to **1000'**.

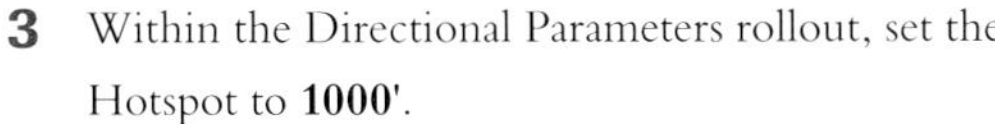

Note: The Hotspot should be large enough to cover the entire ground. The Hotspot determines the radius of the light, and the Falloff will automatically adjust to be slightly larger.

4 Click the Projector map's None button and assign Cellular. To edit the Cellular map, it must be dragged to the Material Editor in an available slot.

5 Drag and drop the Projector Map slot (Cellular) onto an available material slot and, from the pop-up window, choose Instance. Name this map Caustic, click the Cell Color, and set Hue to **150**, Sat to **255**, and Value to **10**.

With such a low Value as 10, this should be a very dark blue and will not light the ground very much.

6 Click the top Division Color and set Hue to **150**, Sat to **255**, and Value to **255**. Click the bottom Division Color and set Hue to **150**, Sat to **50**, and Value to **255**.

With such a high Saturation in the top Division Color, this blue color will be vibrant and light much of the scene. Setting the Value high and the Saturation low in the bottom Division Color will create the brightest color, which will illuminate the caustic spider web pattern.

7 Under Cell Characteristics, select Chips and check Fractal. Set Size to **150**, Spread to **0.3**, and Iterations to **5**.

With the Spread at a low number, the pattern will be very skinny.

8 Go to frame 300 and turn Animate on.

For the spider web pattern to churn and change shape, the Z offset value will be animated from frame 0 to frame 300.

9 Within the Coordinates rollout, set the Offset for Z to **600** and turn Animate off.

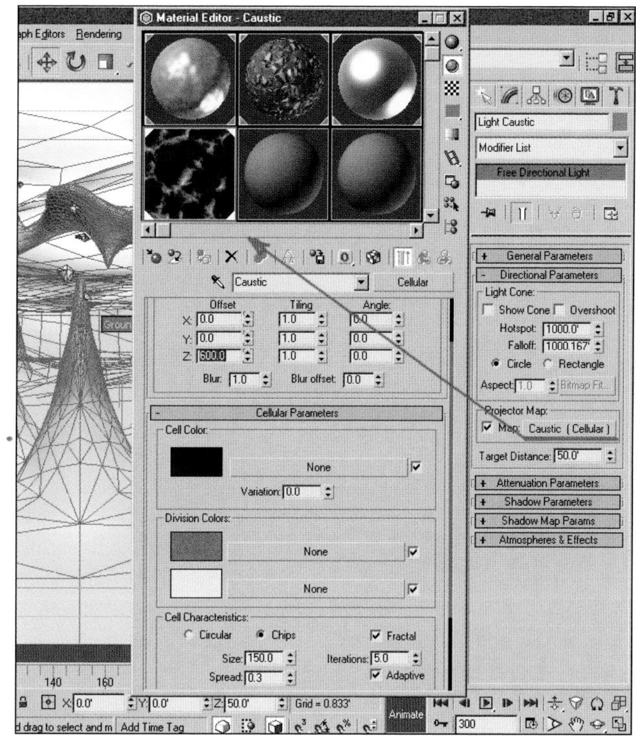

The higher numbers for Offset Z will make the pattern churn faster.

ADJUST THE LIGHT TO REFLECT OFF THE WATER SURFACE

As you look up, you can see the sun through the rippling water. Rays sear down and illuminate the ocean as hills fade in the distance. The water light object is placed below the water and ground. Its light will shine up to reflect off of the glossy water surface.

1 Select the Light Water object, click its color, and set Hue to **150**, Sat to **50**, and Value to **255**. Set the Multiplier to **1.5**.

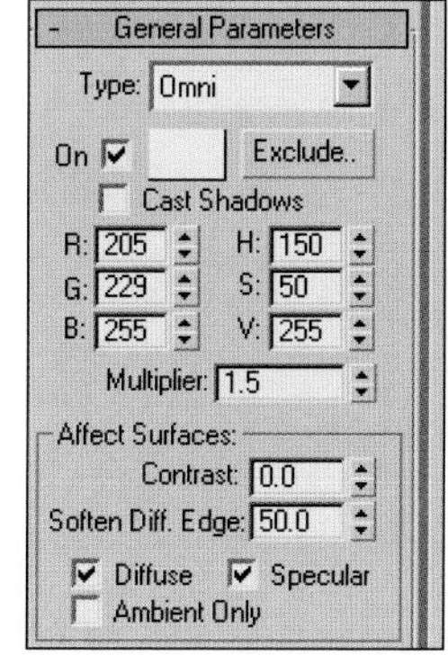

The light will appear as though it were coming from the sun and above the water.

2 Select the Light Fill object, click its color, and set Hue to **150**, Sat to **100**, and Value to **255**. Set the Multiplier to **2**.

3 Within the Attenuation Parameters rollout, under Far Attenuation, set Start to **100'** and End to **150'**. Check both Use and Show.

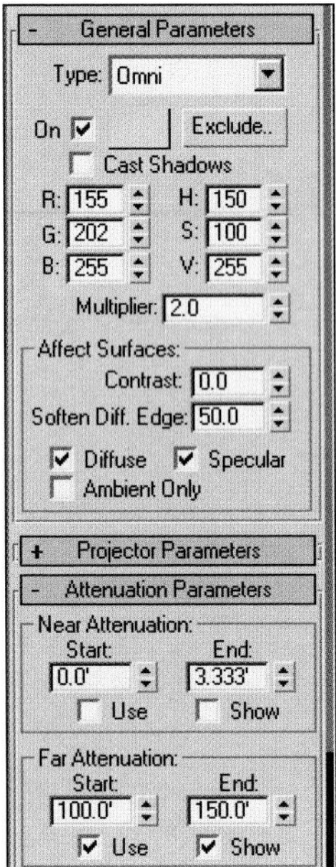

Attenuation keeps the light from illuminating the water or the background.

Add Fog to Simulate the Translucency of Deep Water

Camera settings to the Environment Ranges affect the translucency of the fog. Higher numbers will allow more visibility, unfortunately, this will uncover the edge of the water's horizon line.

1 From the Rendering menu, choose Environment. Within the Atmosphere rollout, click the Add button and choose Fog.

2 Under the Fog Parameters rollout, under Fog, click the color and set Hue to **150**, Sat to **255**, and Value to **180**. Under Standard, check Exponential.

The rendered image will be filled with a deep blue mist.

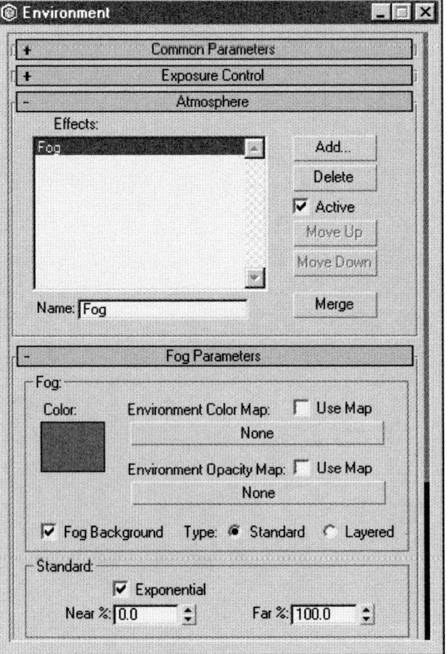

Checking Exponential will cause objects in the distance to lose their detail quicker as they fade into the blue mist. This will also increase the step size, which will help to avoid banding of the fog.

Add Rays of Light Searing Through the Water

Light should appear to illuminate the ocean atmosphere with a glowing mist.

1 Select the Light Rays object, click its color, and set Hue to **150**, Sat to **50**, and Value to **255**. Check Cast Shadows and set the Multiplier to **1.5**.

2 Within the Directional Parameters rollout, set Hotspot to **0.1'** and Falloff to **40'**.

The Falloff will be the width of the light beam. You can vary this amount from 10' to 50'.

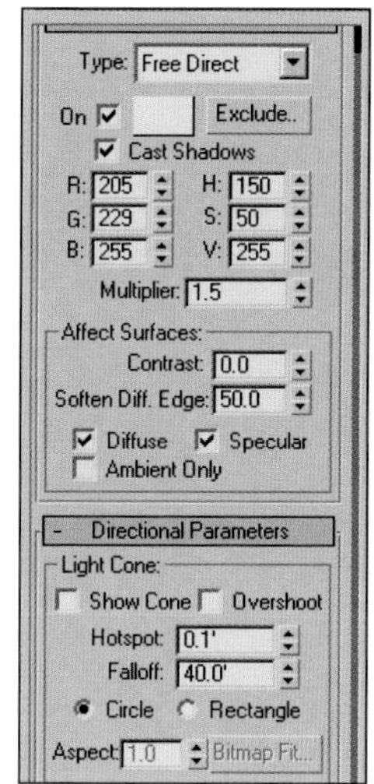

Set the Light Rays parameters.

3 Within the Attenuation Parameters rollout, under Far Attenuation, set Start to **100'**, End to **150**, and check both Use and Show.

The Far Attenuation will taper the strength of the light before it hits the ground. This way, its effect won't cover over the Light Caustics.

4 Within the Atmospheres & Effects rollout, click the Add button and choose Volume Light. Volume Light will be added to the listing. Within this listing, select Volume Light and click the Setup button.

The Environment Editor appears, and Volume Light has been placed below the Fog with the Light Rays object already assigned to the effect. More lights can be assigned to this effect later if needed.

Set the Attenuation parameters.

5 Under Volume, set the Fog Color Hue to **150**, Sat to **50**, and Value to **255**. Set the Density to **0.4** and check Exponential.

This is the same as the light's emitting color.

6 Under Noise, check Noise On, set the Amount to **1**, and select Fractal.

Adding noise to the light will cause the light to break up, as if it were lighting particulate matter in the ocean.

7 Set Uniformity to **1**, Levels to **2**, and Size to **30**.

Lower Uniformity makes the light higher in contrast and dustier looking. Higher Levels take longer to render. Lower Size makes smaller speckles.

Note: An alternative method is to use a Projector map to create streaks in the projection; however, this adds considerably to the render time. A quicker way is to create more lights and add them to this effect.

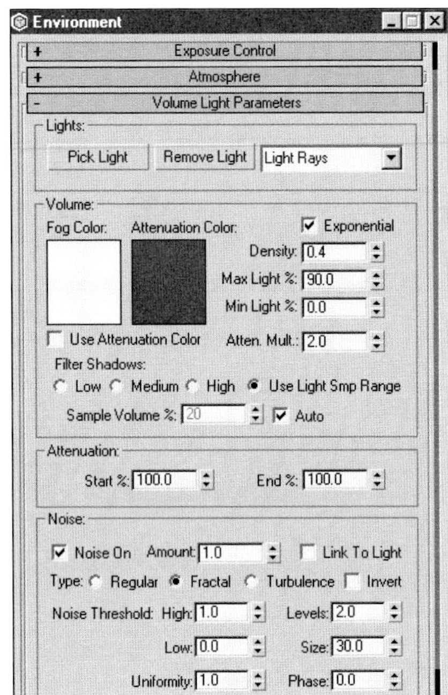

The light will render a misty light-blue fog.

Link the Camera, Light Rays, and Light Water to the Light Fill

When the Light Fill object moves, it controls the position of the camera, Light Water object, and Light Rays object. The camera needs to rotate freely without the Light Rays rotating. So the Light Rays will be linked to the Light Fill instead of the camera. The Z-axis for the Light Rays will not inherit the movement of the Light Fill, so that when the Light Fill moves up or down, the Light Rays object will stay above the water surface where its effect always needs to start.

1 Multiple select the Camera, Light Rays, and Light Water objects. From the toolbar, activate the Select and Link tool, press "H" to Select Parent by Name, and choose the Light Fill object as the parent.

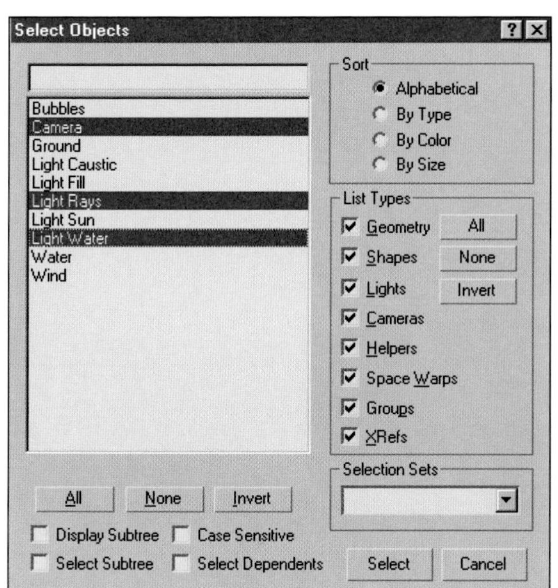

When Selecting by Name, press Ctrl to click one by one and select multiple objects at the same time.

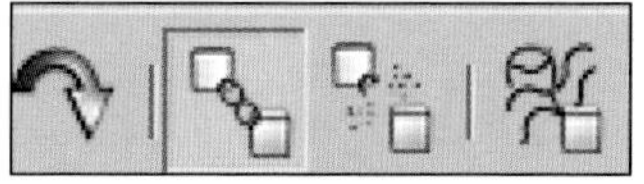

The Select and Link tool. When the Light Fill object changes its position, the linked objects will follow.

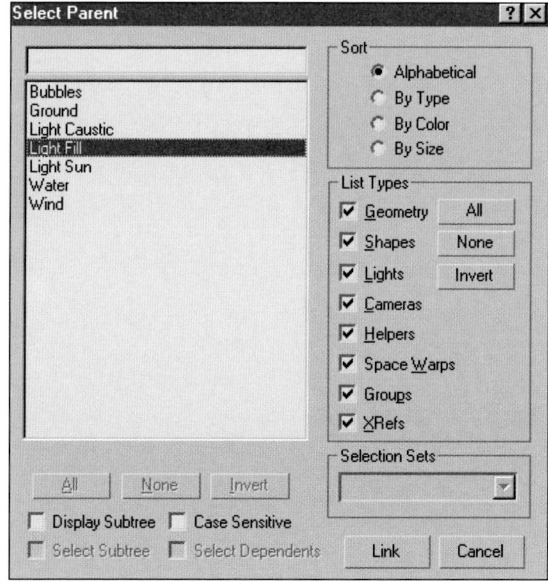

Press "H" to select the Light Fill object as the parent.

2 Activate the Move tool and select the Light Rays object. From the Hierarchy panel, click the Link Info button. Within the Inherit rollout for Move, only uncheck Z, leaving X and Y checked.

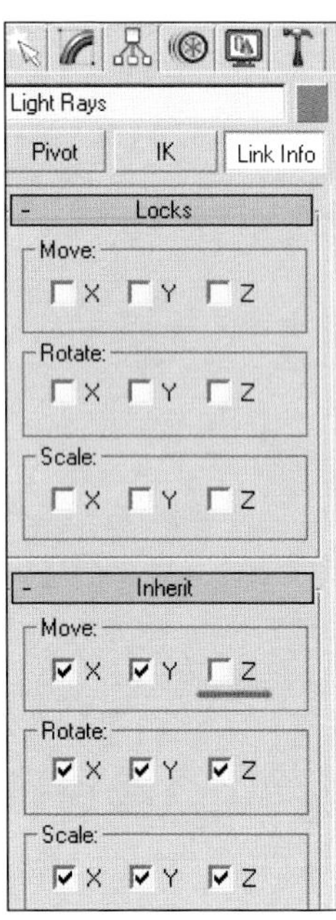

When the Light Rays object follows the animation of the Light Fill object, it will only inherit the X and Y motion, not the Z. This will keep it above the water, even when the Light Fill moves up and down on Z.

Animate the View

By animating the Light Fill object to slowly start and stop, the linked lights and camera will follow.

1 Select the Light Fill object and turn Animate on. Activate the Move tool, go to frame 150, and set the Absolute World position to X = **–20'**, Y = **20'**, and Z = **20'**.

The camera will inherit the X, Y, Z coordinates of the Light Fill object, but the Light Rays will only inherit the X and Y coordinates. This is to prevent the Light Rays object from submerging on the Z-axis and to keep the start of its effect above the water.

Note: Press F1 to search in Help with the keyword "Tangent." Under the topic for Bézier Controllers, you will see a detailed description of all the Tangent types.

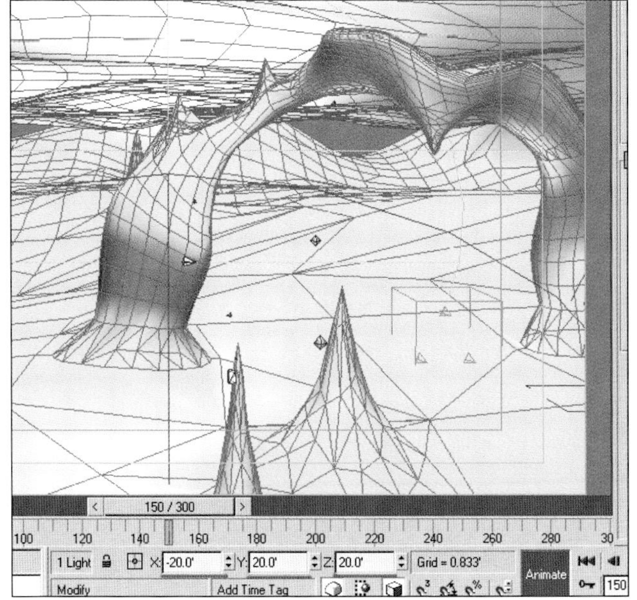

From the bottom of the viewport is a Transform Type In for Absolute World to enter coordinates for X, Y, and Z.

2 Go to frame 300 and set X = **0'**, Y = **100'**, and Z = **10'**.

The camera will dive through the archway, and the rays will stay above the water.

Note: If the blue time slider frame marker covers the red keys, you can still right-click the key to bring up the menu.

3 Turn Animate off and from the Track Bar (below the time slider) on frame 0, right-click the first Key and choose Light Fill: Position. Within the pop-up window for Out, click the pull-down icon to set the Tangent to Slow.

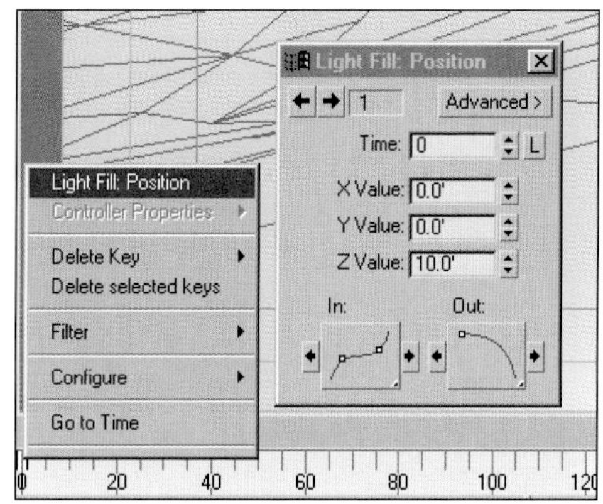

The camera will slowly start on frame 0.

4 From the Track Bar on frame 300, right-click the third key, and choose Light Fill: Position. Within the pop-up window for In, set the Tangent icon to Slow.

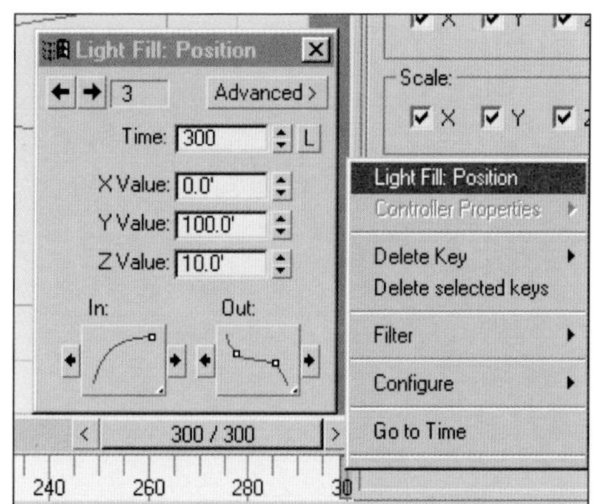

The camera will slowly stop on frame 300.

Render the Scene

The Camera view will render the scene. If rendering times are too long, consider changing some of the parameters listed in the text as timesavers.

1 Make sure the Camera view is Active, press F10 to render the Scene. Within the Render Scene Editor, under Time Output, select Active Time Segment: 0 to 300.

2 Under Output Size, click the 320×240 button. Under Render Output, click the Files button. Save as an AVI file in the location of your choice.

3 In the Video Compression pop-up window, choose Intel Indeo(R) Video 3.2 and set the Compression Quality to **100%**. Click the Render button.

When the rendering is finished or cancelled, go to the Ram Player under the Rendering menu and open to view the rendered file in Channel A.

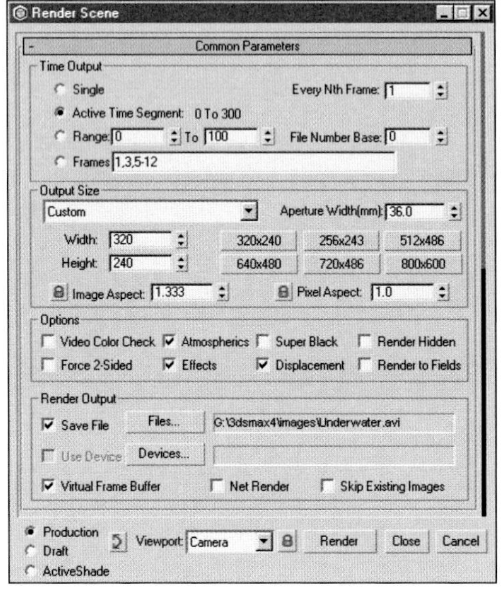

The rendering times will vary and might take a few hours to complete. For each frame, five passes of the Depth of Field will layer a final image. You can disable this along with the Bubble Amount to render faster.

Note: If you live in the Southern California area and you are interested in joining my team of artists, email me at **3dman@charter.net** for a current listing of the schools where I teach 3ds max 4 and plug-ins.

Modifications

I hope you have allowed yourself to explore and make variations in the parameters. Every time you review this exercise, you will get better at adjusting the camera, working with a consistent color palate, animating textures and bubbles, and setting up atmospherics. There is a copy of the finished project called Underwater_Environment_Finished.max on the accompanying CD-ROM.

Demonstrate your creativity and design an original underwater environment. Here are some possibilities:

- Create and model a detailed terrain for the camera to discover.
- Create and animate an interesting sea creature and have the camera follow it through the scene.
- Render many different views and composite the clips together in Video Post.
- Animate the camera changing its focus with Depth of Field.
- Have the bubbles burst out of a creature by setting the start and end times.
- Change the hue used for blue throughout the scene.

Plug-Ins

To enhance the overall realism in the scene, here are some plug-ins that will provide a great way to explore the possibilities.

Free plug-ins:

- Electric from Blur Studios (**www.blur.com**). A procedural Electric map for caustic lighting.
- Dirt from Blur Studios. A procedural Dirt map for the ground texture.

Commercial plug-ins (prices are subject to change):

- FinalRender Stage-0 ($495) from Trinity 3D (**www.Trinity3D.com**). Use global illumination and true raytraced caustics to light the underwater environment.
- QuickDirt ($245) from Digimation (**www.digimation.com**). Design realistic aged objects with dirt, rust, mud, and other deposits on objects.
- Shag: Hair ($495) from Digimation. An environmental effect plug-in that give great control over the shape and animation of underwater grass.
- Stitch ($695) from Digimation. A modifier that simulates the dynamics for leaves of seaweed swaying in the water.
- Splash!Max ($195) from Digimation. Simulate the dynamics needed when a dolphin dives into the water.
- The Essential Textures ($195) from Digimation. Procedural textures to create more interesting coral, sand, and rock.
- Tree Druid ($125) from Digimation. Create animated foliage, trees, and grass.
- Digital Nature Tools ($495) from Digimation. Create realistic skies that can be seen if the camera goes above the water.
- reactor ($1000) from discreet (**www2.discreet.com**). A dynamic simulator that animates realistic collisions with water, rigid and soft bodies, rope, and clothes.

LIGHTING EFFECTS

"The long light shakes across the lakes,

And the wild cataract leaps in glory."

—ALFRED, LORD TENNYSON,

"THE SPLENDOR FALLS ON CASTLE WALLS"

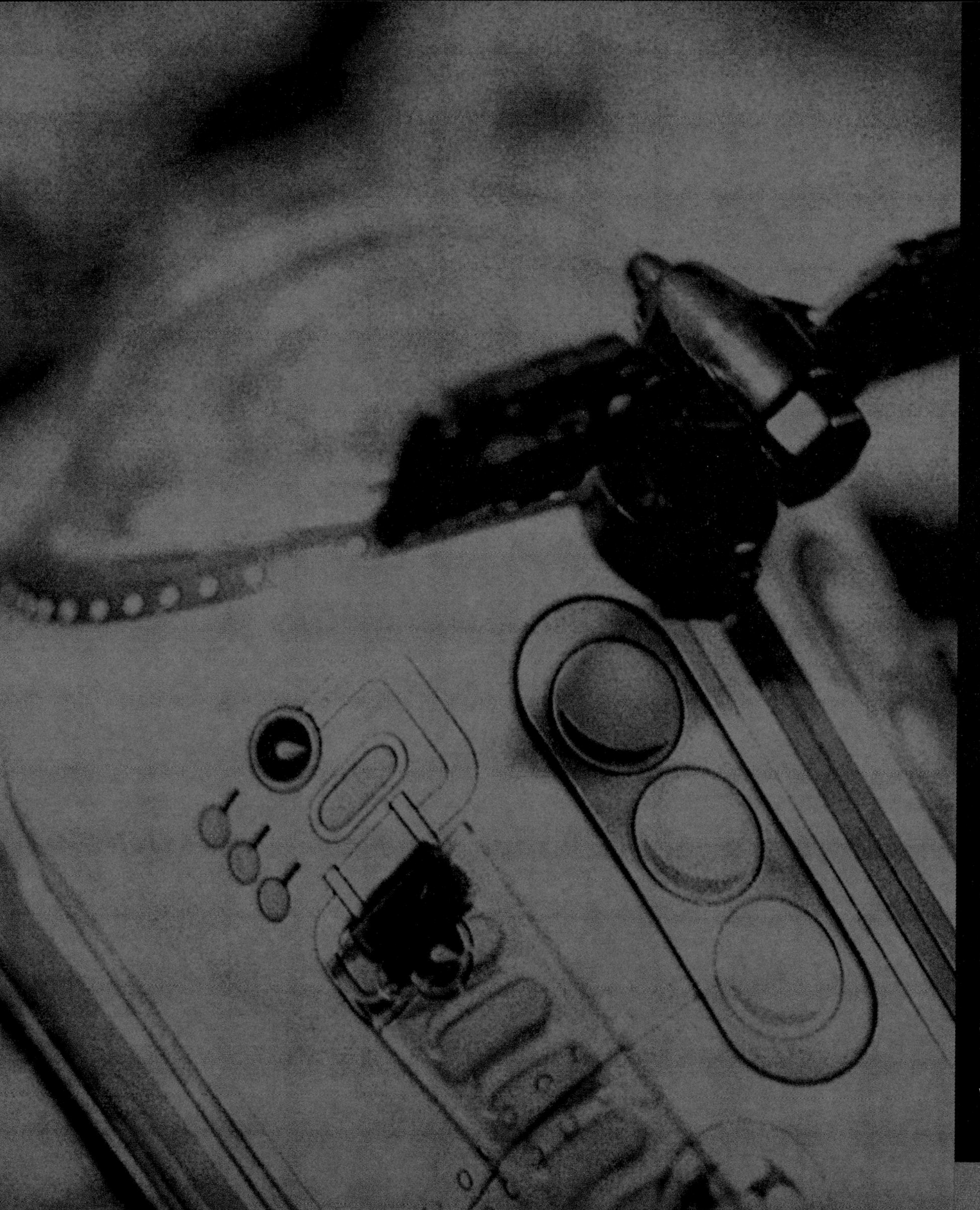

Light a Complex Scene

It has been said that good lighting can't save a bad model, but bad lighting can ruin a good one. Just as in realistic natural media art, light is the medium that defines CG art. Humans are experts in the behavior of light, and their interpretations of CG artwork depend largely on the ways in which light is depicted. When lighting a scene, it is important to depict both the indirect and direct effects of a light source, such as ambient or reflected illumination. It is also useful to consider CG-specific effects such as volumetric lights, which might provide the viewer with cues as to scene composition.

Project 4

Lighting Effects

by Sean Bonney

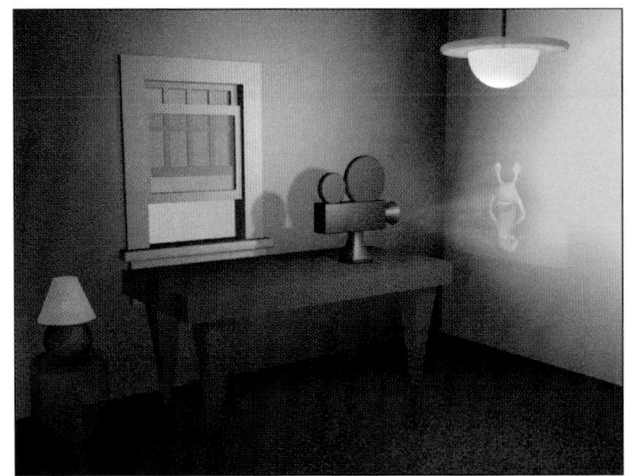

How It Works

In this tutorial, you will light an indoor scene with several artificial and one natural light source. Direct light sources, also known as "key lights," will be created in addition to indirect light sources, or "fill lights." Projection maps will be used, both for the obvious function of projecting an image and to create the illusion of shadow-casting objects.

Getting Started

Start 3ds max 4 and open the file **Lighting.max** from this project's folder on the accompanying CD-ROM. This file contains a simple indoor scene including a few pieces of furniture, two lamps, a film projector, and an open window. View the scene from the Camera viewport to get accustomed to the setup with which you will be working.

This is the interior scene you will be lighting in this tutorial.

General Lighting Setup

In creating a base lighting setup, first consider the direct sources of light. Then add fill lights, taking care not to unbalance the scene by creating obvious hot spots. It is also important to consider the intensity, sharpness, and color of cast shadows.

1 Render a still from the Camera viewport.

  The image will be black because two of the walls in this scene are obscuring the camera.

2 Go to the Top view, select the Wall03 and Wall04 objects, go to the Properties dialog, and uncheck Visible to Camera in the Rendering Control area.

  This will prevent the two walls closest to the camera from appearing at render time.

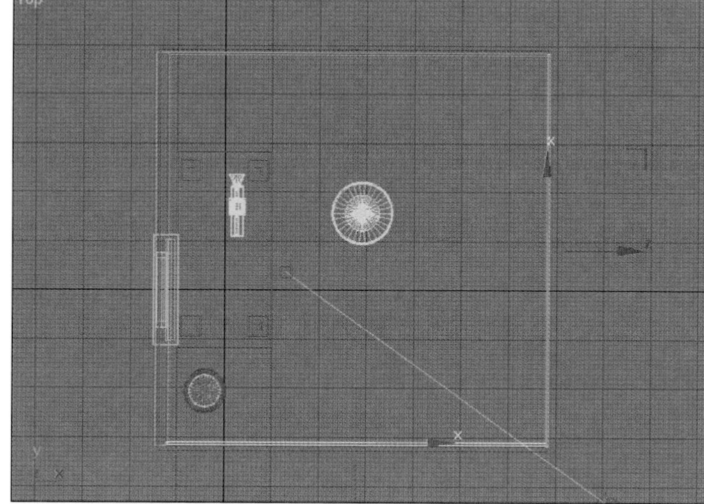

These two walls need to be invisible to the camera so as to not obscure rendering.

One way to begin the lighting setup is to convert the default lighting into editable lights. The first step is to turn on default lighting in the Viewport Configuration dialog.

3 Right-click any viewport label and choose Configure. In the Rendering Method tab, check the Default Lighting box and choose the 2 Lights setup if it is not already selected. Close this dialog. Render a still from the Camera viewport.

Without any lights in this scene, light is being provided by the default lighting solution, which simulates the effects of two omni lights.

In a scene without lights, default lighting creates an even, if bland, illumination.

4 Go to the Views menu and choose Add Default Lights to Scene. Set the following values and click OK:

Add Default Key Light: **On**
Add Default Fill Light: **On**
Distance Scaling: **0.75**

This will create two omnis, named DefaultKeyLight and DefaultFillLight. The Distance Scaling setting determines how far the omnis are placed from the origin, compared to their virtual location before being added to the scene as editable lights.

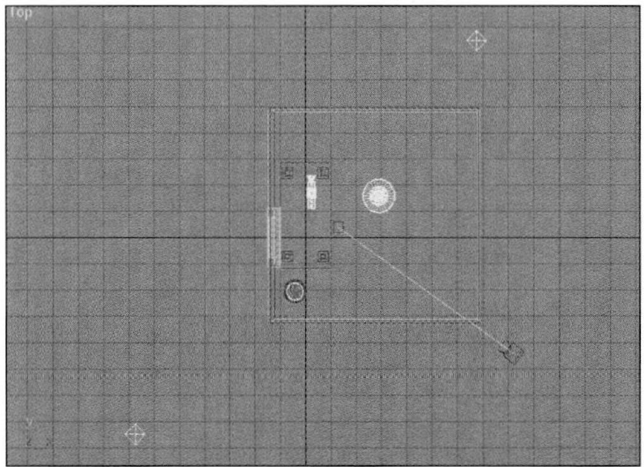

Add the default lights to the scene as editable lights to begin the light setup.

Adding the virtual default lights to the scene creates similar lighting.

Note: If you render another still, you will see similar levels of lighting, but of course, the exact lighting has changed now that the lights have actual positions relative to occluding scene objects.

5 Go to the Front viewport and zoom out to reveal the default fill light positioned below the floor plane. Select this light and move it to X = 150, Y = –250, Z = –130.

The main use for this light will be to fill the room with subtle lighting based on the main light source, the overhead lamp.

Note: A good tactic for placement of a fill light is to place it across the camera plane from the key light so that it will illuminate the sides of scene objects that are not being directly lit, simulating ambient light that is being reflected within the scene.

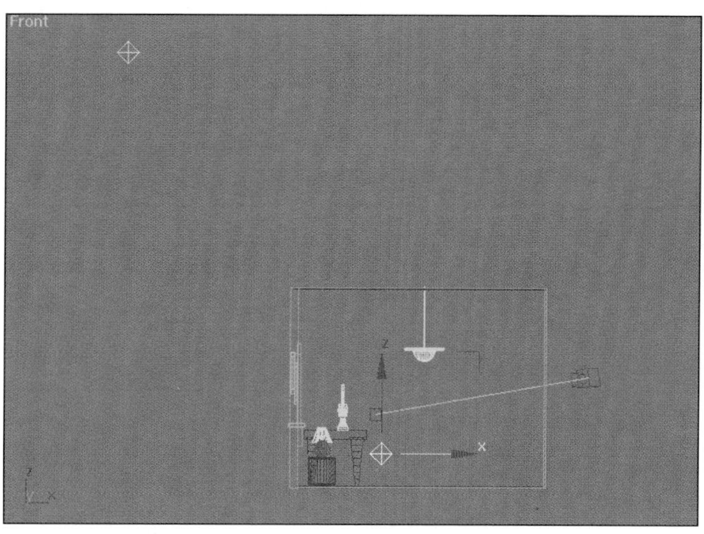

Move the newly created fill light to a position near the floor.

6 Set the following values so this light will give off a subtle illumination:

Color: **R 210, G 220, B 150**
Multiplier: **0.35**
Affect Surfaces
Specular: **Off**

Note: Turning off specular highlights prevents fill lights from creating hotspots that would spoil the illusion that the light they cast is reflected ambient illumination as opposed to a direct light source.

Tweak the fill light to cast a subtle illumination in contrast to the overhead lamp.

7 Select the DefaultKeyLight and move it to a position directly underneath the overhead lamp, at X = 285, Y = 155, Z = 125. Set the following values to create a source of intense, bright light:

Color: **R 255, G 240, B 180**
Multiplier: **1.25**

8 Go to Attenuation Parameters and set the following values to cause this light to fade with distance so that all areas aren't lit equally:

Far Attenuation
  Start: **300**
  End: **590**
  Use: **On**

As the primary source of direct lighting in the scene, this key light will cast shadows.

9 Turn on Cast Shadows in the light's General Parameters rollout and set the following values in the Shadow Parameters rollout:

Object Shadows: **On**
Type: **Shadow Map**
Color: **R 125, G 135, B 60**
Density: **0.7**

Note: Setting the shadow's color to an ambient color and reducing density can prevent shadows from being cast too dark in scenes in which a lot of reflected light is expected, such as indoors. It's even possible to affect the scene's color balance, emotional content, and visual style with the introduction of boldly colored shadows. The second source of interior light is the small lamp on the left side of the camera frame.

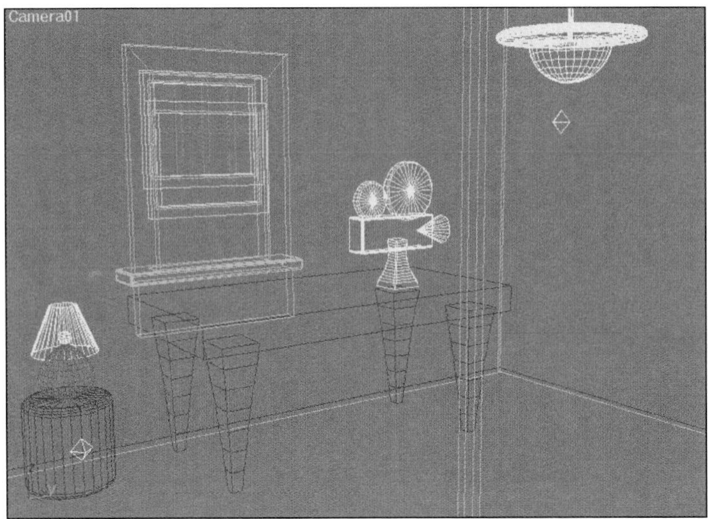

Move the key light to its proper position under the main lamp.

The overhead lamp will provide the majority of the direct lighting for this scene.

10 Clone the DefaultKeyLight using Copy as the method. Name the clone **LampKeyLight** and move it to X = –40, Y = –210, Z = –70 to place it within the lampshade. Set the light's Color to **R 180, G 250, B 245** to give it a unique tint. Reduce the Multiplier to **1.0**.

This light shouldn't cast light as far as the more powerful overhead light.

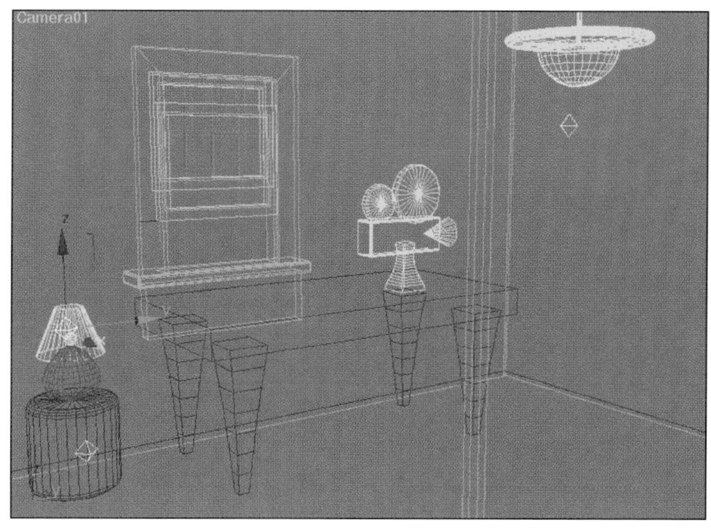

Clone the key light and move it within the lampshade to begin creating a direct source for the small lamp's illumination.

11 To attenuate the light more tightly, set the following values in the Attenuation Parameters rollout:

Far Attenuation
Start: **200**
End: **500**

Note: Light attenuation can also be adjusted by scaling the light object. In fact, nonuniform scaling is the only way to create nonspherical attenuation radii. This lamp's illumination will seem more realistic if visible cones of light are cast from the shade. This will be created with a Volume Light effect. As of 3D Studio MAX 3, environmental effects can be added to lights from the Modify panel.

Reduce the lamp light's attenuation to restrict it to that corner of the room.

The lamp now illuminates its own portion of the room, casting a nice shadow from the lampshade.

12 Go to the Atmospheres & Effects rollout, click the Add button, select the Volume Light effect, and click OK. Select the newly added effect from the Atmospheres & Effects list and click Setup to edit this effect in the Environment dialog.

13 In the Atmosphere rollout, rename this effect **Volume Light: Lamp**. To add ambient coloring to this effect, set the following values in the Volume area:

Attenuation Color: **R 0, G 125, B 75**
Use Attenuation Color: **On**
Density: **1**

Note: Attenuation Color determines the tint of the atmospheric effect as it approaches the selected light's attenuation limit (either Start or End). This is in contrast to the Fog Color, which sets the color of the main body of the effect.

14 To restrict the Volume Light from extending to the far extent of the light's illumination, set End% to **75** in the Attenuation area.

When completing a lighting setup, proper use of attenuation can be very useful in creating a balanced look. Without attenuation, CG lights can easily cast too much light too far by virtue of their perfect illumination model. Compare this to their real-life counterparts, which disperse light quickly, resulting in exponentially reduced visual impact with distance.

The Volume Light effect more clearly delineates the cones of light cast from the lamp.

Note: The Attenuation settings can be useful when you don't want an environmental effect to overwhelm a light's illumination. Reducing the End%, for example, will cause a volume effect to fade away before it reaches the furthest area illuminated.

Projector Light

The film projector in this scene can be said to be the source of a special effect light. Although it will cast subtle general illumination, its main function will be to project an image.

1 Go to the Front viewport and create a Free Spotlight at X = 27, Y = 235, Z = 3. Name this light **Fspot Projector**. Note that the default settings of this light are set to the values of the last light corrected.

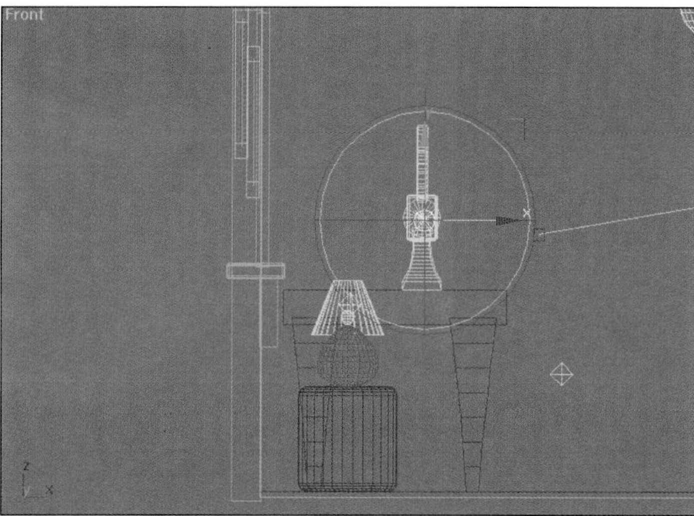

Create a Free Spotlight to serves as the primary light source for the film projector.

2 Go to the Spotlight Parameters rollout and set the light cone type to **Rectangle** to make a more appropriate projection.

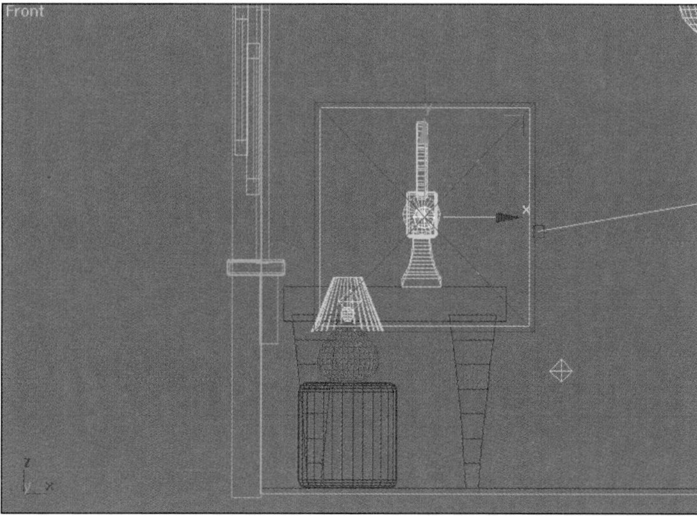

The rectangular light cone type is a more appropriate shape for most projected images.

Note: The image to be projected can be found on the accompanying CD-ROM. Wormy Waving.avi is a 100-frame animation at 320×200 resolution. It depicts a green alien character waving cheerfully. This animation was originally published on the companion CD to the New Rider's book *Inside Studio Max R3: Professional Animation* and was created by a very clever animator.

A prerendered AVI of this curious fellow waving will serve as the virtual film to be projected.

3 To assign this map, first click the Projector Map button and choose Bitmap from the Material/Map Browser. In the Select Bitmap Image dialog, navigate to this project's folder on the accompanying CD-ROM and select **Wormy Waving.avi**.

Note: Projected images can slow down rendering considerably, particularly if they are large animations. Copying the AVI to your hard disk to minimize access time is advised.

4 Drag the map from the Modifier panel to an unused slot in the Material Editor as an Instance and rename it **Wormy Waving**.

This animation has a rather dark background, making it less than ideal for clear projection.

5 Go to the Output rollout and set Output Amount to **1.25** to brighten it up a bit.

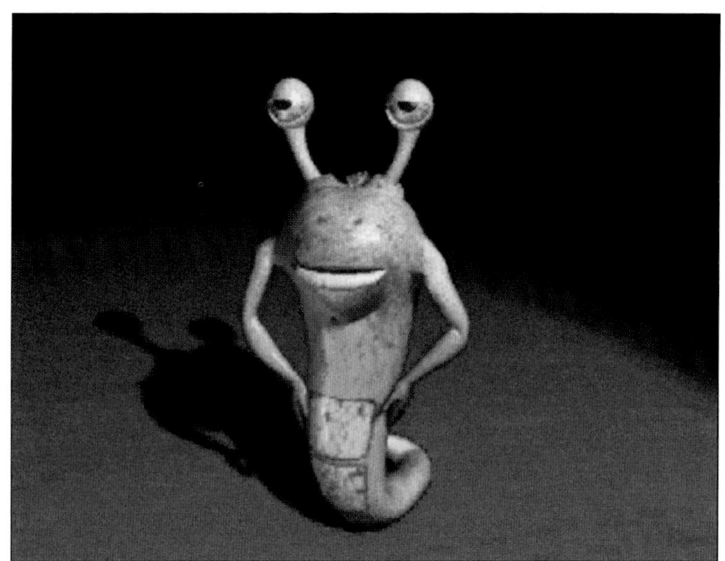

Increase the Output Amount of this map slightly to brighten it and make it project more clearly.

Note: Tweaking the Output Amount in this way usually does not add much rendering time, but in the event that you are working with many large images, it might be beneficial to perform the tweaking prior to loading into max, for example in Photoshop (for still images) or AfterEffects (for animations).

6 Click the Bitmap Fit button to better fit the shape of the projected light to the format of the image. Select the **Wormy Waving.avi** map from the browser (Browse from: Mtl Editor). The Aspect value should change to **1.333**, the proportions of the image.

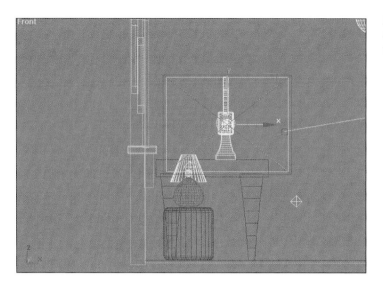

Set the aspect ratio of the light cone to match the proportions of the projected image.

Note: As anyone who has seen a movie that included a working film projector in it knows, all such projectors cast solid cones of light through hazy atmosphere.

7 Add a Volume Light effect to the projector spotlight as you did for LampKeyLight. Name this effect **Volume Light: Projector** and set the following values to create a nice, hazy cone of light:

Volume

- Density: **7**
- Max Light%: **80**

Attenuation

- End%: **90**

A Volume Light effect will be used to create the familiar cone of hazy light.

Note: Volume Light effects assigned to lights that project images automatically reflect the light intensity and color as it changes throughout the image. In other words, the portion of a volume light that is projecting a blue-tinted image will render as blue-tinted fog. The wall that is receiving the projected image looks a little odd because it isn't being illuminated by any diffuse or leaked light from the projector.

8 Clone the DefaultFillLight using Copy as the method. Name the clone **ProjectorFill** and move to X = 30, Y = 440, Z = 0.

9 Set the following values for ProjectorFill to cast a subtle glow around the projected image:

General Parameters

Color: **R 225, G 245, B 185**

Multiplier: **0.5**

Attenuation Parameters

Near Attenuation

Start: **25**

End: **100**

Use: **On**

Far Attenuation

Start: **100**

End: **200**

Use: **On**

Using lights to project images or animations in max is fairly straightforward, thanks to the Projector Map option. The ambient light cast by such a light source and the visual cues to the cone of cast light are useful cues to the source of the projection.

> **Note:** Attenuation settings are very useful for controlling the extent and intensity of lights. Use the Near Attenuation settings to determine how far from the source the light will begin to ramp up to its Multiplier setting. Similarly use the Far settings to control at what distance the light intensity begins to reduce down to zero.

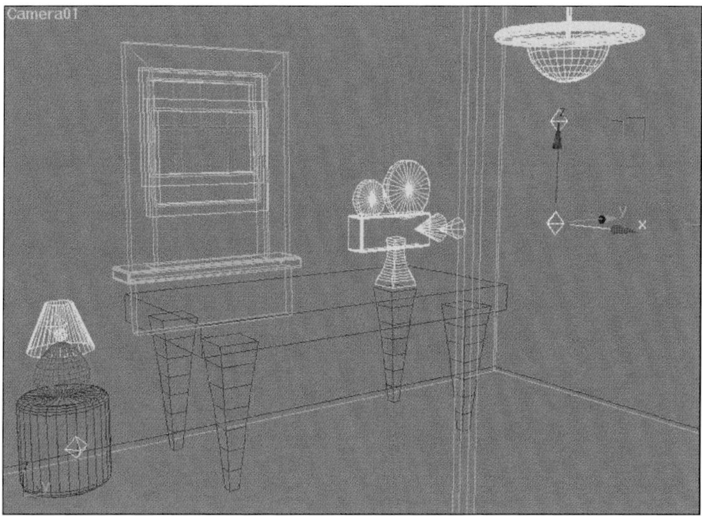

Create another light to fill out the projector's illumination.

Add the fill light near the projector to cast a small amount of ambient light.

Sunlight

The last remaining source of light to be created in this scene is natural light from the open window. In general, direct lights are used for this function because they appear to originate from an infinite distance, resulting in parallel shadows. In this case, the light will be cast through a narrow aperture, so the use of direct lights is not mandatory.

Because there are several lights in this scene and several environmental effects, it might be easier to troubleshoot a new light if all the previous lights are turned off. The best way to do this is to use the Light Lister utility.

1 Go to the menu item Tools and select Light Lister. There will be a brief delay as the Lister collects information on all lights in the scene. To deactivate all lights, clear the check boxes in the On column next to each listed light. Minimize the Light Lister utility. You might want to turn some of the scene lights off to speed test renders. To continue with the tutorial, check On for each light.

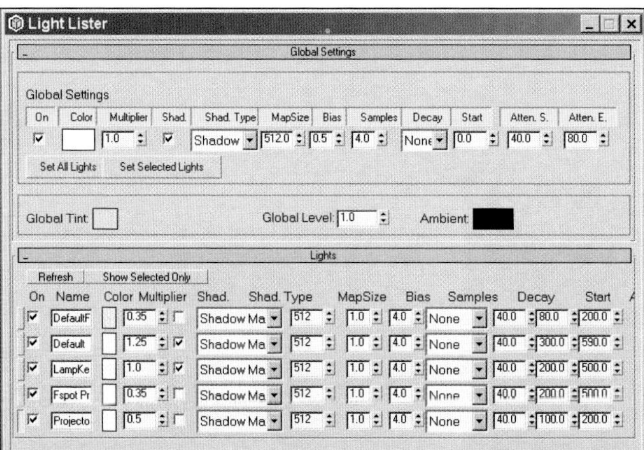

The Light Lister utility gathers controls for most light settings in a single dialog.

2 Go to the Top viewport and create a Target direct light at X = –1000, Y = 550, Z = 650. Name this light **FDirect Sun**. Place the target at X = 130, Y = –100, Z = –200.

This should aim the light into the room through the open window.

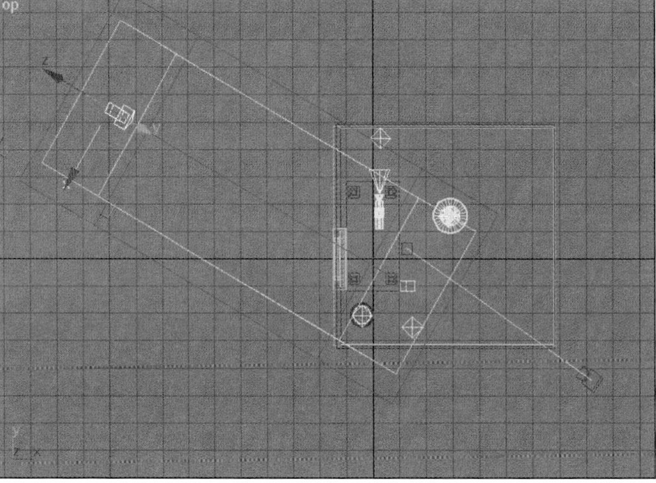

Create a Target direct light to provide a source of sunlight.

3 Set the following values to create a warm, even light:

General Parameters

Cast Shadows: **On**

Color: **R 250, G 245, B 215**

Multiplier: **2.0**

Directional Parameters

Hotspot: **300**

Falloff: **400**

Light Cone Type: **Rectangle**

To make the sunlight break around the window with dimensional shadows, the Shadow Type must be Shadow Map as opposed to Raytraced.

4 Go to the Shadow Parameters rollout and set the following values:

Object Shadows Type: **Shadow Map**
Color: **R 100, G 90, B 0**

Note that the window pane material is not set to two-sided, allowing sunlight to pass through the window panes.

5 Go to the Shadow Map Parameters rollout and check Absolute Map Bias.

Note: Map Bias determines how tightly shadows are cast from objects. The greater the bias, the greater the buffer between objects and their shadows. Absolute Map Bias does not allow for any buffer, creating the most precise shadow possible within the other Shadow Map parameters.

6 Go to the Attenuation Parameters dialog and set the following values:

Far Attenuation
Start: **1300**
End: **1800**
Use: **On**

This will fade the light as it approaches the floor.

Note: Shadow Maps are necessary when using direct lights to cast Volume Lighting effects because Raytraced shadows do not always work properly in this combination.

This direct light will cast a warm, sunny glow through the window, casting characteristic shadows on the table and floor.

7 Add a Volume Light effect to this light, rename the effect **Volume Light: Sunlight**, and set the following values in the Environment dialog:

Attenuation Color: **R 190, G 200, B 0**
Use Attenuation Color: **On**
Density: **2**

8 Set Global Tint to **R 210, G 215, B 130** to tint all of the lights in the scene.

Sunlight has several properties that are usually observed in reality. Most significantly, it originates from a practically infinite distance, so all objects in a scene that receive solar illumination will do so from identical angles. Additionally, it takes on the colors of local atmosphere and background. Often, this is depicted as a warm yellow glow, but consider a wintry, overcast scene in which sunlight might easily be colored a low-saturation blue.

Use Attenuation and Volume Light to link discrete volumetric sun beams to the natural light.

Note: The Light Lister utility is capable of setting a great number of values for scene lights as well as affecting them globally.

Note: Global Tint is very useful for adjusting scene lighting because it enables you to add color to all lights without changing the individual light settings. This function can be helpful in unifying the look of scene.

Animating the Lights

The lights in this scene do not call for elaborate animation. The film projector is the most obvious example of an animated light source, needing only to flicker in intensity to match the expected appearance. For the natural lighting, you will add the mottled effect of sunlight through leaves, again using a Projection map.

1 Select the Fspot Projector light. Before adding noise to the light's brightness, set Multiplier to **0.35**.

2 Turn the Animate button on, go to frame 100, and set Multiplier to **0.3**. Turn the Animate button off.

3 Right-click the light, choose Track View Selected, and expand the tracks.

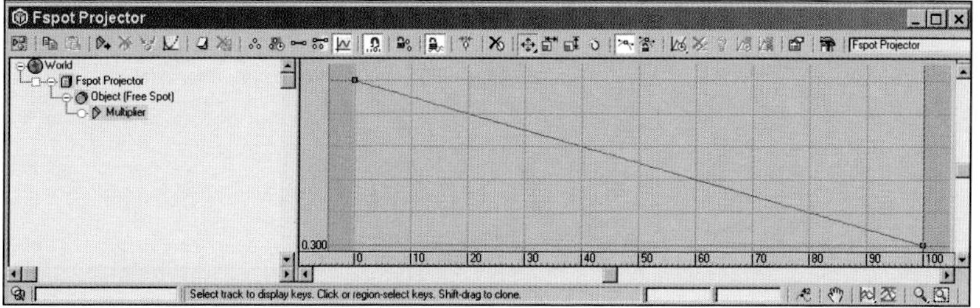

Examine the projector light in Track View to see its base Multiplier track, shown here in Function Curve mode.

4 Apply a Float List controller to the light's Multiplier track to create a slot for additional controllers.

Note: You need to be certain that Show Only: Animated Tracks in the Track View Filter dialog is unchecked because no animation will be set to the available track.

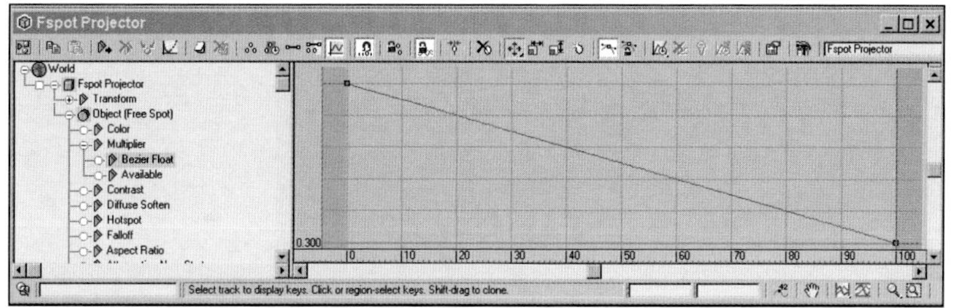

Use the Float List controller to add an available track to the Multiplier track.

5 Apply a Noise Float controller to the newly available track. In the Noise Controller dialog, set the following values:

Strength: **0.5**

Frequency: **0.2**

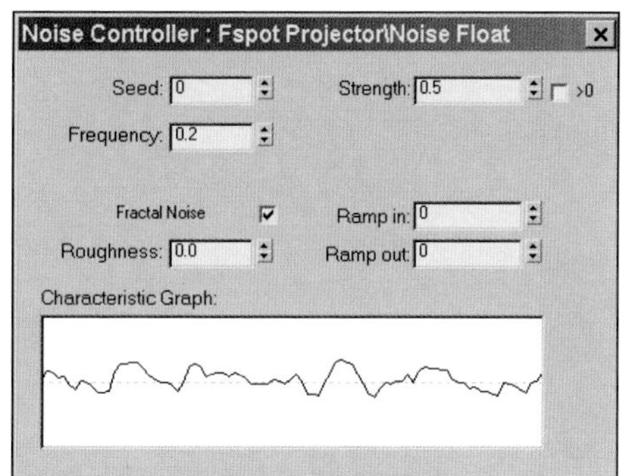

Add a Noise Float controller to blend some random flicker into the projector light's brightness.

6 Select the Multiplier track and go to Function Curves mode to see how the light's brightness will flicker over time. Close Track View.

7 Select the FDirect Sun light and go to the Directional Parameters rollout.

A Noise map will be applied as a projection to modulate the brightness of the light being cast.

8 Click the Projector Map button and apply a Noise map. Drag the map to an unused slot in the Material Editor, choosing Instance as the method. Name this new map **Leaves Shadow** and set the following values to create a mottled light pattern:

Coordinates

Source: **Explicit Map Channel**

Noise Parameters

Size: **0.05**

Noise Threshold

High: **0.8**

Low: **0.15**

Color #1: **R 100, G 100, B 100**

9 Turn on the Animate button, go to frame 25, and set the following values:

Coordinates

Offset

U: **0.2**

V: **0.5**

This will make the material sway over time, as if leaves are being blown by the wind.

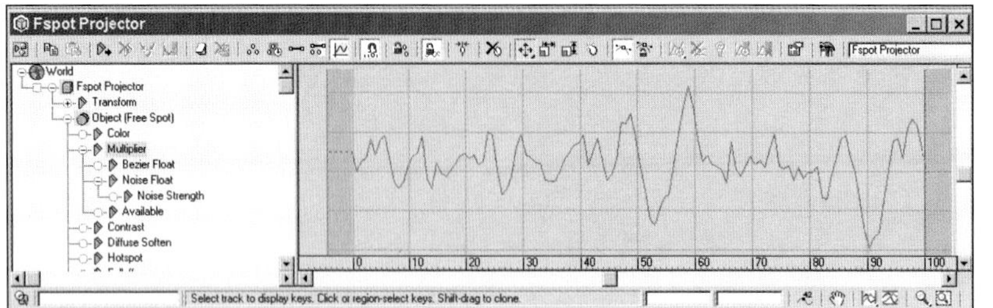

The blended track that will determine the light's Multiplier value.

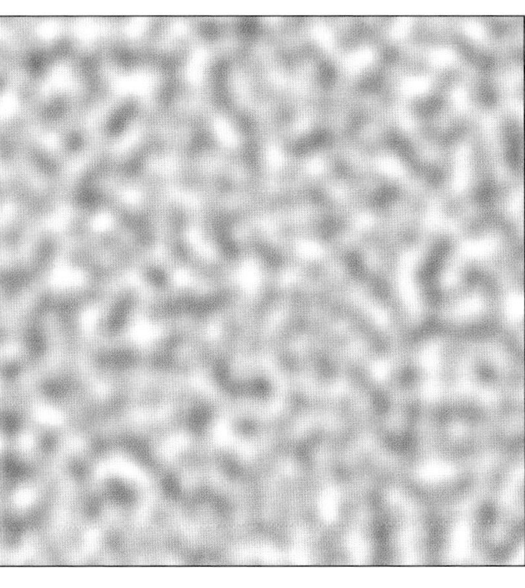

Create a Noise map to provide a mottled shadow pattern to the sunlight.

Note: Using a Projection map to create an artificial shadow layer is similar to the function of a "cookie" in non-CG filmmaking, in which an abstract shape, cut out of plywood, is used to give the impression of leaves or similar objects casting shadows on a scene.

Note: Use Explicit Map Channel as the source whenever you want to apply a map according to a mapping channel as opposed to using World or Object space.

10 Go to frame 50 and set the following values:

Coordinates
  Offset
    U: **0.0**
    V: **0.3**

11 Go to frame 100 and set Phase to **1.0**. Turn the Animate button off. To cycle the panning of the map, open Track View, select the Coordinates, Offset track, and set the Parameter Curve Out-of-Range type to Loop.

Virtually every parameter for lights and their associated maps and atmospheres can be animated. In the preceding section you only touched on a few settings, but it would be simple to expand on that animation, for example, to show accelerated time through the dimming and color change in the natural light.

Modifications

The general practice of balancing a scene's lighting through key and fill lights can be followed as far as needed. Many levels of reflection and quasi-radiosity effects can be rendered through the careful placement of subtle fill lights. Consider using low-intensity colored lights to show the reflection of a surface upon another. For example, a blue reflection cast from the floor in this scene upon the lower walls.

For more exacting outdoor lighting setups, max includes a built-in Sunlight system. Found in the Systems tab of the Create panel, this system enables you to specify hour, time of day, latitude and longitude, and many other factors to generate precise angles of solar illumination. For landscape or architectural work, such accuracy can be essential. Moreover, by paying attention to the characteristic light intensity and color appropriate to specific times of day, the emotional content of a scene can be enhanced.

The Light Lister utility is capable of changing a great number of settings in scene lighting. For example, all or some lights can be set to use specific colors or shadow types.

Global Tinting from the Light Lister utility and Exposure Control environmental effects allow even greater correction of overall scene lighting. These functions are especially useful because they do not affect the settings of individual lights, enabling you to layer rendering changes, much like the Modifier List layers modifiers.

ROPE SWING

"It's because I'm a panda, isn't it?"

—PETEY, THE SEXUAL HARASSMENT PANDA, SOUTH PARK

Soft-Body Dynamics

Soft-body dynamics—such as a sheet waving subtly in the wind or water flowing under a bridge—add a degree of realism to any scene. This added sense of realism allows the brain to take a break and simply partake of the rich visual experience rather than worrying that something "just doesn't look quite right."

In this project, you'll use the new soft-body spring feature found in the Flex modifier to simulate a swinging rope. Flex will also be incorporated into an effect that dynamically simulates a rippling soft-body collision in water.

Project 5

Rope Swing

by Randy M. Kreitzman

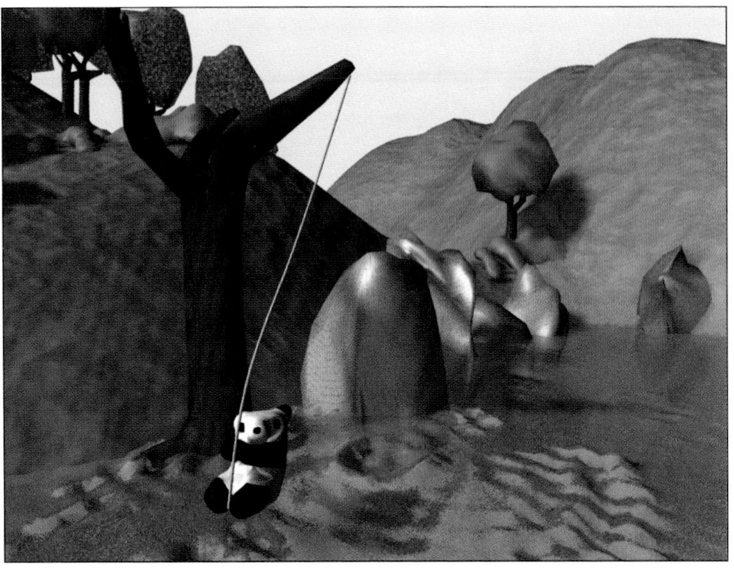

How It Works

This project makes extensive use of the Flex modifier. The rope uses Flex's new soft-body springs to maintain its shape as it is naturally influenced by gravity. The panda bear is a skinned IK rig using the new history independent (HI) IK solver. Each of the panda's limbs is constrained to a different point on the rope via Path Constraints. As the panda's bottom splashes through the water, particles are emitted along the water's surface, selecting the mesh as they move outward in a radial pattern. This selection is deformed with a Push modifier and then sent up to another Flex modifier for the resulting secondary motion that creates the wake and ripples. The end result is a very natural-looking effect that is 100% procedurally generated.

Getting Started

To begin, launch 3ds max 4 and load the scene titled **rope01.max** from the accompanying CD-ROM. This scene contains all the elements you'll need to complete the project (although many components still need to be configured to get things working properly). To speed up interactivity throughout the project, it might help to hide all but the most pertinent components of the scene. So hide the Terrain group and the panda, for starters.

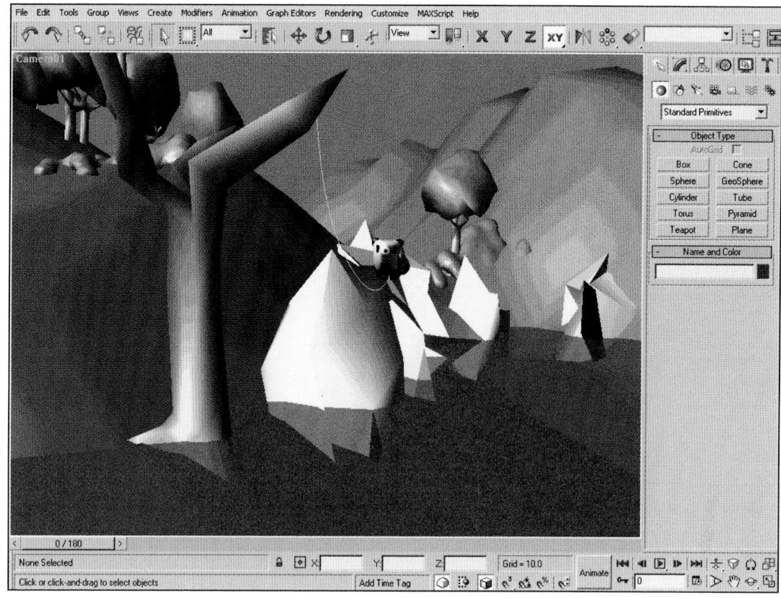

Panda is ready to go.

Flexing the Rope

The rope object is actually a NURBS point curve made up of five control points. In this section, you'll use Flex to set up soft-body springs for each control point. You'll then specify an anchor point for the rope and apply gravity.

1 Select the Rope object. From the Modifiers menu, select Flex from the Animation Modifiers group. Click on the Plus icon next to Flex to display the sub-object levels. Select the Weights & Springs item.

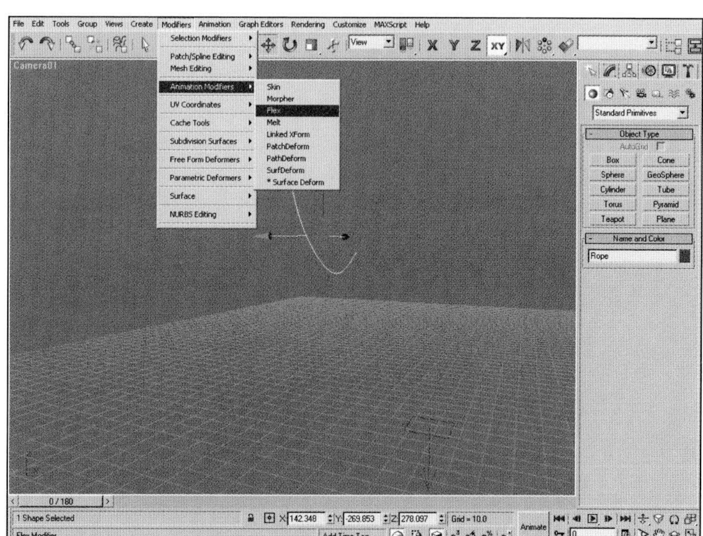

Apply Flex from the Modifiers menu.

2 In the Parameters rollout, turn off both the Use Chase Springs option and the Use Weights option and set Samples to **3**.

Note: You can see the springs between the control points by turning on the Show Springs option in the Advanced Springs rollout. The springs will be displayed only while you're in one of the sub-object levels, however.

3 In the Simple Soft Bodies rollout, click the big Create Simple Soft Body button.

4 In the Forces and Deflectors rollout, click the Forces Add button and select the gravity space warp in the scene. Drag the time slider back and forth to see the animation.

The rope is flexed, but the whole object falls into the lake. You need to specify the top of the rope as an anchor point.

5 In Stack view, select the Edge Vertices sub-object level. Select the control point at the top of the rope to set it as an edge point. Click the Flex item to exit Sub-Object mode and play back the animation to see the new motion.

The only parameters you'll really need to tweak are the Stretch and Stiffness parameters in the Simple Soft Bodies rollout. Each of these parameters controls a different component of the soft-body spring behavior. Stretch indicates the maximum distance between two points. Stiffness controls how rigid each control point is in relation to the next.

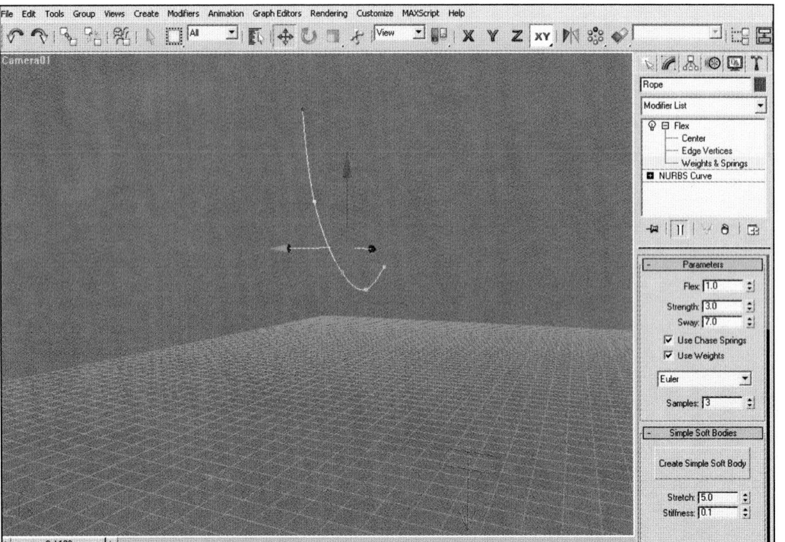

Colored vertices indicate Flex weight value.

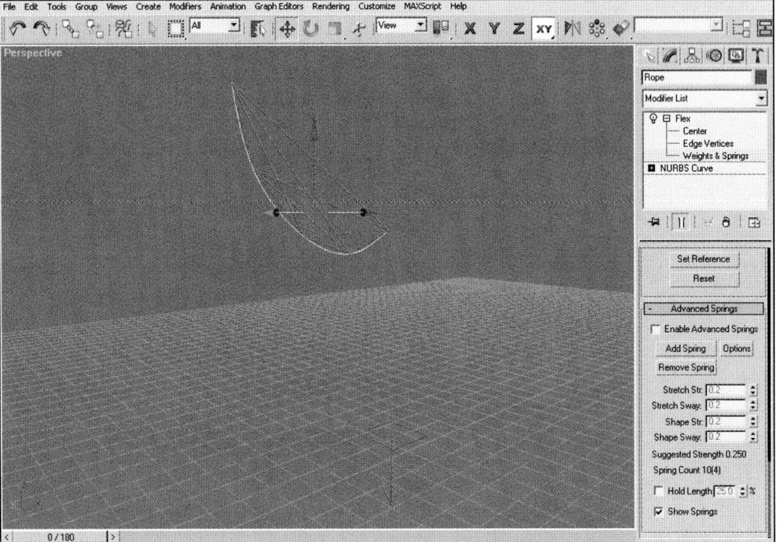

Flex with Show Springs turned on.

6 In the Simple Soft Bodies rollout, adjust the Stretch and Stiffness parameters while the animation is playing back to get a feel for what each control does. The following settings are recommended, but they are by no means mandatory: Stretch = **10.0** and Stiffness = **0.0**.

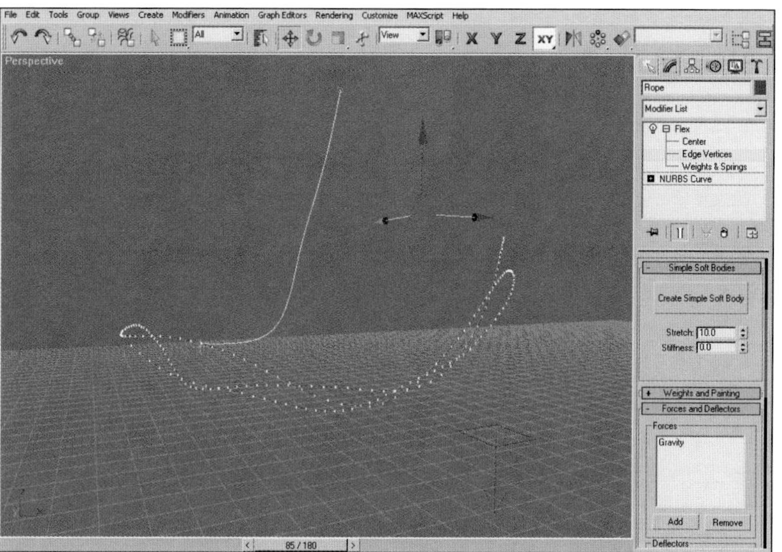

The rope, now anchored by the edge vertex at the top, swings freely.

Attaching the Panda

Now that the basic motion of the rope has been blocked out, it's time to attach the swinging panda. The panda has already been skinned and IK'd for this scene. Each limb uses the history independent HI IK solver new to 3ds max 4. This new IK system uses independent goal objects to manipulate the IK chain into position. You'll use the new Path Constraint to attach the panda's hands, feet, and midsection to the rope. As the rope swings, so will the panda.

1 In the Display panel, press the Unhide by Name button to invoke the Unhide Objects dialog and unhide the three Point helper objects. Select each Point helper one at a time and examine its controller properties in the Motion panel.

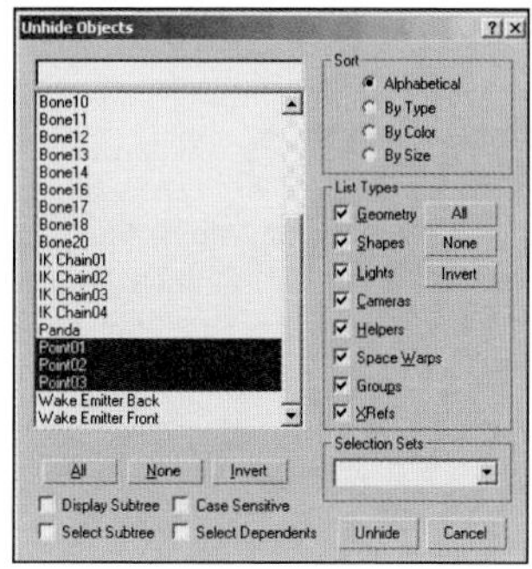

Use the Unhide Objects dialog to unhide multiple objects.

Each Point helper is attached to the rope object by a Path Constraint. Point01 and Point02 will be the anchor points for the panda's hands and feet (respectively), and Point03 will anchor the character's midsection. Point03 also uses a LookAt rotation constraint to maintain its orientation as the rope swings back and forth.

The LookAt Constraint is now a dedicated rotation controller with several new options to explicitly control the direction of the upnode, or pole vector, to prevent flipping. Point03's X-axis is constrained to look at Point02, while its Y-axis upnode attempts to maintain alignment with the world Y-axis. This ensures that Point03 (and, hence, the panda's midsection) will not flip as it passes back and forth across the steep vertical section of the rope over the course of the animation.

Note: Constraints are a new class of controllers that explicitly reference other objects in the scene. Both the Path and LookAt Constraints have been completely overhauled for 3ds max 4. Each constraint offers the ability to reference multiple weighted targets. Constraints can be assigned from either the Animation/Constraints menu or the Motion panel.

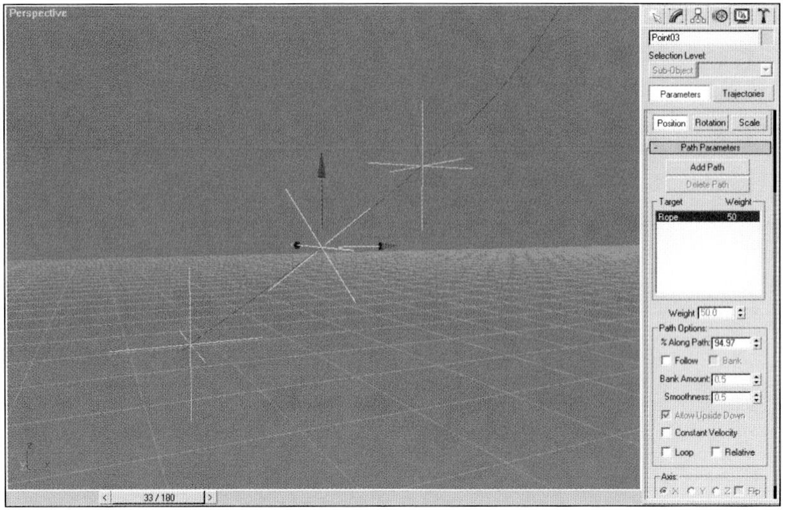

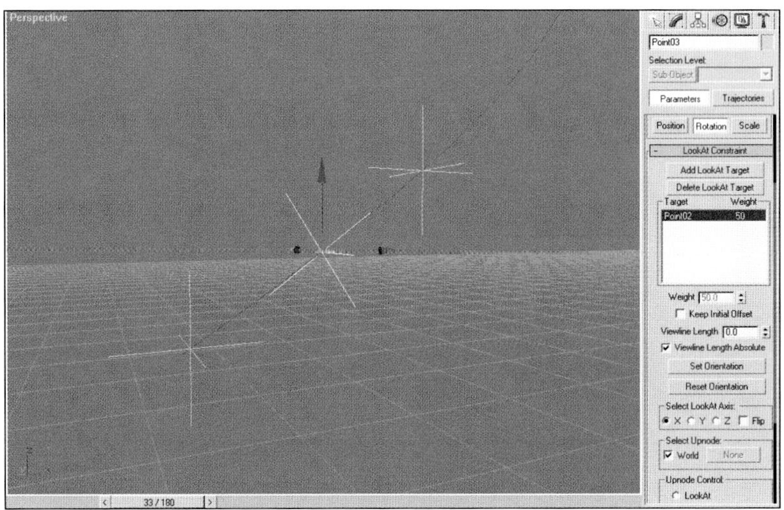

Examine the Path and LookAt Constraint parameters.

2 Drag the time slider back and forth and examine how each Point helper is constrained to the rope throughout its motion.

3 In the Display panel, press the Hide by Name button to invoke the Hide Objects dialog and unhide each of the Bone objects and the four IK chains.

4 Go to frame 0 and use the Select and Link tool to link IK Chain01-02 to Point02. Link IK Chain03-04 to Point01. Link Bone01 (the skeleton's root) to Point03. Then scrub the time slider and examine how the skeleton moves with the rope.

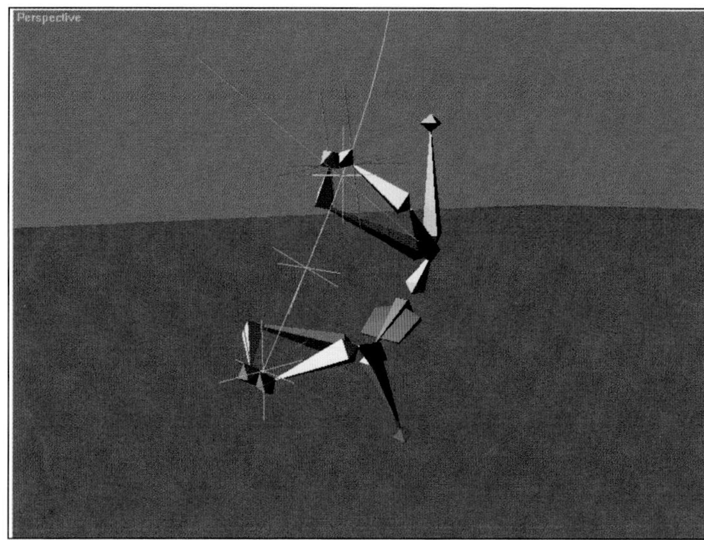

Panda's skeleton swings through the air.

Note: Bone16, the bone used to control the panda's head, is LookAt constrained to the camera in the scene (Camera01). This helps to enhance the realism of the panda swinging back and forth on the rope.

5 In the Display panel, press the Hide by Name button to invoke the Hide Objects dialog and hide all the Bone objects. Then, unhide the panda skin.

6 Select and move any of the Point helpers up and down along the rope. Select and move any of the IK Chain objects to move the limbs.

Because the IK goals are hierarchically linked to the path constrained Point helpers, they inherit the rope's motion, but they are also free to move independently. This would enable you to animate the panda's hand waving to the camera, for instance.

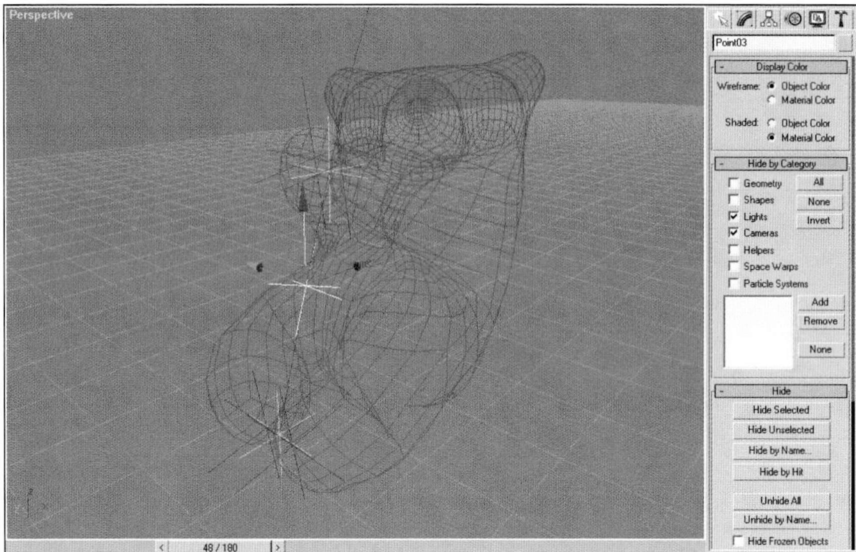

Move the Point helpers to adjust the panda's position.

7 Hide the Point helpers and IK Chain objects in preparation for the next exercise.

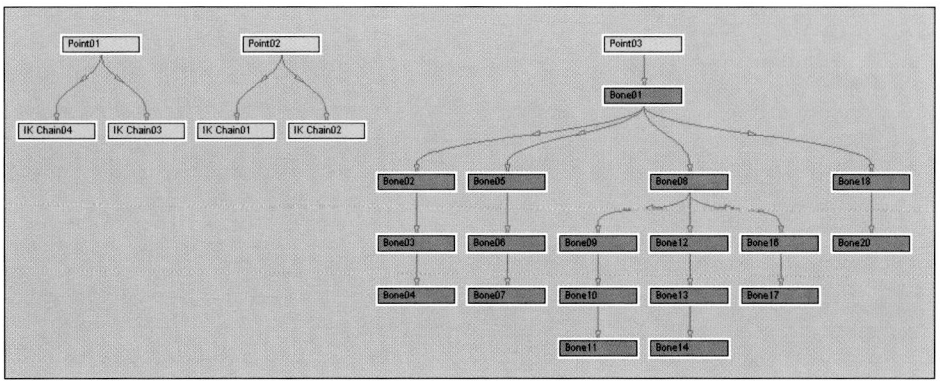

This schematic view demonstrates linkage hierarchy.

MAKING A SPLASH

For the final effect, the panda splashes down and drags his bottom through the water, creating natural ripples that radiate outward and a wake that trails behind. You'll take great advantage of the 3ds max 4 geometry pipeline as you procedurally generate this effect from scratch, without the use of any additional plug-ins. SuperSpray emitters will leave a trail of particles across the surface of the water, selecting portions of the mesh as they go. The selected mesh is deformed using a Push modifier and then passed up the stack to Flex, which handles the secondary motion.

1 Unhide both of the Wake Emitter objects and play back the animation.

Concentric rings of particles radiate outward from the two emitters. The two emitters are configured identically, but they are rotated 180 degrees from one another to distribute particles in opposite directions.

Note: This step requires considerable resources. Slower computers might have difficulty playing the animation.

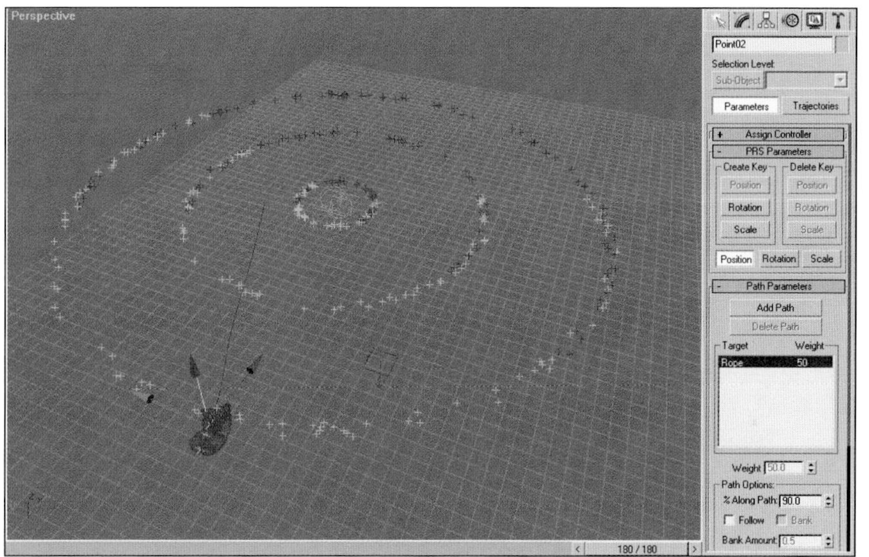

Particle waves radiate outward in concentric rings.

2 Select either emitter and examine its properties in the Modify panel.

In the Basic Parameters rollout, note that the emitter is configured to spread particles over a 120-degree span, which produces a pattern slightly greater than semicircular. This allows the particles to be projected to a point just behind the emitter, overlapping the other emitter's pattern of particles.

In the Object Motion Inheritance rollout, note that the Influence value has been decreased to 0. This parameter controls the degree to which an emitter's motion can influence a particle after it has been emitted. When this value is set to 0, each particle is simply emitted and left to go its own way.

In the Particle Generation rollout, note that the Use Rate spinner flashes a value of 40 as the particles are periodically emitted. This happens because the particle system's Birth Rate parameter is controlled by a MaxScript expression.

3 Right-click in the Use Rate spinner field and select Show in Track View toward the bottom of the quad menu.

4 Right-click on the range bar of the Birth Rate track to bring up the Script Controller expression window.

This is a simple expression that tests the position of Bone20, which happens to be the panda's tailbone. If Bone20 dips below Z:0 (sea level, in this case), 40 particles per frame are emitted for as long as the bone is below the surface. If the bone's elevation is greater than zero, no particles are emitted. This saves precious computational energy, which will be put to use later on.

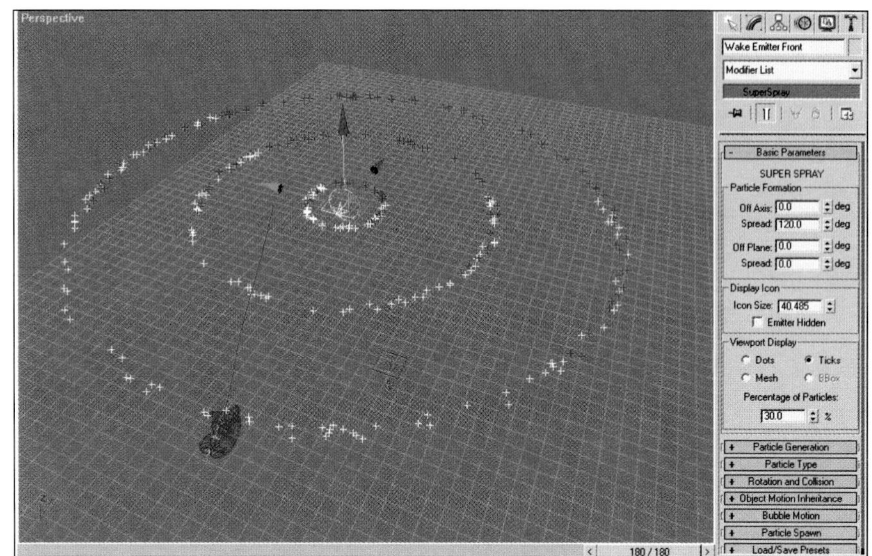

Examining particle emitter properties.

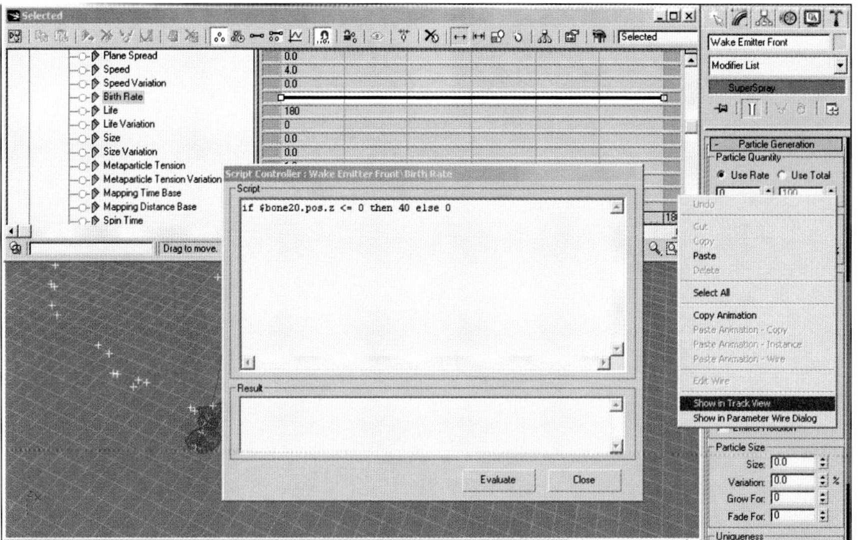

Use Show in Track View to display scripted controller properties.

Note: The scripted controller on the Birth Rate track is instanced between the two particle emitters. If you change the expression in one controller, the controller on the other particle system is automatically updated. This means you don't have to fuss around replacing multiple controllers with the same expression every time you want to change the effect.

5 Close Track View (and the Script Controller expression window along with it) and go to frame 0.

6 Unhide Bone20. Select both emitters, using the Select by Name dialog if necessary. Select and link both emitters to Bone20 and play back the animation.

When the emitters are attached to the panda's tailbone, they leave a nice trail of particles across the surface of the water. This distribution of particles will now be used to select and deform the water itself.

Note: Each emitter's rotational link inheritance has been turned off in the Hierarchy\Link Info panel. This ensures that the emitters stay flat in respect to the surface of the water. The goal is for the projected particles to radiate outward but to run parallel to the surface.

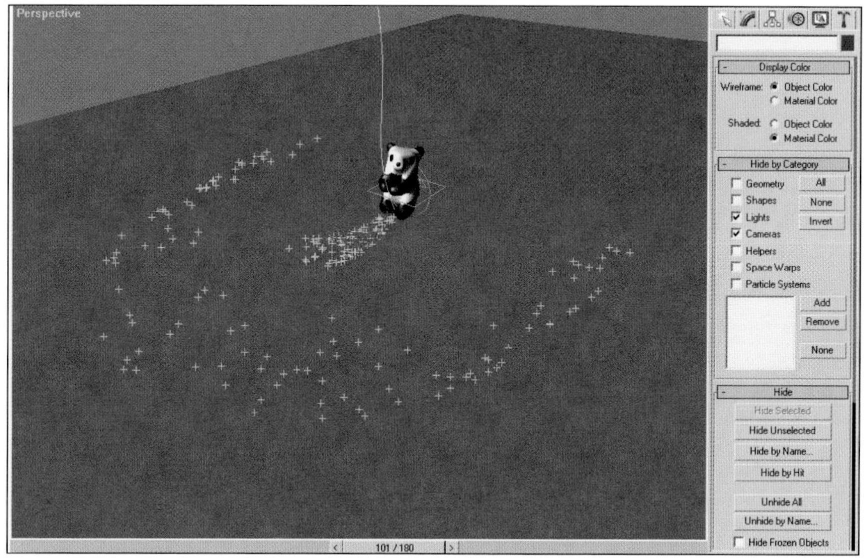

Moving emitters leave a trail of particles on the water's surface.

Deforming the Water

The next step in creating a realistic soft-body water effect is to convert the motion of the particles into actual deformation of the water mesh itself. You'll use a couple of Volume Select modifiers to select the water mesh based on the positions of the emitted particles. This selection is passed up the stack to a Push modifier, which projects the mesh upward. This animated deformation is then handed off to another Flex modifier to create secondary motion, generating ripples.

1. Select the Water object. From the Modifiers menu, select Volume Select from the Selection Modifiers group.
2. In the new modifier's Parameters rollout, change the Stack Selection Level to Vertex. In the Select By group, change the selection type to Mesh Object. Click the Mesh Object button labeled "None" and pick Wake Emitter Front in the scene. In the Soft Selection rollout, enable Use Soft Selection.
3. In Stack view, right-click the Vol. Select entry and choose Rename. Change the name to **Vol. Select Front**.
4. From the Modifiers menu, apply a second Volume Select modifier. As you did in the above procedure, change the Stack Selection Level to Vertex and the Select By type to Mesh Object, picking Wake Emitter Back as the selection object. Enable Use Soft Selection.

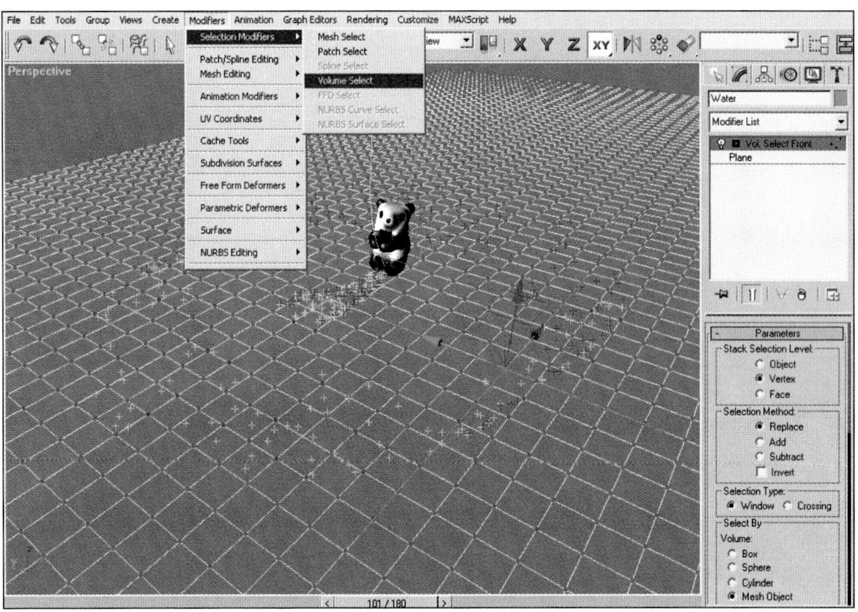

Apply a Volume Select modifier to the Water object.

Note: It is sometimes easier to copy or paste an existing modifier with your preset parameters than to create a new one from scratch using its default values. You can do this by right-clicking on an existing modifier in Stack view and then selecting the Copy and Paste options.

5 Rename the new Vol. Select to **Vol. Select Back** and change Vol. Select Back's Selection Method to Add.

As each particle moves outward from the splash point, Vol. Select assigns a weighted (soft) selection to the vertices near its position. The closer the particle is to the mesh, the stronger the selection becomes. Each Vol. Select references a particle emitter in the scene. Vol. Select Back's Add selection method simply adds its selection to the incoming selection from Vol. Select Front, shown here.

6 From the Modifiers menu, select Push from the Parametric Deformers group. Adjust the Push Value to see how the modifier affects the incoming soft selection. Set the Push Value to **7.0** and play back the animation.

7 From the Modifiers menu, select Flex from the Animation Modifiers group. In the Parameters rollout, set Strength to **5.0**, Sway to **4.0**, and Samples to **2**. Uncheck Use Weights. In the Advanced Parameters rollout, check Affect All Points.

The Flex modifier takes the incoming deformation generated by Push and creates secondary motion, generating ripples. The Strength and Sway values control the ripples' frequency and damping, respectively. Because you've turned off the Use Weights option, the entire surface of the water mesh is weighted equally. The Affect All Points option applies the Flex motion to all selected and unselected vertices in the mesh.

The collection of modifiers needed to generate the procedural wave requires a significant amount of computation. To speed up playback in the viewports, you can use the new Point Cache modifier on top of the Water object's stack.

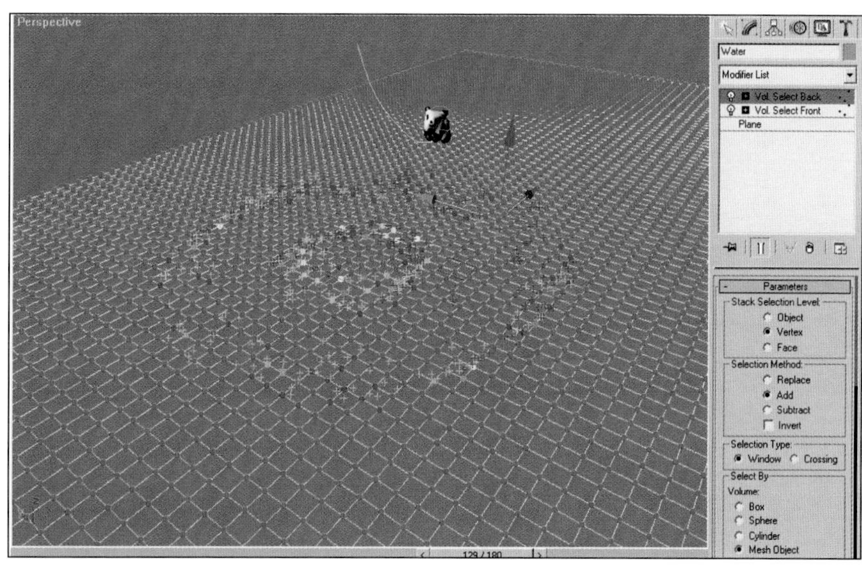

Volume Select displays its weighted soft-selection in varying degrees of color.

Note: It may be difficult to see the effect of the Push modifier on such a low-resolution mesh. Keep in mind that the effect you see will automatically be refined to a much higher resolution at render time because the Plane object is set to render at four times its viewport density.

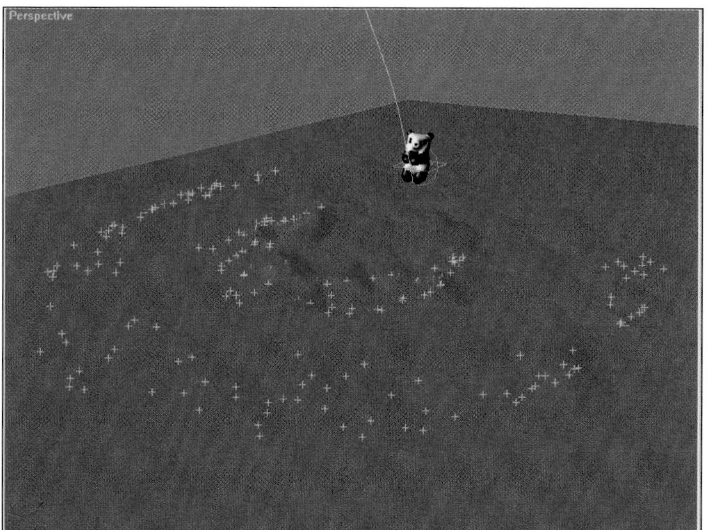

Flex secondary motion creates ripples on low-resolution mesh.

Note: If Affect All Points were not checked, the Flex motion would be applied to only the current sub-object selection at any given point in time. Because the current selection travels with each wave of particles, Flex would only be applied to the vertices in that wave. For this effect, you need the Flex motion on the portions of the mesh that the selection wave has passed through.

8 From the Modifiers menu, select Point Cache from the Cache Tools group. In the modifier's Record Cache group, click the Record button. Specify a .pts file and click Save.

Depending on the speed of your computer, this process may take up to several minutes to complete. A status indicator in the modifier's Record Cache group reports how many frames have been cached during the operation.

9 When all frames have been recorded, click the Disable Modifiers Below button and play back the animation.

The Point Cache modifier saves the position over time of each vertex on the Water object to a file on your hard disk. During playback, Point Cache reads this data from the file and repositions each vertex accordingly. Because all the modifiers below Point Cache have been turned off, the procedural overhead has been lowered substantially, thereby speeding up playback in the viewport.

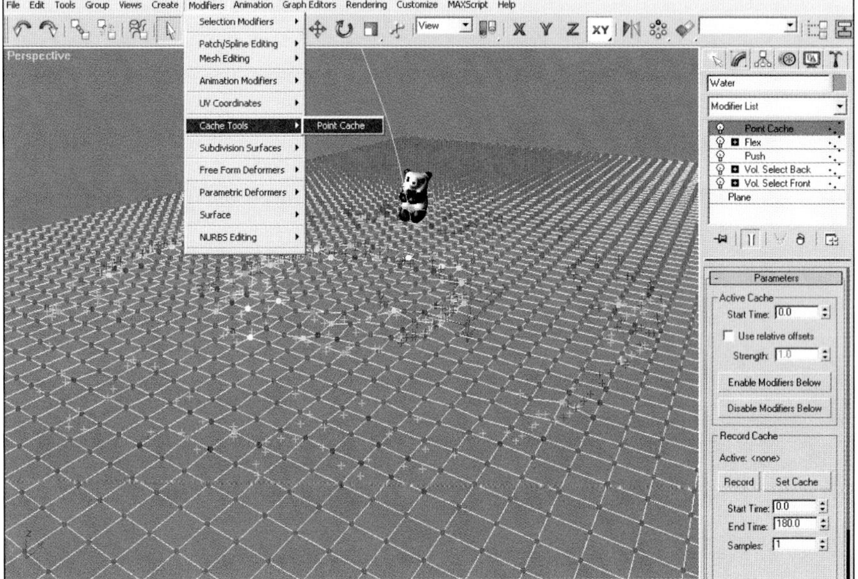

Apply the Point Cache modifier.

Note: To speed up viewport playback even more, you can hide both of the particle emitters.

Before you render the scene, remember to re-enable all the modifiers below Point Cache and then turn Point Cache off. This is necessary because the water object (plane) is set to render at four times its viewport density. If Point Cache were left enabled, it would have only one-fourth the data required to properly deform the mesh, resulting in a rather unsightly mess.

To see the final result of this project, load **rope02.max** from the accompanying CD-ROM, or play **rope.avi**, also on the CD-ROM.

Play back the animation using Point Cache.

Note: You need the Ligos Indeo 5.11 codec to view the AVI on the accompanying CD-ROM. You can download it for free from **http://www.ligos.com/indeo/**.

Modifications

To add an additional bit of realism to the scene, you could procedurally control the Speed parameter of the particle emitters. This would be very similar to the technique used to control the particle Birth Rate, except you'd use the tailbone's velocity to control the speed of the particles. Hint: You'll find a Wake Velocity track in Track View's Global Tracks.

Try animating the panda's IK goals to move his limbs while he's swinging on the rope. You could have him wave to the camera or, perhaps, carry a flag that waves in the wind.

Try adding a Drag force to the Flex forces list to slow the rope down over time. To make it more interesting, you could procedurally control the drag strength so that the rope slows down only when the panda's tail is in the water.

JELLYFISH

"To All Who Come To This Happy Place: Welcome."

—THE FIRST LINE FROM THE PLAQUE IN DISNEYLAND'S TOWN SQUARE

Bringing Jellyfish to Life

There are thousands of jellyfish species out in the sea, and they come in all shapes and sizes. 3ds max 4 offers just as many tools to help re-create and animate these incredible animals. By using a combination of simple keyframing, a few modifiers, and an environmental trick or two, this tutorial will guide you through bringing these gelatinous creatures to life. The simple methods introduced here can be used to add realism to many other types of animation, organic and nonorganic alike.

Project 6

Jellyfish

by Michael Reiser, MD

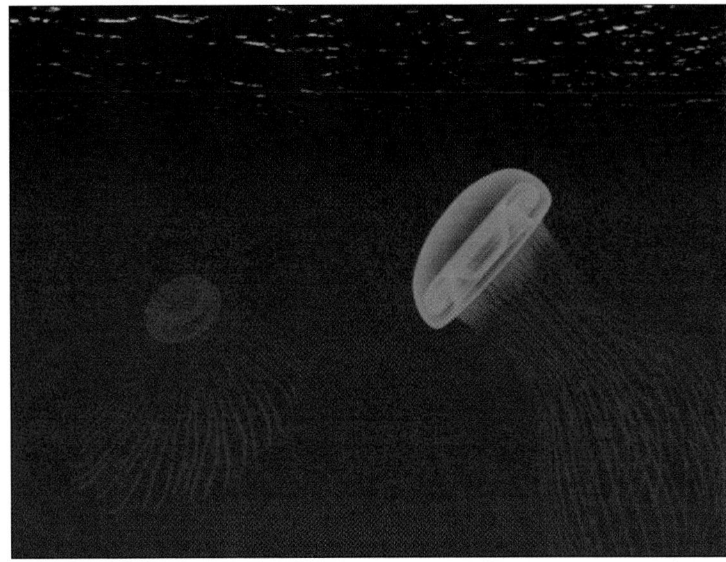

How It Works

It's good practice to maximize efficiency while trying to maintain a sufficient amount of detail to accomplish a task. In an attempt to keep to this good practice, this tutorial does not involve any complicated models, extremely complex textures, or too many keyframes. For instance, the jellyfish model is a simple double-sided lathed spline with a few Opacity maps to give the illusion of tentacles. The body texture is a simple Falloff material. In addition, there are only a few manually placed keyframes, as the majority of the secondary motion is contributed by combining the Flex and Noise modifiers. Finally, the background is a combination of a volumetric light and Raytrace material simulating the undersurface of the ocean, giving a surprisingly realistic environment.

Getting Started

The setup for this tutorial is not very complex. The animated objects in the scene consist of a simple mesh object and a short spline. The environment is created using two plane objects and a single volumetric light. As you follow along, I encourage you to complete the project on your own. The image file for the tentacles as well as the mesh object and final scene are, of course, available on the accompanying CD-ROM. You might want to add the scenes and meshes to the appropriate 3ds max 4 subdirectories for easy access.

Creating the Jellyfish Object

In this first portion of the tutorial, you are going to model the jellyfish and produce the few keyframes that will define its motion. The first thing to do is load in a background image that will act as our template as well as the initial guide for the animation.

> **Note:** Most of the time when animating living creatures, you are trying to convince an audience that this collection of polygons is alive. This, as you know, is not easy. I suggest that you take the time to seek out the real thing (if it exists, of course) and study its motion. For those nonexistent creatures, find something similar in nature to study. For this jellyfish tutorial, I went out and bought a few videotapes. Ideally, I could have gone to the local aquarium to see them in true form. The point is, do whatever you can to take the time to study your subject's motion. The payback is invaluable to your final product, and this jellyfish project is no exception.

1 Click the Views tab on the main max 4 menu. Scroll down to the Viewport Background option. Under Background Source, click the Files option. Guide the browser to the **Jelly_Spline.tif** file on the accompanying CD-ROM. Open this file.

2 In the Viewport Background dialog box, select the Match Bitmap, Display Background, and Lock Zoom/Pan options. Change the viewport to Front. Click OK.

3 Zoom and Pan until the image fits into the viewport. You might want to turn off the Show Grid option for the Front viewport. I also suggest changing the layout to a three-view option with the background drawing in the larger window.

Notice in the image that the lines representing the tentacles are numbered 1–7. These numbers are there to show the order of tentacle motion over time. For instance, Spline01 moves to the position of Line02 over a set period of time and so on. You will use this as a guide for animating the tentacles. Though there are many ways to create a jellyfish-type creature in max 4, I found that producing the model using the following steps kept the scene more interactive and processor friendly.

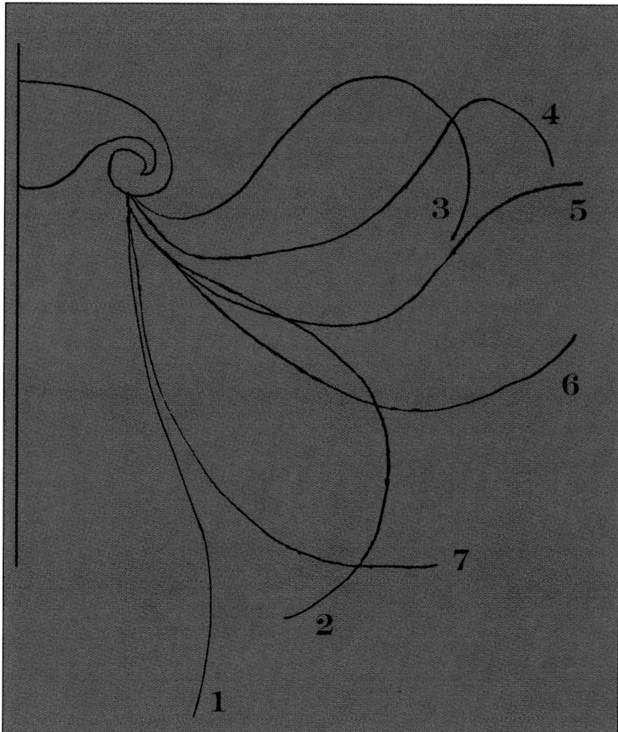

The background template.

Note: The background image represents one-half slice of the jellyfish prior to being lathed. Let me explain why I created this and how it will help us out greatly. After making hundreds of sample scenes, it became painfully clear that the best way to create the effect I wanted was going to involve some keyframing. After studying the videotapes over and over again, a pattern emerged that demonstrated the motion I was going for. This background drawing represents that motion.

4 To start modeling the jellyfish, use the Line tool under Create/Shapes/Line. Before creating the line, change the Creation Method subtypes as follows:

Initial Type: **Smooth**
Drag Type: **Bézier**

This will give you smooth control when drawing the rounded corners for the organic look you are going for.

5 In the Front viewport, create the outline by tracing over the jellyfish body. End this line by right-clicking and create a separate line that traces over the line labeled 01.

Keep the spline simple. I suggest no more than four vertices for the tentacle portion.

6 With the spline selected, go to the Modify panel and use the Attach tool to connect the two splines into one object. Name this spline object something original, like **Jellyfish**.

Next you will give the jellyfish its basic motion.

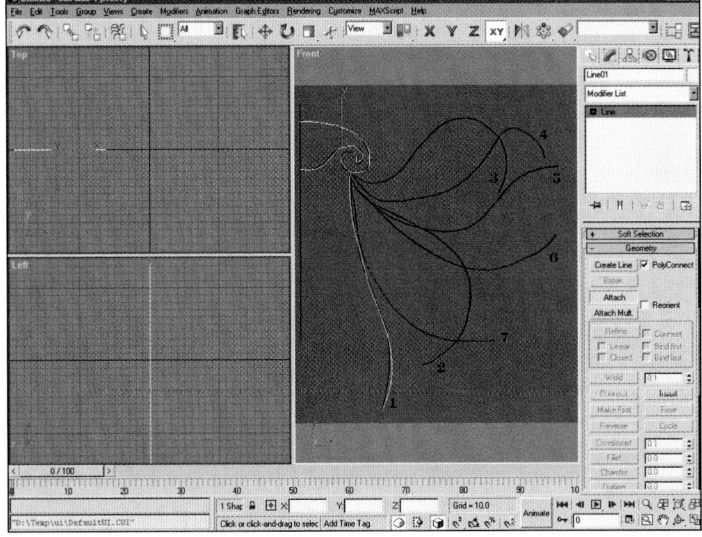

New spline overlying the background image.

Note: I like to have Ghosting active to get a feel for the animation while I am creating it. To activate Ghosting, click on Show Ghosting under the Views tab.

7 With the new spline selected, open the Modify panel. You will notice that the selected item is highlighted in gray, and there is a small plus sign to the left of it. Click the plus sign to expand the item subtree.

Note: 3ds max has given the Modify panel a slightly new look to help with workflow.

Note: Clicking the plus sign is the new way to access the sub-objects for the selected item. You will see that this is a wonderful new addition, and you will be using this extensively throughout the tutorial.

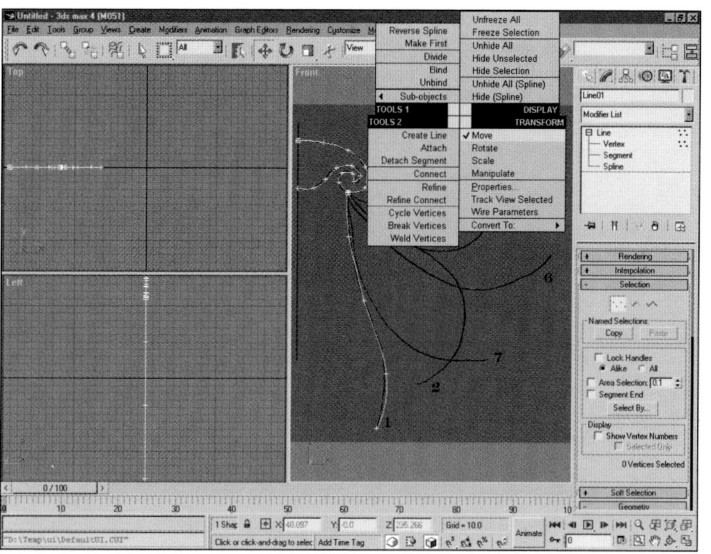

3ds max 4's new Modify panels.

Note: It is always a good idea to save often. You might also want to give your saves a description of where in the project each particular save is from. Undo is a great thing, but saving is better.

8 Select and highlight the Vertex subtree option for the jellyfish spline. Click the Time Configuration button next to the animation controls. Change the Length option to 210 frames (or 7 seconds). Click OK.

This was the approximate time it took for the jellyfish that I studied to go through their motion.

9 Turn on the Animate button and move the time slider to 30 frames. Move each of the tentacle vertices so that they approximate the background drawing for tentacle number 02. You might need to use the Bézier-type curve to match the background template.

10 Move the time slider to 60 frames and move the tentacle vertices to approximate the position of tentacle number 03. Repeat this action of increasing the time slider by 30 frames and then moving the vertices until you have reached the end of the numbered tentacles. Your last key should be at 210. Turn off the Animate button.

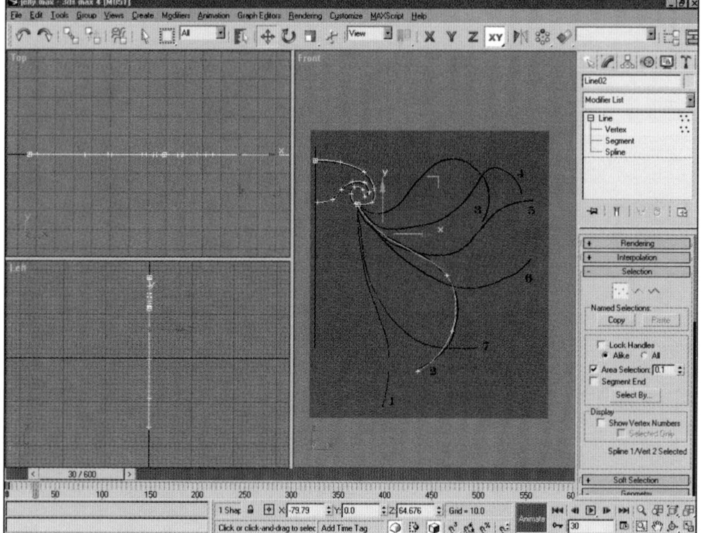

The spline in its new position.

11 Play the animation in the Front viewport.

You should have a spline that has a flowing motion that is clean and skip free.

What you have animated so far is one jellyfish "cycle." The tentacles "pull up" and then "push down." You want the jellyfish to do this twice.

12 Right-click in any viewport while the mouse is over the jellyfish spline. From the Tool Tip menu box, choose the Track View selected option.

Note: 3ds max 4 offers a number of interesting ways to repeat a cycle, and as always, I suggest using the fastest and easiest way that will get the job done. Introduced in previous releases of 3D Studio MAX, the Block controller could be used to seamlessly combine each jellyfish cycle. However, for this animation, it might be a bit much, as my intent is to repeat this motion only once more. If, however, you intend to have the motion repeat a number of times, you might want to look into using the Block controller. You will use what is called the Master point controller. This is a set of Master keyframes, and each controls a subset of individual vertex keyframes that have been animated in groups much like our tentacle example. It is important to remember that you don't lose control of the individual keys when using the Master point controller. If need be, you still have the capability to manipulate the individual keys.

13 Right-click over the spline in Track View and choose the Expand tracks option. Scroll down to the Master branch under Object.

You will notice that each of the individual spline vertices is a subset of the Master point controller. The green keys in line with the Master controller will control the subset of vertices underneath. By selecting one Master key, you have the capability to change the timing and thus the animation of the entire subgroup of vertices.

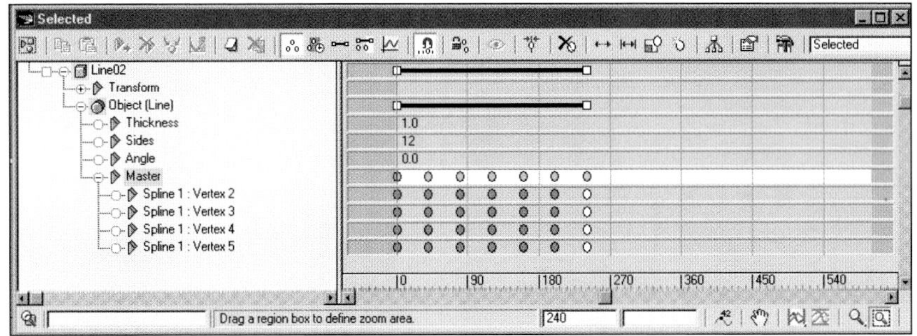

The Master point controller.

14 Select all of the green Master keys in Track View to repeat the jellyfish cycle. Now hold down the Shift key while you click, hold, and drag the group of keys so that the new set begins just as the first is ending. In this example, the first copied key should be placed at 210.

If you would like to change the timing of the animation, choose Master keys individually and change them to your liking. You will probably have to adjust the individual keys to smooth out your changes.

Note: I do caution, however, that moving Master keys does more than just change the timing of the animation. The in-and-out behavior is also influenced as the keys are moved closer or farther apart from each other in Track View.

15 Play the animation and the motion will repeat twice.

You can copy the cycle over and over until you have as many motion cycles as you need. Bear in mind that you will have to increase the animation length as well.

16 Turn off the background image in the Front view; you will no longer be using it. The basic motion of the jellyfish tentacles is complete.

Note: To access the properties of the subkeys under each Master key, select a single Master key and right-click. A Key Info panel appears, giving you the option to change various parameters for each subkey.

Lathing the Spline into a 3D Object

Now that the animation for the spline is complete, you need to give it 3D form. To do this, you will lathe the spline into the jellyfish shape.

1 To the right of the Modifier List heading, there is a drop-down list. Open the entire Modifier List and select the Lathe modifier under the Patch/Spline Editing section.

The Lathe modifier has now been added to the top of the modifier stack.

2 Open the Lathe modifier sub-objects by clicking the plus sign to the left of it.

3 Highlight the Axis sub-object. Move the Axis sub-object in the Front viewport until the shape resembles that of a jellyfish.

It is very important to make sure you have checked the Generate Mapping Coordinates option near the bottom of the Lathe rollout.

4 Select the Patch option as well. Keeping the object as a mesh will result in mapping errors.

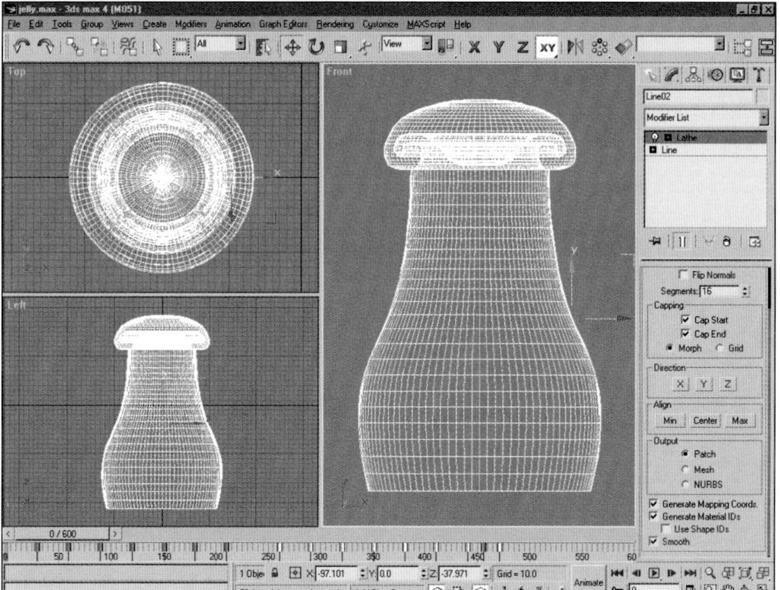

The lathed object.

5 Go to the Hierarchy panel and open the Pivot submenu. Under the Adjust Pivot rollout, choose the Affect Pivot Only option. In the Front viewport, adjust the pivot point so that it sits at the apex of the jellyfish bell.

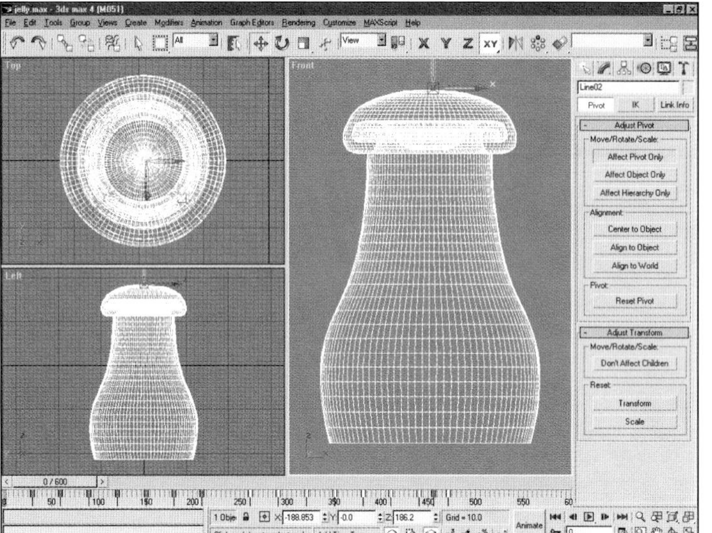

The pivot point in proper position.

6 Apply an Edit Patch modifier to the top of the modifier stack. Open the sub-object list for the Edit Patch modifier and highlight Vertex. In the Front viewport, select the vertices that make up the fringe of the jellyfish skirt.

7 Open the Soft Selection option and adjust the falloff so that the soft effect extends to just below the bell of the Jellyfish.

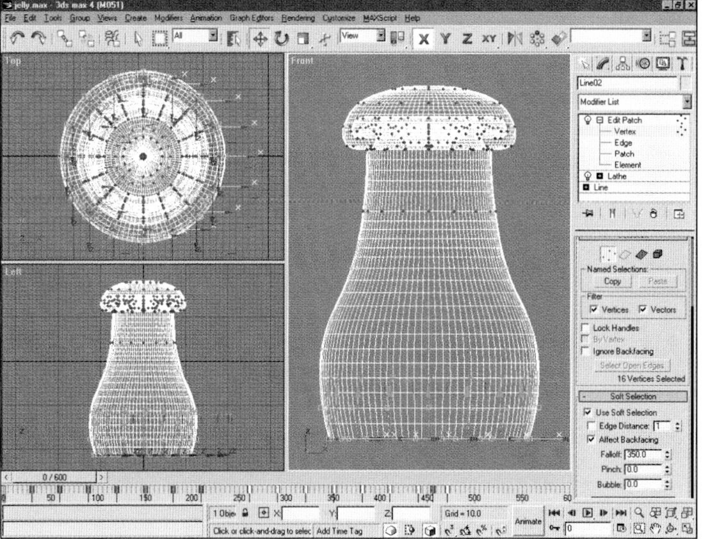

The selected vertices.

8 In the same modifier, deselect the Vertex sub-object and select the Patch sub-object. In the Front viewport, select the Patches that make up the skirt of the jellyfish.

Don't be concerned about the vertices you selected previously. As long as you do not change that selection, max 4 will remember the selection when the time comes to use it.

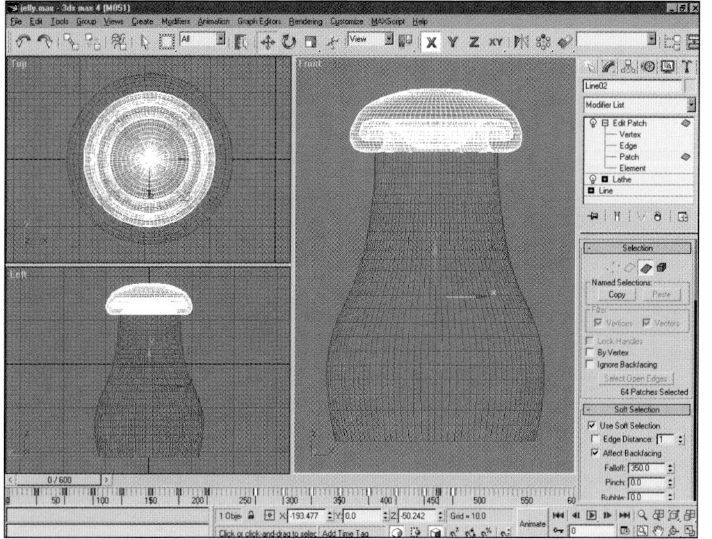

The selected skirt polygons.

Setting Up the Jellyfish Materials

The jellyfish materials themselves are very simple, but the material setup can be a little tricky. In this portion of the tutorial, you are going to assign a Multi/Sub-Object material to the jellyfish subsections.

1 Open the Material Editor. Change the material type for the fist Material slot from Standard to Multi/Sub-Object. At the pop-up menu, choose to keep the old material as a submaterial. Set the number of materials to **2**. Change the color splotches next to each material and name them as well. Something like **Body** and **Tentacles** will do fine.

2 Open the Edit Patch modifier and activate the Patch sub-object, if it is not still active.

The patches that make up the tentacle skirt should be highlighted, reflecting the selection you made earlier.

3 Drag the Skirt material from the Multi/Sub-Object Basic Parameters rollout to the selected patches in the viewport.

The color of the material in the shaded view should change to match the Tentacle sub-object material.

4 With the patches of the jellyfish skirt still selected, go to the Edit menu on the main max 4 toolbar and click the Select Invert option.

The bell of the jellyfish should now be selected.

5 Drag the Body material to this patch selection.

This area should also change color to match that of the Body sub-object material.

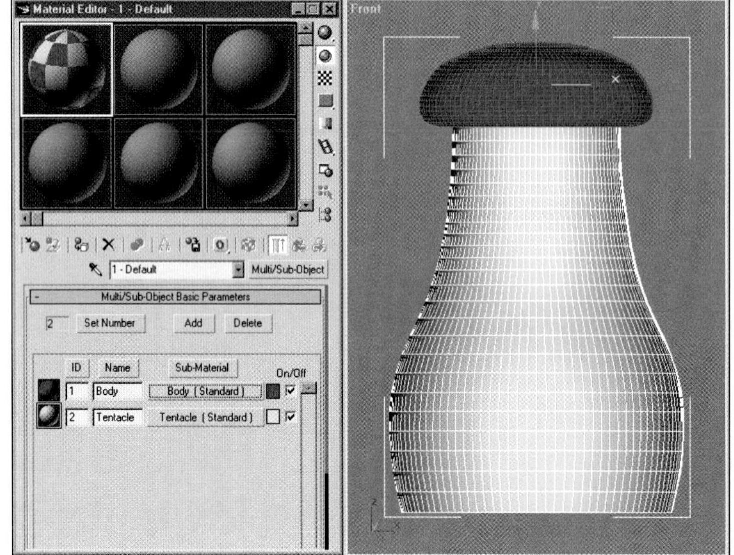

Apply the Multi/Sub-Object materials to the jellyfish.

Making the Jellyfish Materials

Now that the jellyfish setup is complete you can move on to actually making the materials. This section will discuss the jellyfish Body material as well as the materials and methods for producing the tentacles.

1 Click the Body material in the Multi/Sub-Object material menu. Change the diffuse color to be a dusky light blue.

Don't use anything too powerful. You want these creatures to seem as though they are part of the environment.

2 Set the remaining material properties to the settings in the accompanying figure.

3 Open the Maps rollout for the Body material. Click the Map button next to the Opacity channel. Choose Falloff material when the Material/Map browser appears. Leave the Falloff parameters at their default settings and return to the parent material.

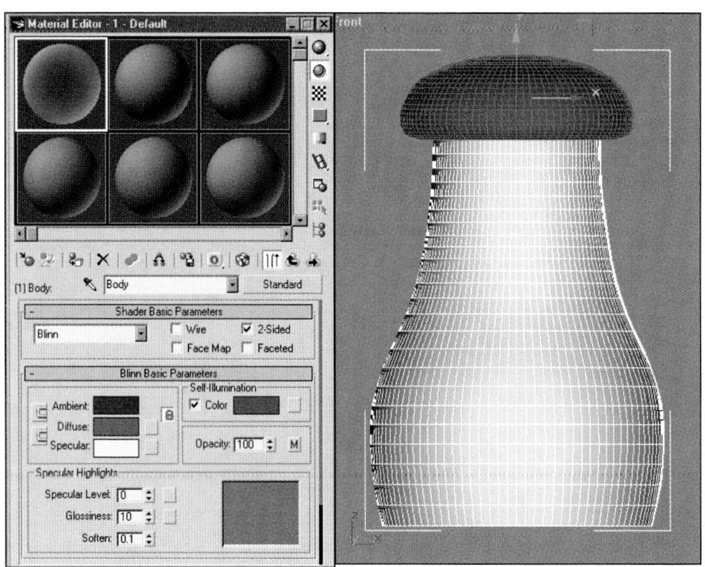

The Body material basic parameters.

4 Open the second material in the Multi/Sub-Object material. For the tentacle color to match the body, use similar diffuse and ambient colors for the second Multi/Sub-Object material.

5 Open the Opacity map channel in the material Basic Parameter section. Click the Map button to bring up the Material/Map browser. Select the Bitmap option and click OK. Browse to and select **Tentacle_Map.tif** from the accompanying CD-ROM and click Open.

6 Copy this Opacity map to the Specular Level and Glossiness channels.

This will keep the transparent areas from giving any reflection and giving away the illusion.

7 With the Tentacle material selected, click the Show Map in Viewport button in the Material Editor.

The viewport should obey the Opacity map and only show the tentacles in the viewports in which Smooth + Highlights is activated.

If the background is washing out, use the Tentacle map in the Self-Illumination slot to give a slight glow to the jellyfish. Use this sparingly, as it can ruin the effect.

That's all that is needed to produce the material for our jellyfish. If you intend to do extreme close-ups, you might want to increase the size of your bitmaps to add more detail. Here, however, at this distance, these maps will do the job. If you make a test render of jellyfish, you should have something similar to this figure.

Note: Depending on how you drew the original spline, the bitmap might be upside down. If you need to fix this, adjust the angle for the bitmap in the coordinate section to correct this problem. For this example, **–90** in the W will work.

Test render of jellyfish with the materials applied.

Animation

The Flex modifier contributes subtle secondary motion to the keyframes you produced earlier. The actual forward motion of the jellyfish will be controlled by a Constrain to Path motion controller. By placing keys in the Path Percent option, you will keyframe the jellyfish along the path. And finally, you will add a Noise modifier to the top of the modifier stack to add a little bit of chaos.

1. Return to the Shapes button under the Create tab and create a simple spline that gently curves upward along the World Z-axis. Bring the interpolation up from the default value of 6.

   This spline does not need to be very long.

2. With the Jellyfish selected, open the Animation menu from the main tool bar and choose the Constraints submenu. From the submenu choose the Path Constraint option. You will notice a little dotted line following your mouse pointer. Drag this until you select the spline you just drew.

   This constrains the jellyfish to the path you created.

3. Change the path options so that the Follow and Bank options are both checked.

   You might need to change the axis so that the mesh is lined up properly to the spline.

4. Click the Play button.

   You will notice that max has generated keys so that the jellyfish now moves along the spline for the length of the animation. The rollout for the Constrain to Path motion controller can be found under the Motion tab.

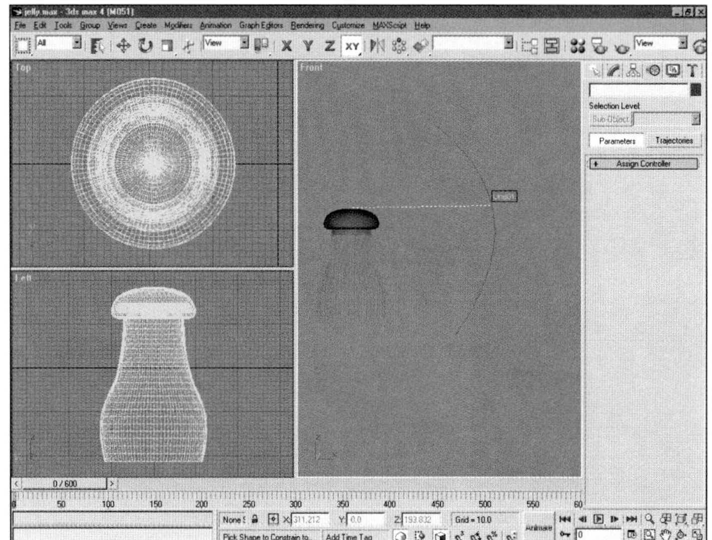

The Constrain tool.

5 Right-click the jellyfish in any of the viewports. Choose the Track View selected option. When Track View appears, right-click the Jellyfish object and choose the Expand Tracks option. Double-click the Percent parameter found under Path Constraint. Choose the Function Curves button from the Track View menu bar.

6 Use the Add Keys option from the top menu and, by clicking the motion path itself, create five or six evenly spaced keys across the length of the animation in Track View. Adjust these keys as shown in the figure.

The forward motion along the motion path needs to coincide with the keys set for the tentacle motion. As the jellyfish "pulls" its tentacles, it has little forward momentum and motion. During this time, the slope of the line in Track View is decreased. As the tentacles "push" the jellyfish through the water, the slope of the line in Track View should increase. Adjust the keys in Track View while playing the animation to work interactively with your animation.

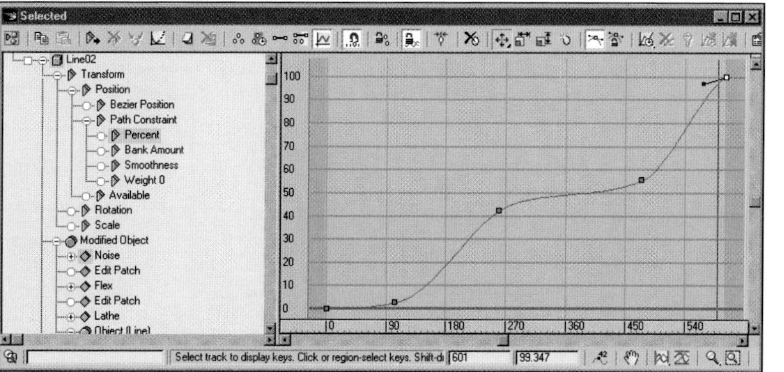

The Track View showing the positions of the keys.

Note: A sloping line should span the Track View graph window. If not, you might need to adjust the window by clicking Zoom Value Extents and Zoom Horizontal Extents from the bottom toolbar. This line represents the percentage of distance the jellyfish has traveled along the spline as compared to time.

Note: Notice that as the slope of the line decreases so does the distance the jellyfish travels along the path. This is how you are going to animate the to-and-fro motion that is typical of a jellyfish.

The Flex Modifier

The Flex modifier, in my opinion, is one of the most versatile yet simple modifiers in the 3ds max 4 arsenal. Flex is great for adding realistic secondary motion to objects such as bouncing ears or a jiggling potbelly. As the jellyfish speeds up and slows down along its motion path, the tentacles and body will sway and wave in such a way that it appears the jellyfish is swimming through a viscous medium.

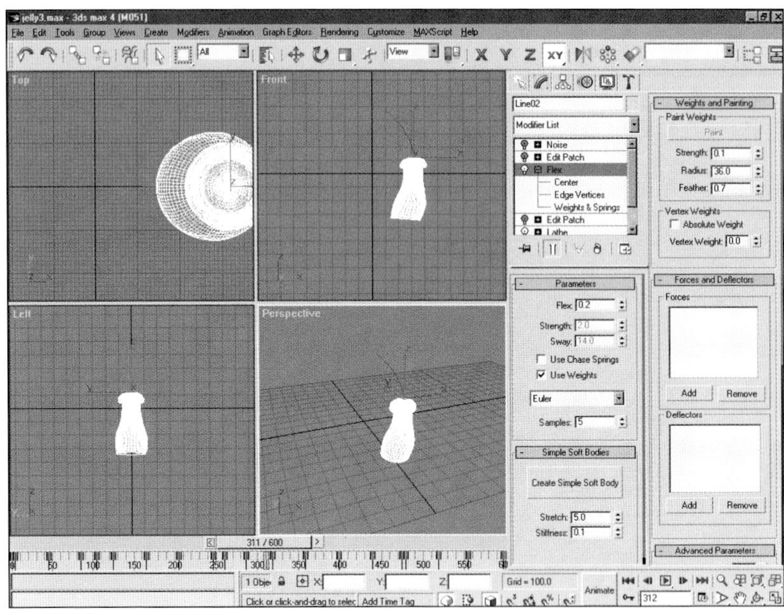

The Flex panel.

1 With the jellyfish patch selected, go to the modifier list and apply Flex. Open the Flex subtree and select the Center option.

You will see that all the vertices are now a rainbow of colors ranging from blue to red. These colors represent falloff values for Flex's influence. In this instance, the Red vertices are under the least influence, while Blue vertices are under the greatest. If the Flex Center sub-object is not in proper position, move it to an area above the jellyfish so that the bell has its inferior portions slightly green. To add a little chaos, you might want to have this slightly off center.

2 Change the Parameters in Flex to match the accompanying figure. Make a preview.

Depending on how it worked out, you will probably want to adjust these settings to your liking.

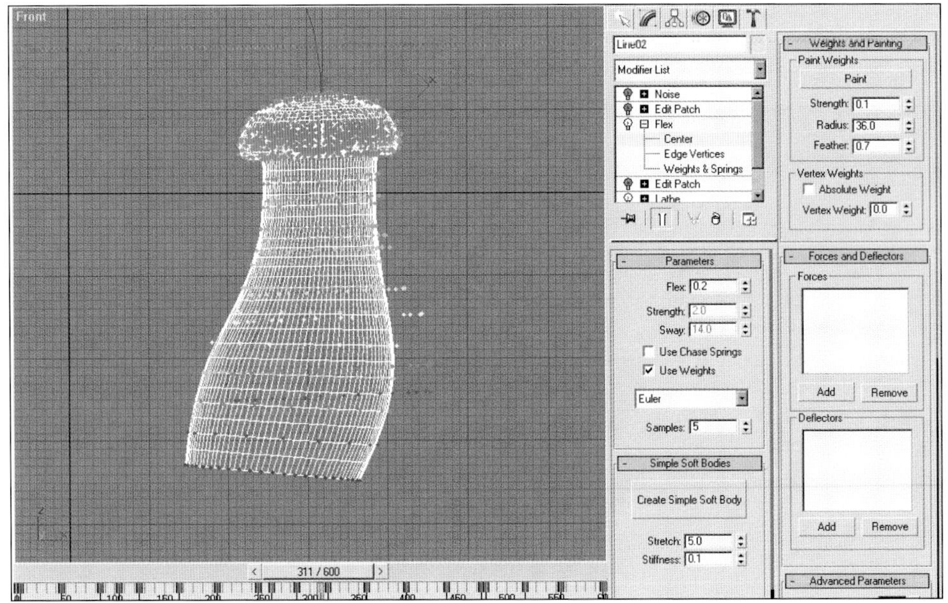

The Flex modifier applied.

Add a Little Chaos with Noise

The animation so far looks pretty good. You have a jellyfish pulsating through the water on its long journey to nowhere. You will notice, however, that the skirt on the jellyfish is too regular. The Flex modifier added a nice sway to the jellyfish's skirt, but it's still not very natural. You need to add a bit of chaos so that the tentacles will wiggle a bit as the jellyfish moves through the water.

1 Go to the top of the modifier stack and apply a second Edit Patch modifier. Click the Vertex branch of the Edit Patch subtree and notice that the vertices you selected earlier are again selected.

Note: Had you not made the Vertex selection earlier, it would be much more difficult given the jellyfish's new position. However, now when you apply the Noise modifier, it will act on these selected vertices.

2 With the Vertex branch of Edit Patch modifier still highlighted, add a Noise modifier to the top of the stack. Change the settings so that they are similar to the figure. Play the animation.

Notice that the vertices at the edge of the skirt are jumping all over the place. This is not the effect you are going for.

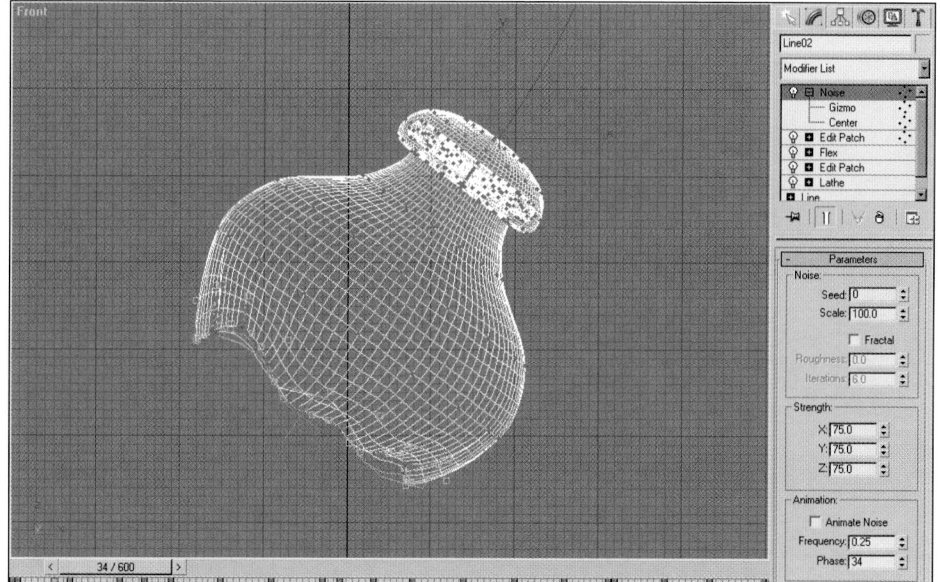

Noise parameters.

3 Go back to the last Edit Patch modifier and choose Use Soft Selection under the Soft Selection rollout. Adjust the Falloff until the yellow vertices are just under the bell. Go back to the top of the modifier stack and play the animation once more.

Now the tentacle movement has a natural falloff.

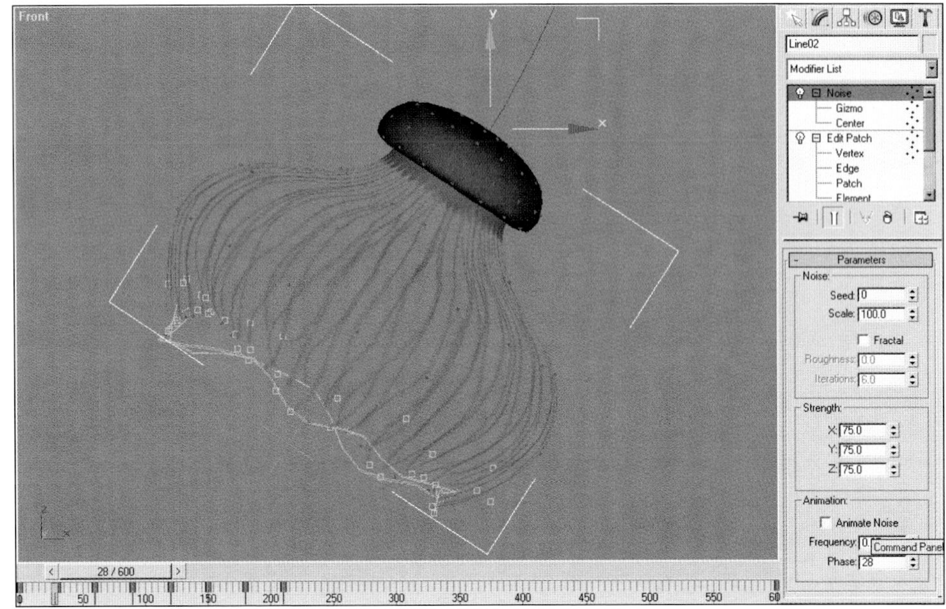

Noise applied to vertex selection.

Just Add Water

You need to give this little guy a home to swim in. There are more ways to make an underwater ocean scene in 3ds max 4 than there are types of jellyfish! The method I am proposing here is fast and gives surprisingly realistic results. The basic environmental scene will consist of two separate plane mesh objects and a single volumetric light.

Note: See Project 3, "Underwater Scene," for more details on creating underwater scenes in 3ds max 4.

Here you will add the needed objects to the scene to create the underwater world. To help speed up test renders, hide the jellyfish mesh and motion path.

1 Place a free camera in the Front viewport. Change the Perspective view to Camera.

2 In the Top viewport, create a plane object that is large enough to extend to the camera's vanishing point. Name the plane object **Ocean**. Make a copy of the ocean object and move it on its Z-axis so that it is above the ocean object. Use the uniform scale tool and decrease the size to about one-fifth of the original. Name this object **Sky**.

3 Move the camera on its Z-axis so that it is just below the surface of the ocean object.

You might have to move the camera a bit so that it is in proper position. Have the sky object just out of view above the camera.

4 In the Top viewport, create a Free Directional light. It should be pointing in the negative Z direction. Move it so that it sits between the two plane objects.

5 Open the Material Editor. Select an empty Material slot and change its color to a pure white. Select the two-sided option. Change the Self-Illumination option to pure white by clicking the color splotch and dragging the color bar to pure white. Apply this material to the Sky plane object.

6 Choose another empty Material slot and change the material type to Raytrace by clicking the button in the right-hand corner that reads Standard. Select Raytrace from the list of material types and click OK. Change the Raytrace values to match the accompanying figure. Make sure to check the 2-sided option.

7 In the Raytrace material, open the Maps rollout and click the Transparency button. Select Falloff from the Material/Map browser and leave the defaults as is.

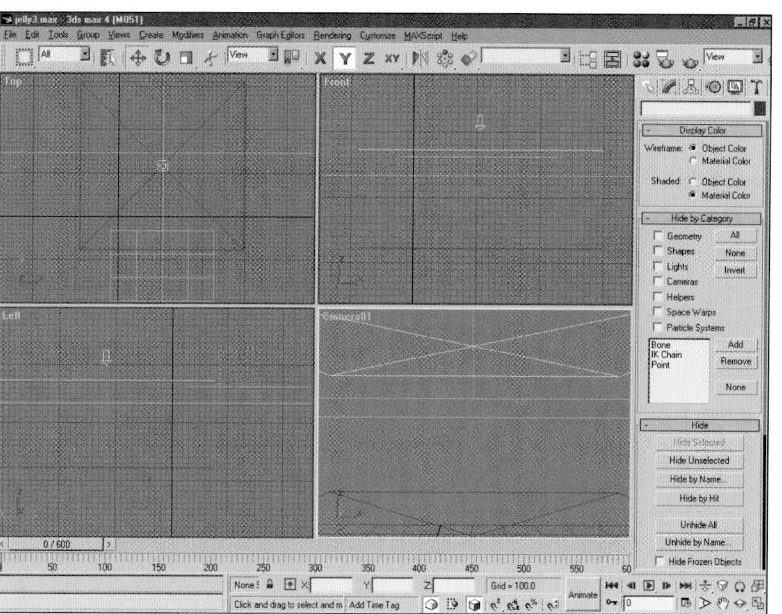

The underwater scene setup.

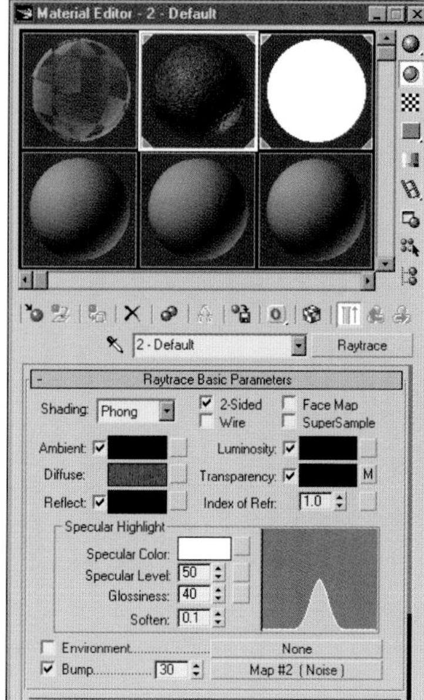

The Raytrace parameters.

8 Place a Noise map within the Raytrace bump channel. Change the noise type to Turbulence and change the size to **10**. Apply this material to the ocean object.

Depending on the camera distance from the ocean surface object, the correct size for the Noise modifier might vary.

9 Select the light and open its Modify panel. Make the light a pure white. Under the Directional properties, change the shape to Rectangle. Adjust the size of the falloff so that it encompasses the size of the ocean object.

10 In the Attenuation Parameters rollout, check Use and Show under Far Attenuation. Adjust the Start and End spinners so that the area of attenuation covers the vanishing point from the camera's perspective.

11 The next thing to do is change the light into a volume light. To do this, open the Rendering menu on the main max 4 menu bar. Select the Environment option. Change the background color to a dark navy blue.

12 Click Add in the Environment Atmosphere section. Select Volume Light from the pop-up menu and click OK.

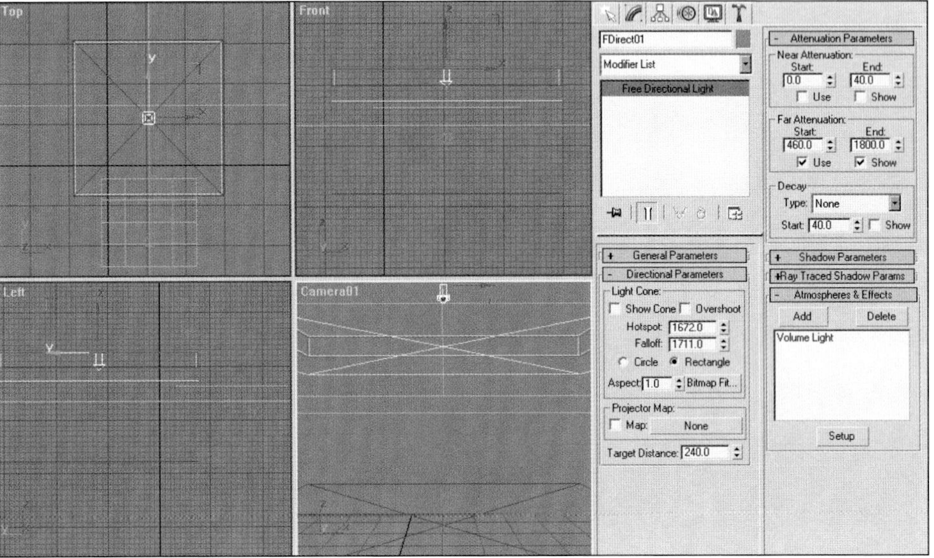

Light panel showing settings.

13 Click the Pick Light button and choose Free Directional Light.

14 Check the Exponential option and change the density to **2**. Drag an instance of the background color you just created to the attenuation color for the volume light. Create a volume light color that is a slightly lighter version of the attenuation color.

These colors should represent the lightest and darkest colors in the scene, as shown in the figure.

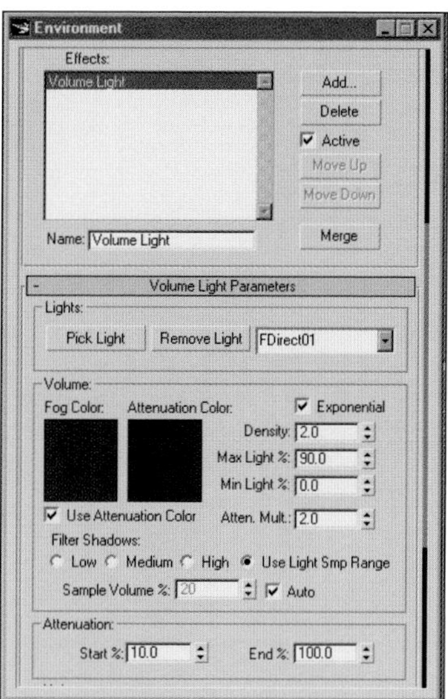

The Environment Atmosphere panel.

15 Make a test render.

Final environment render.

16 Unhide all of the objects in the scene. You might have to change the position of the objects to get everything right. Make another test render. Adjust objects as needed and make a final render.

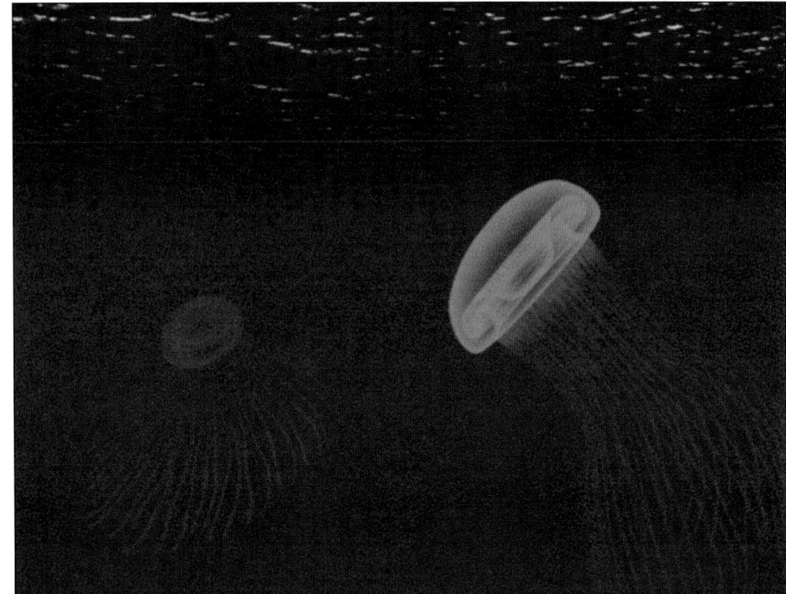

Final project render.

MODIFICATIONS

I hope this tutorial has opened your eyes to some different ways of animating as well as to the use of certain materials. The following are some alternative methods to completing this exercise. They tend to be more processor and memory intensive, so plan accordingly. As I stated in the beginning of the tutorial, I prefer to use meshes and materials that will produce decent results without taxing my system or my time. But for those of you who have mammoth systems, here you go!

One of the problems with using Opacity maps is that they tend to flatten out when viewed sideways. (That's the price you pay for faster renderings.) To add detail to the tentacles so that they don't flatten out, try adding a Displace modifier after lathe in the modifier stack. To get an effect that is worthwhile, you will need to use the High Detail Mesh subdivision option. I will warn you that this will send your rendering times through the roof, so beware.

Of course, you don't have to use Opacity maps at all. You could model the tentacles. Try making and animating a tentacle spline using the same techniques you used here. Only this time use the Lofting tool to model the tentacle. Use the Array tool to produce a number of tentacles that can be attached or linked to a jellyfish bell. This, again, will increase the rendering time but will give good results because the tentacles have true depth. For jellyfish close-ups, this might be the method of choice. A more processor friendly way of modeling the tentacles is to use the renderable option for splines. When doing this, use a gradient as an Opacity map to have the tentacles fade off at their ends.

The ocean environment is fun to create but tends to be memory intensive. If you can, try to find some video footage and composite the jellyfish into it. This is far less memory intensive, but it also means you have to have some basic editing abilities.

Lastly, enable the new Multi-Pass Depth of Field effect. This gives great results but, as with many great effects, will slow down render times.

Good luck!

Note: For information on compositing images into video footage, see Project 13, "Camera Matching."

CHARACTER ANIMATION USING INVERSE KINEMATICS

"That wasn't flying! That was falling with style!"

—WOODY, *TOY STORY*

Character Animation Tools

If you have ever tried setting up a character, you understand how difficult the task can be. Things you might never have thought of before come into play. Things like when to use inverse kinematics (IK) instead of forward kinematics (FK), or how to make a straightforward and easy setup that everyone can use. A good setup can be a daunting task, so much so that you can make a career out of it. This chapter will explore how 3ds max 4 has come to the rescue and will demonstrate how some aspects of character setup have never been easier.

Project 7

Character Animation Using Inverse Kinematics

by Michael Reiser, MD

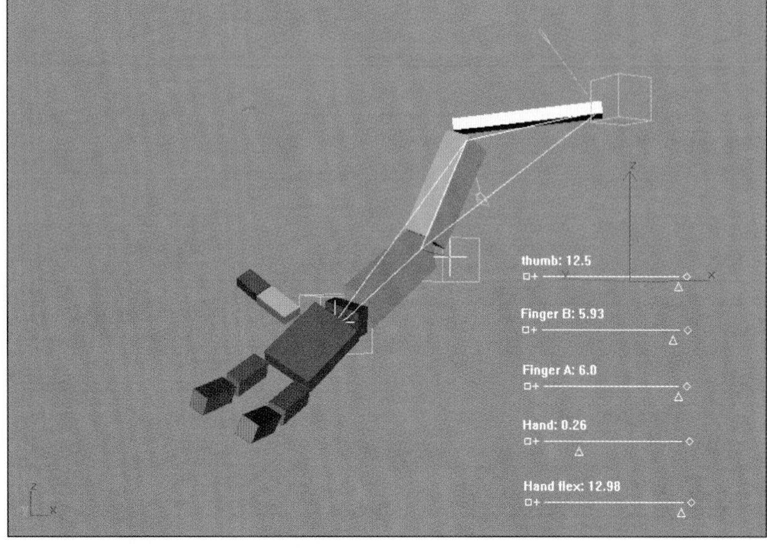

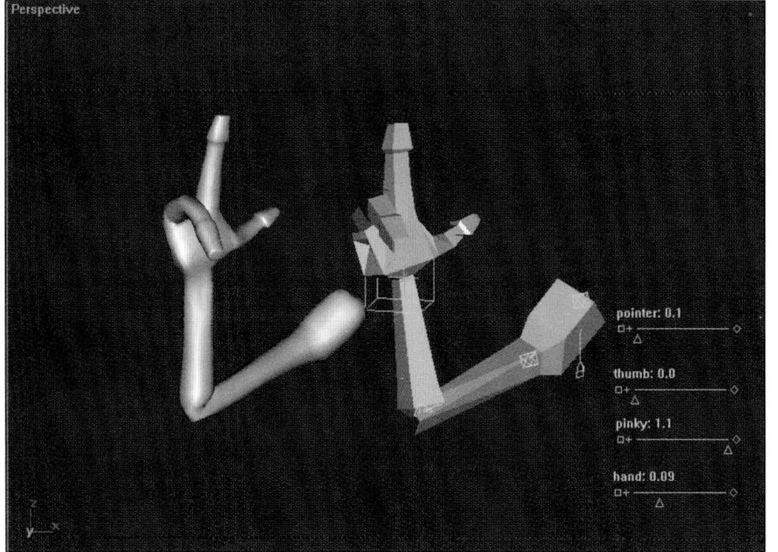

How It Works

The best way to demonstrate some of the new character-animation tools is to show them in action. This chapter is divided into two distinct sections. The first section explores some aspects of the new IK tools available and how they apply to our simple project. The second explains how the new manipulators can be used in conjunction with a preexisting hierarchy to give incredible control over items such as fingers and morph targets. In the end, you will have a simple setup that is powerful and easy to use.

GETTING STARTED

Included on the accompanying CD-ROM is a file called Arm_Hierarchy.max. This is a simple hierarchical setup using boxes to represent an arm and a hand. The pivot points have been moved and the boxes rotated to a "natural" resting pose. Because one can use almost any object as a bone, I have started the practice of creating my own skeletons out of primitive objects and linking them accordingly. This might seem to be an archaic practice, but it is a personal preference, and I suggest using whatever works for you. In this chapter, you will not be going into the new bone enhancements that 3ds max 4 offers. You should, however, take the time to explore some of the changes. If you liked using bones before, you are going to love using them now!

In addition to the basic setup, there is a final version of the project called Final_mesh.max on the accompanying CD. If you prefer, use this file and reverse engineer the scene. I have found that max is pretty forgiving is this respect. Most of the parameters that will be created can be changed and manipulated. You should easily be able to pick apart aspects of the scene and see how they were built.

The arm in a natural resting position.

Note: Normally, the resting pose of a bone setup is made to match the overlying geometry. Here, because I will be discussing the setup itself, I chose a pose that reflects an arm in a relaxed position.

APPLYING IK CHAINS TO THE ARM

Before you get started, some terminology needs to be clarified. If you are new to the 3D world, the terms inverse kinematics (IK) and forward kinematics (FK) might not mean much to you. Both terms, FK and IK, describe how a hierarchical setup (meaning linked in a parent-child relationship) responds to the movement of an individual link. In the case of FK, if a link is rotated, the following links (its children) will react to the rotation; however, the proceeding links will remain still and unaffected by the rotation. The manipulation of the chain is in a "forward" direction. On the other hand, IK is more or less the opposite. By manipulating the last link in an IK chain, the rest of the chain follows much like pulling on the end of a real chain. Both methods are used in most character setups, and our example is no different.

Note: If you need further explanation of IK or FK, refer to the max Help files or to example scenes shipped with max.

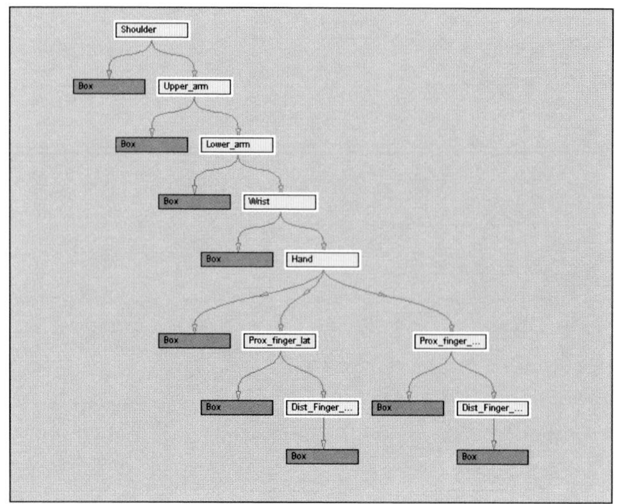

The Schematic view.

One more thing that needs to be clarified is the naming method used for the arm setup. I have included an image of the Schematic view to help with the arm's naming conventions. As you can see, there is a shoulder, upper and lower arm, wrist, hand, and fingers. Only two fingers are described in the tutorial to make the length of this tutorial tolerable. The final version of the project has a thumb as well that was created in an identical fashion as the other fingers.

The first thing you will do is place a few IK solvers across the shoulder and arm.

1 Load the file **Arm_Hierarchy.max** from the accompanying CD-ROM.

You will see that it is a relatively simple hierarchical setup. The first thing you will do is add an IK solver to the arm. The purpose of this first IK chain is for large or gross motions of the arm.

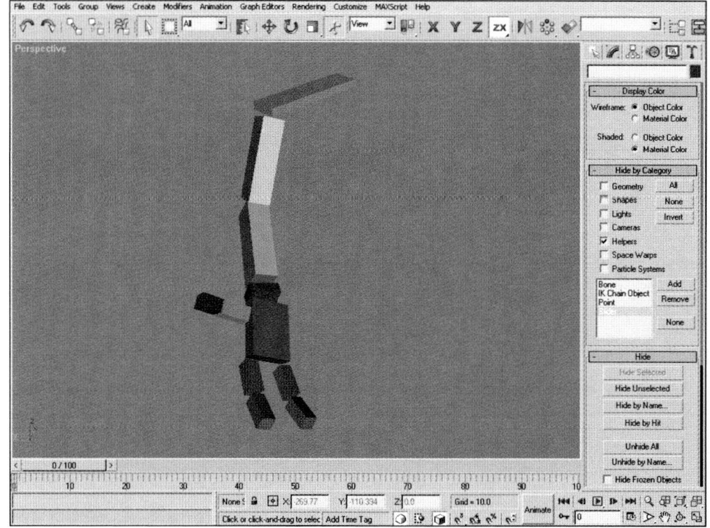

The arm setup.

2 Select the Upper_arm object. From the main toolbar, select Animation/IK Solvers/**HI Solver.** In the active viewport, drag the Rubber Band helper to the wrist and left-click.

Here you will now see a new addition to max. A line is drawn from the shoulder to the wrist as well as through each of the links in the IK chain. At the end of this chain is a white crosshair. This is the goal of the IK chain, and it can be moved around to control the hierarchy. Grab it and give it a try. You will immediately notice how clean and predictable the motion is.

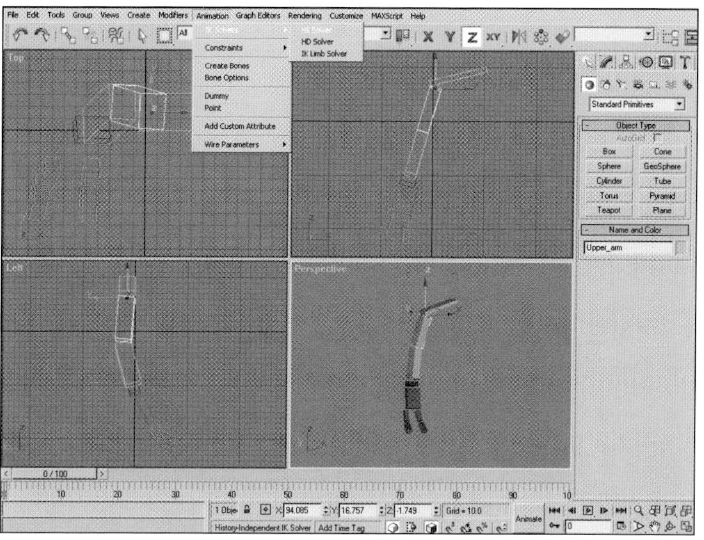

Select HI Solver from the Animation menu.

Note: The IK solution used here is new. The HI stands for history independent. In earlier versions of max, the IK solutions used calculations from previous positions of the chain to adjust and recalculate the current chain position. This "old" way is now called HD, for history dependent. The new HI solver seems very stable, fast, and predictable. As advertised, it is just as fast early in an animation as it is thousands of frames later. This is one of the reasons why it is recommended for use in character animation. The white lines you see do more than just show you the links involved in the solution. They also help define a plane that in turn helps define an angle known as the "swivel angle." This angle is used by the IK solver and can be changed using a spinner in the IK Solver Properties rollout or adjusted directly in the viewport with its manipulator. (I will discuss the new manipulators a little later.) If you feel that your IK chain is not rotating in the plane in which you intended, try adjusting the swivel angle until the chain reacts correctly.

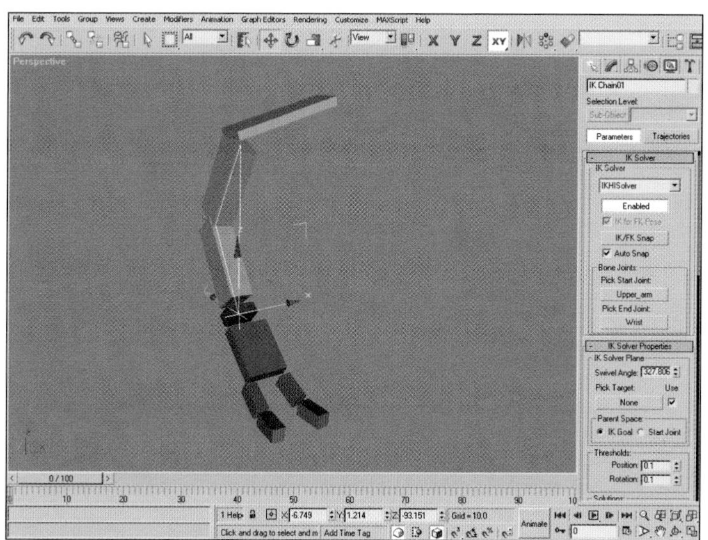

The applied IK solver.

Note: The end-effector displayed in earlier versions of max is still there; however, it is hidden and a goal object is displayed in its place. If you want, there are controls to have the end-effector enabled and visible.

3 Link a Dummy object to the IK goal (the white crosshair) using the standard Linking tool. The Dummy object is easier to select and gives an animator a nice control device.

Rename the dummy object **Wrist_control**.

4 Add an overlapping IK chain and select the Shoulder object to activate it.

A great addition to max is allowing multiple overlapping IK chains. Each can be controlled individually by separate goals, giving unprecedented IK control.

5 From the same menu, select Animation/IK Solvers/IK Limb Solver. Drag the Rubber Band helper to the Lower_arm object.

Don't attempt to move this goal just yet. You will first link it to another Dummy object. This IK solver looks very similar to the previous one. However, this particular IK solution is written explicitly for hierarchies that contain no more than three links. It is fast and predictable and is a great solution to simple setups.

6 With the shoulder goal still active, link a separate Dummy object and name it **Shoulder_control**. Link Shoulder_control as a parent to the previous dummy object, Wrist_control.

Now, when the Shoulder_control dummy is moved, the Wrist_control dummy should move with it.

These two control objects give a fast and simple method for animating the shoulder as well as gross motion of the arm.

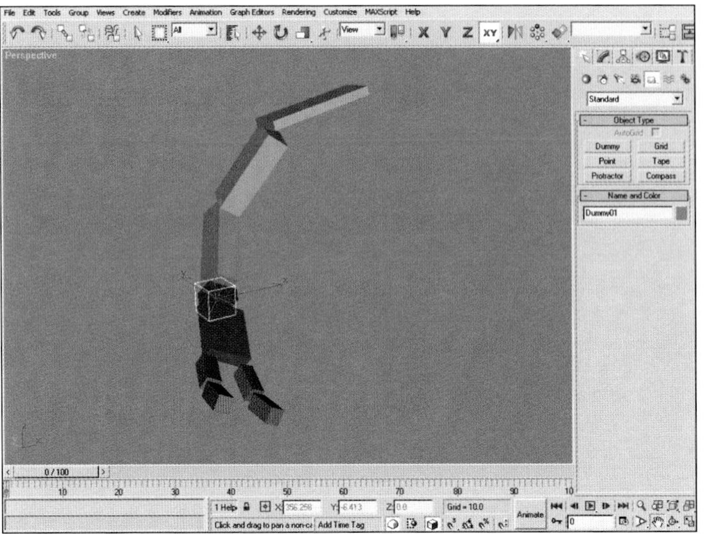

The Dummy object linked to the Goal object.

Note: Don't feel as if you need to use dummy objects as controls. Point objects or any nonrenderable geometry works well too. Try using text objects that describe the IK chain and goal to which they are linked.

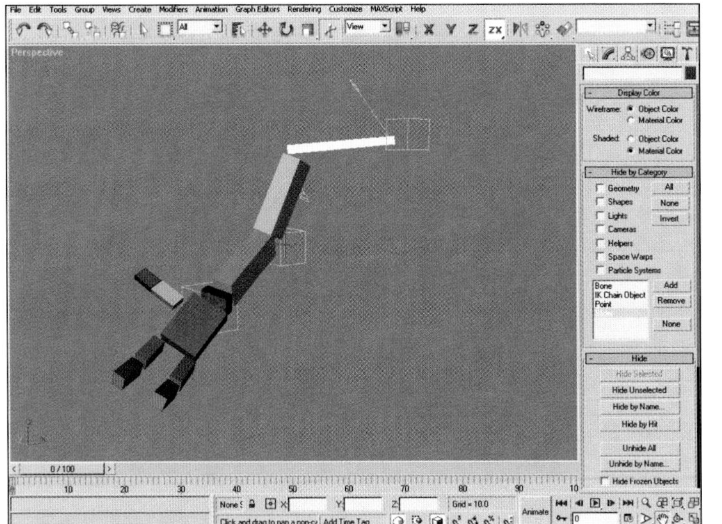

The project so far.

Note: I have added a third Dummy object to the arm as the Root object, to which all other Dummy objects are linked. This is a good idea for any character setup because it enables you to grab one object and move the entire character. This object is called Total Control in Final_Arm.max.

7 Click the Select and Manipulate button from the main toolbar or from the Quad toolbox to activate the viewport display of the Swivel Angle manipulator.

The manipulator is a tabbed handle bar that allows for the adjustment of the swivel angle. Used in combination with the previously set up control objects, full range of motion for the arm is easy to achieve.

8 Activate the Select and Manipulate button and adjust the wrist's swivel angle in the viewport.

Notice how you can externally rotate the arm while keeping the IK chain control intact.

As you can see, the addition of only two IK solvers to a simple arm hierarchy has led to a nice little IK setup. There is no unexpected jumping or snapping of the chain. The motion is smooth and predictable. There are, however, some areas such as the hand and fingers that need to have some control. Luckily max 4 has the answer.

Note: The use of overlapping IK chains comes in very handy when animating things like tentacles as well. Truly, the uses are endless. How did we ever live without them!

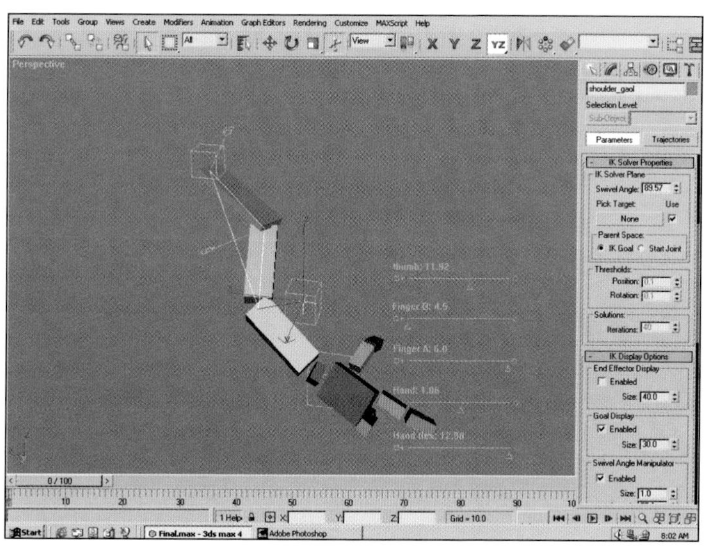

The Swivel Angle control.

Controlling the Hand and Fingers with FK

With all the new IK controls being introduced, people new to the field get the impression that FK is no longer used in character animation. This couldn't be farther from the truth. To show how FK is alive and well in max, the hand and fingers in your setup will be controlled using forward kinematics. There is, however, a new twist. Here you will add controllers called manipulators that will make flexing individual fingers and thumbs, a sometimes frustrating task, an interactive delight!

1 From the Create tab, select the Helpers button. From the drop-down list, select Manipulators. Click the Slider button. Create three sliders in the front viewport.

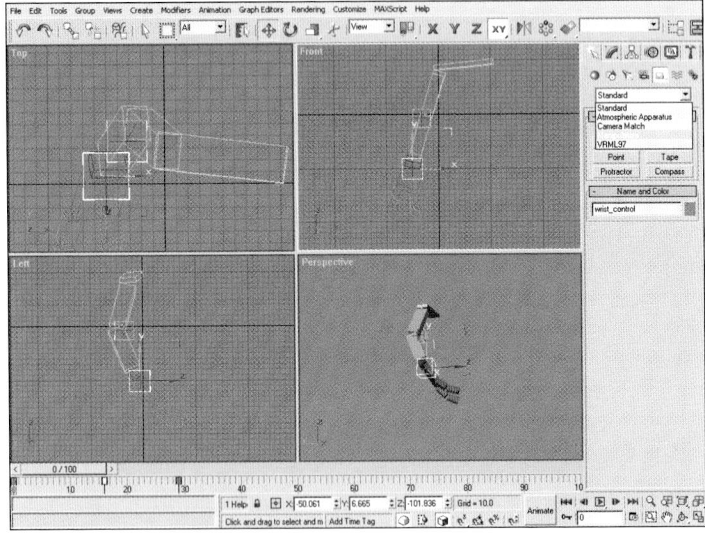

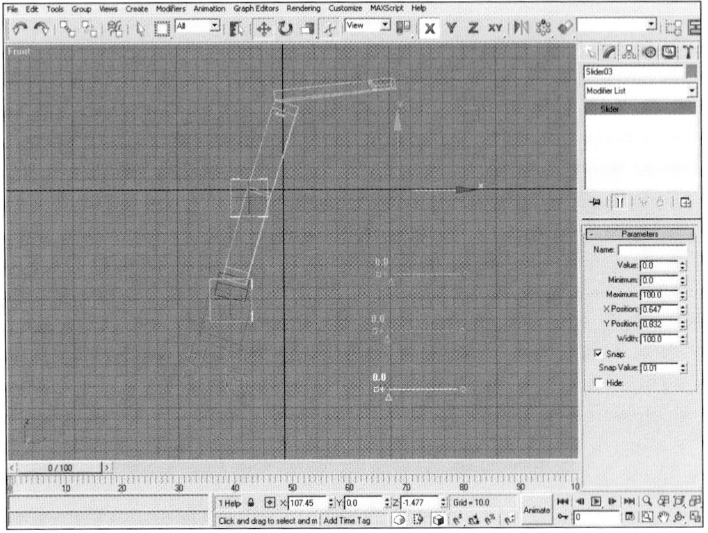

Create the sliders and place them in the Front viewport.

2 Select one of the sliders and open the Modify panel. Type **Hand** in the Name field and press Enter. You will see the name Hand appear for the slider you selected. For convenience, name the other two sliders now as well. Something like **Finger A** and **Finger B** will do just fine. Don't worry about the other settings right now.

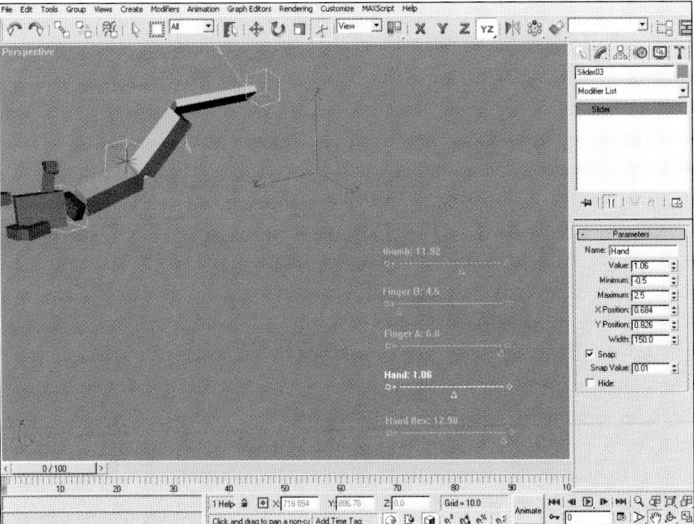

Name the sliders.

3 Select Local for the reference coordinate system. With the Select and Manipulate option off on the main toolbar, select the Hand slider. Right-click the slider and select the Wire Parameters option.

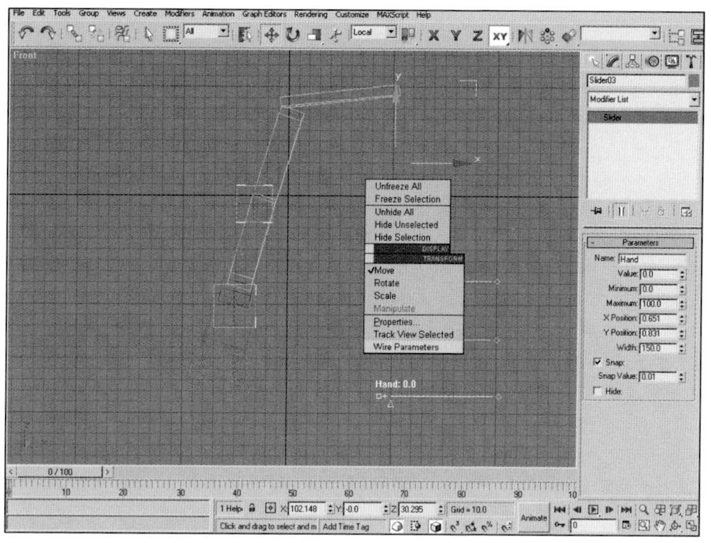

Wire parameters selected from the Quad menu.

4 From the small pop-up menu, choose Object (Slider)/Value. From the Rubber Band tool that now appears, select the Hand object. Another pop-up menu appears. This time choose Transform/FK Sub-Control/Rotation/Y Rotation.

In the menu that appears, you will see that Value and Y Rotation are selected for the slider and hand objects, respectively. You can change these settings, but for now leave them as they are.

Note: If you can't access the Y Rotation option, check the Rotation Controller. It should be set to Euler XYZ controller, not TCB rotation, to access the XYZ coordinates.

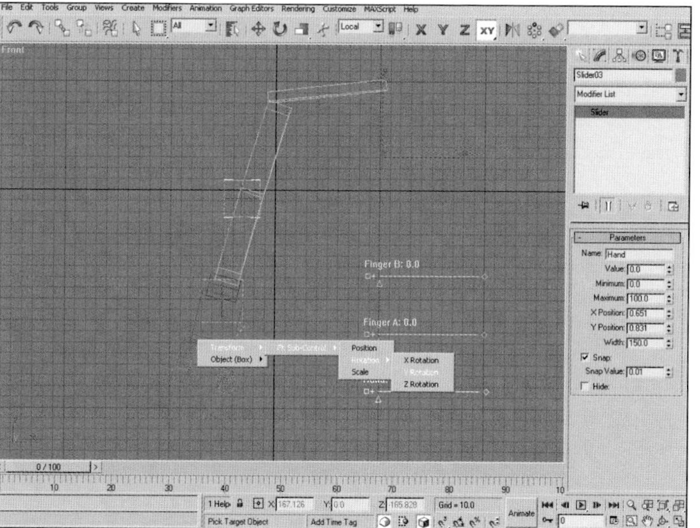

The pop-up menu selection.

5 Choose the arrow that directs the control from the slider to the hand object. Select the Connect button to join, or "wire," the two parameters together. Close the Wire Parameters dialog box.

Note: If you get error messages when trying to connect parameters, it most likely has to do with the rotation type you have set for the objects. You must change the rotation to Euler XYZ for the sliders to work on that object. Go to the Motion panel to assign the Euler rotational controller. You might want to have this as your default controller. It is not as smooth as some other rotational controllers, but you can use it with sliders as well as adjust it in Track View. See the max Help files for information on assigning motion controllers.

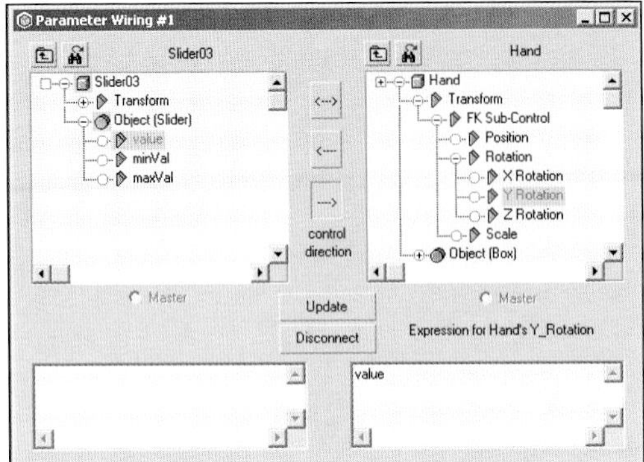

The Wire Parameters dialog box.

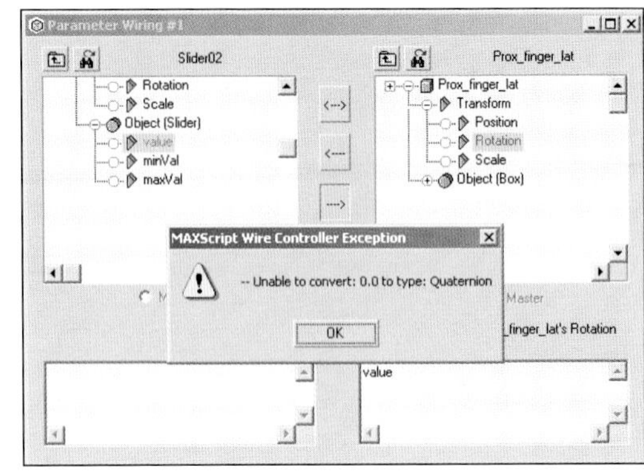

The error message.

Note: For more details on Parameter Wiring, see the max Help files.

6 Activate the Select and Manipulate button from the main toolbar or by right-clicking and selecting it from the Quad menu in the active viewport. Drag the slider triangle and see how the hand spins out of control.

To fix this, you need to adjust the range of the slider.

7 Turn off the Select and Manipulate option. Select the Hand slider and go to the Modify panel. Use the Value spinner to see the range for which to set the Minimum and Maximum spinners. For the hand example, use **–0.5** as the Minimum and **2.5** as the Maximum.

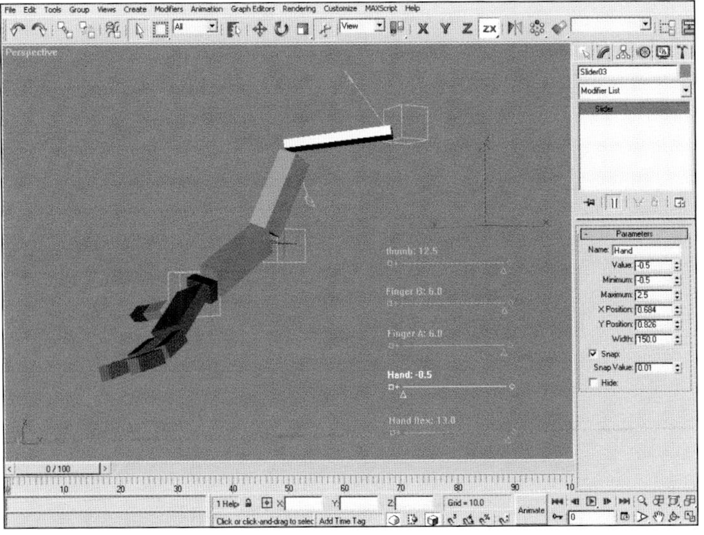

The Hand Slider rollout in the Modify panel.

8 Turn the Select and Manipulate option back on. Now adjust the Hand slider triangle and see that the hand rotates with much more control within the limits you set.

The fingers use the same method with a few additions.

9 With the Select and Manipulate option off, select one of the Finger sliders. Right-click and choose the Wire Parameters option. As before, select Object (Slider)/Value. Use the Rubber Band to select the base of the finger. Again, pick Transform/Rotation/X Rotation.

Notice that you choose to use the X-axis this time to simulate the curling of the fingers.

10 Click Connect from the Wire Parameters menu then close the menu.

This is where it is slightly different. Don't bother going to the Modify panel to correct the rotation.

11 Repeat the actions outlined in step 9 using the same slider. This time, however, choose the second, more distal portion of the same finger. Assign the same slider to its X-axis rotation as well. Now you can go the Modify panel to adjust the Minimum and Maximum values for the finger. Use a Minimum of **4.5** and a Maximum of **6.0**.

Notice that by combining the rotation through one slider, the hierarchy is respected and the rotations react accordingly.

12 Simply repeat the previous steps for the second finger using the third slider. I added a second slider to the hand as a control for its X-axis rotation as well adding a thumb to the setup.

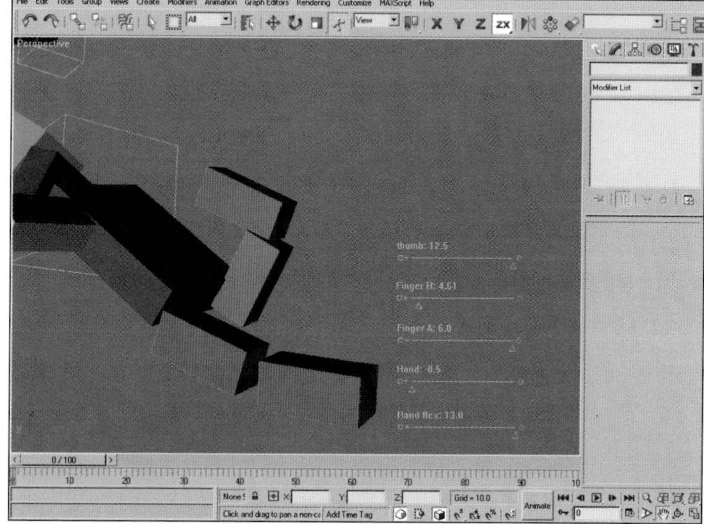

The curled finger.

Note: Notice that I have added a thumb and an additional slider to the arm. Using these steps, you can add any number of appendages on the fly, without changing any of the existing setup.

Note: You could just as well have used Plane Angle manipulators to adjust the hand or fingers. I prefer to use the sliders, however, because sliders can be named for easy identification and they become active in whatever viewport you are working in. The Plane Angle manipulator may have a useful function in facial animation interacting with individual bones.

Combining Sliders, Morph Targets, and Bones

The true power in any character-animation package is the capability to combine different animation tools into a seamless character setup. Not only has 3ds max 4 brought you all the character-animation tools you could ever hope for, it also gives you the capability to combine them into a setup that is predictable and easy to use. Earlier I described how to create a hierarchy using a combination of IK and FK as well as incorporating sliders to help with ease of use and increase productivity. That example dealt solely with the skeleton of the character. In addition to bones, morph targets play a large role in character animation. Morph targets, however, work on the mesh itself and have nothing really to do with the skeleton setup. Here you will add a Morph slider to the previous setup to show how easy flexing some muscle can be.

Note: The Skin modifier will not be discussed here in detail. It is, however, a very powerful modifier and should be studied in great detail if you plan to do any character work.

1 Open the file called **Final_mesh.max** from the accompanying CD-ROM.

This is the same hierarchy you previously created. The difference, as you can see, is that this arm has some flesh added. I used the Skin modifier to apply the model of a cartoon arm I created. (Àla Gumby!) Move the separate control objects and sliders around to get a feel for the setup. Try hiding the Bone objects to see the mesh move more naturally.

Before you can use objects as bones in max, you have to give them the correct properties.

2 Select all of the boxes that make up the arm, hand, and fingers. When they are highlighted, right-click in the viewport and select Properties from the Quad menu. In the lower-right corner of the Properties pop-up menu is a section called Bones. Toggle the Bone option to On. Close the Properties panel.

These objects can now be used as bones.

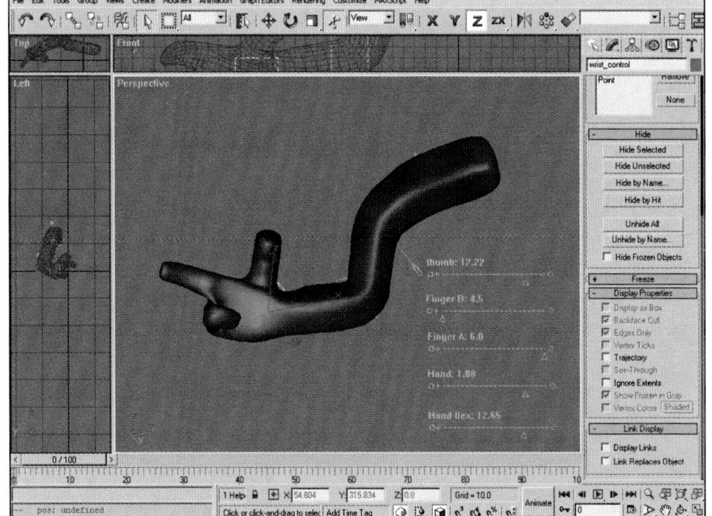

The mesh arm posed with Bone objects hidden.

The only differences between this scene and the previous setup are the addition of the overlying mesh using the Skin modifier and a single morph target. There is another mesh hidden from view that is a copy of the arm mesh. This copy has been slightly altered and (using the Morpher modifier) is the morph target for the arm mesh.

3 Go to the Display panel and unhide this mesh. Hide it again when you are done.

As you can see, all that was done was to distort the object so that the upper arm is slightly bulged.

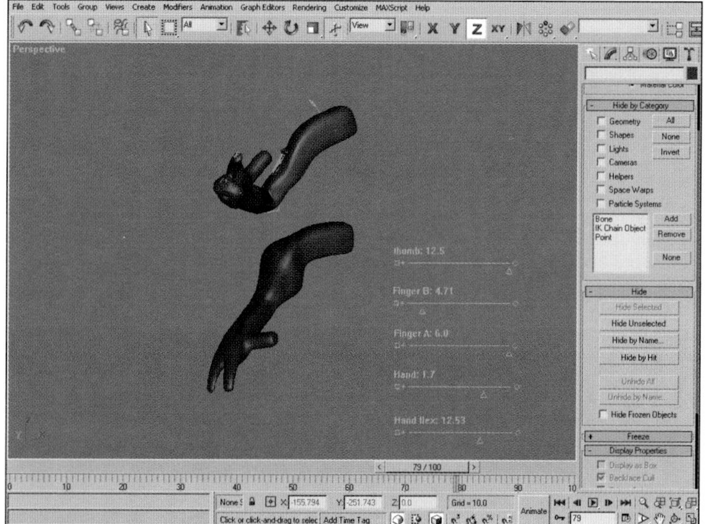

Morph target.

4 Select the visible Mesh object that is encasing the bone setup. With it highlighted, go to the Modify panel and take a look at the modifiers that are applied.

Three modifiers have been applied to the mesh. At the top of the stack is the Skin modifier. The second modifier in the stack is the Morpher modifier, and last is the MeshSmooth modifier. The morph target already exists, and the Morpher modifier is applied and works fine.

Note: The modifier order is very important when working with morph targets and skin. Remember that max works in order, from the first modifier applied to the last. In this example, max first applied the MeshSmooth modifier. (It is important for this to be the time when copies are made for morph targets. If you later decide to change the mesh density in MeshSmooth, remember to change your morph targets as well.) The next modifier in the stack is the Morpher modifier. The thing to consider when using Morpher is not to have the morph targets change so much that the transformed vertices will lie outside of the bones influence in the next modifier, Skin. In the end, what you are really doing is boning the morph targets. All you see is the end result at the top of the modifier stack, but how max got there is very important. If you are getting bad results, return to your modifier stack and see if the modifier order is correct.

5. Move the arm around and try it. Go to the Modify panel and adjust the first spinner for the morph target.

   No matter what position the arm is in, the mesh morphs correctly. So why bother changing anything by adding a slider? The answer is workflow. By getting as many controls as possible close to where the animator will use them, he or she spends less time clicking through menus trying to find the right spinner.

6. Add a slider to the active viewport as previously outlined. Name it **Morph target**.

7. Turn off the Select and Manipulate option from the main toolbar. Right-click and choose the Wire Parameters option from the Quad menu. At the pop-up menu, select Object (Slider)/Value.

8. Drag the Rubber Band pick tool to the Mesh object and left-click when you are over it. From the pop-up menu, select Modified Object/ Morpher/[1] Box04 (Target Available). At the Parameter Wiring dialog box, select the left to right arrow and click Connect. Close the window.

9. Turn on the Select and Manipulate option. Move the new Morph target slider and see the arm update in the viewport.

   Notice how fast and easy it is to move the dummy controls and swivel angle controls and use the individual sliders, all from the active viewport.

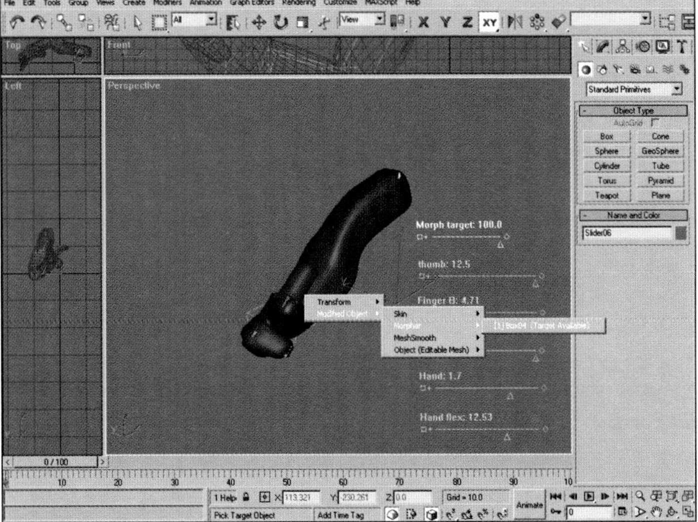

Linking the Morph slider to the Morph object.

This project has covered a number of new additions and enhancements to the 3ds max 4 character animation tools. These tools and their applications in our examples were simple, but they obviously have more complicated potential uses. The addition of overlapping IK, not to mention the new IK solvers and manipulators, has brought 3ds max 4 to the forefront of character animation.

Check out arm_exam.avi on the CD-ROM to see these animation techniques in action.

Note: An additional step that will help you out is grouping the sliders. You can imagine that having sliders for the entire character would become very crowded pretty fast. Once you have grouped the sliders, use Hide By Name and Unhide By Name to bring them up as you need them.

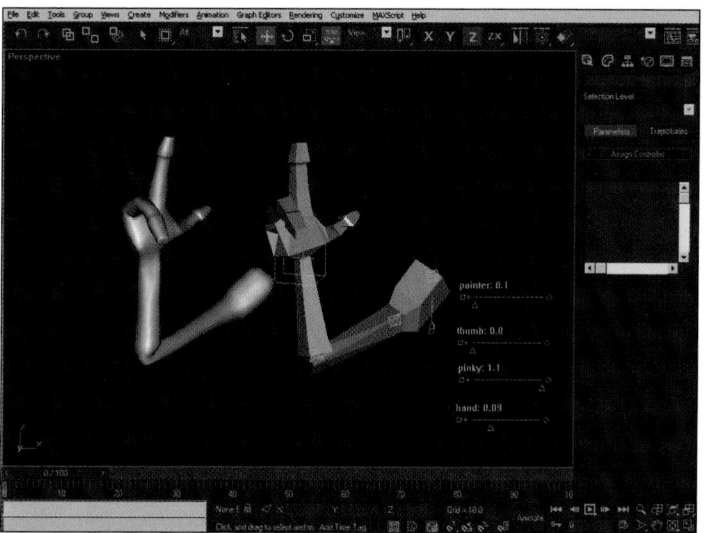

Another arm created using IK techniques.

Modifications

As you can imagine, the uses for the new IK solvers and manipulators are endless. These techniques can be used in character facial expression as well as character dialogue. Try using a slider in combination with a jawbone and mouth morph target. Wire the FK rotation of the lower jawbone and a morph target for a phonetic mouth shape to the same slider. You will find, as you are using the slider for morphing, that the jaw will move as well. If this does not give you enough control and you want to separate the controls, have all the phonetic morph targets on different sliders and jaw rotation on another.

Instead of using geometry changed into a usable bone, you could, of course, use max bones instead. In 3ds max 4, there have been extensive additions and enhancements to the existing bone tools. Try the preceding setup, but this time build it with bones instead. Use the IK solvers and sliders just as you did above.

The capability to use overlapping IK chains can help with creating realistic, complicated hierarchies such as centipede bodies, insect legs, tentacles, and so on. Overlapping IK chains could be used to create complex robotic arms with pistons. We will probably see a large number of applications for the use of these new tools as people start to solve their individual animation problems. So start solving! I cannot wait to see some of the applications!

MECHANICAL MACHINE

"Does your dog bite?"

—INSPECTOR CLOUSEAU (PETER SELLERS) TO CONCIERGE

IN *REVENGE OF THE PINK PANTHER*

Making a Rube Goldberg-Style Animation

Rube Goldberg was a cartoonist/illustrator/inventor who designed fanciful mechanical contraptions using mundane household objects. He would take a simple task and proceed to make it convoluted and ridiculous, but always fascinating to watch. This tutorial will take some of the mystery out of complicated non-organic animation by presenting methods for both the mechanically inclined and the mechanically inept!

Project 8

Mechanical Machine

by Sue Blackman

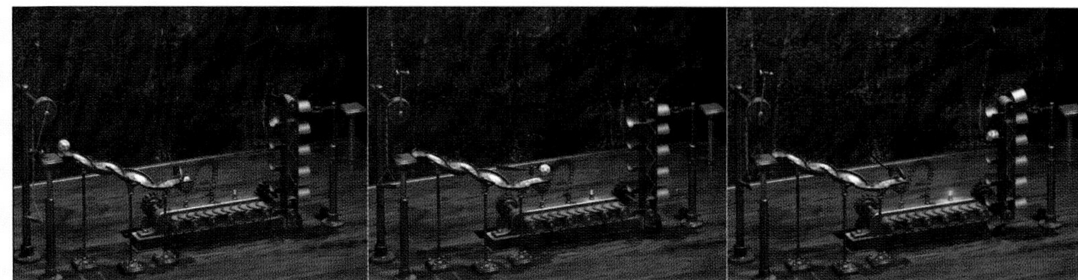

How It Works

In this project, you will become familiar with several useful controller types in 3ds max 4, including Path Constraint, Attachment controller, Link Constraint, and Wiring. By breaking the animated parts into logical modules, you will be able to concentrate on one technique at a time and see useful variations on each. Do not let the term "mechanical" scare you off; this tutorial is written for the "right-brainers" as well as the "gear heads" among us!

Getting Started

One beauty of creating animations on the computer is that you can let the computer take care of many of the repetitive tasks and logical relationships. In this exercise, you will become familiar with several 3ds max 4 controllers, but to make your task easier, you will also be using a few extra tools. You will need the following:

- Roller from HABWare, a plug-in that rolls an object along a path.
- Key_Shifter from Stefan Didak, a MaxScript that offsets Path Constraint objects along a path.
- An equation provided by Swami*, BSEE, aka "codeWarrior()"

Because this tutorial is rather lengthy, most of the objects in the scene and their materials have been created for you. You must follow several steps before starting this tutorial:

Note: For more information on these tools, read the text files that accompany them or visit the authors' Web sites:

- Harald Blab/HABWare: **http://www.habware.at**.
- Stefan Didak: **sdidak@euronet.nl, sdidak@bart.nl, http://www.sdidak.com/**.
- Swami*: A "pixel guy for hire," who can be contacted for script and equation writing at **swami@cfl.rr.com**.

1. Install **Roller.dlc** into your 3ds max 4 Plug-ins directory. As is true during any plug-in installation, you must exit and restart max to load the new lines of code.
2. Put the Key_Shifter MaxScript into the MaxScripts folder for easy access.
3. Put the maps for this project in the MAX Maps, Misc. folder.
4. Start 3ds max4 and open the file **MechanicalMachine01.max** from this project's folder on the accompanying CD-ROM.

Note: You might not want to put the extra files into your max folders, in which case you must create a path to enable max to find them.

5 To view the finished animation, open the file **MechanicalMachine.avi** from the accompanying CD-ROM. The supporting objects will be merged in at the end of the project from Supports.max. Most of the objects you will be dealing with are currently hidden.

This project makes extensive use of selection sets for easier organization.

A few spare parts.

Non-Linear Option: In case you don't want to work *straight* through this tutorial or you prefer to skip sections containing techniques with which you are already familiar, incremental files corresponding to the beginning of each section have been provided. For example, if you complete the section called "Give It a Whack!" but want to skip the "Down the Chute" section, you can load the file SpinTheSpoon.max and continue at the "Spin the Spoon" section.

Pull Here to Start

One of the main goals with mechanical animation—whether realistic or fantasy—is to make max do much of the work for you. For the pulley mechanism, you will animate only the string being pulled, and max will take care of the rest. This gives you the freedom to adjust the timing on one object without worrying about the rest of the objects. In mechanical animation as well as character animation, timing is everything!

For this section, you should see the Pulley, String, and Line String objects.

1 In any viewport, select the String object and add the Animation modifier, ***Path Deform** (not the Object Space version, Path Deform). Click Pick Path and choose Line String. Then click Move to Path.

2 In the Front viewport, select Line String and break the leftmost vertex to break the string off the circular path. The string should then be in place. Select the string object.

3 Set the *Path Deform Percent to **–60**.

This will give you a clear view of the end face of the string in the Top viewport, which will be important later when you use the Attachment controller to attach a dummy to the string.

4 Under Helpers, create a small dummy. Name it **Dummy Pulley End**.

5 Open the Motion panel, open the Assign Controller rollout, highlight Position, and click the Assign to Controller button. Choose Attachment.

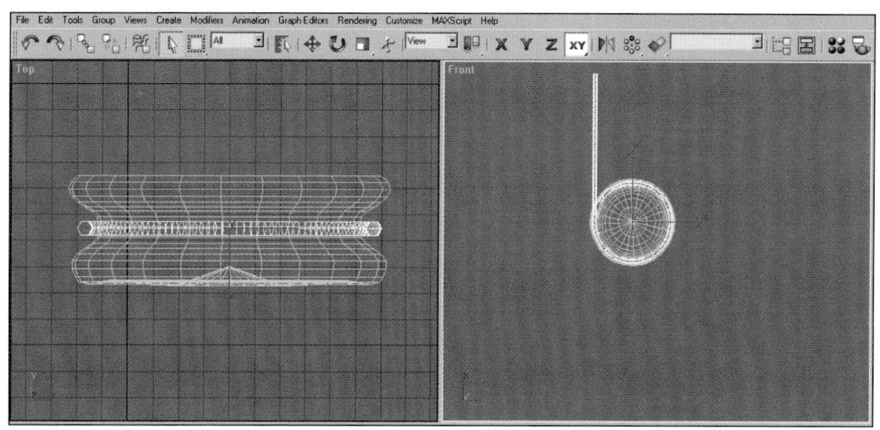

A clear view of the end face in the Top viewport.

Note: Most of the dummies you will create in this exercise will be positioned by controllers. So unless it's specifically noted, the viewport in which they are created will make no difference.

6 For Pick Object, select String. Turn on the Set Position button. In the Top viewport, click the mouse button over the end face. The dummy should jump to the face.

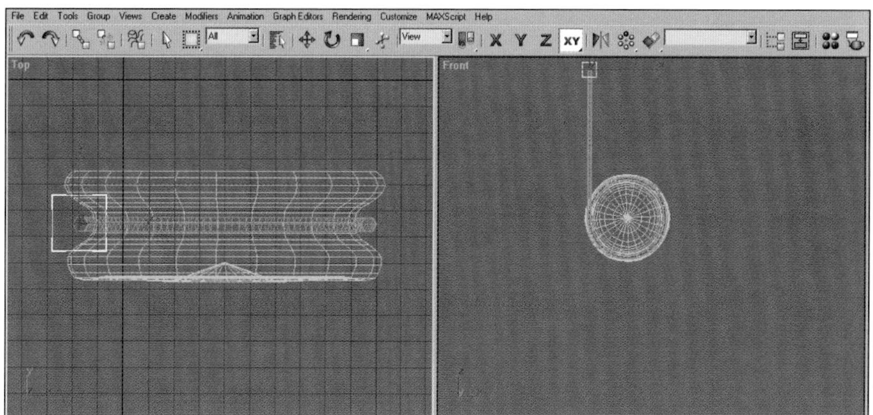

The dummy is attached to the correct face.

Note: Unlike Link, which links one object to the transform axis of another, the Attachment controller links the object to the selected face. Try moving the String along the path and notice that the string's transform axis does not move. Therefore, *linking* the dummy to the string would leave it motionless.

7 Select the String and change the Percent to **25** so Dummy Pull End is at a 6 o' clock position in the Front viewport.

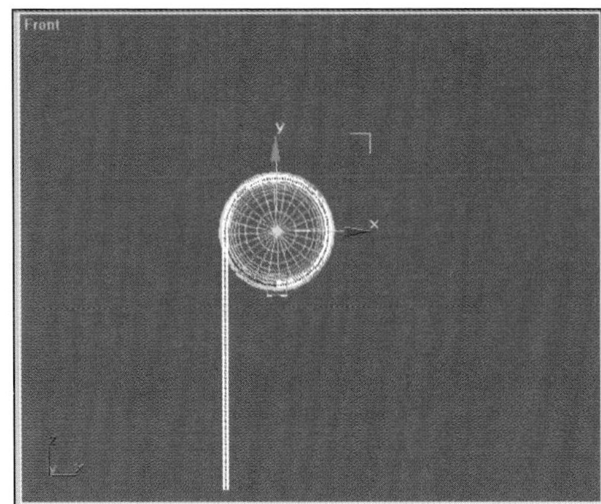

String with the dummy at 6 o' clock position.

ANIMATE THE STRING

The pulley is spring-loaded, so after you "pull it down," it will spring back. This will be adjusted in Track View, where most mechanical animation is refined. Learning to "read" the function curves is essential to making *believable* animations.

1 Select the String object and turn on the Animate button. Move the time slider to frame 13 and change the percent to **78**. Go to frame 28 and set the Percent to **25**. Turn off Animate. Then click Play to observe the result. The timing is okay, but the action could be snappier.

2 Right-click on the String object and choose Track View Selected. Open String and highlight Percent along path. Click the Function Curves button.

You should see an upside down U-shaped curve. Use Zoom Region to zoom in on the curve if you want.

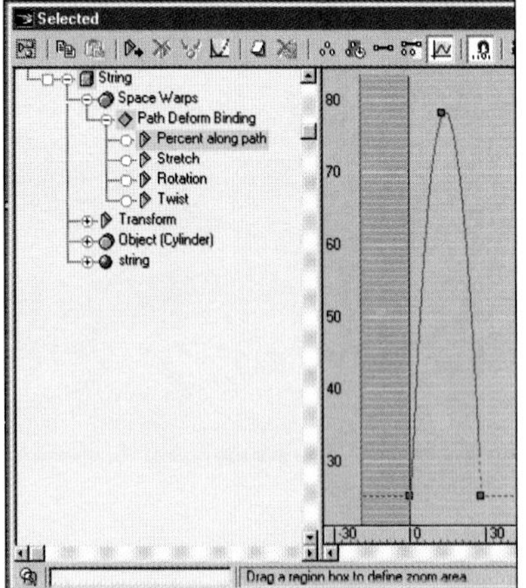

Function curve for Percent Along Path.

3 Select the second key and right-click over it to bring up the Properties dialog. Open the In: flyout and select the Fast interpolation tangent. Do the same for the tangent on the Out: flyout.

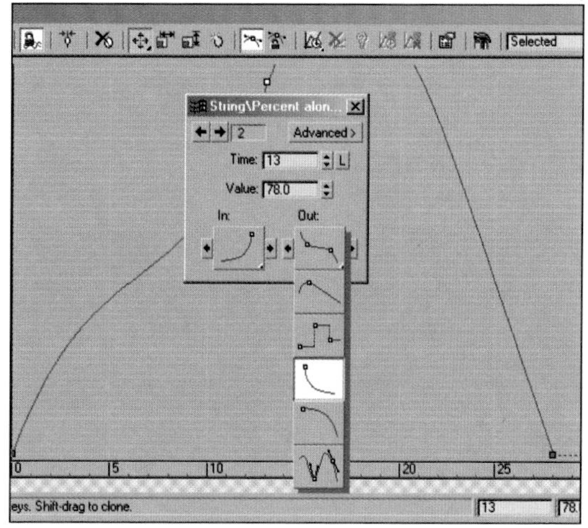

Fast interpolation tangent for Key 2 out type.

4 Move to Key 1 by clicking the left arrow at the top of the dialog. Set its Out: tangent type to Slow. Then change Key 3's In: tangent to Slow.

Note: All these preset tangent types can be confusing at first. If you look at the function curve graph, you see time on the horizontal axis and value on the vertical axis. Therefore, the important thing to remember about the function curve is just that: *Horizontal is slow, vertical is fast.* Later you will use the Custom tangent type to achieve better control over animation.

5 Close Track View and click the Play button to observe the changes. The string snaps back as if it were attached to a spring.

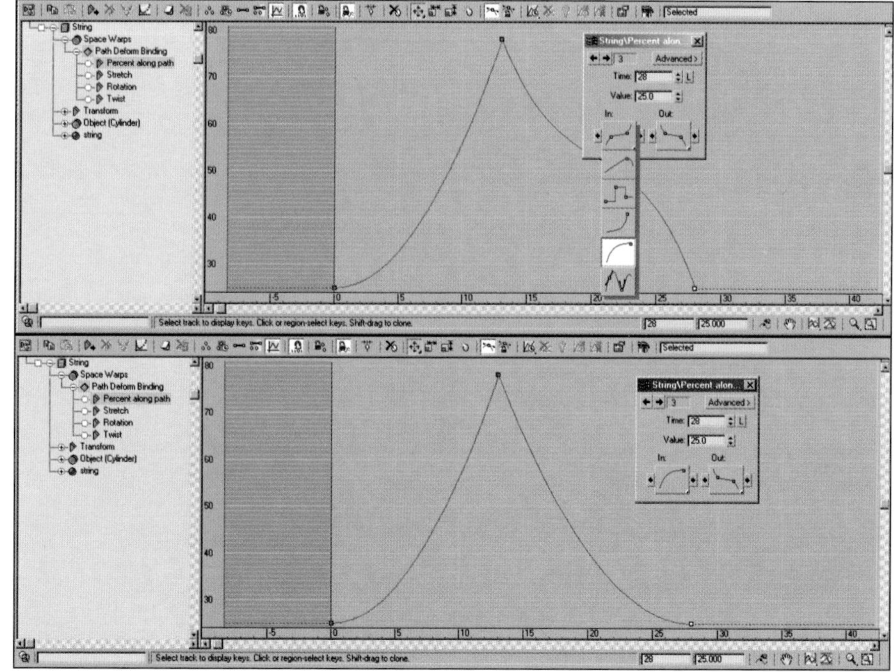

The altered function curve.

Attach the String to the Pulley

The pulley needs to rotate as the string's position on the path changes. There are a few different ways to do this, but you will be using the LookAt Constraint in this part of the project.

1 Create a small dummy and name it **Dummy Rotate Pulley**. Use the Align button to center it to the pulley. In the Left viewport, use the Align button to center it on the *X-axis only* to Dummy Pulley End.

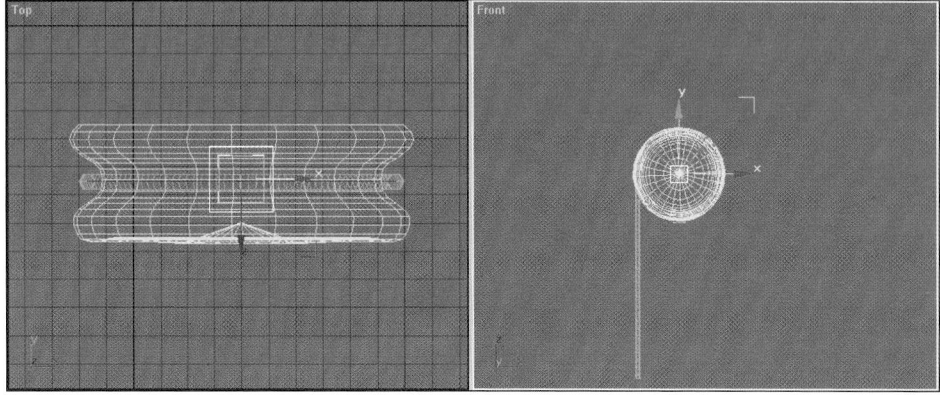

The dummy is centered on pulley and Dummy Pulley End.

2 In the Motion panel, assign a LookAt Constraint to the Rotation track of Dummy Rotate Pulley. Set the following parameters if they have not already been set by default:

Select LookAt Axis: **X**
Select Upnode: **World**
Upnode Control: **Axis Alignment**
Source Axis: **Y**
Aligned to Upnode Axis: **Y**

3 For Add LookAt Target, choose **Dummy Pulley End**. Scrub the time slider to observe the results.

4 Link the Pulley to Dummy Rotate Pulley.

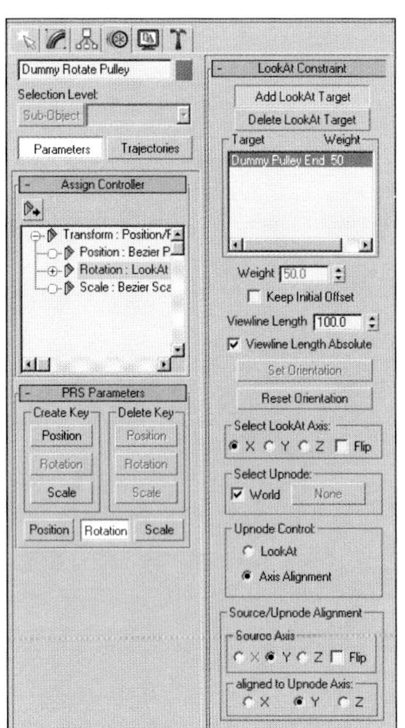

The LookAt panel configuration with the panel expanded to the left.

Give It a Whack!

This section adds the pulley assembly's cosmetic elements. As with Dummy Pulley End (see "Pull Here to Start"), the handle will be *attached* to the path-deformed String object rather than *linked*.

1 Unhide the By Name option and choose Selection Set/Pulley Accessories.

You should see Handle and Hammer.

2 Link the hammer to the Pulley. At frame 13, rotate the hammer so it is approximately at a 5:30 position. You will fine-tune it later. Return to frame 0.

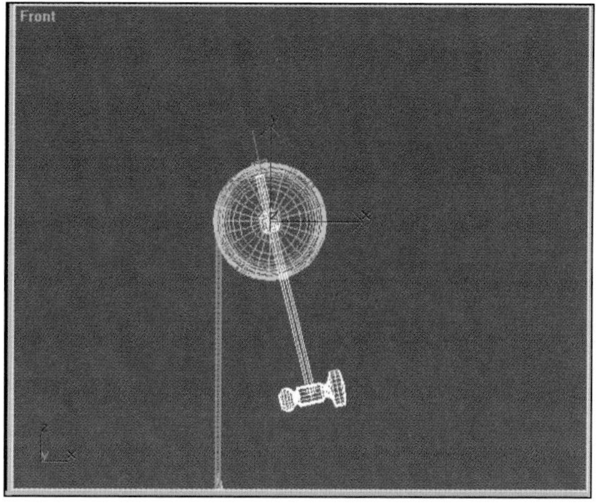

The hammer is in approximate position.

3 Use the Attachment controller to attach the handle assembly to the end of the string. Rotate the handle to the correct alignment. To align the handle's *position*, because it is being "controlled," you must use Affect Object Only in the Hierarchy panel.

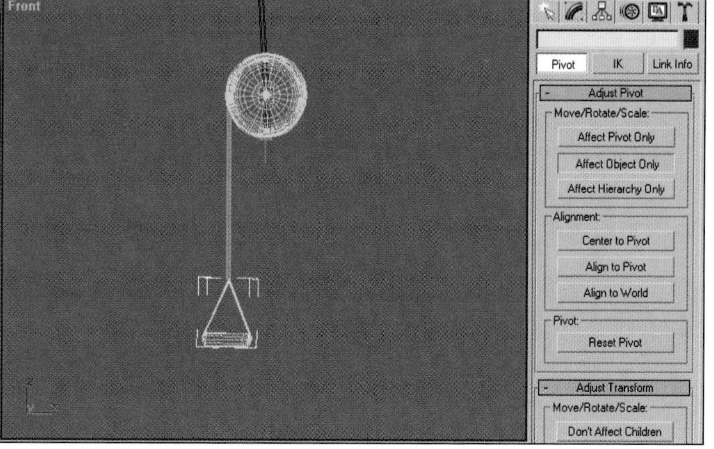

Use Affect Object Only to reposition the handle.

Note: If you find this alignment technique frustrating, consider *attaching* a dummy to the string end and linking the handle to it.

4 Select all and create a Named Selection Set called **Pulley Assembly**. Be sure to click Enter to complete the set after typing the name.

You can add a little movement to the handle at this point if you like, or you can skip steps five and six and go to the next section.

5 At frame 80, turn on the Animate button and rotate the handle slightly on the Y-axis in the Front or Left viewport, view coordinate system.

6 At frame 160, rotate the handle back in the other direction.

7 Repeat step 5 at frame 240, step 6 at frame 320, and step 5 again at frame 400, decreasing the rotation each time. Turn the Animate button off.

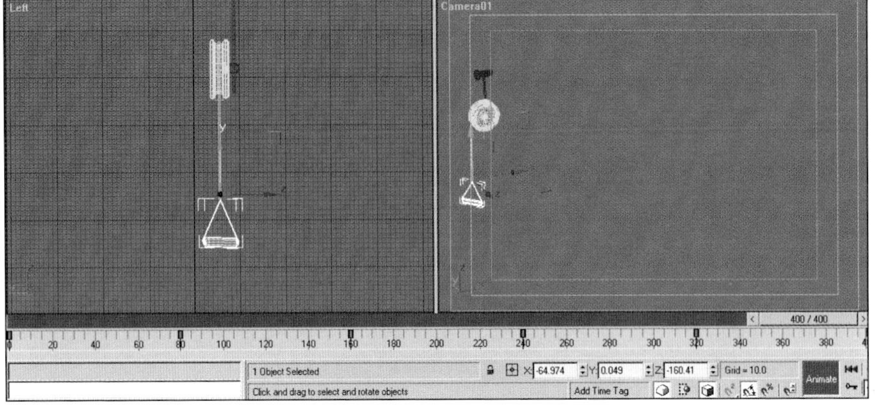

Track Bar keys for the moving handle.

Down the Chute!

By now you may have noticed a certain affinity for dummies. Although they are rarely ever *strictly* necessary, they provide a great amount of design flexibility. It is easy to link a multitude of objects (lights, particle systems, and so on) to one dummy and retain their individual behaviors as they travel together along a path. In this project, you will link only one object, the ball, but in this case, the dummies enable you to keep the various parts of the animation as independent units. The only animation on the ball itself will be the link information, which makes it very easy to replace it with any object of similar size or shape.

1 Unhide the selection set, Chute Assembly. You should have Chute, Line Chute, Ball, and Start Platform.

   As you may have guessed, Chute was a loft object made with Line Chute as its path and then collapsed. Before you can use Line Chute as the path for the ball, you must extend it up onto the platform.

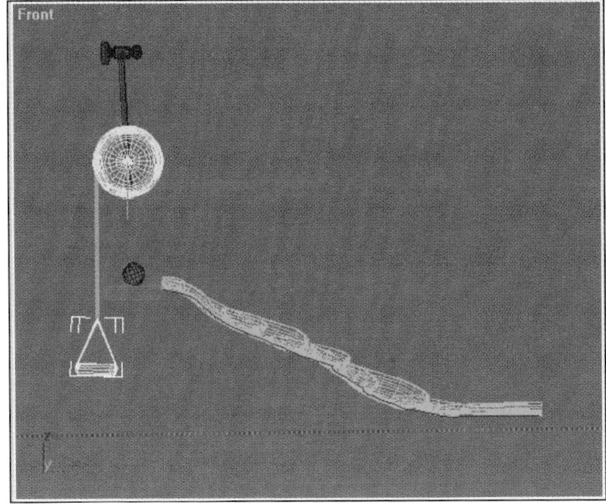

The Chute Assembly.

2 In the Front viewport, select the line and position the top vertex to the center of the platform. Adjust the Bézier handle to give the line a smooth, slightly upward transition onto the chute. In the Front viewport, select the bottom end vertex and raise it until it is even with the chute edge so the ball will lift into the spoon.

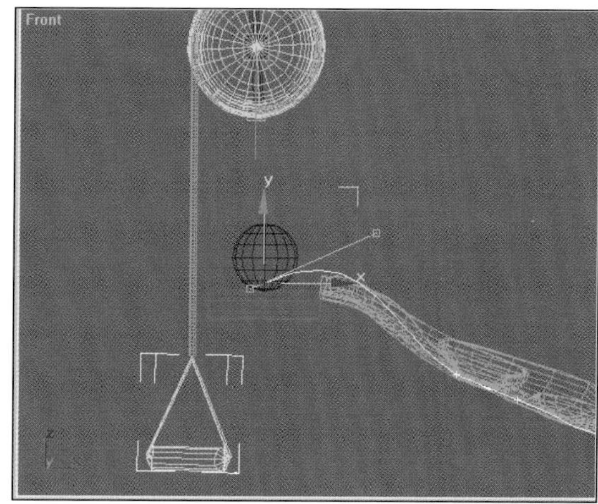

The adjusted top vertex for Line Chute.

3 Create a dummy approximately the size of the ball. Name it **Dummy Down Chute**.

4 In the Motion panel, assign a Roll Along Path (not Follow [Roll Along Path]) controller to the dummy's Position channel. Check Add Offset Radius and set the Radius to **30** (the ball's radius). Click the Pick Path button and select Line Chute.

Roll Along Path automatically sets keys at the beginning and end of the total animation, but you will need to adjust these so the dummy will roll down the chute at the proper time and speed. You can easily do this in Track Bar, a sort of "mini" Track View.

Note: If you are unable to locate Roll Along Path, make sure Roller.dlc has been copied into the Plug-ins folder; if you have put it somewhere else, make sure you configure a path to its location. Remember that max will have to be restarted to load any new plug-ins. Save your file before restarting max.

5 In Track Bar, move the start key to frame 12 and the end key to 47.

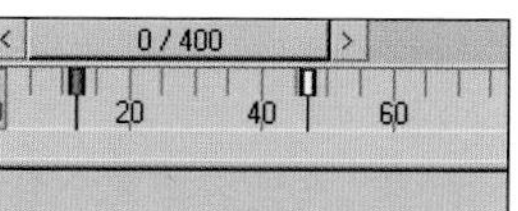

Move the keys in the Track Bar.

6 Under Edit on the menu bar, choose Edit Named Selections. Select Chute Assembly in the left window and remove the ball. Click the Add button and add Dummy Down Chute to the selection set. Click OK.

Keeping each module organized as a selection set (unlike grouping) enables you to animate individual objects and hide and unhide objects or sets at will.

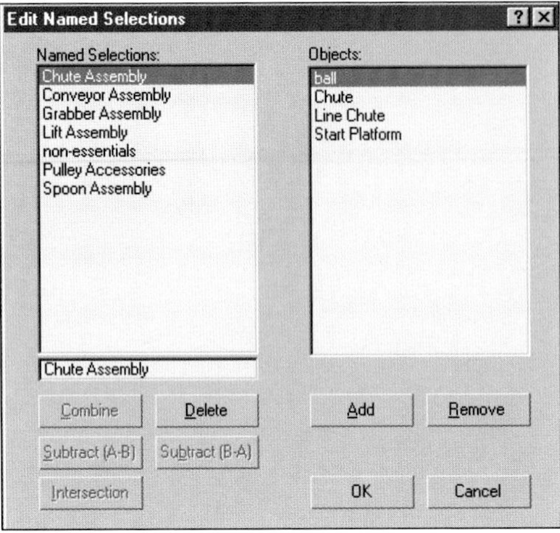

The Edit Named Selection dialog.

Spin the Spoon

Although the ball spinning with the spoon is highly improbable, no one ever seems to mind! After all, what fun is a 3D program if you can't take a bit of poetic license every now and then?

1 Unhide the Spoon Assembly selection set. You should have two objects: Spoon and Line Drop from Spoon.

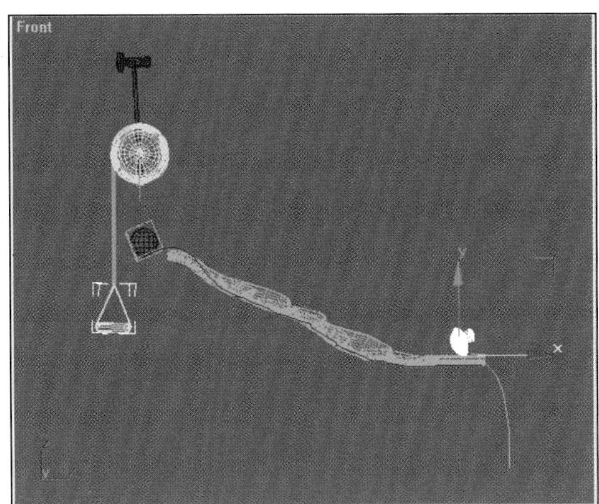

The spoon assembly.

2 In the Camera viewport, select the Spoon and go to frame 46. Right-click on the time slider to bring up the Create Key dialog, clear the Position and Scale check boxes, and click OK to set a rotation key. Go to frame 120 and turn on Animate. Click the Select and Rotate button. With the camera active, toggle the Transform Type to Offset mode and enter **1080** in the Z field. Turn off the Animate button.

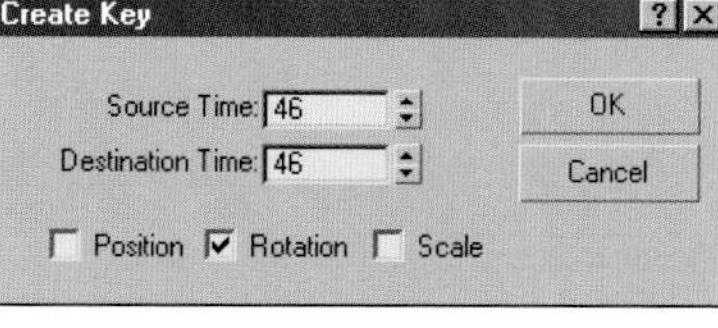

The Create Key dialog appears when you right-click the time slider.

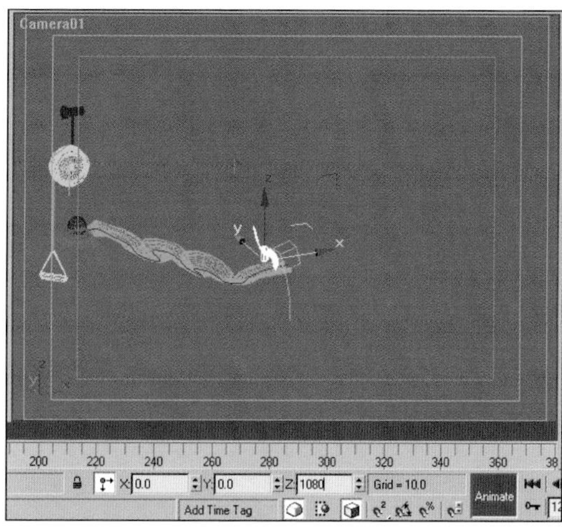

The Transform Type-In area.

Note: In 3ds max 4, rotation functions have been rewritten so that it is now possible to rotate objects more than 180 degrees without cumbersome workarounds.

3 Open Track View for the spoon. Note that the spoon has an Euler rotation controller, which allows access to its X, Y, and Z function curves. Highlight the Z Rotation track.

Note the straight line from start to end key. This indicates a constant velocity for the spinning spoon. Because the spin should start out fast and then gradually slow to a stop, the curve must be adjusted.

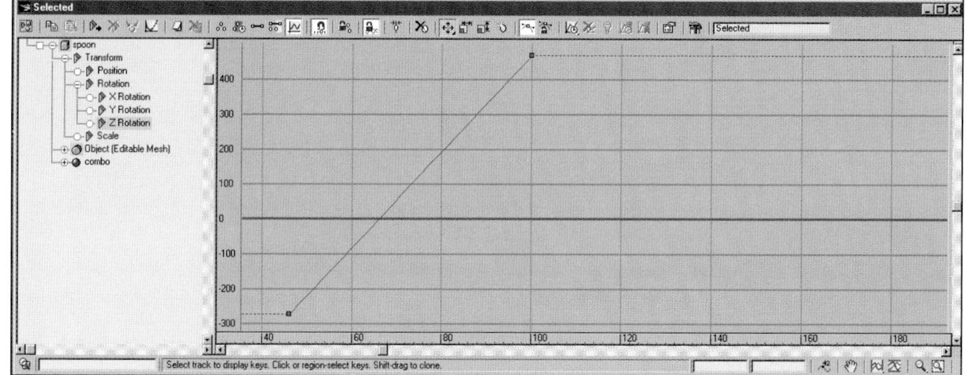

Straight function "curve."

4 Turn on Edit Keys mode and select both keys. Right-click to bring up the Properties dialog. Change the Tangent interpolation type for In: to Custom. The Out: value also changes. Zoom Region to show about half the window.

You will now be able to adjust the curve with the familiar Bézier handles. Remembering that *vertical is fast and horizontal is slow*, adjust the curve so that it starts out steep and then slows to horizontal at the end.

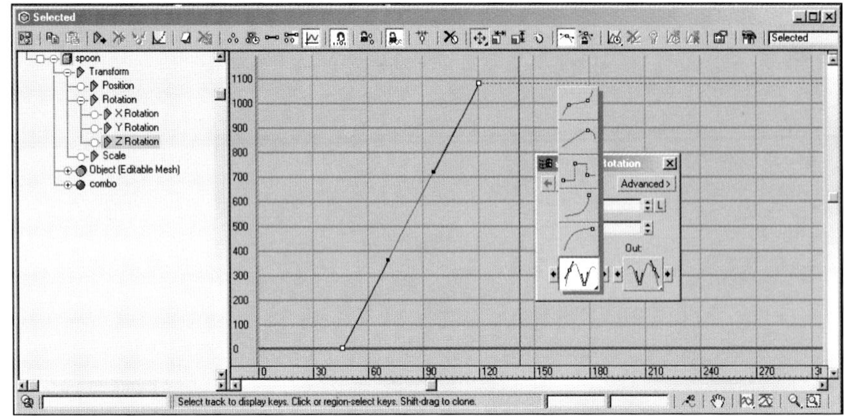

Custom tangent type.

5 Click Play. Adjust the handles for the start key until the spoon's starting velocity looks correct in relation to the speed of the ball/dummy as it hits the spoon. Close Track View.

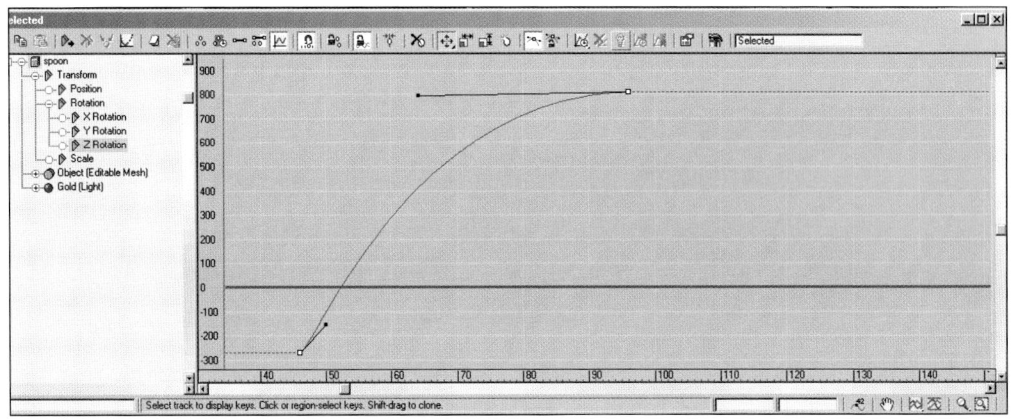

The corrected curve.

Get the Ball Moving

Now that you have a couple of modules completed, it is time to link up the ball. Because the ball will be passed to various dummies and objects during the animation, you will use a Link constraint to achieve dynamic linking.

1 Zoom extends all, go to frame 0, and select the ball. In the Motion panel, highlight Transform and change the controller type to Link Constraint. Click the Add Link button and pick Dummy Down Chute. Turn off Add Link.

2 Check the ball position at frame 13. It may be necessary to rotate the hammer back so it will hit the ball correctly. Make sure the animate button is *not* on.

3 Go to frame 46. This is where the spoon needs to take control of the ball.

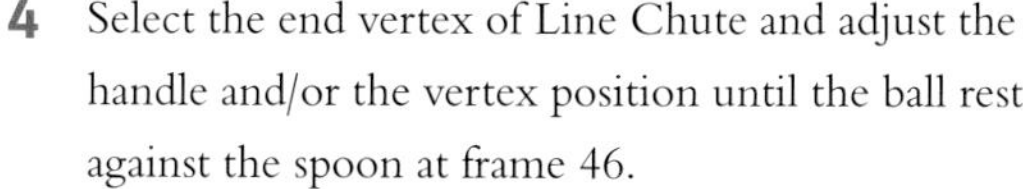

4 Select the end vertex of Line Chute and adjust the handle and/or the vertex position until the ball rests against the spoon at frame 46.

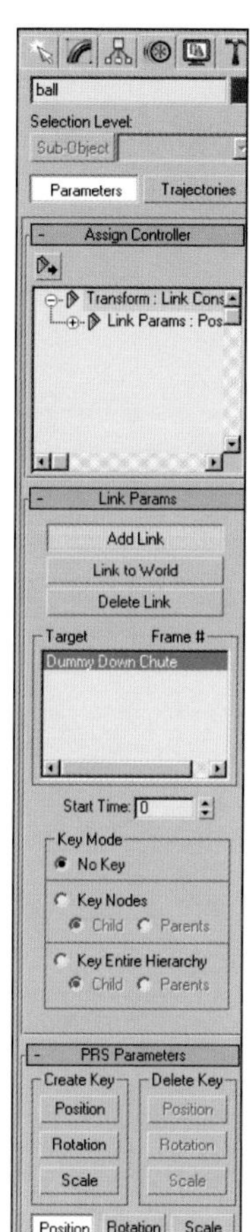

The Link Constraint panel.

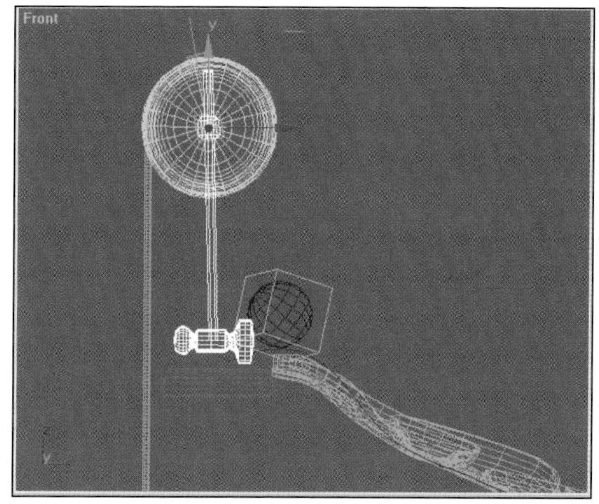

Hammer and ball position at frame 13.

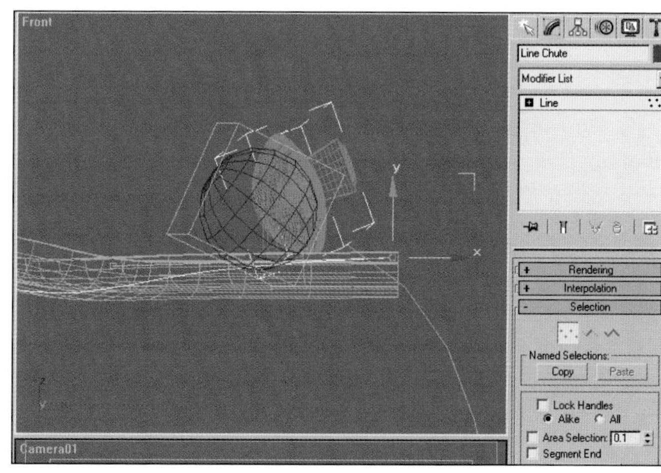

Adjust the end vertex and its handle to bring the ball up against the spoon.

5 Back in the Motion panel with the ball selected, at frame 46, click Add Link and select the spoon. Then turn off Add Link, return to frame 0, and click the Play button.

The ball now passes from the chute dummy to the spoon!

6 Hide the Chute Assembly selection set and the Pulley Assembly selection set.

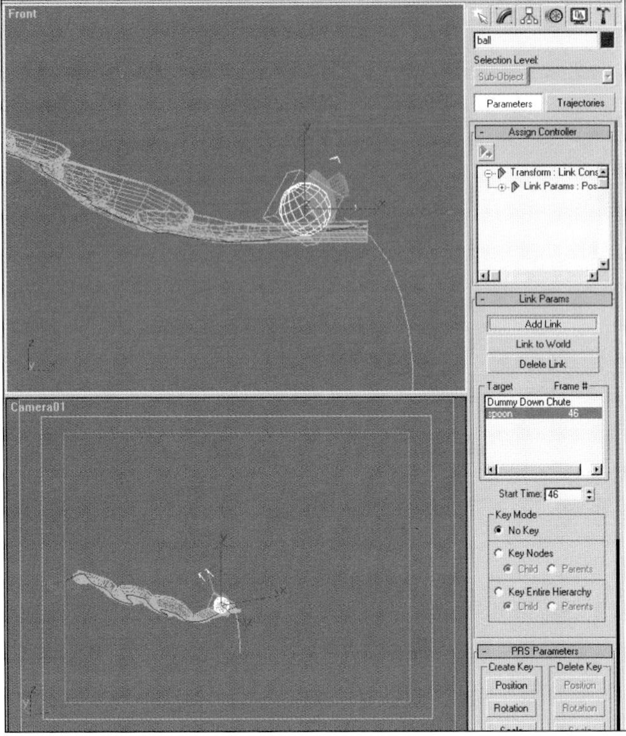

The Link Constraint panel. The ball is linked to the spoon at frame 46.

Break Out the Conveyor Belt

No self-respecting "mechanical" animation would be caught dead without a conveyor belt, and this one is no exception. This conveyor belt uses the same technique as the string on a path. But first you need to get the ball to land on it.

1 Create a dummy and name it **Dummy Drop from Spoon**. By frame 78, the spoon has slowed enough that the ball ought to drop out.

2 Put a Path Constraint on Dummy Drop from Spoon with Line Drop from Spoon as the path. Be sure to check Follow and Allow Upside Down.

3 Open Track View in Function Curve mode, and then move the Percent Along Path start key to frame 78 and the end key to frame 88. Add a bit of bounce to the ball by adding keys at frames 94, 99, 103, and 106. Move the key at 94 down just a little and the key at 103 down a little less. This sends the dummy back up the path.

4 Change all key In/Out Tangents to Custom and adjust the handles so that the dummy spends very little time on the "ground." Also, adjust its curve to be slow at first and then faster at the end. When you finish, close Track View.

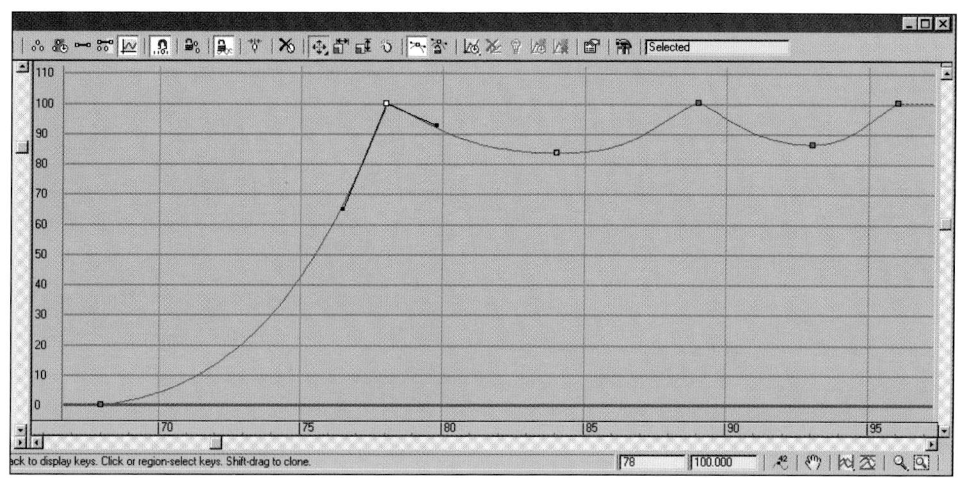

The function curve with low "bounces."

Tip: To change the handles from Bézier to Bézier Corner, hold the Shift key and move a handle. It becomes a Bézier Corner type! You can also use the Lock Tangents button. This technique also works on spline vertices and in the Loft Deformations windows.

5 Move the Track View window aside so the spoon is visible in the Top viewport. Go to frame 68 and adjust the spoon's end rotation key handle to deliver the ball to the dummy at frame 68.

Note that the ball does not have to be centered on the dummy. Select the ball and add the Dummy Drop from Spoon link in the Motion panel.

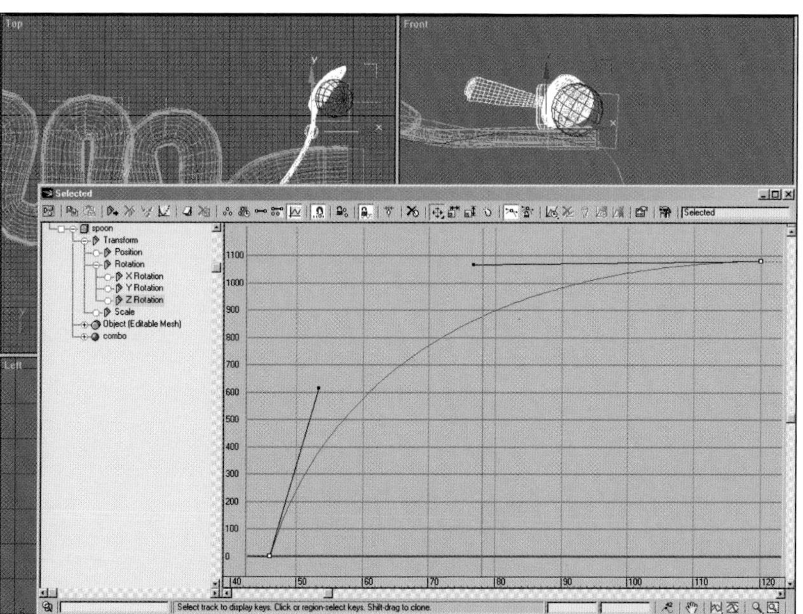

The spoon's position adjusted using the end rotation key handles.

6 Unhide the Conveyor Assembly selection set. You should have these objects: Gear01, Gear02, Wheel, Conveyor Belt, Line Conveyor Belt, and Line Space Wheels.

7 Select Conveyor Belt and add a Path Deform. Click Pick Path and choose Line Conveyor Belt. Then click Move To Path.

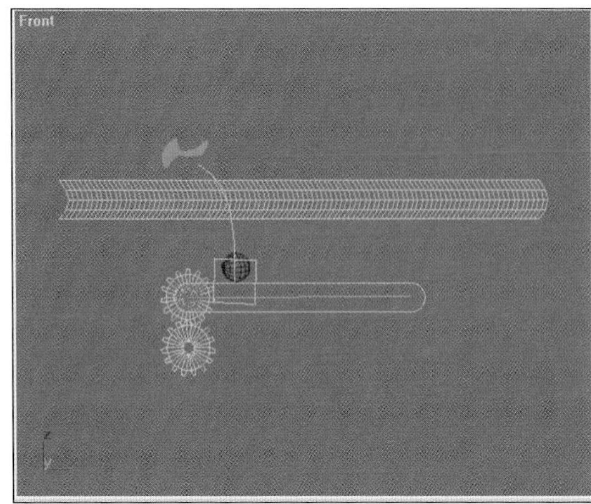

The Conveyor Belt Assembly.

8 Choose X as the Path Deform axis and set the Rotation to **–90**. Set Stretch to **1.119** to close the gap.

9 With Conveyor Belt still selected, open Track View and create a key in the Path Deform Binding: Percent Along Path track at frame 46 with a value **0**. Create another key at 67 with a value **–12**.

After the speed is set, the movement needs to loop.

Tip: You can type both frames and values into the text boxes at the lower-right of the window. If you choose to create these keys in the Track Bar, max might create a key at frame 0 that will have to be deleted.

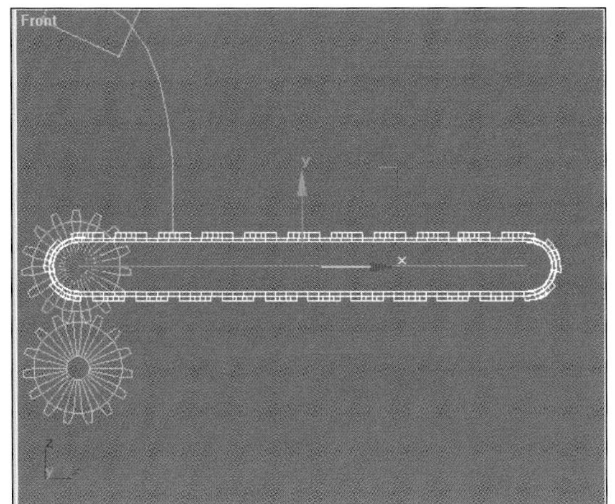

The Conveyor Belt is in place.

10 Click the Parameter Out-of-Range button and choose Relative Repeat for the Out type.

With the Out value set to Relative Repeat and the In value set as Constant, the motion will start at frame 46 ("triggered" by the spinning spoon) and then continue for the rest of the animation.

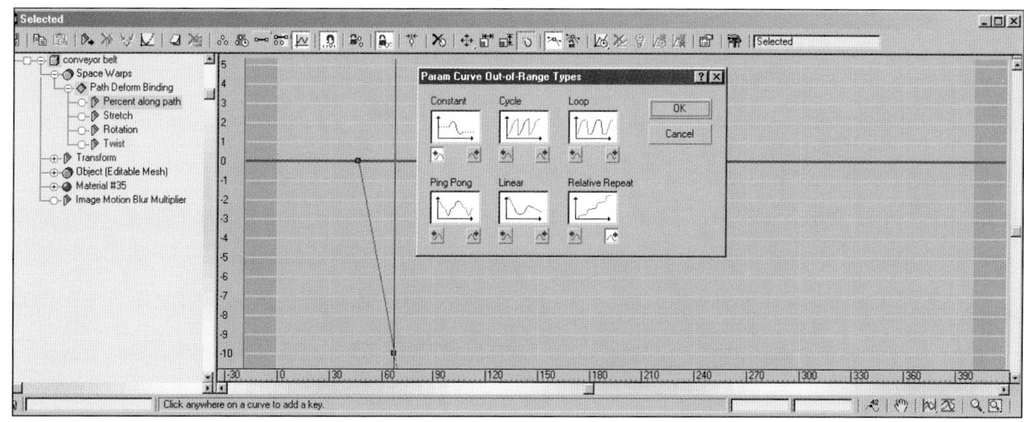

Parameter Out-of-Range Types dialog.

Rotate the Gears and Wheels

Because this is max and not "real" life, you will get the wheels and gears rotating by doing a bit of "backward" engineering. The method used in this section is for "right-brain artist types." No tricky mathematical formula is required, but you can still get 3ds max 4 to do the grunt work if it is set up properly!

You need a way to compare the rotation of the belt (actually the Percent Along Path) with the rotation of the wheel. You will make a couple of helper objects (small spheres in this case) to assist with this task. You will visually compare their location and alignment while adjusting the wheel rotation to the travel of the conveyor belt. It will be relatively easy to wire the gears to the wheel rotation.

1 Go to frame 0 and create two small spheres in the Front viewport. Select Smooth and Highlight to make it easier to see things. Use the Attachment controller to attach and move (Set Position) one of the spheres to the edge of the conveyor belt, just below the wheel. Use the Align button to center the second one on the first, and then move it directly above the first, over the edge of the wheel, and link it to the wheel.

Helper spheres: one is *attached* to the belt, and one is *linked* to the wheel.

2 In the Front viewport, select the wheel. Right-click and choose Wire Parameters/Transforms/Rotation/ Y Rotation. Then "connect" it to the Conveyor Belt /Space Warp/Path Deform Binding/Percent Along Path. The Parameter Wiring dialog appears.

3 In the Parameter Wiring dialog, click the left-facing arrow so the Percent Along Path of the conveyor belt "controls" the Y rotation of the wheel. Click Connect. Leaving the dialog open, reposition the sphere if necessary and scrub the time slider.

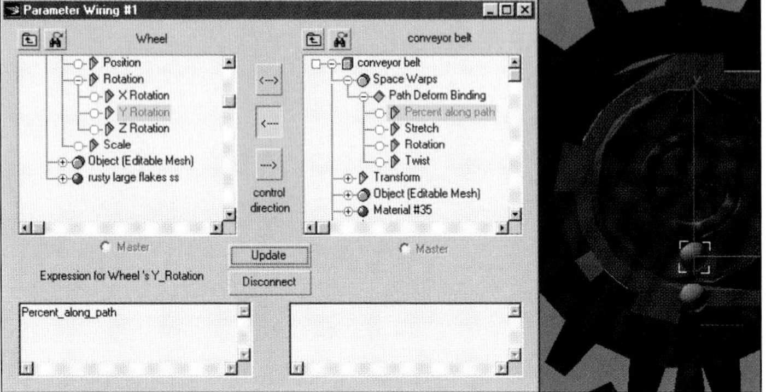

The Parameter Wiring dialog.

If the wheel actually controlled the belt speed, you would expect the two spheres to stay aligned as you scrubbed the time slider, until the belt sphere reached the flat area.

4 In the Parameter Wiring dialog, under Expression for Wheel's Y Rotation, add ***40** to the expression to give the wheel more speed in order to properly synchronize with the moving conveyor belt. Add a minus (–) to the front of the equation to reverse the direction, and then click Update. This will give the wheel more speed so that it will properly synchronize with the moving conveyor belt.

Note: At the time of this writing, there was an intermittent problem with wiring. If you are experiencing problems, go to **www.discreet.com** and download the latest patch for 3ds max 4. If nothing happens when you click Connect or Update, perform a Hold and then a Fetch to activate the wiring.

5 Move the time slider by increments to check on your adjustment. A setting of 40 is a bit fast, so try **38** (do not forget to click the Update button).

Note: Return to frame 0 before clicking the Connect or Update button to retain the relative positions of the objects.

Although it's not exact, 38 will be fine for this short animation. If you needed the belt to be animated for several full rotations, you could get a more accurate value by checking the spheres' alignment at the last pass against their alignment at the start.

6 Delete the two "helper" spheres. Close the Parameter Wiring dialog.

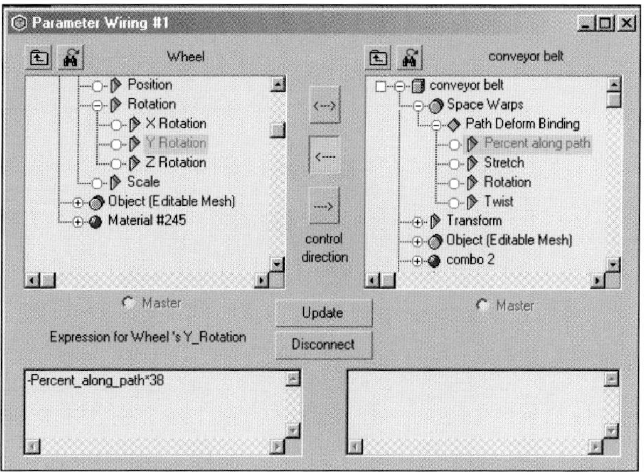

The corrected parameters.

7 Link Gear01 to the wheel. Select Gear02 *and* Wheel. From the Animate menu, open the Parameter Wiring dialog. Note that the selected objects are highlighted.

This is another way to access the wiring dialog, and this method can be used in conjunction with a hotkey instead of the menu bar for increased efficiency.

8 To wire Gear 02, highlight it's Y Rotation on the left side and Wheel's Y Rotation on the right side. Click the arrow that points from the *controlling* object (Wheel) to the *controlled* object (Gear 02) and click Connect.

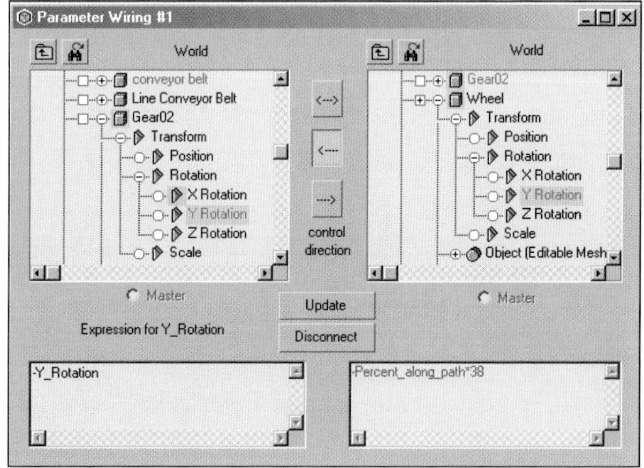

Gear02's wiring parameters.

9 Scrub the time slider. Both gears rotate in the same direction. You need to put a minus (–) in front of the active equation and click Update to reverse the direction of Gear 02.

Note: If the gears do not mesh properly, adjust the rotation in the Hierarchy panel according to the pulley handle.

10 Select Wheel and choose the Spacing tool in the Array pull-down list or from the Tools menu. Pick Line Space Wheels as the path. Make six instances and click Apply. Close the dialog.

The spacing tool does not include the original wheel in its calculations, so you need to delete Wheel06. The animation is copied, but the actual wiring controller is not. You need to wire each of the new wheels individually. They can all be wired to the Wheel object, or they can be daisychained to it.

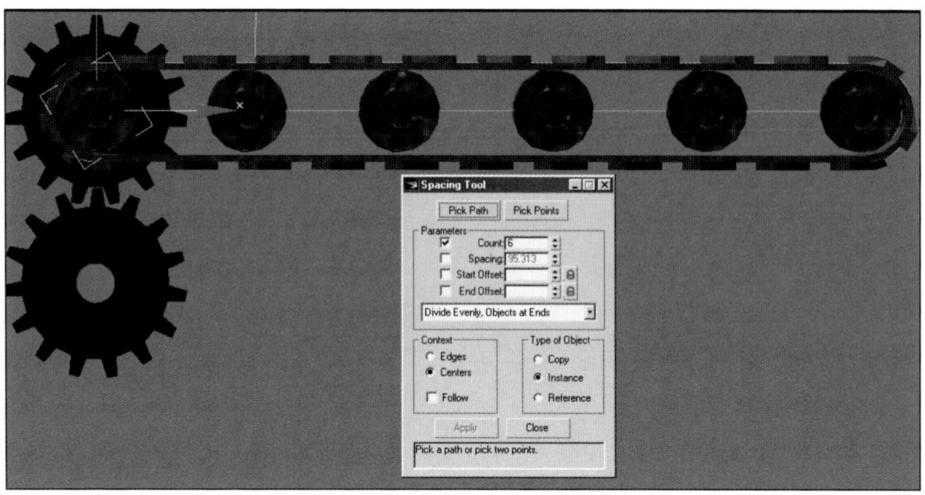

The Spacing Tool dialog.

Moving Right Along

It is time to send the ball on down the conveyor belt!

1 If the ball is too low, go to frame 110 or so. Select Dummy Drop From Spoon. Open Track View and select the top keys. Set the Move Keys constraint to vertical and move the selected keys down until the ball touches the conveyor belt surface (not the treads). If it is too high, move the Line Drop From Spoon up. Close Track View. Your eye tells you the ball should move down the belt even as it bounces.

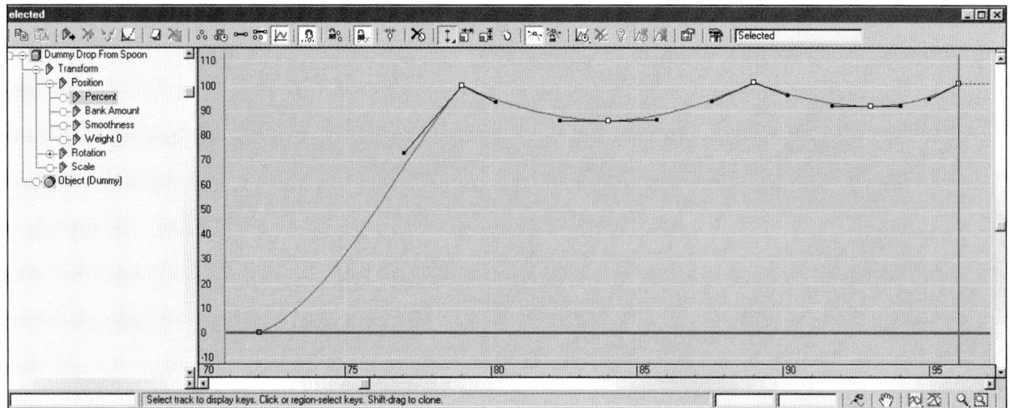

Adjust the landing position.

2 Select Line Drop From Spoon at frame 88 and set a position key for it. Turn on the Animate button and go to frame 106, where the bouncing has stopped, and then move the line about 35 units along the conveyor belt.

3 Create a dummy and name it **Dummy Conveyor Belt**. Put an Attachment controller on it with Conveyor Belt as the control object, and then position it so that it is aligned to the ball in the Top viewport at frame 106 when the ball stops bouncing.

4 Select the ball and Add Link to pass control of it to Dummy Conveyor Belt at frame 106.

5 Select Dummy Drop From Spoon, add it to the Spoon Assembly selection set, and hide that set.

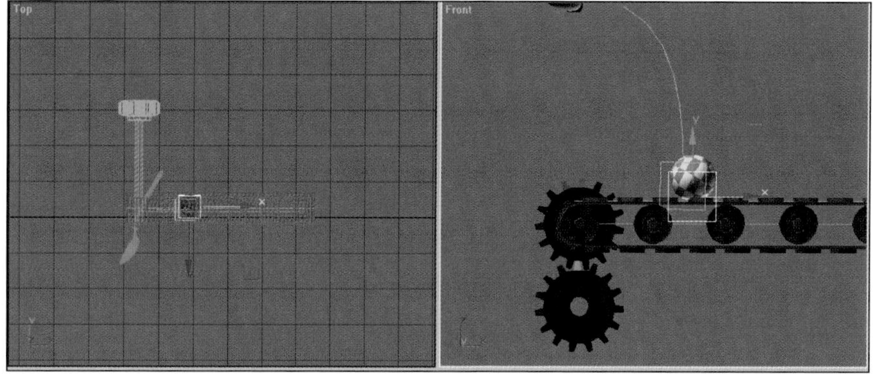

Align the conveyor dummy.

ANOTHER BELT...

This time you will animate the belt the mathematical way by using Expression controllers. The inestimable scripting guru, Swami, has provided a useful equation to control this conveyor belt using the rotation of the rollers.

1 Unhide the Lift Assembly selection set. You should see the following objects: Gear 03, Gear 04, Lift, Line Lift, Lift Cup, and Sphere 01.

Let us suppose somewhere under the table the rotation has been "geared down" so the wheel controlling the Lift belt is slower than the conveyor belt wheels.

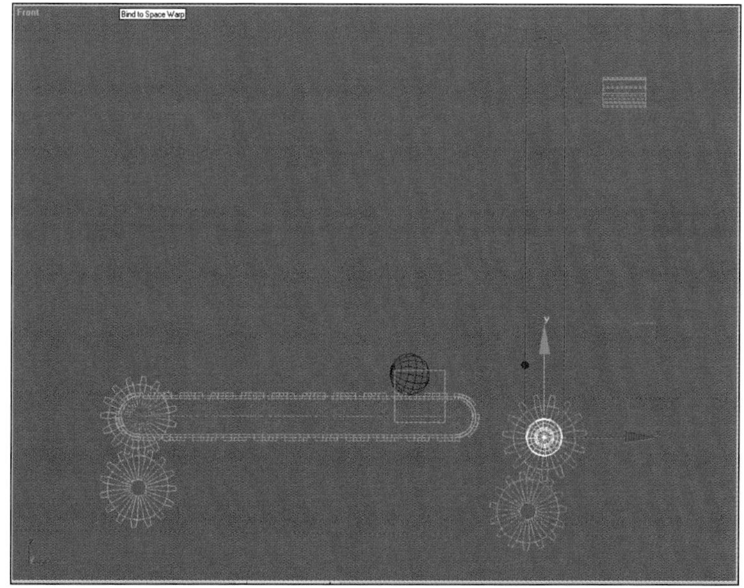

The lift assembly: The lift belt already contains a *PathDeform modifier.

2 Wire Lift Wheel's Y rotation to any of the conveyor wheels' Y rotation and add ***–75** to the equation. Do not forget to update.

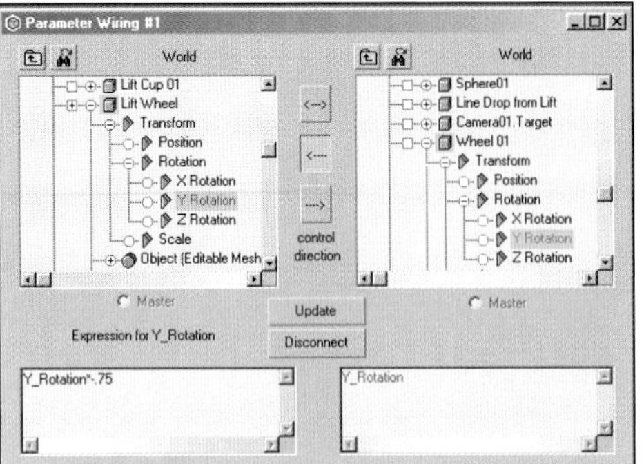

The Wiring dialog for Lift Wheel.

3 Link Gear03 to Lift Wheel. Wire Gear04's Y rotation to Lift Wheel's Y rotation and reverse it with a minus sign. Because a linked object *has* no animation keys of its own, wiring to a linked object will *produce* no animation.

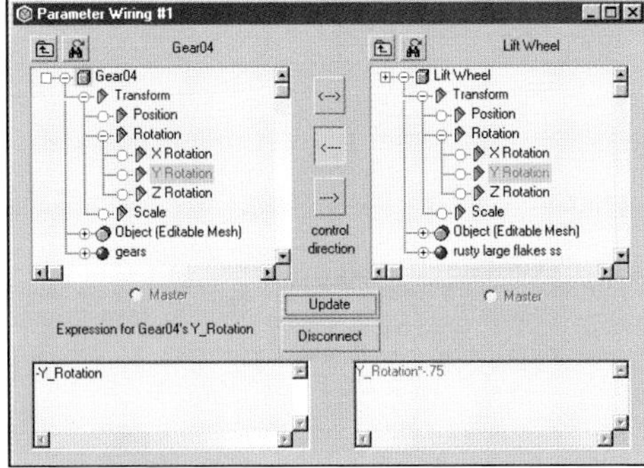

Gear04's wiring dialog.

4 Shift+copy to create Lift Wheel01 and move it to the top end of the lift. Wire its Y rotation to Lift Wheel.

5 Select Lift Belt, and in Track View, change its Percent Along Path controller to Float Expression. In the Expression Controller dialog, you need to create three Scalar variables for the equation. To do so, either assign a constant value or select another object's value to use as the controller. Create the following variables:

- **w**, the belt length. Assign to Constant. You can find the value by selecting the Line Lift in the viewport and choosing Measure in the Utilities panel. Its Z dimension should measure 613.337 units, which is the value you will use as w.
- **r**, the lift radius/width. Assign to Constant. This value should be 54.301 units.
- **t**, the lift wheel angle. Assign to Controller. Choose Lift Wheel's Y Rotation.

6 Enter the equation **–t*r/2/((w–2*r)+pi*r)** and click Evaluate. Scrub the time slider to see the results. The belt's rotation should now be controlled by Wheel's Y rotation. Be sure to include the descriptions of the variables in the Description section.

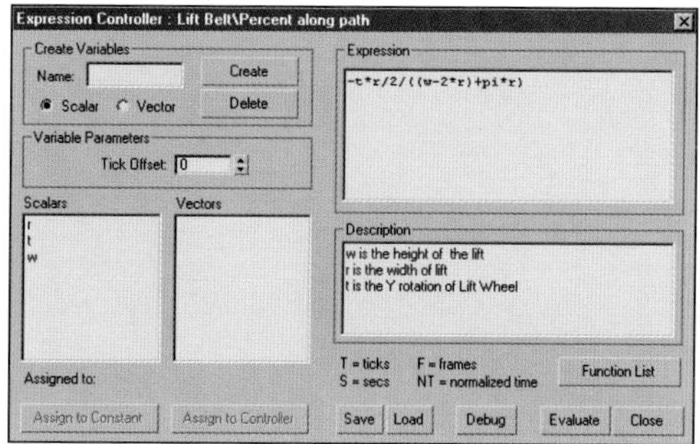

The Expression Controller dialog for controlling the lift belt Percent Along Path with the lift wheel's rotation.

Note: Sometimes real-time playback in the viewport shows a strobing effect. Manually scrub the time slider to assure yourself that the rotation is correct.

Up, Up and Away!

At the time of this writing, Larry Minton's very useful Attachment 2 controller was not available, or you could easily attach the Lift Cups to the Lift object itself. Gimble Lock causes them to flip when using the standard Attachment controller, so another method must be used. It requires a bit more work, but it enables you to make use of a very handy little MaxScript by Stefan Didak. As usual in max, there are several ways to solve a problem.

1 Select Lift Cup01. Add a Path constraint with Line Lift as the path. Check the Follow and Allow Upside Down Loop, and Constant check boxes.

2 At frame 300, Rotate Lift Cup01 until its orientation is correct—tipped slightly upward. In Track View, set or move the start key to 46. In the Parameter Out of Range dialog, set the In *and* Out types to Relative Repeat. Close Track View. Go to frame 46.

3 Select the helper object, Sphere01, and move it to line up with the corner of Lift Cup01. (It has an attachment controller, so you will need to Set Position to move it.) Because its position was set at frame 0 and you are at frame 46, a dialog appears, asking "Are you sure you want to animate the position of this object?" Click OK and delete the original key at frame 0.

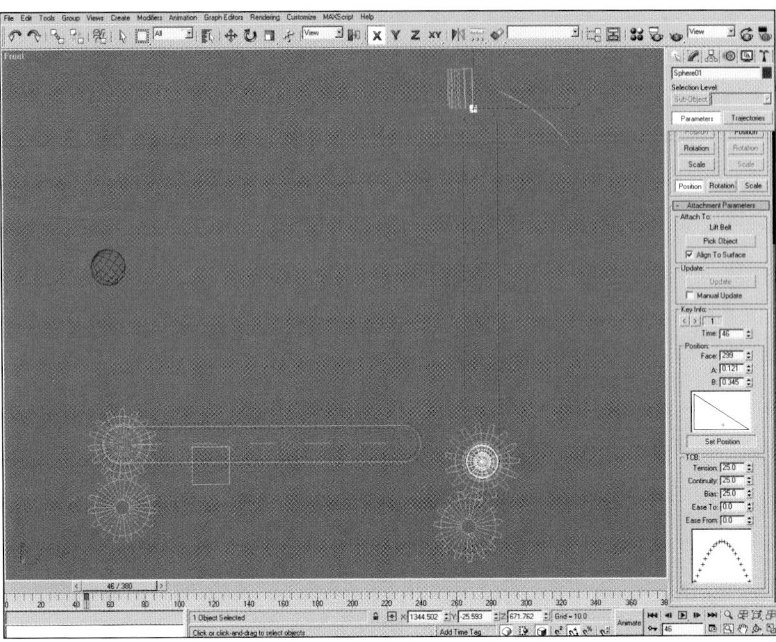

Lift Cup01 with Path constraint: Sphere01 is lined up with Set Position.

4 Go to frame 199, where the sphere has made a complete circuit since frame 46. In the Track Bar, move Lift Cup01's end key backward (to the left) until the cup aligns with the sphere (frame 199). The sphere is a helper that should make the travel of the lift belt easier to gauge. Delete Sphere01. Go to frame 46.

5 Choose either Select and Rotate or Select and Scale. *Do not use Select and Move*. Select Lift Cup01, hold down the Shift key, and click on the cup to make 11 more instances. They should all be in the same place. Select all the cups.

6 Do a Hold. In the Utilities panel, choose MaxScript and click the Run Script button. Choose Key_Shifter.ms. In the dialog that appears, click the Selected button, set Shift Keys to **13**, and click Shift Time. Then close the dialog window.

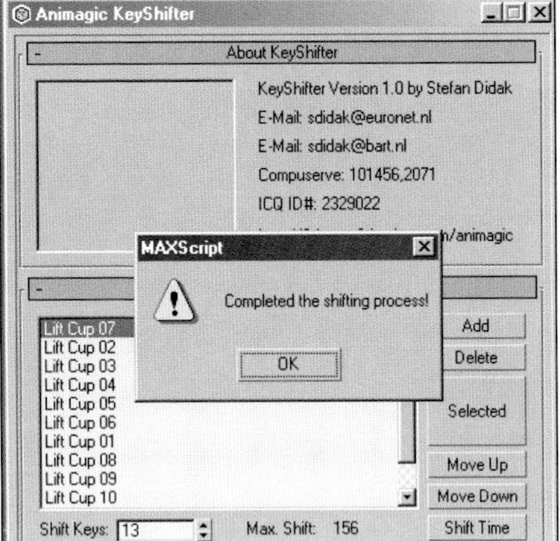

The KeyShifter dialog.

Note: Because 153 (the circuit time) is not evenly divisible by 12 (the number of cups), there is a different gap between two of the cups.

Note: The script does not add this action to the Undo stack, so if you make a mistake, you should Fetch and go back to step 6.

7 Go to frame 162. To pass the ball to the closest cup, you might have to shift the keys for all the cups. Select all the cups and open Track View Selected. In Edit Keys, click the Show Subtree button and move all the cup keys to the left until the cup is in position to receive the ball at frame 162. Close Track View.

The cups rotate nicely, but nothing else in the animation starts moving until frame 46, so the cups should do the same. To "catch" each lift cup at the proper starting position, you must add a key at frame 46 for each cup's track *before* you set the In Parameter Out of Range type to constant.

8 Go to frame 46 and turn on the Animate button. Select (*not* Select and Move) each cup and set a key at frame 46 for each one by clicking the Percent spinner up once and down once. This method works well for setting a non-transform animation key. Delete the middle keys in the Track Bar as you go.

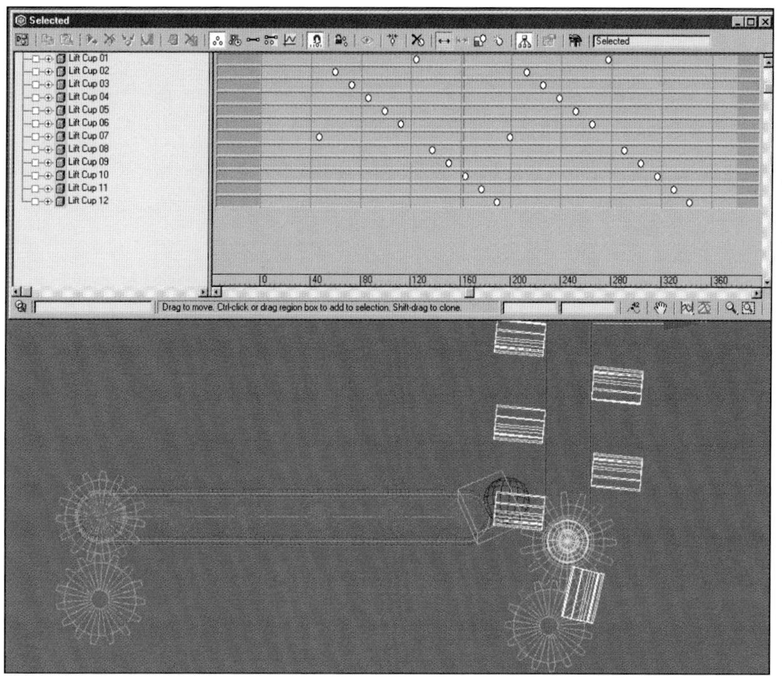

Shift keys to align a cup with the ball at frame 162.

9 You can now change the In Parameter Out of Range type to Constant. The cups retain their relative positions and do not start moving until frame 46.

If you were to pass the ball directly to the cup, it would be stuck on the edge of the cup. In order to allow the ball to settle or roll into the cup, you need to make a dummy.

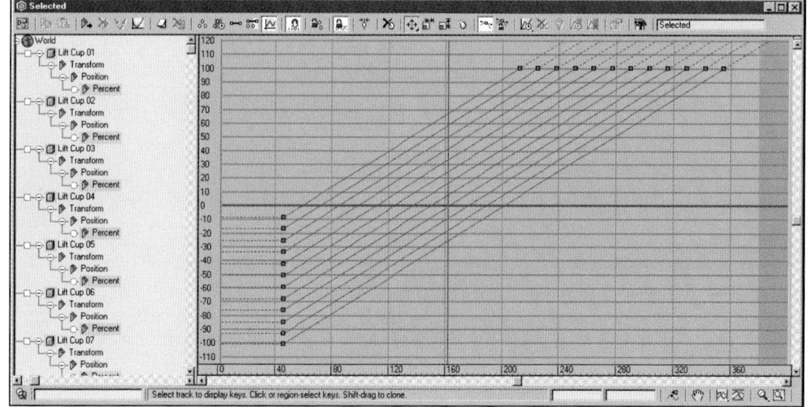

In Function Curves, you can see that the lift cups have new keys at frame 46, the middle keys have been deleted, and no movement will occur until frame 46.

Note: Because of the nature of many of these techniques, slight variations may prevent your frame numbers from matching up exactly with the frame numbers in the tutorial. If that is the case, simply add or subtract the offset and continue.

10 Make a dummy, name it **Dummy Lift**, and align it with the ball. Link it to the cup at frame 162. Set a position and a rotation key for the dummy at frame 162.

11 Select the ball and Add Link to Dummy Lift. Turn on Animate and go to frame 173. Move (or Move and Rotate) the dummy until the ball rests against the lift. Center it in the cup, and then turn off Animate.

12 Add Dummy Conveyor Belt, Lift Wheel01, and the conveyor wheels to the Conveyor Belt Assembly selection set and hide it. If you have not already done so, delete Sphere01.

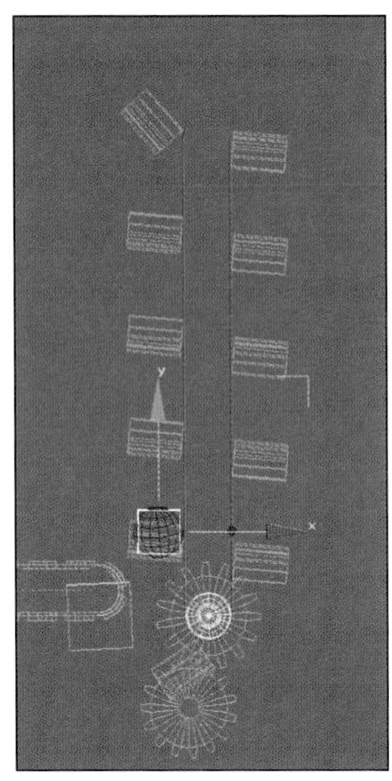

The dummy with the ball resting against the lift belt at frame 173.

Toss That Ball

This is another case in which a dummy on a path will provide more control than straight animation. Keyframing an object's position in each frame rarely yields smooth animation. By adjusting the path vertices and their handles, you can control the speed and the position *and* have a smooth animation—all at once!

1 Unhide the Grabber Assembly selection set. You should see the following objects: Line Drop From Lift, Claw Right, Claw Left, Grabber Assembly, and End Platform.

2 Create a dummy and name it **Dummy Drop From Lift**. Put a Path constraint on it and choose the Line Drop From Lift for the path. Check Follow, Allow Upside Down.

3 In the Track Bar, set its start key to **228** and its end key to **233**. Select the ball and Add Link at frame 228 to Dummy Drop From Lift.

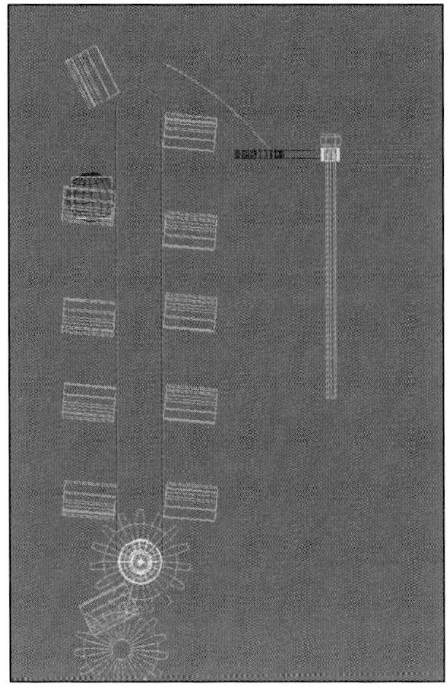

The Grabber Assembly.

4 Select the dummy. In Track View, make the curve steeper at the end to give the ball some extra speed.

5 Adjust the path's end vertex so the ball seats well in the grabber claws. Step through the frames one at a time and adjust the handles, if necessary, so the ball does not go through the cup as it is thrown out.

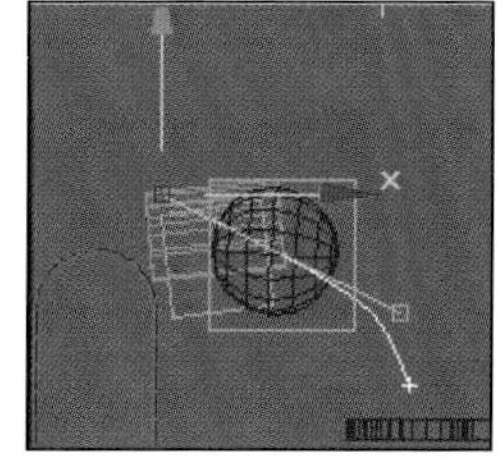

Adjust the path to seat the ball in the grabber claws.

ARTICULATE THE GRABBER CLAW ASSEMBLY

If you would like more practice manipulating position and rotation keys for objects that need to stop and start repeatedly, you can consult Bonus Project 5 on the accompanying CD-ROM to find instructions and figures for setting up a timeline and adjusting position and rotation track animation for the grabber claws. The default interpolation that max provides can often produce quite unexpected results. The bonus section deals with many of the pitfalls that can occur when you use this type of animation.

You can skip the actual animation by merging in the finished grabber assembly. Note the slight secondary motion that's added as the grabber goes up and down.

1 Delete Grabber sleeve, Claw Left, Claw Right, and End Platform. Merge the completed Grabber Assembly from the file **ArticulateTheGrabberClawAssembly.max**.

   You should see the following items: Grabber Sleeve, Claw Left, Claw Right, and End Platform.

2 You might find it necessary to shift the merged object's animation keys slightly so that the animation matches your timing. You can do this carefully in the Track Bar.

3 Add Link the ball to either of the grabber claws at frame 233 and the platform at frame 263.

4 When you are happy with the results, unhide all and make a preview of the entire animation. Adjust as necessary and add subtle nuances anywhere you want.

Let 'er Rip!

It is time to see the results of your labor. Animating this many objects is very time consuming, so the support objects, materials, and lighting have been provided for you. You might want to render the entire scene in Draft mode with the maps and shadows turned off before you include all the "bells and whistles." Now finish it up!

1 In Environment, you will notice there is a map already in place. Check Use Map. Unhide all.

Originally, there was geometry in the scene with a complex material that added a considerable amount of render time. Because there are no shadows that affect it and the camera is stationary, it is much more efficient to render it out in the scene by itself and bring it back in as a background bitmap.

The background image.

2 To add all the support objects, merge the contents of **Support.max** into your scene. Everything should be in place, but you should double check just in case you have inadvertently moved anything.

This file also contains a duplicate camera in case Camera01 has been moved.

Add the support objects.

3 The small green light on the gear housing has some noise on both Omni Green's multiplier and the Light Bulb material. Select Omni Green and in its Atmospheres & Effects rollout, click Add, highlight Volume Light, select Existing, and click OK.

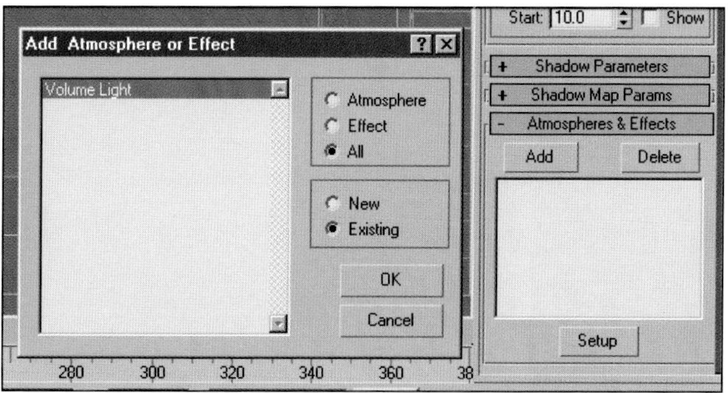

Add the existing Volume Light effect to Omni Green.

4 Open Track View, highlight Multiplier under Omni Green, and click the Copy Controller button. Under Environment/Volume Light, select Density and Paste and choose Instance. The density of the volume light now uses the same values as the light's multiplier and the Bulb material's self illumination.

5 The coil has noise on the interior vertices of its deform path. Check out Track View to see why the various "noises" do not start until frame 46 when everything gets under way.

Feel free to experiment with any other objects. There is some motion blur on the gears and the conveyor belt. You might want to add Blur to the ball or any other moving object.

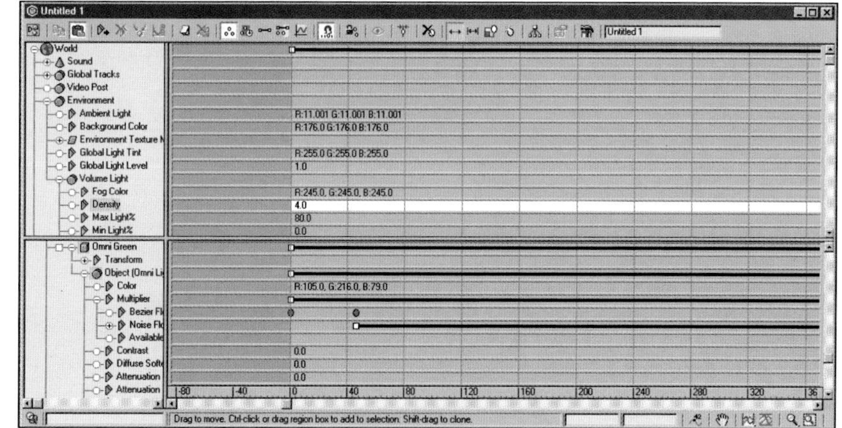

Copy Omni Green's Multiplier track to Volume Light's Density track.

6 Change the render from Draft to Production for the final render to include the mapping, shadows, and the volume light effect.

The finished file, which is named **MechanicalMachineComplete.max**, can be found on the accompanying CD-ROM.

The completed machine.

Modifications

Anyone familiar with "Rube Goldberg"-type wacky machines probably has a bunch of ideas for adding more stuff to this little animation. Here are a few suggestions to get you started thinking.

Add some spin to the ball as it hits the conveyor belt, and anywhere else you would expect to see some rotation. Remember to set a key where each rotation starts before animating the spin. The conveyor belt timing was left a bit long to enable you to add to the animation without having to change the timing. You might want to have a particle system spray the ball as it travels along the conveyor belt, animating a color change. Perhaps another assembly could swing over to affix a label to the ball as it travels past.

Alternatively, have the ball's landing on the end platform "trigger" the various components to stop moving. Hint: Do this in Track View.

Another idea would be to have a nozzle (the Hose object would be ideal here) inflate the ball when it reaches the end platform (possibly to the point of bursting).

To really get into the "Rube" spirit, you could turn the end platform into a ski jump and have the ball land in a basket that is attached to a balloon so it is joggled loose, causing the balloon to rise, flipping the toggle for a fan as it rises, which turns it on and blows the balloon towards a knife assembly that cuts the string, dumping the ball onto a plate on a scale that trips a hammer that comes down and squashes the ball flat and tips the plate, allowing the ball to slide off and land on its edge so that it rolls down a track, triggering colored lights as it goes... well you get the idea! The wackier the better, and each section can be designed to function independently or to be triggered by a previous module.

Rube actually used many non-mechanical things in his assemblies—birds, boots, tires—you name it, he made use of it! Many schools hold annual "Rube Goldberg" contests to see who can use the most steps to complete a given simple task! Board games and even computer games have been inspired by his creative inventions. An .avi of the preliminary test for this animation, RubeTea.avi, is included on the accompanying CD-ROM.

To read more about Rube Goldburg, his cartoons, and his inventions, visit **http://www.rube.iscool.net/**.

Enjoy!

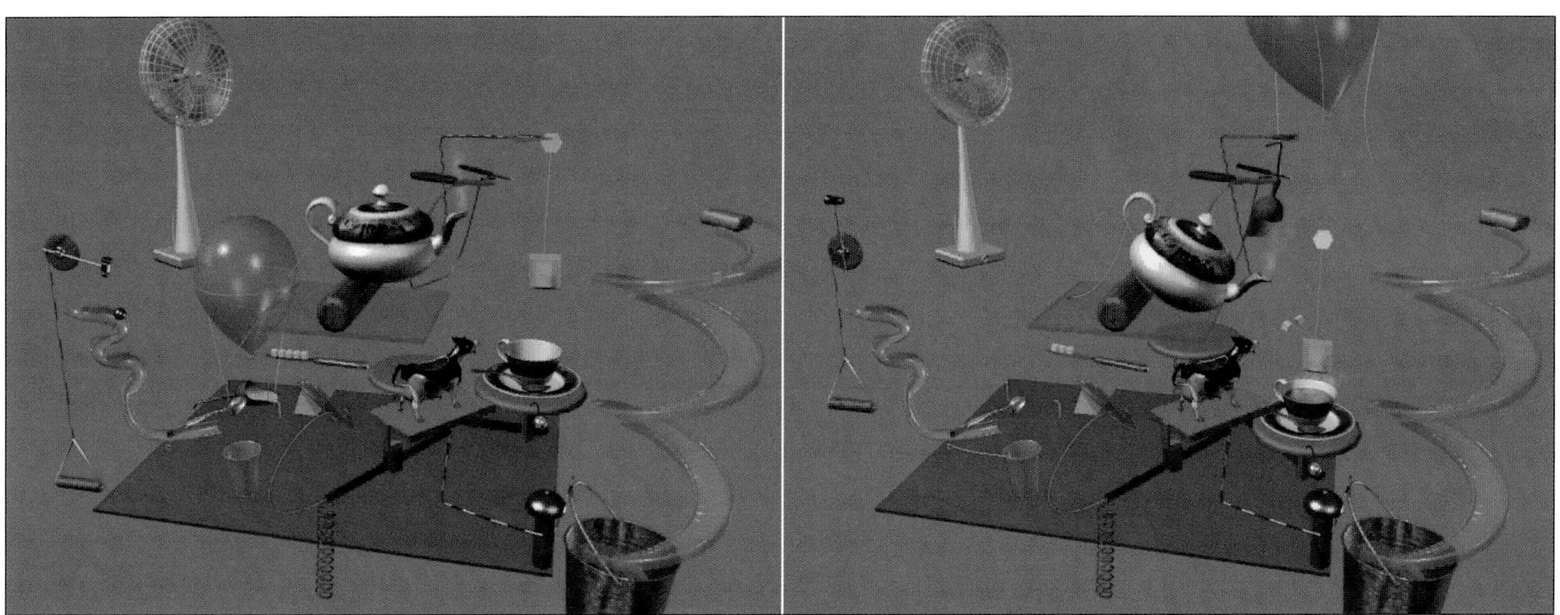

Making a cup of British tea, Rube Goldberg style.

STORMY SEA

"Crushed thirty feet upwards, the waters flashed ...like heaps of fountains, then brokenly sank in a shower of flakes, leaving the circling surface creamed like new milk ..."

—HERMAN MELVILLE, *MOBY DICK*

Create a Stormy Seascape

The successful effects film *The Perfect Storm* relied heavily on computer-generated imagery to re-create the impact of the legendary storm that formed in the North Atlantic in October of 1991. There are very specific wave dynamics that exist in heavy seas, and even though most people couldn't accurately describe them, if the effect isn't set up properly, something will appear to be wrong. The primary task is to separate the propagation of the waves through the body of water from the relatively motionless aspect of the water itself.

Project 9

Stormy Sea

by Sean Bonney

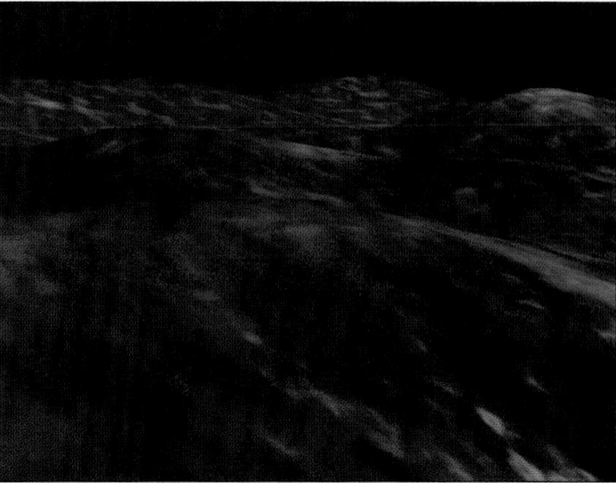

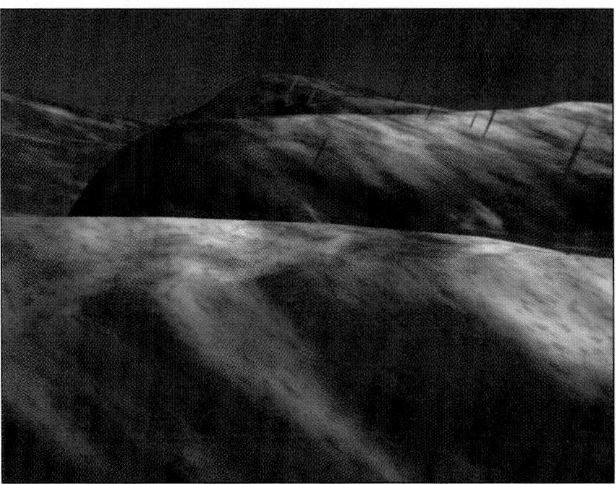

How It Works

In this tutorial, you will create a stormy seascape using displacement as the primary tool for the animation of large swells of water. You will create detailed textures in the Material Editor to both color the water appropriately and enhance the perceived surface perturbations associated with heavy weather. You will use a simple but convincing cloning trick to create a layer of floating foam. Finally, you will add atmosphere and depth to the scene with distance-based fog and particle rain.

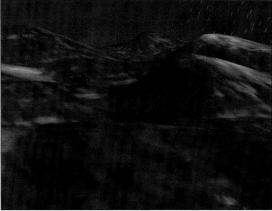

Getting Started

Start 3ds max 4 and open the file **StormySea.max** from this project's folder on the accompanying CD-ROM.

Creating a Heaving Sea

The main tool for creating the large swells found in a stormy sea will be displacement. You will animate a Noise map to serve as a blueprint for wave formation and will align the Displace gizmo in such a way as to create the expected trough/peak pattern.

1 Create a plane to serve as the basis for your seascape at X = 0, Y = 0, Z = 0. Name this object **Sea**. Set the following values:

Length: **1000**
Width: **1000**
Length Segs: **20**
Width Segs: **20**
Generate Mapping Coords: **On**

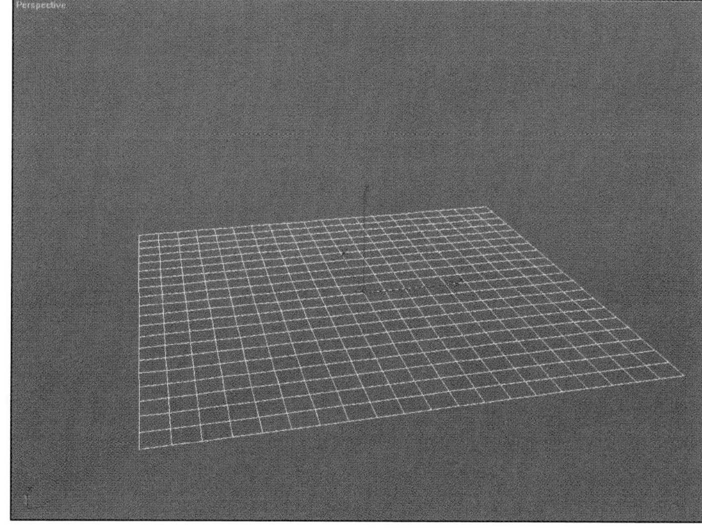

Create a plane to serve as the basis for the sea.

2 To ensure that this plane is rendered with sufficient faces, set Density to **3**.

The Render Multipliers settings enable you to specify factors by which to change key values at render time. If the entire plane is displaced to create the waves, the edges will sometimes come into view. To prevent this, select only the center portion of the object to displace.

3 Apply a Volume Select modifier. Set the following values:

Stack Selection Level: **Vertex**
Select by: **Cylinder**

Note: The Edit Mesh modifier can be used to achieve the same selection but with a higher computational cost. It is advisable to use Volume Select when possible.

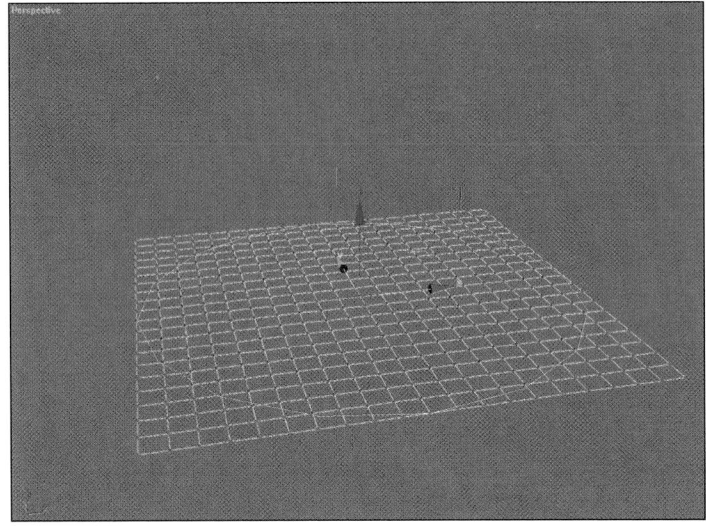

Apply a Volume Select modifier to restrict future modifiers to affect only the center of the plane.

4 Go to Gizmo/Sub-Object mode. Go to the Top viewport and Non-uniformly Scale the gizmo 85% in the XY View plane.

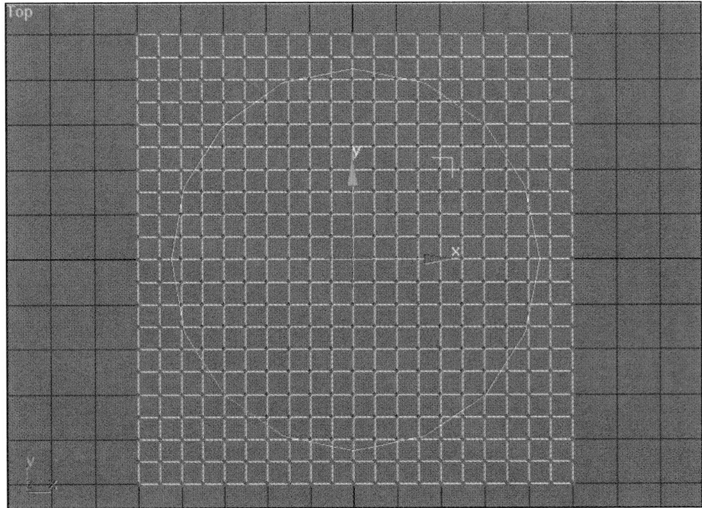

Reduce the size of the Selection gizmo to exclude the edges of the plane.

5 Exit Sub-Object mode. To gradate the effect a bit, go to the Soft Selection rollout and set the following values:

Soft Selection: **On**

Falloff: **70**

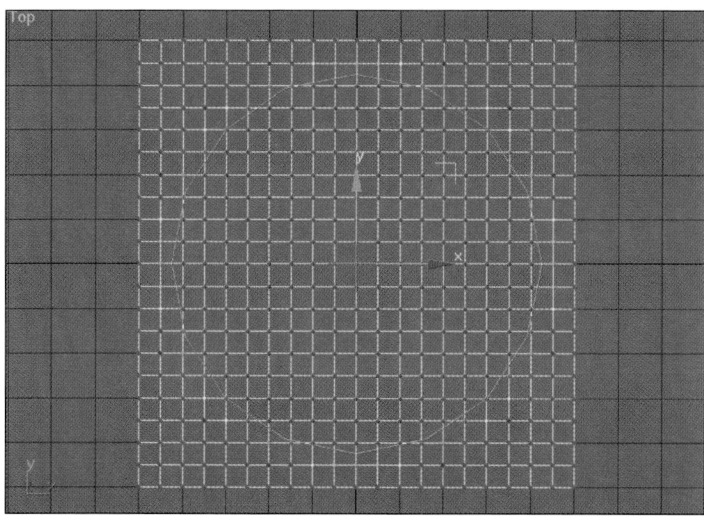

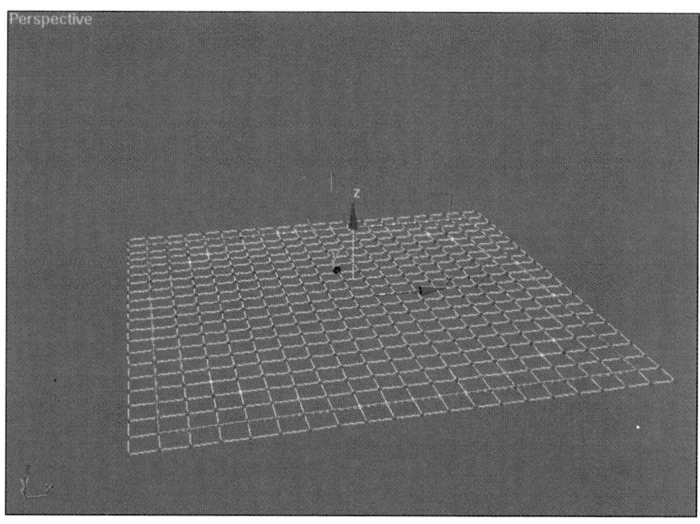

Activate Soft Selection to gradually fade the selection.

6 Apply a Displace modifier. Set Strength to **300**. In the Map area of the Modifier rollout, set Length and Width to **900**. Check the box labeled Apply Mapping to apply the Displace modifier's mapping as a UV mapping channel.

Note: Applying Displacement mapping as a UV channel can be useful when it becomes necessary to align materials with displacement.

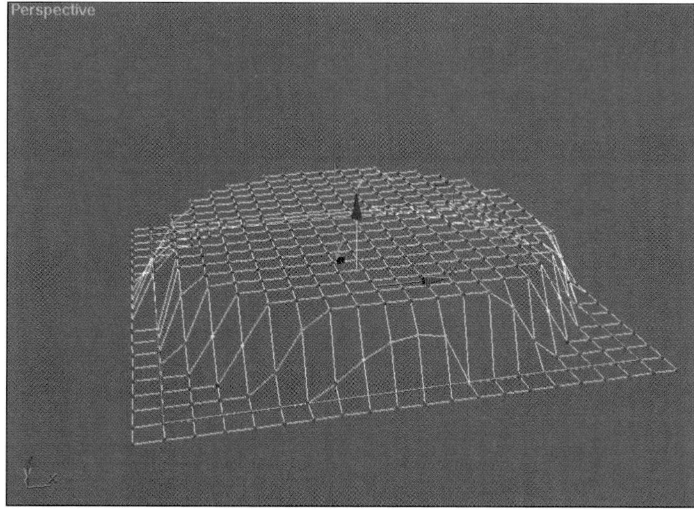

Apply a Displace modifier to create the actual waves.

7 In the Channel area, set Map Channel to **2**.

This will create a UV mapping channel separate from the first channel, which was set up in the Plane object's Creation panel. This mapping channel will also be used to apply materials based on the Displacement map.

8 Click the button labeled None under Maps and select a Noise map.

This map will be used to determine the shape of the waves and will serve as the basis for several textures.

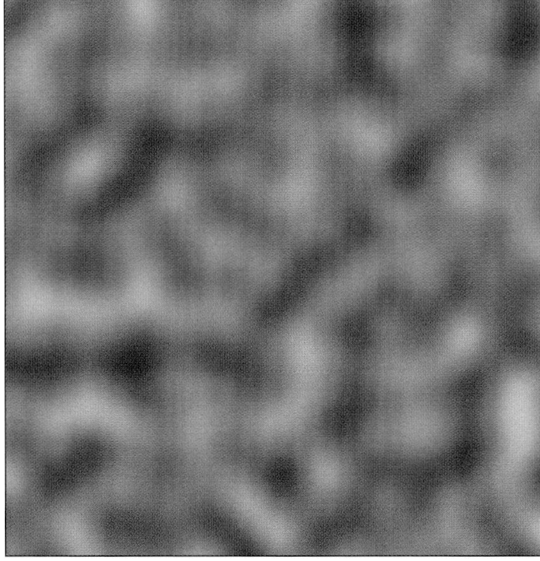
The waves will be created by a Noise map, shown here at its default settings.

9 Open the Material Editor and drag the Noise map to an unused material slot, choosing Instance as the method. Name this material **Big Waves** and set the following values to ensure that this map creates displacement according to the Displace gizmo's orientation:

Source: **Explicit Mapping Channel**
Map Channel: **2**

10 In the Noise Parameters rollout, set Size to **0.1**.

This Displacement map needs to slowly roll through the course of the animation.

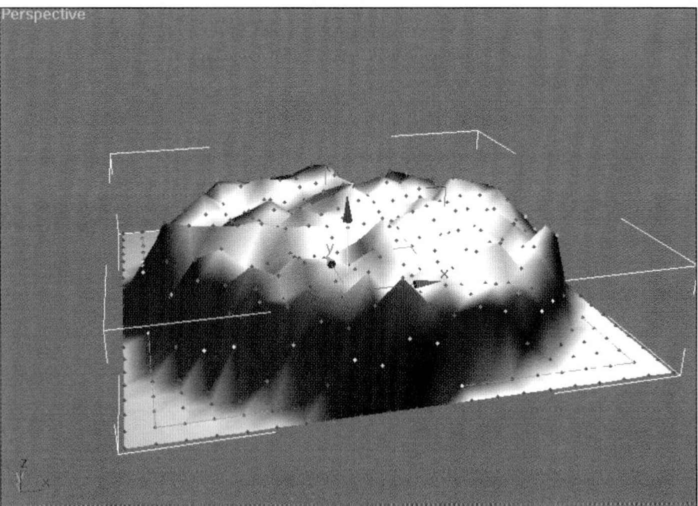

Displace the waves using the Noise map.

11 Turn Animate on, go to frame 200, and set the following values:

Coordinates
- U, Offset: **–0.05**

Noise Parameters
- Phase: **0.75**

Turn the Animate button off.

12 Go to the Camera viewport and scrub the time slider to see the waves slowly undulate.

Of course, the rendered resolution will be three times that shown in the viewport due to the Render Multiplier setting in the Plane object's Creation panel.

The waves are being displaced vertically along the View Z-axis. This is due to the Displace gizmo's alignment along the View XY plane. To create the illusion of powerful swells being propelled by wind, you need to rotate the Displace gizmo.

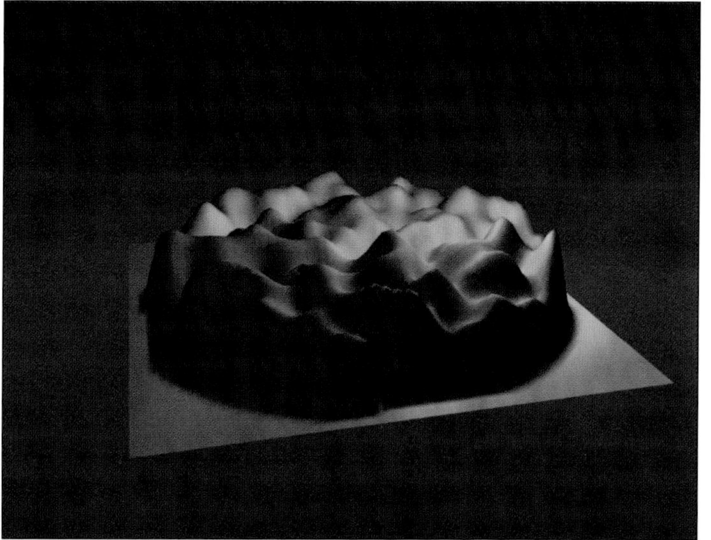

Increasing the Render Multiplier results in smoother meshes at render time without having to work with high-resolution objects in the scene.

13 Go to the Front viewport and select the Displace gizmo. Rotate the gizmo 50 degrees on the View Z-axis. The waves are now being pushed at an angle.

These wave forms will suffice for the heavy swells that define the large-scale texture of a stormy sea. The smaller-scale definition will be created in textures.

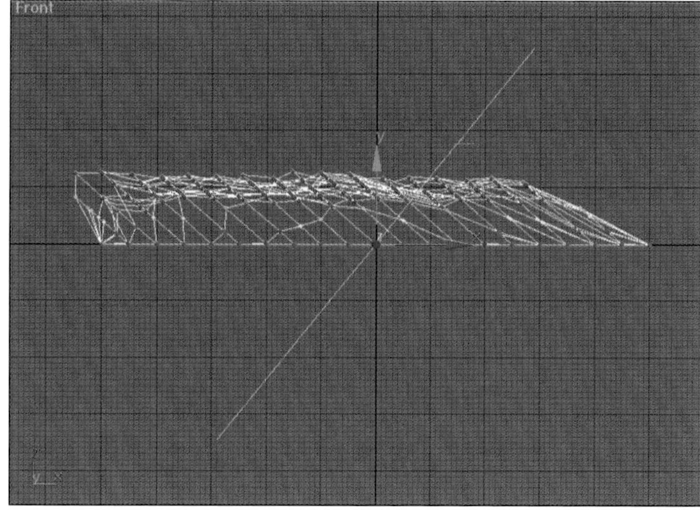

Rotate the Displace gizmo to create wave forms that appear to be "pushed" across the sea.

Texture the Sea

The textures used to enhance an effect are obviously crucial. Textures become even more important when they are used to create a level of surface reality to compliment the actual surface's geometric characteristics, as is the case with the foamy crests and bumps you will set up in this section.

1 Select an unused material slot and name it **Waves**. Assign this material to the Sea object. Set the following values in the Basic Parameters rollout:

Self Illumination: **25**
Specular Highlights
  Specular Level: **40**
  Glossiness: **40**

Note: Later in this section, a custom Specular map will be created. However, it will only partially determine specular values in this material.

Create a shiny, subtly self-illuminating material as the basis for the water texture.

2 Assign a Mix map to the Diffuse channel; name it **Wave Diffuse Color**.

In this channel, you will mix a map for the overall color with a map for the foam typically found along the wave crests.

3 Assign a Noise map to the Color #1 slot and name it **Wave Base Color**. Set the following values in the Coordinates rollout:

Source: **Explicit Mapping Channel**
Map Channel: **1**

Note: The UV channel for this map is the original mapping set up in the Creation panel, as opposed to the mapping created within the Displace modifier. Also, it is necessary to choose Explicit Mapping Channel whenever UV mapping channels are being used.

4 In the Tiling area, set the following values:

Tiling
U: **0.5**
V: **2.0**

Stretching the map with these values compensates for the distortion created by the Displace modifier. This map will be a small-scale turbulence map.

5 Set the color distribution weighted slightly toward the Color #1 slot. Set the following values in the Noise Parameters rollout:

Noise Type: **Turbulence**
Size: **0.025**
Noise Threshold
Low: **0.2**

6 Set Color #1 to **R 20, G 35, B 45**.

This map will be colored with deep sea colors, along with a subtle mix of bright white to support the illusion of random crests of foam.

7 Assign a map to the Color #2 slot. While in the Material/Map Browser, select Browse From Mtl Editor. Clone the Wave Base Color map as a Copy. Remaining in the Color #2 slot, rename this map **Foam**.

The values in the Coordinates area can remain unchanged, ensuring that this map tiles the same way its parent map does.

Create a blue-green Noise map to provide the overall sea texture.

8 Set the following values in the Noise Parameters rollout:

Noise Type: **Fractal**
Size: **0.02**

Noise Threshold
High: **0.75**
Low: **0.4**

Color #1: **R 45, G 60, B 60**
Color #2: **White**

This will create a mostly sea-green map with small touches of white.

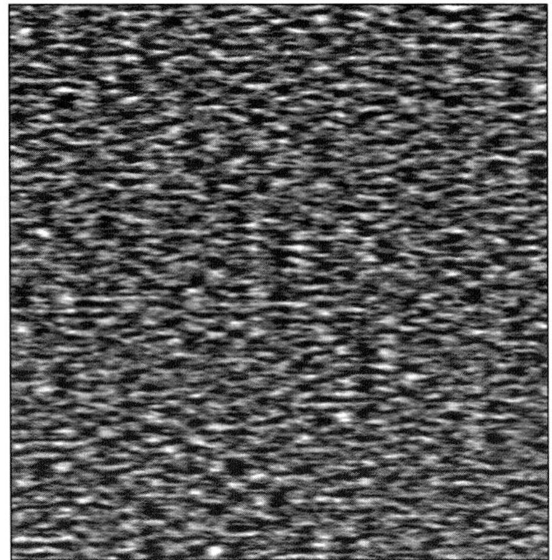

This sea map, flecked with foam, will be applied in select areas of the parent Noise map.

Combining the two Noise maps, shown here at the Wave Base Color level, adds a level of detail.

9 Go up to the Wave Diffuse Color map. Assign a Speckle map to the Color #2 slot and name it **Foam**. This map will provide a bubbly white texture for the wave crests. Set the following values:

Source: **Explicit Mapping Channel**

Speckle Parameters
Size: **0.01**
Color #1: **R 85, G 100, B 115**
Color #2: **R 215, G 235, B 235**

This bubbly blue-white map will create the foam usually seen along wave crests.

Note: The Material/Map Navigator is a very handy and quick method for moving within a material hierarchy. Additionally, it displays an easy-to-read summary of the selected material.

10 Go up the Wave Diffuse Color slot and drag the Big Waves map created earlier for the Displace modifier to the Mix Amount slot. Use Copy as the method of cloning. Name the new map **Wave Color Mix Amt**.

This map will determine which areas of the material are colored with the base color and which with the foam color.

Using a modified clone of the Displacement map enables you to mix Diffuse maps based on wave height so that only the highest areas of the sea will have the foam color applied.

11 In the Wave Color Mix Amt map, set the following values:

Source

Map Channel: **1**

Noise Threshold

Low: **0.55**

Raising the Low threshold value reduces the amount of the Color #2 value applied. Color #2 represents the Foam map and will only be applied when the Noise map is at its very highest value.

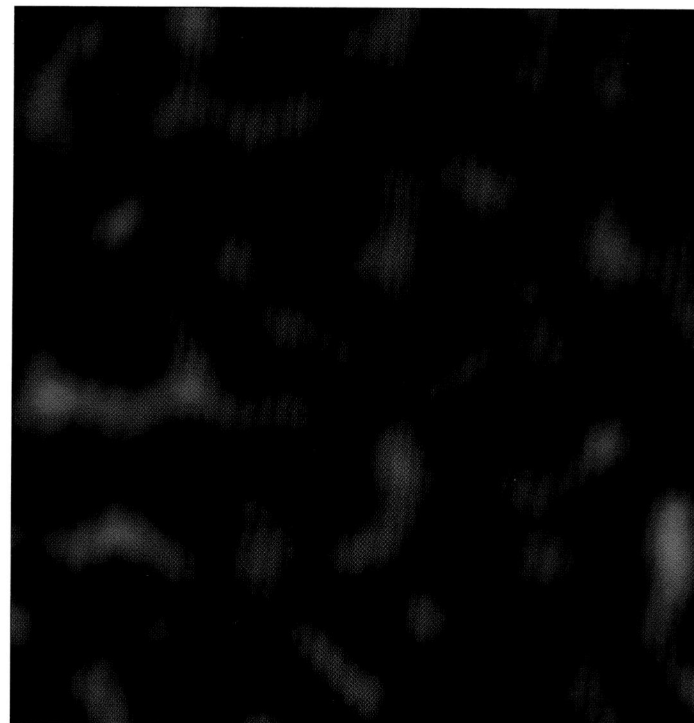

Modify a clone of the Displacement map to serve as a guide for mixing wave textures with foam textures.

12 Go up to the Wave Diffuse Color map. In the Mixing Curve area, set the following values:

Use Curve: **On**

Transition zone

Upper: **0.4**

Lower: **0**

Lowering the Upper transition value forces the maps to mix along a much steeper curve so that the boundary between the two textures will be sharp and closely aligned with the transition to the highest level of the waves.

13 Go up to the root Waves material and set the Bump channel amount to **25**. Assign a Speckle map to the Bump channel.

This small-scale Bump map will create the small peaks and valleys that are created on the surface of water by gusts of wind.

14 Name this map **Waves Small Bumps**. Set the following values:

Coordinates

Source: **Explicit Mapping Channel**

Speckle Parameters

Size: **0.35**

Color #1: **White**

Color #2: **R 40, G 40, B 40**

15 Go up to the root Waves material and set the Specular Level channel amount in the Maps rollout to **50**. Drag the Waves Small Bumps map to the Specular channel, using Copy as the method.

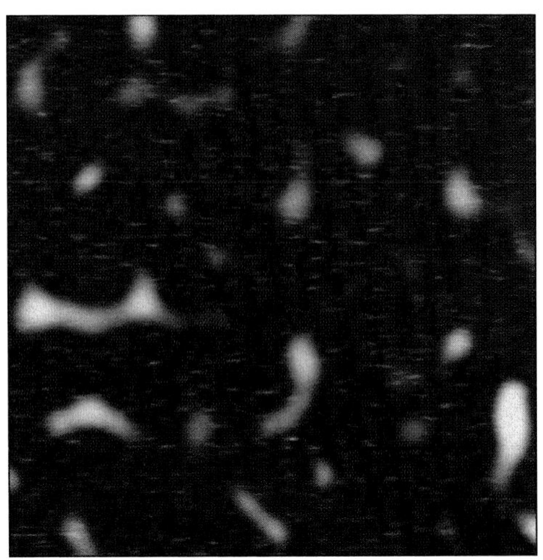

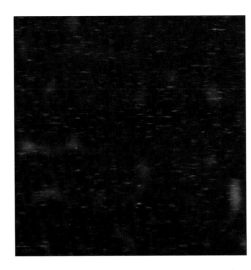

Lowering the transition value for the Mix map intensifies the contrast between the mixed maps.

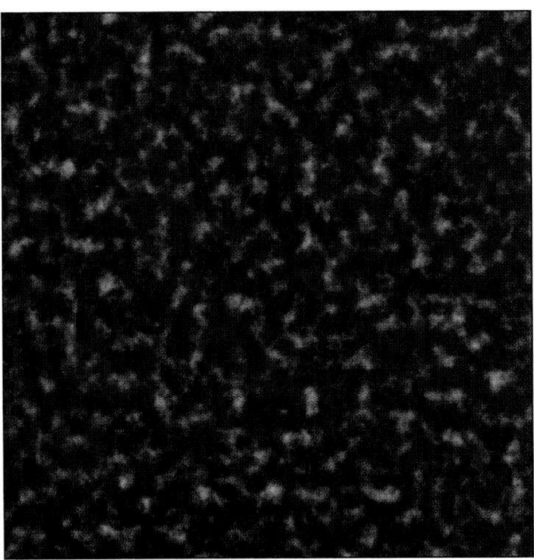

This Speckle map will create the surface texture of the sea and represent the small-scale waves.

Note: Cloning between the Bump and Specular Level (and occasionally Glossiness) channels is a common method for enhancing the "shine" factor in a material. This method makes it easy for the portions of a surface pushed highest by the Bump channel to also be the shiniest.

16 Name the new map **Waves Specular**. You can keep the cloned values with these exceptions:

Color #1: **R 140, G 140, B 140**
Color #2: **Black**

It is necessary to tone down the color values because the colors used to create strong distinctions for the Bump channel would be far too bright for the Specular channel, resulting in a high-gloss surface.

Clone the Bump channel to the Specular channel to enhance the perceived surface texture of the sea.

These textures go a long way toward creating the convincing illusion of a stormy sea. It is important to note that the Displacement map was used in giving the material an additional level of realism.

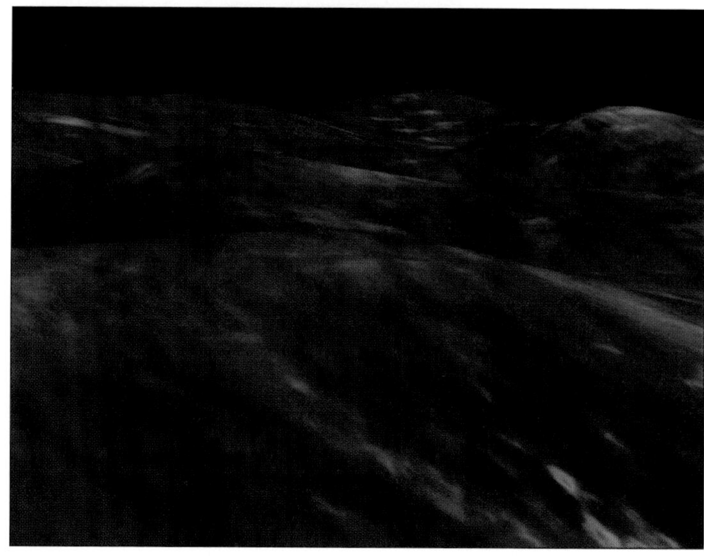

The sea's texture, as shown from the camera's perspective.

Add a Layer of Foam

The surface of a large body of water can become quite messy and frothy under the influence of high winds and large waves. Foam is churned up by the water's action and moves about on the surface seemingly independent of the motion of larger swells. In this section, you will use a relatively simple but effective method to create this layer of froth.

1 Go to the Camera viewport, select the Sea object, and clone it using Copy as the method. Name the clone **Foam** and move it one unit on the View Z-axis so that it rests just above the sea.

In terms of geometry, this object will behave exactly as the sea does, but an entirely different material will be used to give it the appearance of floating, shifting foam.

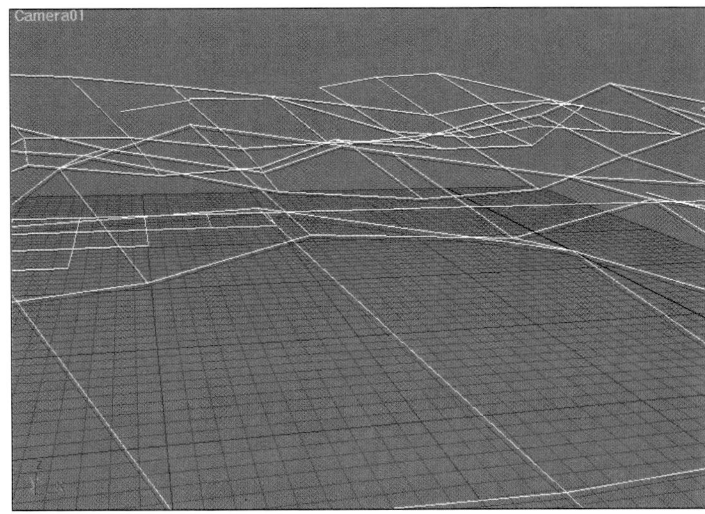

Create a clone of the Sea object to serve as a layer of foam.

2 Go to the Material Editor, select an unused material slot, and name it **Foam**. Assign this material to the Foam object. Set the following values:

Diffuse: **R 150, G 185, B 210**
Glossiness: **0**

The main function of this material will be to apply opacity to the diffuse color. Assign a Noise map to the Opacity slot.

Note: By default, the Ambient and Diffuse colors should be locked. Usually, the only time these colors are set separately is to tweak the material color that appears in shadowed areas.

3 Name this new map **Foam Opacity**. Set the following values:

Coordinates

Source: **Explicit Mapping Channel**

Noise Parameters

Noise Type: **Fractal**

Size: **0.075**

Noise Threshold

High: **1**

Low: **0.27**

This high-contrast map will be used like a mask to randomize the distribution of a smaller-scale Noise map. In this way, the foam will not appear to remain absolutely constant as it flows across the waves.

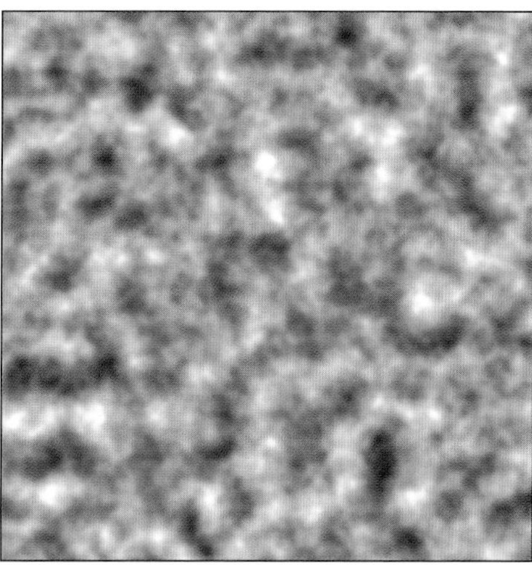

This large-scale Noise map will determine where the foam is applied, as opposed to determining the actual shape of the foam.

4 Apply a Noise map to the Color #1 slot. Name this map **Foam Opacity Detail**. Set the following details:

Coordinates

Source: **Explicit Mapping Channel**

Noise Parameters

Noise Type: **Fractal**

Size: **0.01**

Noise Threshold

High: **0.65**

Low: **0.5**

Create a small-scale Noise map to control the shape of the foam, as masked by the parent map.

5 This map needs to be very dark so as to only add subtle touches of foam. Set the following color values:

Color #1: **Black**

Color #2: **R 55, G 55, B 55**

6 Turn the Animate button on and go to frame 200. Set the following keys in the Foam Opacity Detail map:

Offset

U: **–0.1**

Noise Parameters

Phase: **0.3**

This will give the proper appearance. The foam needs to flow slowly against the waves, cycling in phase as well.

7 Go up a level to the Foam Opacity map and set the following keys:

Offset

U: **–0.25**

Noise Parameters

Phase: **0.25**

These two maps will cycle slowly as they pan across the waves' surface. Turn the Animate button off.

By adding this semitransparent layer of foam, the illusion of proper wave mechanics is supported. The waves should appear to be propagating in force without necessarily moving the water. Anyone who has dropped a cork or similar object into heavy swells can attest that the cork, along with the surrounding water, rises and falls as the waves' energy passes.

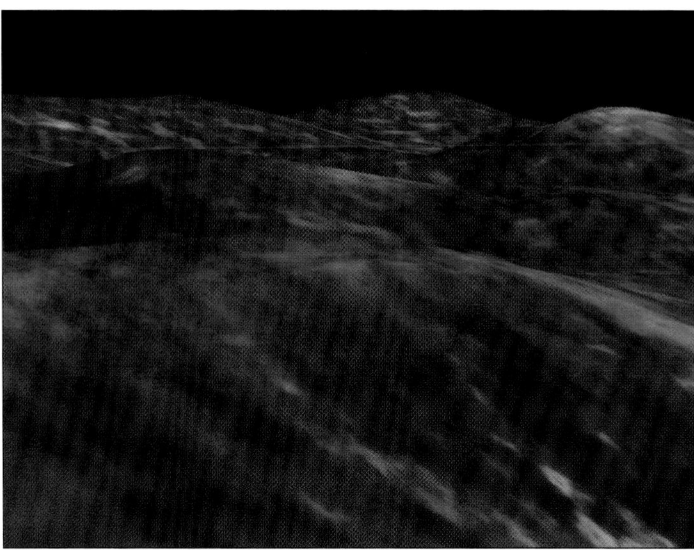

The Foam object adds an interesting dynamic to the surface of the water, especially as it animates.

Note: If you want to preview how the material will animate, the Create Material Preview function in the Material Editor is a very handy tool for this purpose. You will find a rendered preview of the waves material in this project's folder on the accompanying CD; it is called **Waves Preview.avi**.

Add Atmosphere to the Storm

A scene like this seems a little bare without the swirling fog, clouds, and dark skies associated with stormy weather. In this section, you will add an Environment map and distance-based fog.

1 Open the Environment dialog. Click the Environment Map button in the Background area and assign a Gradient map.

2 Drag the map to an unused slot in the Material Editor, using Instance as the method of cloning. Name this map **Sky Gradient** and set the following color values:

Gradient Parameters

Color #1: **R 15, G 20, B 35**

Color #2: **R 40, G 95, B 95**

Color #3: **R 40, G 55, B 80**

Note: The purpose of this map is to provide an overall color for the sky. If it appears a bit too intense at this stage, that is acceptable because fog will be layered over it later in this section.

3 To add a bit of swirl to this map, set the following values in the Noise area under Gradient Parameters:

Amount: **0.2**

Size: **2.0**

This map needs to cycle slowly as if it were being pushed by the wind.

Use a Gradient to provide a suitably swirled and gloomy background.

4 Turn the Animate button on, go to frame 200, and set the Noise Phase to **0.35**. Turn the Animate button off.

The fog for this scene will be based on the distance from the camera.

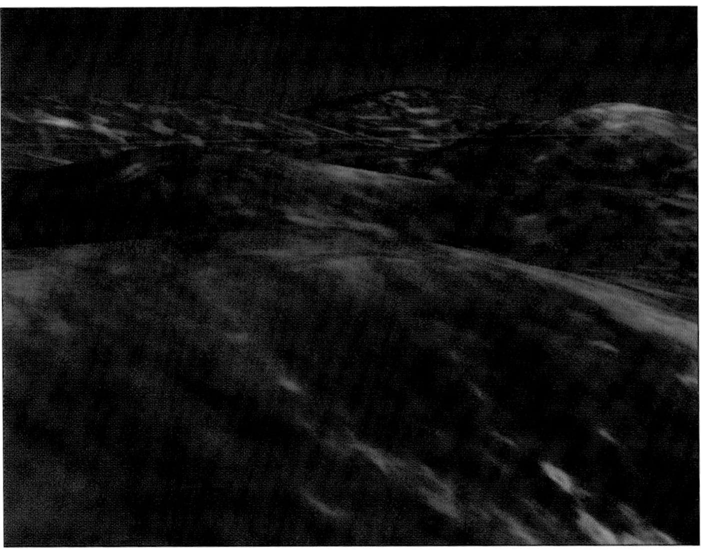

An appropriate background texture adds a subtle touch to the scene.

5 Select the camera and go to the Modifier panel. To set the fog range close to the camera and extending beyond the limit of the waves, set the following values:

Environment Ranges

Near Range: **50**

Far Range: **1000**

6 Go back to the Environment dialog and add a Fog effect. Set the Fog Color to **R 50, G 75, B 85**.

Note: A good general rule for fog color is to pick a color that is similar to the background colors and general palette. For low-light scenes, try lowering the Saturation and Value. Conversely, scenes with bright lighting might call for brighter fog colors.

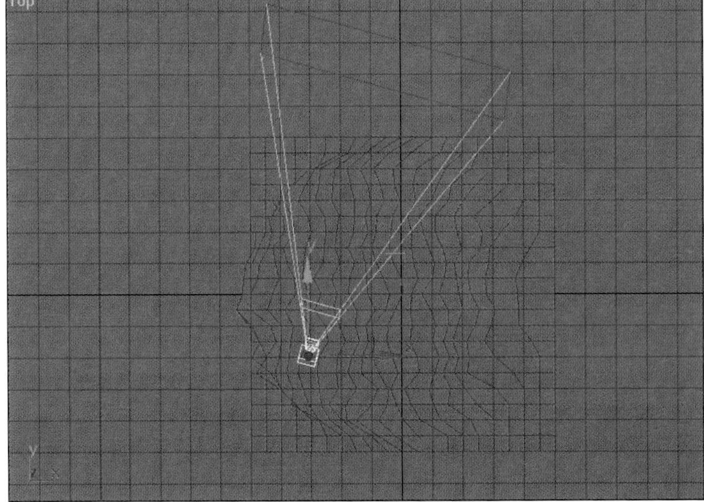

The camera's Environment Ranges will determine at what distance the fog is applied, shown here with Show checked.

7 In the Standard area, set the following values so that the fog will be nearly transparent at the camera's Near Environment Range and will be at 90% Opacity at the Far Range:

Exponential: **On**
Near%: **15**
Far%: **90**

> **Note:** The Exponential check box increases the sampling rate to avoid banding. This should only be used when applying fog in a scene that includes transparent objects.

8 Click the Environment Opacity Map button and assign a Gradient map. Check the Use Map button.

The degree of opacity will be determined by an Environment map before the preceding percentages are applied.

9 Drag the new map to an unused Material Editor slot and name it **Camera Fog Opacity**. To apply this image to the scene using shrink-wrap style mapping, set the following values:

Coordinates
    Environ: **On**
    Mapping: **Shrink-wrap Environment**

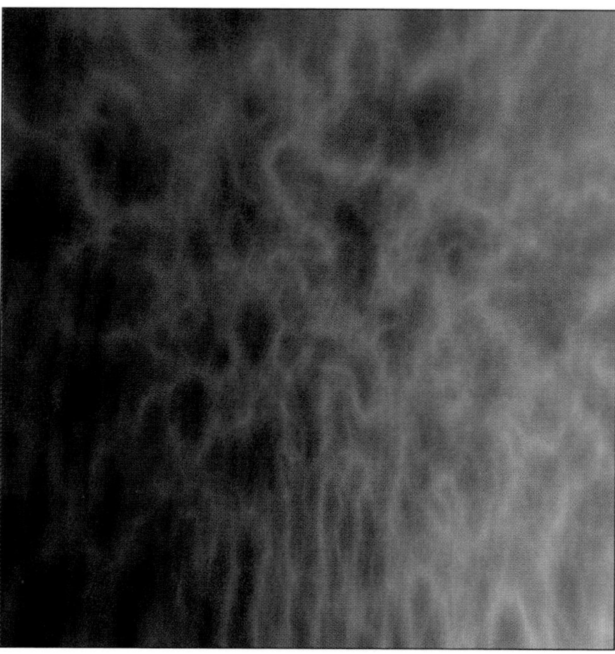

The Opacity map will cycle across the scene similarly to the Sky Gradient background map, creating a fog effect.

10 Set the following noise values in the Gradient Parameters rollout to add some character to this body of fog:

Noise
    Amount: **0.35**
    Type: **Turbulence**
    Size: **0.75**

This Opacity map will be animated to cycle across the scene in a style similar to the Sky Gradient background map.

11 Turn the Animate button on, go to frame 200, and set Noise Phase to **0.7**. Turn the Animate button off.

Fog is being used in this scene to represent a specific meteorological event. Scenes that don't depict heavy weather can benefit from fog as well. Even relatively clear air contains a large amount of suspended dust and water vapor that contributes to distance haze.

The addition of distance-based fog adds appropriate weather and a moody depth to the scene.

Make It Rain

The final bit of weather to add to this scene is a quick burst of rain. The particles representing individual drops of rain will be spawned from a moving emitter, which will be keyed to sweep through the camera's field of view. This will add to the illusion of stormy weather and will reinforce the depth of the scene as rain sweeps across the waves.

1 Go to the Top viewport and create a plane at X = 330, Y = 345, Z = 360. Name this object **Rain Emitter**. Set the following values:

Length: **250**
Width: **400**
Length Segs: **1**
Width Segs: **1**

This mesh will serve as an emitter for the rain particles. Unlike other emitter types, the actual vertex count does not factor into particle spawning.

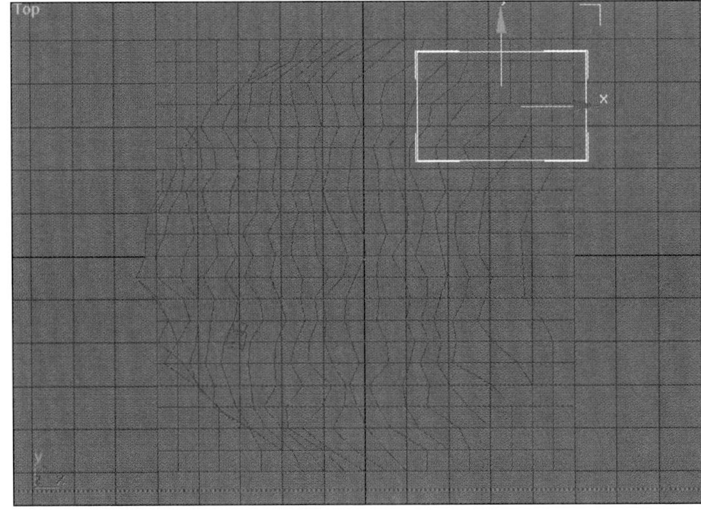

Create a plane to serve as a particle emitter.

2 Right-click the Rain Emitter object, select Properties, and clear the Renderable check box to ensure that this object does not inadvertently render. Go to frame 200 and turn the Animate button on. Move the object to X = 20, Y = –30, Z = 360.

This will move the rain through the scene.

Note: The display of an object's trajectory can be activated either through the Display Properties rollout in the Display panel or by right-clicking on the object, opening its Properties dialog, and checking the appropriate box in the Display Properties area.

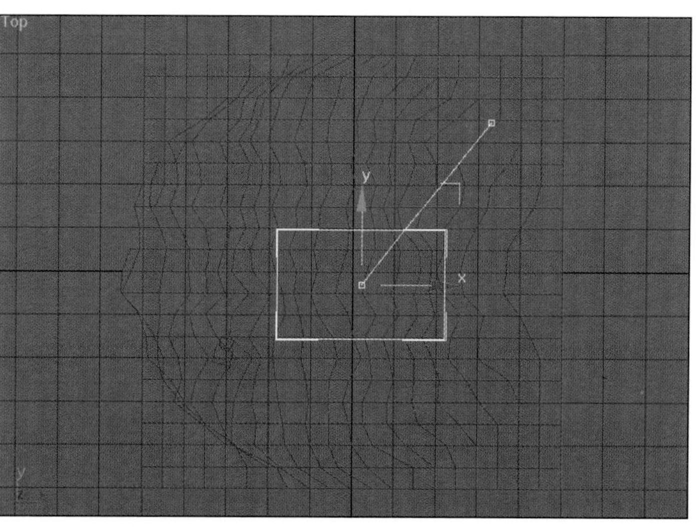

Key the emitter to move across the scene, shown here in Trajectory mode.

3 Create a PCloud particle system. The position of the icon is not significant.

4 In the Basic Parameters rollout, click the Pick Object button and choose the Rain Emitter object.

Note: Under Viewport Display, you might want to reduce Percentage of Particles to a low amount (such as 10%), depending on computer speed available.

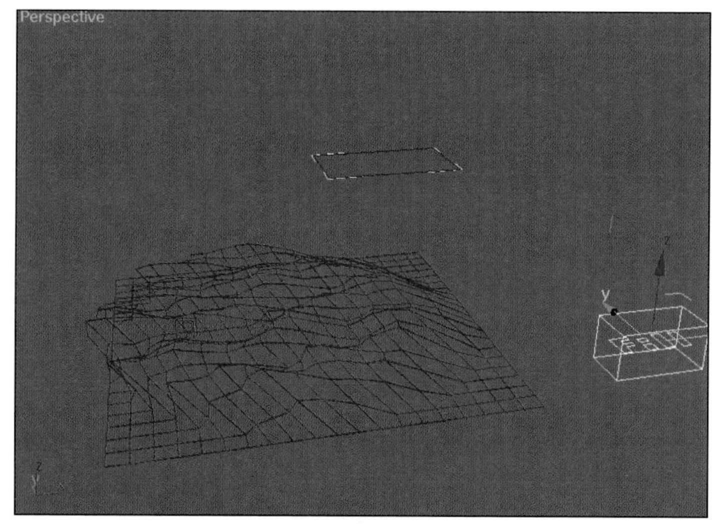

Create a PCloud particle system to control the properties of the spawned particles.

5 Go to the Particle Generation rollout and set the following values to generate a constant stream of particles dropping at a steep angle through the scene:

Particle Quantity

Use Rate: **55**

Particle Motion

Speed: **20**

Variation: **20**

Direction Vector: **On**

X: **–0.5**

Y: **0**

Z: **–1**

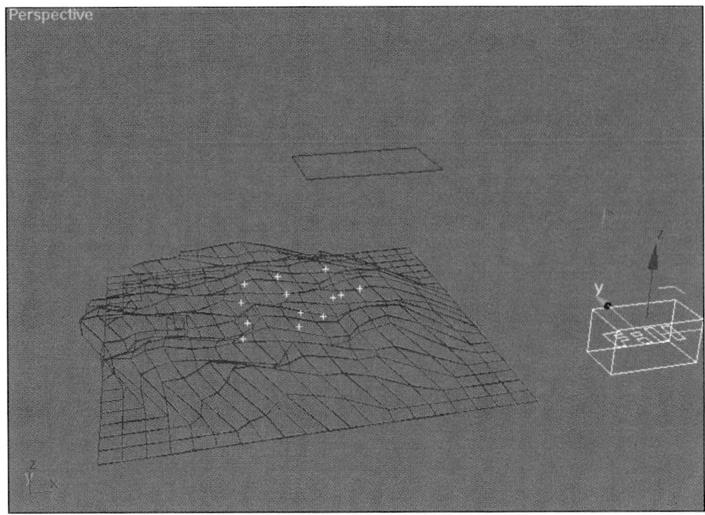

Set the Direction Vector to send the particles through the camera's window at a steep angle, shown at frame 25.

6 Set the following values in the Particle Timing area:

Emit Stop: **200**

Display Until: **200**

Life: **20**

This will ensure that particles die out soon after passing through the water (to save on computation) and that they are displayed throughout the length of the scene.

7 Set Particle Size to **5**. Then go to the Particle Type rollout and set the Standard Particles type to Facing.

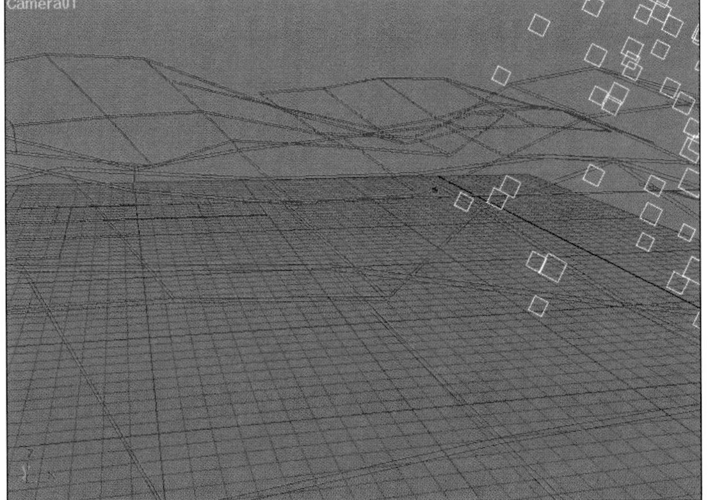

Use Facing particles to represent the rain.

Note: Facing particles render more quickly than mesh or MetaParticles and are a good choice when flat, decorative (as opposed to dimensional) sprite effects are called for.

8 Go to the Mat'l Mapping and Source area and click the Get Material From button to assign the PCloud icon's material (created later in this section) to the rain particles.

9 Select an unused slot in the Material Editor, name it **Rain**, and assign it to the PCloud icon. Set the following values:

Face Map: **On**

Diffuse Color: **R 170, G 190, B 195**

Specular Highlights

Specular Level: **0**

Glossiness: **0**

10 Assign a Gradient map to the Opacity channel and name it **Rain Opacity**. To compress this gradient horizontally, set U, Tiling to **12**.

The main function of this map will be in the Opacity channel, where a gradient will be used to create the illusion of streaking rain drops.

PCloud emitters are very useful when an overall emission area is needed (for example, in rain, snow, or vapor that is created from a limited area).

Note: Face mapping is the preferred mapping type for Facing particles because it applies the material evenly across the particle without tiling or distortion.

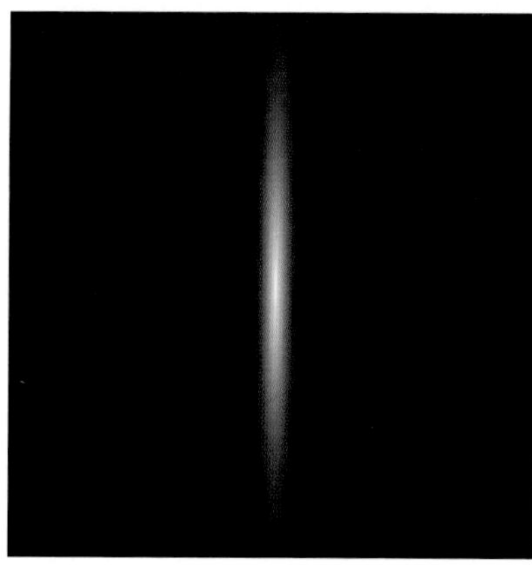

Use Facing particles to represent the rain.

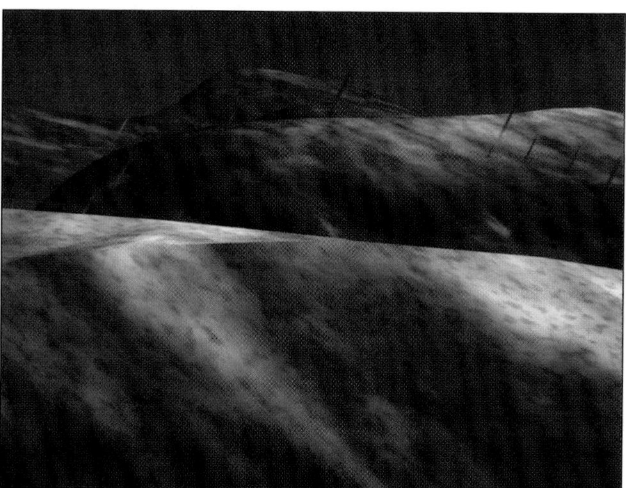

The rain adds both realism and depth to the scene, shown here at frame 200.

Modifications

It would be a simple matter to make this watery surface more detailed. By increasing the resolution of the original plane (in conjunction with a higher Render Density Multiplier) to provide a sufficiently dense mesh, it should be possible to use the Bump channel created in this tutorial as an additional Displacement map.

By using Atmospheric Apparati to contain fog, specific clouds could be keyed to pass through the scene, perhaps in conjunction with the movement of other objects such as ships.

The rain burst could be enhanced with the use of Object Mutations and an Object Deflector so that rain drops could spawn a splash effect upon impact with the sea. Note that the rain drops would need to be represented by Instanced Geometry in that case.

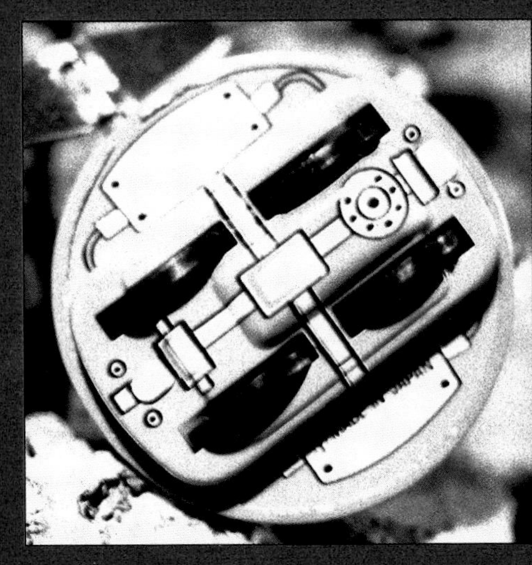

GAME TEXTURES

"Pieces of ruin...rusty struts that had held a bath, a line of tiles above the struts, a fireplace with a metal cowl, collages of layers of wallpaper. Fallen slabs of floor...a thick rusty girder protruded for yards...Sharp bricks...piled on the girder...Something lay under the bricks. Eyes. A face."

—RAMSEY CAMPBELL, *THE DOLL WHO ATE HIS MOTHER*

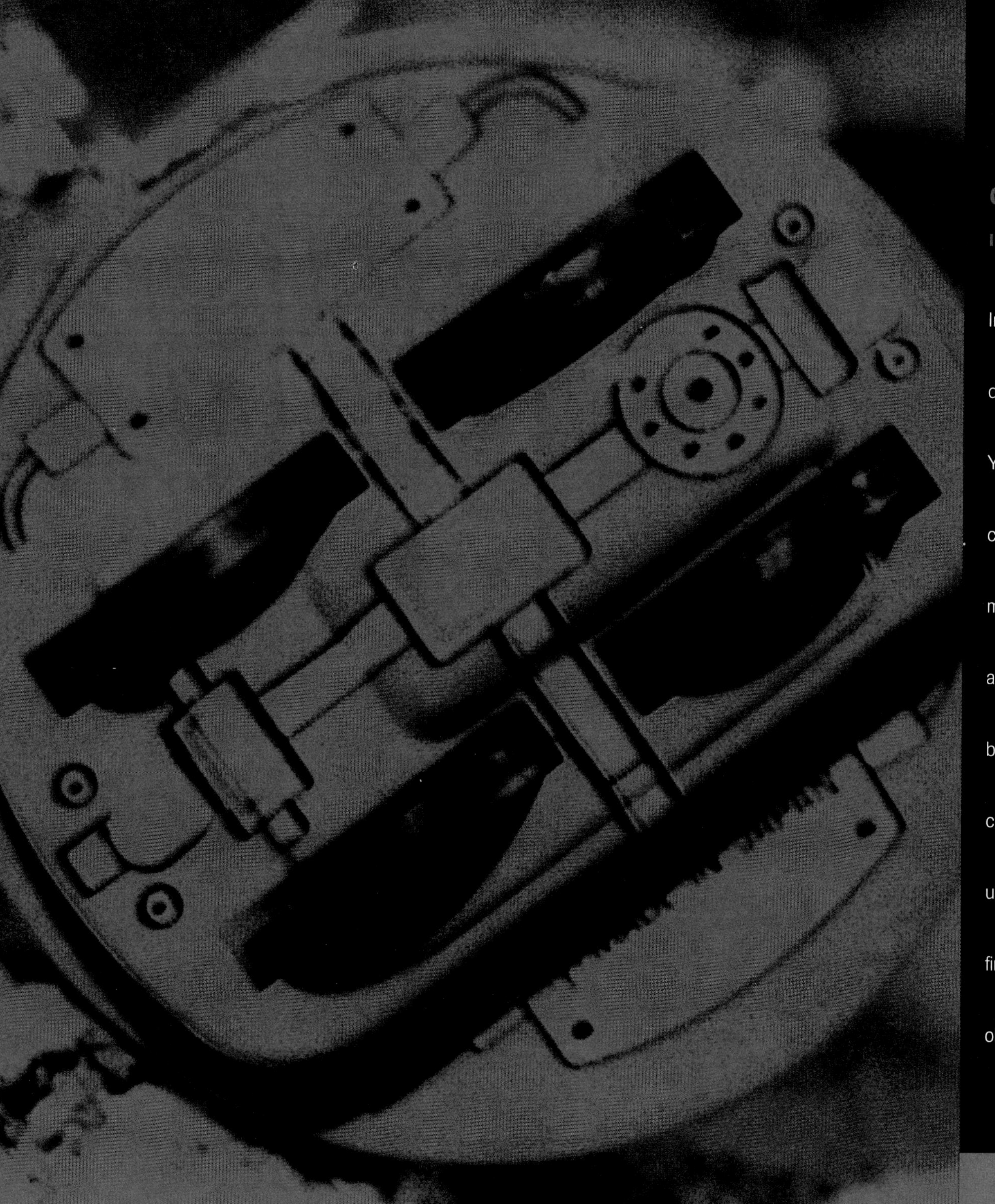

Create Custom Textures for Use in Games

In this tutorial, you will create a texture designed for use in current 3D game engines. You will take advantage of Material Editor capabilities to construct a detailed, layered material and employ some simple geometry to add complexity. You will light the texture to bring out the three-dimensionality of it without creating distracting hotspots. Finally, you will use an exterior image-editing application to fine-tune the texture and blend out any obvious seams.

Project 10

Game Textures

by Sean Bonney

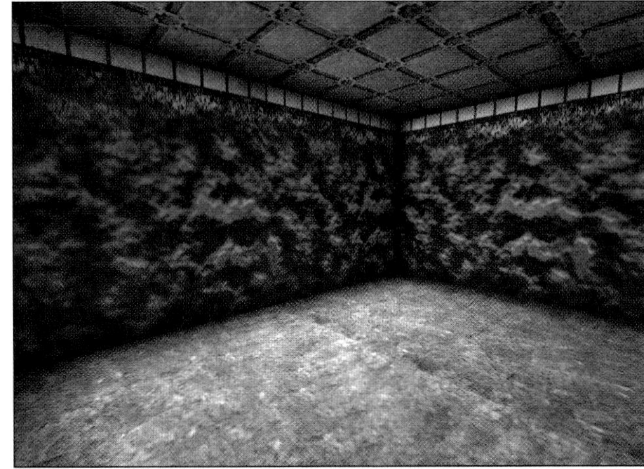

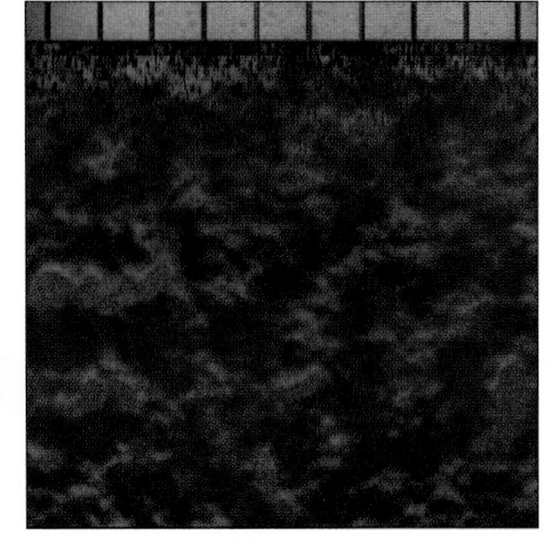

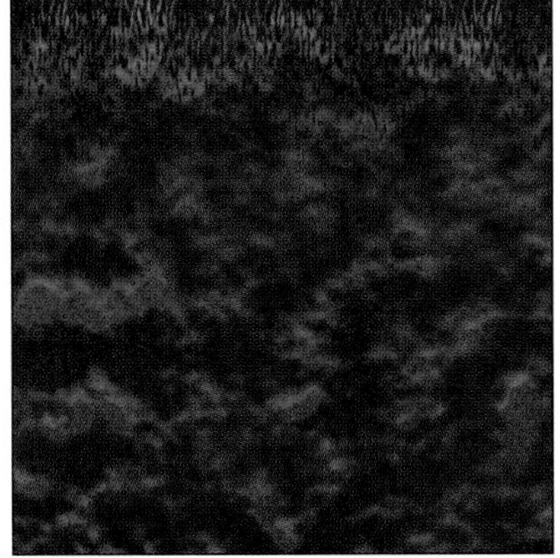

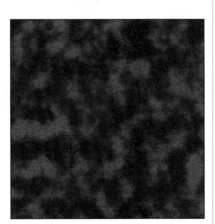

Getting Started

Start 3ds max 4 and open the file **GameTextures.max** from this project's folder on the accompanying CD-ROM.

A few scene objects have been provided for you, but initially you will work in the Material Editor.

Creating a Rusty Metal Texture in the Material Editor

3ds max 4's Material Editor is a very powerful tool for creating custom textures; you can create textures for game use almost without leaving the Material Editor. In this section, you will create a complex, realistic-looking material.

1 Open the Material Editor, select a new material, and name it **Old Metal**.

2 Set the Bump Amount to **35**, assign a Noise map to the Bump channel, and set the following values:

Source: **Explicit Map Channel**

Noise Parameters

Noise Type: **Fractal**

Noise Threshold

High: **0.65**

Low: **0.4**

Size: **0.1**

Note: The explicit mapping channel isn't strictly necessary when creating texture to be applied to simple, nonanimated objects. The primary benefit of explicit mapping is that materials will "stick" to objects as they deform or animate. However, explicit mapping makes it much easier to animate scene objects, if necessary, without the extensive rescaling required when converting from Object or World space. For this reason, it is a good practice to employ explicit mapping whenever three-dimensional mapping isn't required.

3 Name this map **Metal Bump #1**. These settings will result in a pitted Bump map of medium density. Moving the Noise Threshold settings close together means the boundary between the Color #1 and Color #2 areas will be sharp, simulating a layered material.

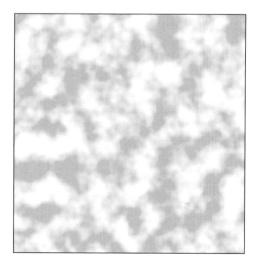

Create a high-contrast Bump map that will serve as a basis for this new material. Here it is shown rendered directly from the Material Editor.

Note: It is highly recommended that you name every material and map you create with a meaningful, unique name. This will facilitate navigating through the material hierarchy as well as finding specific maps to clone.

4 Set Color #1 to **R 196, G 196, B 196**. This will be a relatively high area of bump relief.

5 Assign another Noise map to the Color #2 Maps slot. Name this new map **Metal Bump #2**. Set the following values:

Source: **Explicit Map Channel**

Noise Parameters

Noise Type: **Fractal**

Noise Threshold

High: **0.8**

Low: **0.3**

Size: **0.001**

This map will appear only in the areas of the main Bump map that would have used Color #2. This is a good way to add random detail to specific areas of a map.

Create a Bump map with a very small scale that will appear in parts of the main Bump map.

6 Set the following color values for the colors of the Metal Bump #2 noise:

Color #1: **R 192, G 192, B 192**
Color #2: **R 0, G 0, B 0**

7 To preview the result, right-click on the Sample Window and choose Render Map. Set the desired dimensions of the render and click the Render button.

Note: Render Map always renders at the current level in the material hierarchy, so rendering while Metal Bump #2 is the active level will only show that detail texture. Going up a level to the main Bump map will show the effects of mixing both maps.

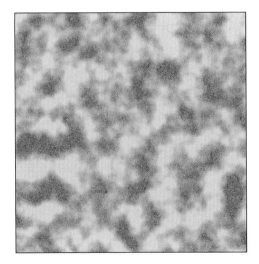

Combining the two Noise maps yields a more realistic level of complexity.

8 Go to the Diffuse channel. In the Material/Map Browser, choose Browse From: Mtl Editor and select the Metal Bump #1 Noise map. Click OK and choose Copy as the method. As this multilevel map is already being used to determine the division between the two "layers" of material, it will prove useful in other channels as well. Rename this map **Metal Rust #1**.

> **Note:** It is recommended that you rename maps when cloning them to avoid confusion.

9 Go down to the Color #2 Map slot, rename this map **Metal Rust #2**, and set the following color values:

Color #1: **R 80, G 90, B 90**

Color #2: **R 40, G 45, B 45**

Change the color values for the map previously used in the Bump channel to adapt it for the Diffuse channel.

> **Note:** Given how subtle and small-scale this map is, the degree of perturbation might appear very different depending on how large the rendered preview is.

10 To add some color detail to the rust areas of the material, go up to the Metal Rust #1 map and assign a Noise map to the Color #1 slot. Name this map **Metal Rust #3** and set the following values:

Source: **Explicit Map Channel**

Noise Parameters

- Noise Type: **Fractal**
- Noise Threshold
  - High: **1.0**
  - Low: **0.4**
- Size: **0.01**

11 For this color detail, you will combine two dark-reddish colors:

Color #1: **R 45, G 15, B 10**
Color #2: **R 95, G 45, B 10**

12 Go up to the root Old Metal material. Once again, you will use Metal Bump #1 as the basis for another channel, this time the Specular channel.

13 Go to the Specular Color channel and clone the Metal Bump #1 map, choosing Copy as the method. Rename this map **Metal Specular #1**.

14 You won't need the secondary Noise map. To deactivate it, you could simply clear the check box next to the Color #2 Maps slot. To avoid confusion with the material hierarchy, drag the None map from the Color #1 slot to the Color #2 slot (the method does not matter).

15 The previous operation should have returned you to the Metal Specular #1 map. The current color values are much too bright to make realistic metal specular levels, especially the Color #1 value, which will be applied in the rusted and presumably less shiny areas. Set the following color values:

Color #1: **R 60, G 60, B 60**
Color #2: **R 200, G 200, B 200**

Metal Rust #3, a rust-colored Noise map.

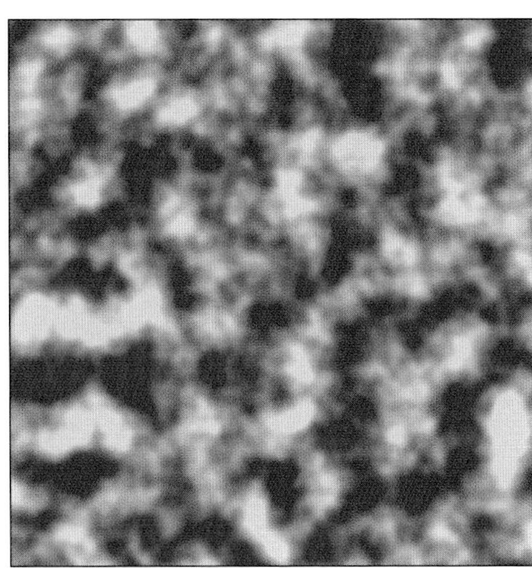

Clone the Bump channel and tweak to create an appropriate Specular map.

16 To check the material hierarchy, open the Material/Map Navigator. In addition to proving quick access to any map in a material, this dialog shows a simple summary of material.

Check the Material/Map Navigator to gain an overall look at material hierarchy.

The Material Editor contains many capabilities for realistic texture creation. This is particularly true when you consider the value of cloning maps and building several channels in a material from a base map. In reality, different parts of a surface will present varying surface properties, so your texture creation will benefit when you consider a strategy for duplicating the properties of real-life materials.

Adding Details to a Base Texture

Adding specific details, such as mechanical panels to a metal surface or corrosion effects to an edge of a surface, can add quite a bit of visual interest to a material.

In this section, you will add a row of dripping rust to the top edge of the metal texture you created in the preceding section.

1 Select a new material and name it **Rust Drip**.

2 Assign a Noise map to the Diffuse channel, name it **Rust Drip Color**, and set the following values:

Source: **Explicit Map Channel**

Noise Parameters

Noise Type: **Regular**

Noise Threshold

High: **0.8**

Low: **0.3**

Size: **0.05**

This map will consist entirely of very dark rust colors. When it is blended with the Old Metal texture in a later step, this color will provide the added layer of detail.

3 Set the following color values:

Color #1: **R 0, G 4, B 5**

Color #2: **R 23, G 23, B 25**

4 To compress this map horizontally and give it a more streaked appearance, set the following values:

Coordinates
  Tiling
    U: **5.0**
    V: **0.5**

5 Select a new material and name it **Metal Blend**. Select a Blend material.

Create a drippy stain map to be blended as a texture detail.

6 Drag the Old Metal material onto the Material 1 slot, using Instance as the method. Drag the Rust Drip material onto the Material 2 slot, using Instance as the method.

7 Assign a Gradient map to the Mask slot and name this map **Metal Blend Mask**. To make this map approximate a vertical drippy pattern, set U Tiling to **5**.

8 The current colors set for this gradient will have the rust at the bottom. To invert this, drag the Color #1 swatch onto the Color #3 swatch, choosing Swap as the method. Set Color #2 to **R 60, G 60, B 60**. Set Color 2 Position to **0.85**.

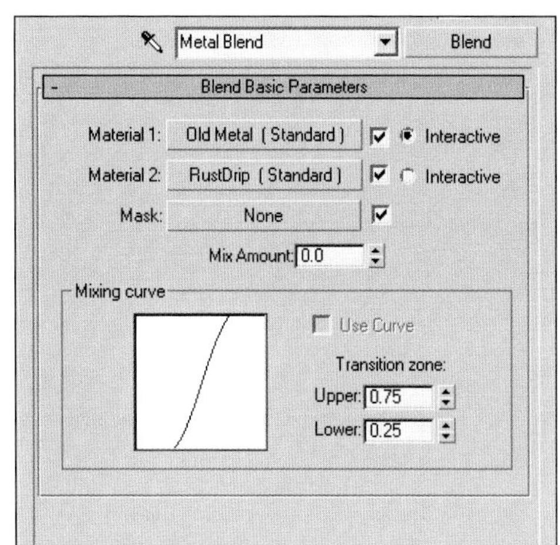

Use the Blend material to combine the two materials previously created.

9 To make this mask as irregular as possible, set a large amount of noise in the Gradient Parameters:

Noise

Amount: **0.5**

Type: **Fractal**

Size: **0.5**

10 Assign the Metal Blend material to the Box01 object.

Using a Blend material is only one of several methods you might employ to combine materials in the Material Editor. Composite materials, Top/Bottom materials, Mask maps, and Mix maps can also be used to differing effect to combine materials or maps.

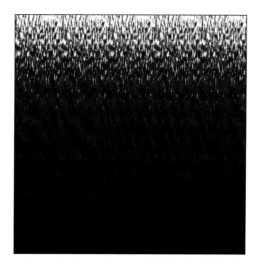

Create a streaked Gradient map to function as the mask for the Rust material.

Rendering Maps for Output

After you have set up a material, rendering it to a file useable in a game engine is fairly straightforward. The main consideration is lighting. One of the reasons for making realistically lit materials is to simulate the effect of lighting, so it is important to take advantage of lighting cues like Bump and Specular maps.

The complimentary consideration for lighting is to avoid giving very strong cues as to lighting sources. Because textures will almost always be tiled multiple times across a surface, it is important that lighting be as even as possible; otherwise, bright highlights will obviously repeat.

In this scene, a box and camera have been set up to facilitate rendering. Note that the camera is aimed directly at the box and is placed so that the box exactly fits the frame horizontally.

A simple camera setup for rendering textures applied to the box.

1 Render a still from the Camera viewport, specifying a custom Output Size of:

Width: **256**

Height: **256**

Rendering without lights in a scene uses a default lighting setup that is very bright and even. To get more visual interest out of your texture, you will want to create a set of lights that will bring out the surface properties and textures in your material without creating any obvious hotspots.

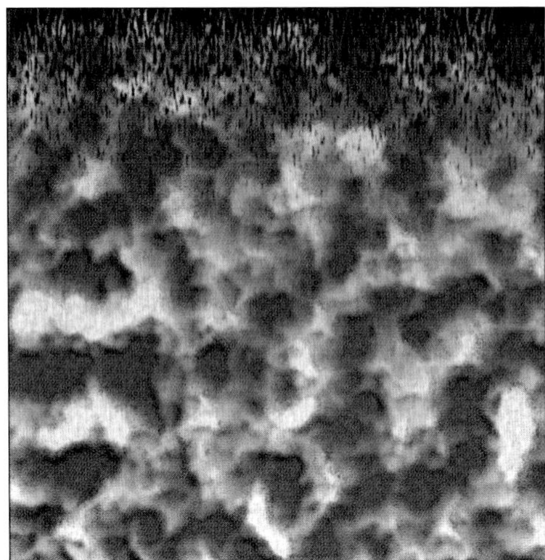

Rendering an image without any lights uses the default lighting preset, which is typically much brighter than desirable.

Note: For reasons that have their roots in the history of computer programming, the resolution of 256 pixels by 256 pixels is the most common texture size employed in game engines. As more powerful video cards reach the market, this value will most likely increase to 512×512 or even 1024×1024, but at the time of this printing, it is best to stick with 256×256.

2 Make certain that the Camera viewport is active. On the toolbar, select Rendering/ActiveShade Floater. This brings up a floating render window set to the Output Size of your last render. Small progress bars on the top and right side of the window show progress toward a complete render.

Note: ActiveShade is a very useful tool for tweaking lighting and materials. The ActiveShade rendering is updated interactively to reflect changes to material settings, colors, and light position and settings. Changes to scene composition or geometry will not be reflected. Note that the ActiveShade render is a close approximation of the final render but will necessarily be a little coarser than the final.

Open an ActiveShade floater to quickly preview lighting changes.

3 Create an omni light at X = 300, Y = –200, Z = 300. Name this light **Omni Key 01**. Set the following values:

Color: **R 215, G 240, B 255**
Multiplier: **0.35**

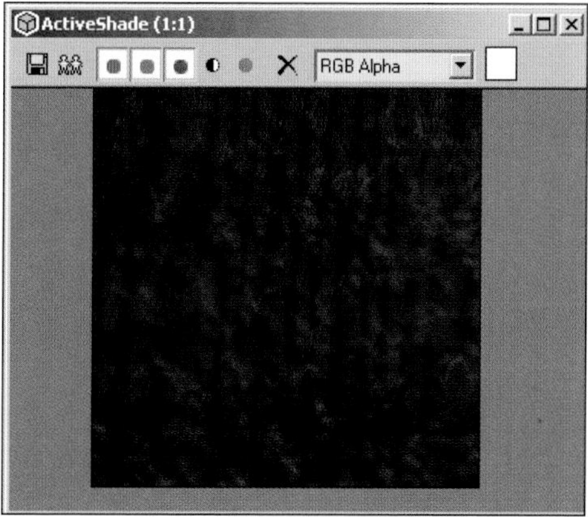

Create an omni light to serve as a key light, reflected here in the Activeshade floater.

Note: The ActiveShade floater is updated to reflect changes in lighting. If you want to keep the rendering from continually updating, right-click in the Activeshade window and uncheck Auto Update. Once Auto Update is deactivated, choosing Update from the quad menu will re-render the image.

4 Clone this light using Instance as the method and move to X = –300. These two omni's will provide the main, or key, lighting.

Clone the omni to provide overall key lighting without hotspots.

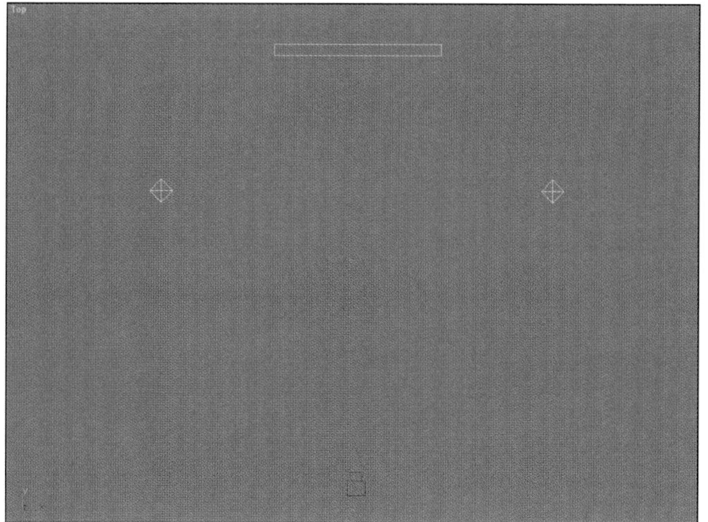

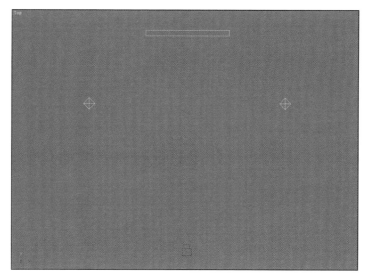

The two omni key lights are evenly placed across the texture.

5 Some of the rust color is being washed out, so add another omni at X = 0, Y = –200, Z = –275 to act as a fill light. Name this light **Omni Fill 01** and set the following values:

Color: **R 115, G 75, B 60**
Multiplier: **1**

6 To keep this light from adding highlights to the surface, uncheck Specular in the General Parameters rollout. Leave Diffuse checked; this will force this light to only affect the diffuse color of the surface without adding specular highlights.

This light is too subtle to be clearly reflected in the ActiveShade viewport on an update. To show this light's effect, right-click the ActiveShade window and choose Initialize.

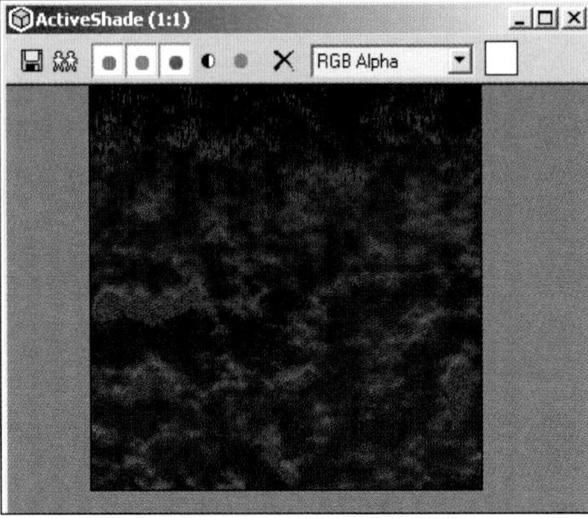

Create a fill light to bring out some of the diffuse color that might be washed out by the key lights.

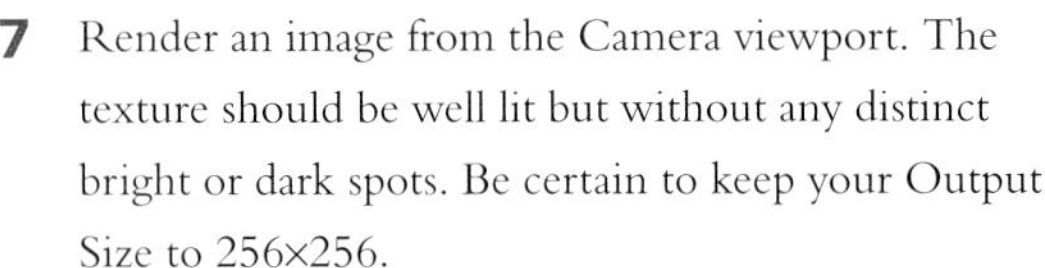

7 Render an image from the Camera viewport. The texture should be well lit but without any distinct bright or dark spots. Be certain to keep your Output Size to 256×256.

The rendered texture, well lit but without obvious bright or dark spots.

Rendering textures for use in game engines requires special attention to lighting and framing. The priority is to create an image that will require the least amount of postprocessing. In some cases, you might want to render a larger image, for example 512×512. If you expect to be doing a lot of touch-up after rendering, a better image may be obtained by editing the larger image and reducing to final resolution afterward.

Adding Geometric Details to a Texture

Textures designed for application to wall surfaces in game use very often contain trim detail along the top or bottom edges of the texture. This is often used to imply the existence of supporting architectural detail without adding actual polygons to a scene. The most straightforward method for adding this kind of detail in 3ds max 4 is by adding geometry to support a texture.

1 Go to the Left viewport and create a Box at X = 128, Y = –5, Z = 118. Name this object **Top Trim** and set the following dimensions:

Length: **20**
Width: **10**
Height: **256**
Generate Mapping Coordinates: **On**

This will place the box across the top edge of the texture area, as seen from the camera.

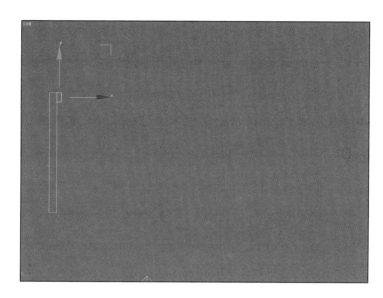

Create a simple box to serve as a geometric detail along the top edge of the texture.

Note: Strong shadow demarcations between surfaces in game textures can add definition and character to a texture and are usually desirable.

2 Select a new material and name it **Top Trim**. Set the following values:

Specular Highlights
    Specular Level: **35**
    Glossiness: **20**

Assign this material to the Top Trim object. The top trim piece will be textured with a bright, shiny metal surface.

3 Set the Bump channel amount to **60** and assign a Gradient Ramp map to the Bump channel. Name this map **Top Trim Bump** and set the following values:

Tiling
U: **10**

Angle
W: **90**

This will result in a repeating pattern across the trim piece to simulate a machined part.

4 In the Gradient Ramp parameters, set the following flags (right-click an existing flag to bring up its properties or double-click in the gradient to create a new flag):

Position: **0**	Color: **Black**
Position: **5**	Color: **White**
Position: **95**	Color: **White**
Position: **100**	Color: **Black**

This gradient will give the appearance of a flat surface broken by regular grooves. You will use this base pattern to create a Diffuse channel with varying colors, depending on the bump height.

5 Go up to the root Top Trim material and drag the Bump map to the Diffuse channel, choosing Copy as the method.

6 Assign a Mix map to the Diffuse channel, choosing Keep Old Map as Sub-map. This will result in the gradient being assigned to the Color #1 slot.

Use a mechanical-style Gradient map to imply a machined surface.

7 Rename this map **Trim Diffuse** and drag the gradient from the Color #1 slot to the Mix Amount slot, choosing Swap as the method. Rename the Mix Amount texture to **Trim Diffuse Mix Amnt**.

The gradient amount will determine which of the two Mix maps will be applied.

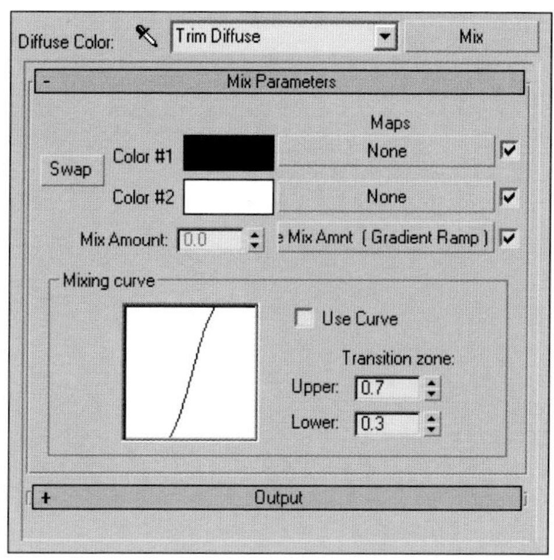

Once you have completed the cloning operation, the Bump channel will have been copied to the Diffuse channel's Mix Amount slot.

8 Go up to the Trim Diffuse map and assign a Noise map to the Color #1 slot. Name this map **Trim Color #1** and set the following values:

Noise Parameters
- Noise Type: **Fractal**
- Noise Threshold
  - High: **0.9**
  - Low: **0.25**
  - Size: **5.0**

9 Set the following color values:

Color #1: **R 25, G 65, B 75**
Color #2: **R 15, G 35, B 40**

This map will provide a general dark blue surface.

Create a dark blue Noise map to be applied in the grooved areas.

10 Go up to the Trim Diffuse map and drag the Trim Color #1 map from the Color #1 slot to the Color #2 slot. Be sure to choose Instance as the method.

11 Assign an RGB Tint map to the Color #2 slot, choosing Keep Old Map as Sub-map. Name this map **Trim Tint #1**. This method will enable you to change the color of the map without loosing the reference to the original.

Note: Because both maps are instances of each other, this is one example of a situation in which renaming cloned maps is not useful.

12 To add a green tint to this color, set the following colors in the RGB Tint map:

R: **R 255, G 100, B 100**
G: **R 70, G 200, B 70**
B: **R 75, G 75, B 105**

Use an RGB Tint map to color the instanced Noise map.

There is no limit to the sorts of interesting details that can be added to textures with even simple geometry. Even without applying such detailed materials, simple boxes and cylinders can add visual interest.

Lighting Geometric Details

Lighting small geometric details can be a bit tricky because of the need to light small areas without overly affecting the rest of the texture. In this section, you will use small radius lights to light the top trim object.

1 Create an omni light at X = 110, Y = –30, Z = 120. Name this light **Omni Trim 01**. Set the following values:

Cast Shadows: **On**
Color: **White**
Multiplier: **1**

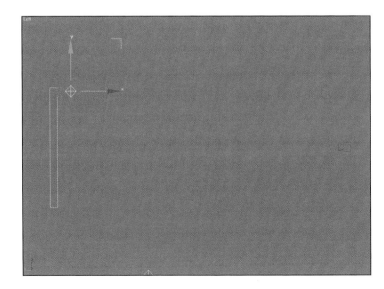

Place an Omni light very close to the trim object.

2 Uncheck Specular, leaving Diffuse checked. This will keep the trim lighting from adding undesirable specular highlights.

3 Go to the Shadow Parameters rollout. Be certain that Shadow Map is the chosen shadow type and increase shadow Density to **5**. Usually, such a high shadow density would be excessive, but this light will be constrained to a very small area of effect.

4 In the Shadow Map Parameters rollout, set Bias to **0.1** to make the Shadow map tighter.

5 In the Attenuation Parameters rollout, set the following values to limit this light to a small sphere of effect:

Far Attenuation
  Start: **30**
  End: **60**
  Use: **On**

If you render a still from the Camera viewport, you will see that the trim is being lit and is casting a shadow, but only in the area immediately surrounding the Omni Trim 01 light. Several of these lights will be needed to complete the detail lighting.

6 Click the Array button on the Toolbar and enter the following values in the Array dialog:

Incremental
  X: **–50**

Type of Object: **Instance**

Array Dimensions
  1D: **On**
    Count: **5**

7 Click OK to create four clones of the trim light, spaced evenly across the trim object.

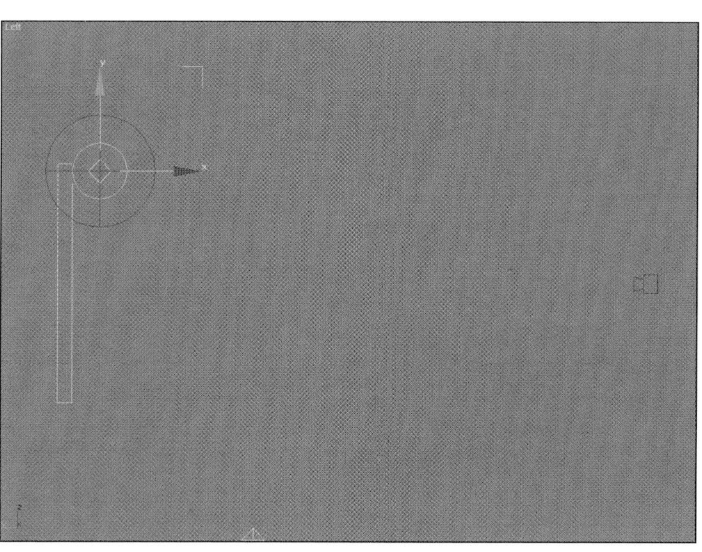

Use Attenuation to restrict the omni's area of effect to a small area.

This small-radius omni light serves as the beginning of a lighting solution for the trim geometry.

When lighting small-detail objects or parts of a texture, it is essential to avoid excessive leaking of light across the body of the texture. Arrays of lights can be useful when small amounts of dispersed lights are needed.

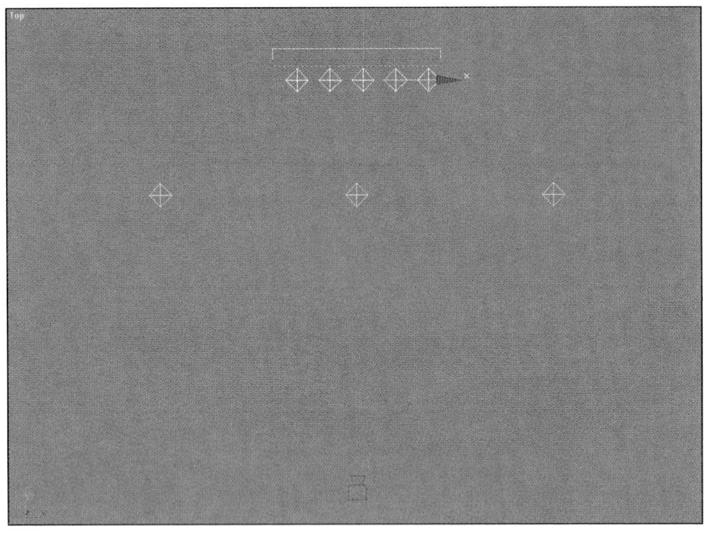

Use the Array tool to create a series of instanced lights.

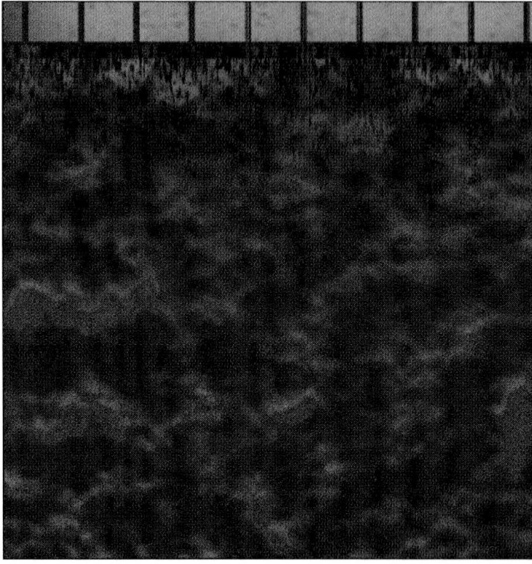

A series of attenuated omni lights can be used to light a small area of the image without overly affecting the overall lighting.

Tiling Textures

The texture, as it renders at this point, has one flaw that must be addressed. If it is applied across a large surface, the left and right edges of the texture will not blend together. In other words, the texture does not tile correctly. This is a difficult issue to address within 3ds max 4; a standalone image-editing application like Adobe Photoshop or Corel (formerly Metacreations) Painter is designed to address this sort of issue. For this section, correcting tiling will be shown using Adobe Photoshop, arguably the most popular image-editing application.

1 Render a still to file from the Camera viewport with Output Size still set to 256×256. The TIFF format will translate well into Photoshop, although most game engines will not accept TIFFs.

2 Load the image into Photoshop.

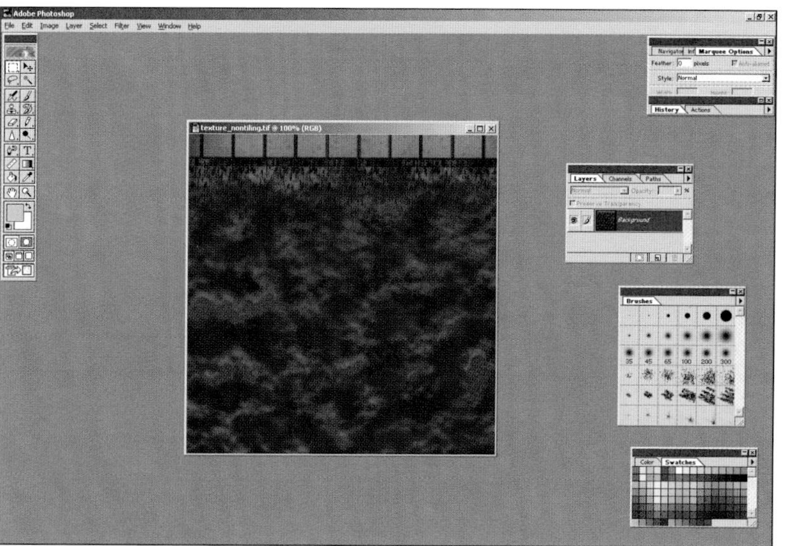

Photoshop is a very useful application for image editing.

3 To bring the right and left edges into the frame, go to Filter/Other/Offset. Enter the following values in the Offset dialog:

Horizontal: **32**
Vertical: **0**
Undefined Areas: **Wrap Around**

Click OK to apply the filter. Note that a visible seam appears on the left side of the image. This seam needs to be blended before the texture will tile correctly.

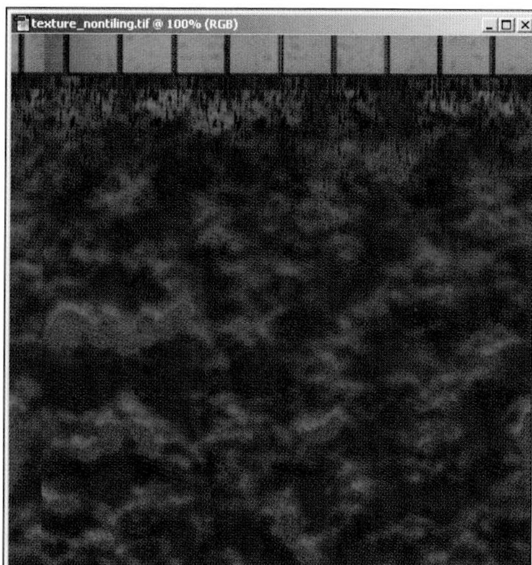

Use the Offset filter to bring the texture seam into the frame.

4 Select the Rubber Stamp tool (keyboard shortcut S). In the Rubber Stamp Options floater, set Opacity to **50%**.

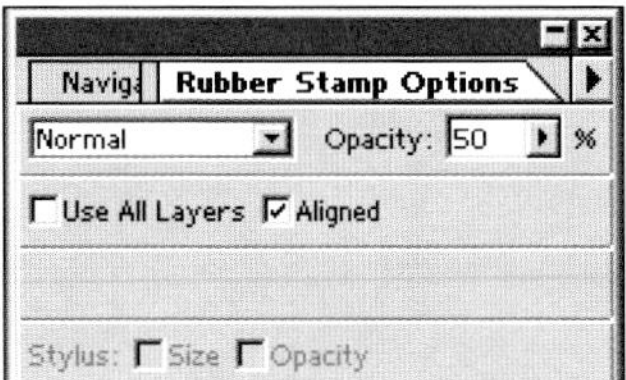

The Rubber Stamp tool is very useful for blending texture edges.

5 Hold down the Alt key and click in the image to define a source area and then paint over the seam. A good strategy is to use source areas that are similar to the target area. For example, to smooth over a rusty area, use a rusty area from another part of the image. The blended area might become noticeably blurrier than the rest of the image.

6 To correct this, select the Sharpen tool (keyboard shortcut R). In the Sharpen Options floater, set Opacity to **25%**.

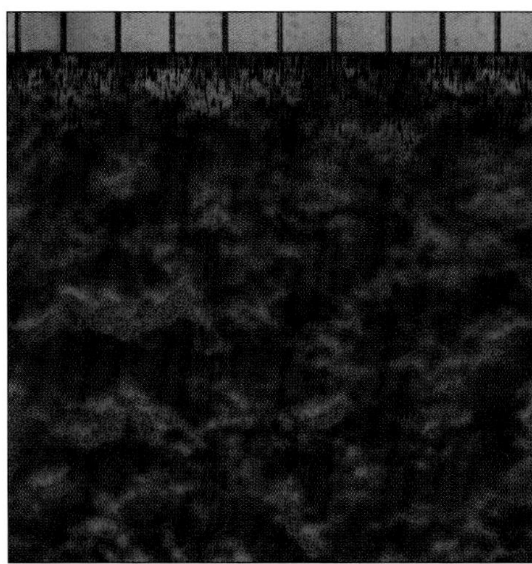

Paint over the texture seam with the Rubber Stamp tool.

7 Paint carefully over the blurred areas of the image until the entire image is equally sharp.

The procedure for blending edges in textures should be fairly similar for other image-editing applications. The basic strategy is to copy over the visible seam with seamless texture, making the edge essentially invisible.

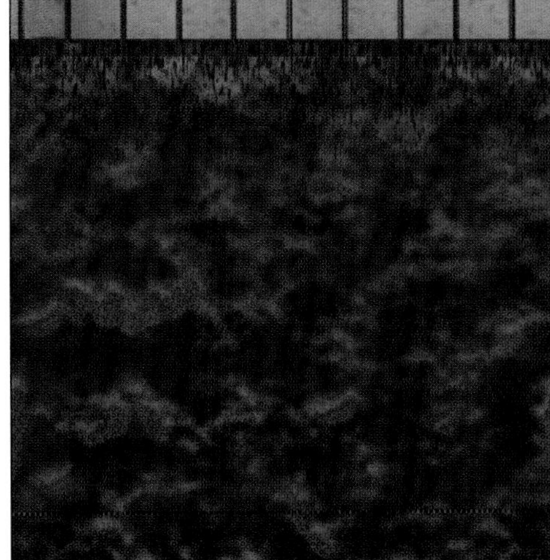

Use the Sharpen tool to regain detail in the blended areas.

Image Formats for Game Engines

Although the acceptable image formats for game engine use are dependent on the target engine, in most cases, a resolution of 256×256 pixels is acceptable. Additionally, many game engines only support 8-bit color (256 individual colors), although 16-bit color (65,536 colors) will be widely supported as more powerful video hardware becomes commonplace. Standard Windows bitmaps (files with .BMP extensions) are among the most widely supported file formats.

In the pictured example, the texture created in this tutorial was exported as an 8-bit Windows bitmap, imported into the Unreal game engine, and applied across a wall as a horizontally tiling texture. The Unreal engine, created by Epic (**www.epicgames.com**), has been popularized by the very successful 3D action games Unreal and Unreal Tournament and is one of the most visually sophisticated game engines for 3D games.

The final texture as displayed in the Unreal game engine.

Modifications

The Material Editor contains many map options that can be used to create a variety of textures appropriate for game use. The Bricks, Cellular, Perlin Marble, and Speckle maps are a few examples of maps that could easily be rendered as useable textures. Try to create textures that imply a lot of 3D information, with the use of Bump and Specular channels, and materials that build upon base textures to create believable material complexity.

TABLE OF NAILS

"You take away all obstacles. Without them to strengthen us, we will weaken and die."

—CAPTAIN KIRK IN THE *STAR TREK* EPISODE, "METAMORPHOSIS"

Using MaxScript for Automation

This tutorial touches on several of max's features, but the heart of it is a script that will automate a repetitive task. The script will also itself "write" MaxScript and set up optimizations using MaxScript's event callback mechanism. Additionally, you will create a complex material and animate part of it. The animation will be a chain reaction starting with a few keyframes set on a material map, driving a Displace modifier, which in turn moves a series of scripted objects.

Project 11

Table of Nails

by Richard Katz

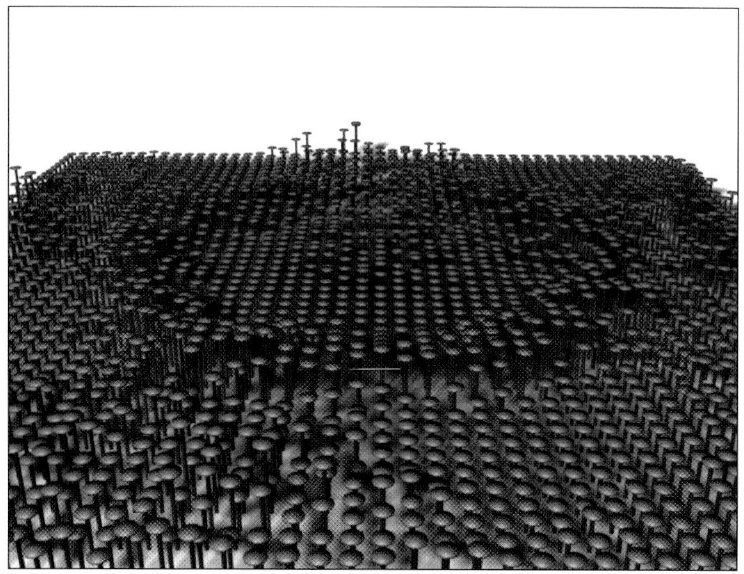

How It Works

You start with a nonrendering plane primitive and a simple nail model. You will apply a Displace modifier to the plane and create a Displacement map representing a cityscape. You'll add to the Displacement map a Radial Gradient Ramp that you'll use to animate several of the flags to reveal a devastating tidal wave that could be disastrous for the inhabitants of your little metropolis.

But how do you get your one little nail to multiply? Here's where you apply MaxScript's greatest use—automation. You will write a script to copy the nail thousands of times and program each one to follow a vertex on the plane.

Have you ever worked with a scene that was calculating thousands of controller scripts simultaneously? It's not pretty. You'll add a few lines to the script that will keep the nails hidden until rendered.

Getting Started

You can break this project into four parts. The first part is building the geometry you will need to complete the project. After you create the geometry, the second part will be creating the materials, the third part will be writing the script, and the fourth part will be running the script.

1. In a new max scene, create a plane primitive in the Top view with these parameters:

   Length: **200**
   Width: **200**
   Length Segments: **50**
   Width Segments: **50**

2. Right-click the plane and select Properties. Uncheck the Renderable parameter and click OK.

3. Apply a Displace modifier to the plane.

> **Note:** A finished version of this project, Nailwave.avi, can be found on the accompanying CD-ROM.

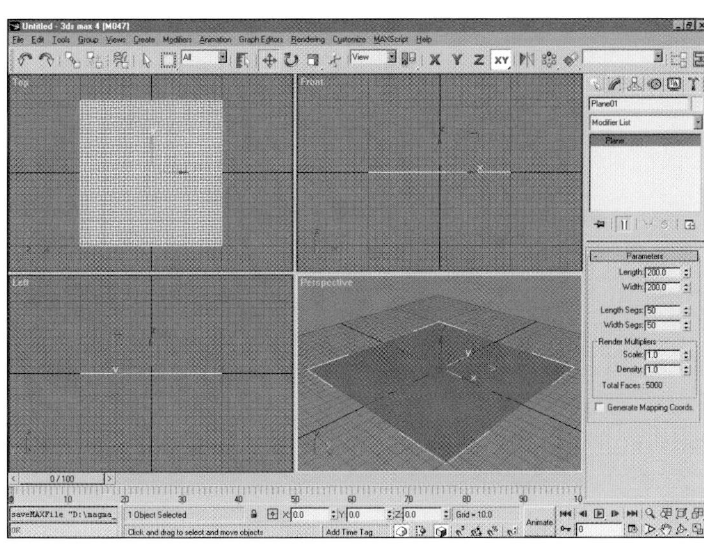

Create a plane primitive.

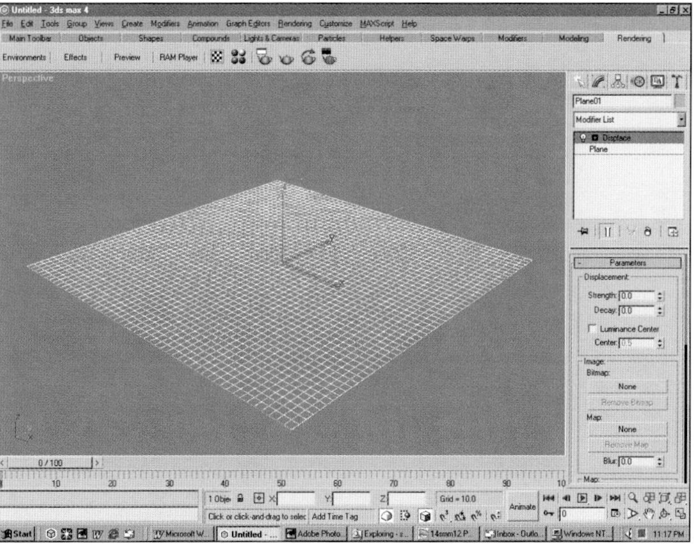

The plane with the Displace modifier applied.

4 Create a cylinder primitive in the Top view with the following parameters:

Radius: **1.6**

Height: **20.0**

Height Segments: **4**

Sides: **10**

Name it **Nail**.

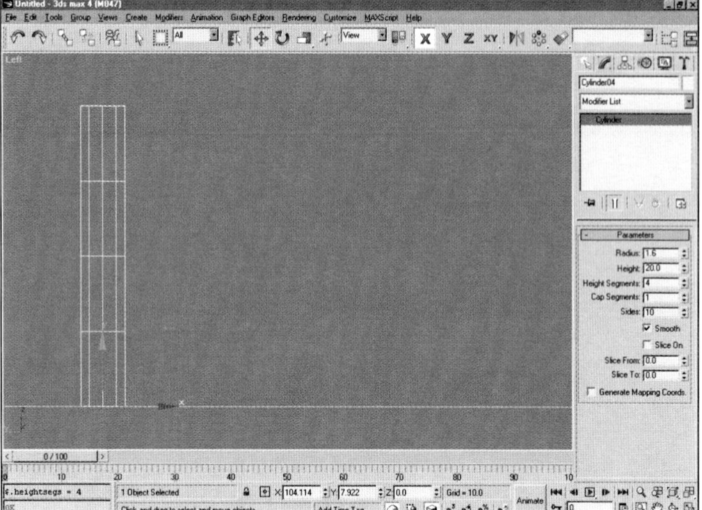

Create a cylinder primitive.

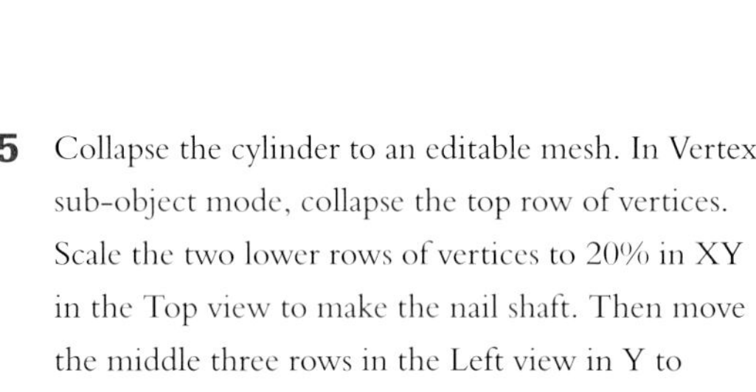

5 Collapse the cylinder to an editable mesh. In Vertex sub-object mode, collapse the top row of vertices. Scale the two lower rows of vertices to 20% in XY in the Top view to make the nail shaft. Then move the middle three rows in the Left view in Y to form the nail.

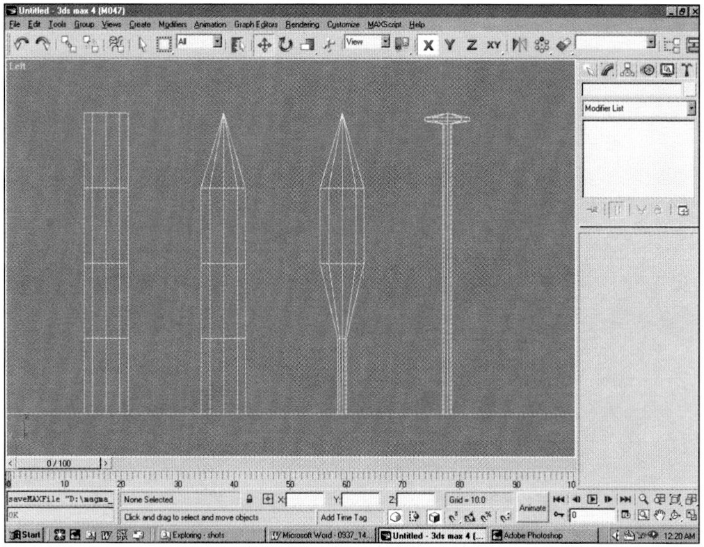

Scaling and moving the vertices to transform the cylinder into the nail.

6 In the Top view, create a box around the plane with the following parameters:

Length: **220**
Width: **220**
Height: **25**

This will act as a backdrop for the nails when you render.

7 Move the box down to Z= –10.

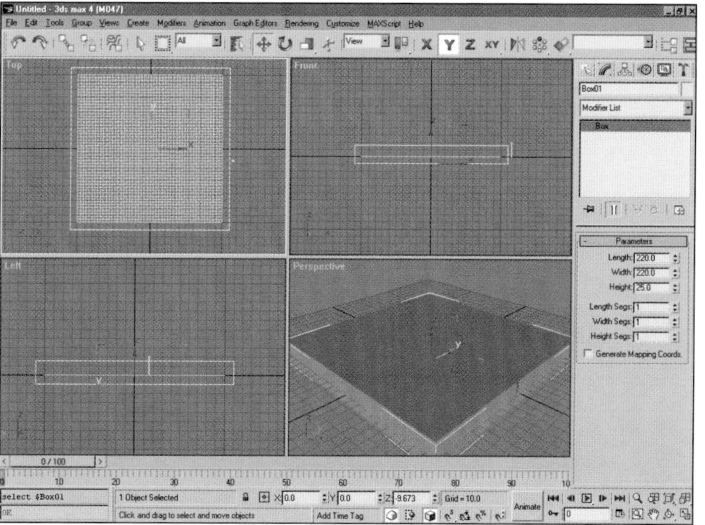

Create a box primitive.

SET UP THE MATERIALS

Now that you have created the objects, you will need to make materials to define how the objects will appear in the final render. You will also create the Displacement map to be animated later.

1 Open the Material Editor. Create a semi-shiny material and assign it to the nail object:

Specular Level: **30**
Glossiness: **25**

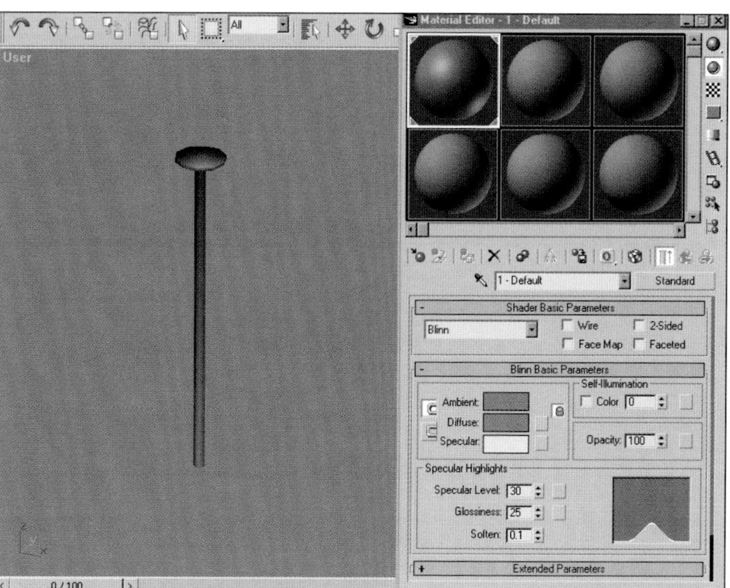

Set the Nail material Specular Highlights properties.

2 Create a simple material for the table. Keep it fairly matte to contrast with the nails. Assign this material to the box.

Specular Level: **0**

Glossiness: **10**

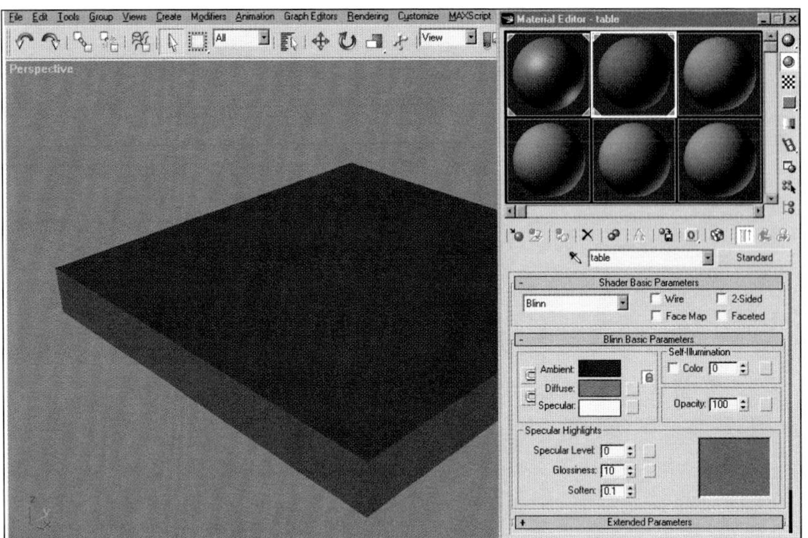

Set the Specular Highlights properties for the Table material.

3 Open the Material/Map Browser. Click and drag a new composite map to a slot in the Material Editor. Name the map **displacement map**.

Because this is a map and not a material, you cannot assign it to an object. After you have created and animated this map, you will assign it to the Displace modifier you applied to the plane in the preceding section.

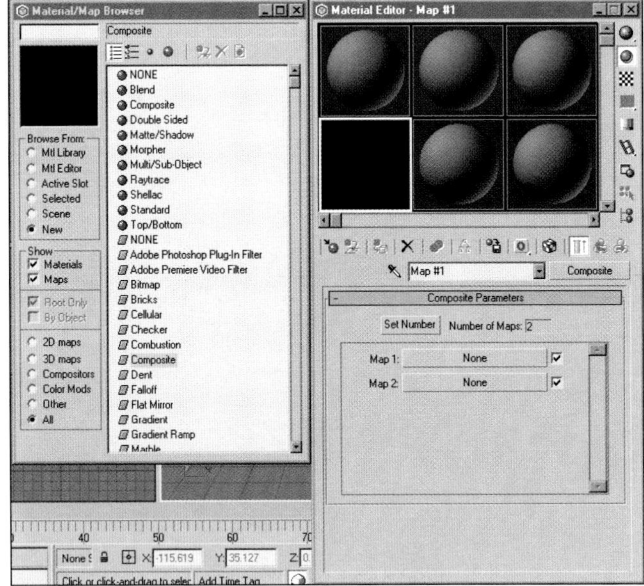

Create a new composite map in the Material Editor.

4 Create a Mask map for the first slot for the cityscape. Name the Mask map **city**.

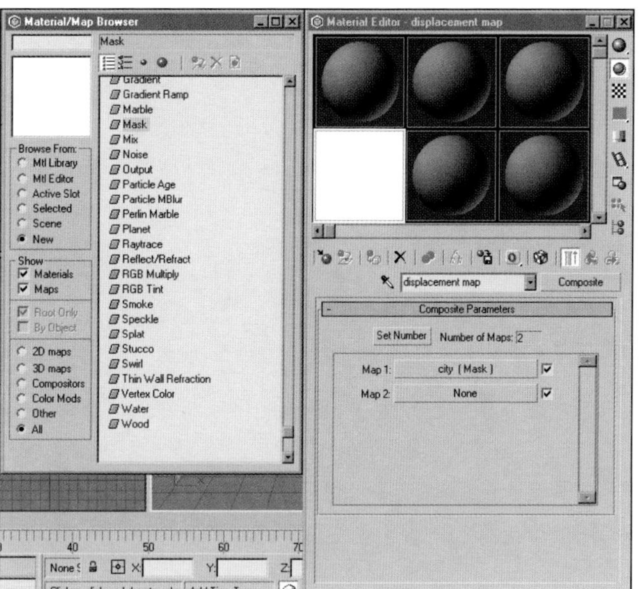

Create a Mask map in the Map 1 slot of the Composite map.

5 Create a Noise map in the Map slot of the city Mask map with these settings:

Type: **Turbulence**
Size: **8**
High: **0.44**
Low: **0.11**
Color #1: **R 33, G 33, B 33**

Name the map **buildings**.

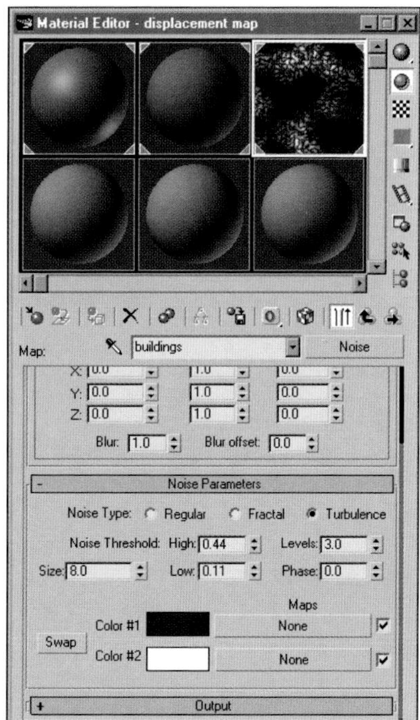

Noise Parameters for the buildings map.

6 Navigate up a level, back to the city Mask map. Create a Noise map in the Mask slot for the water. Name this map **water**. Give it the following settings:

Type: **Regular**

Size: **64**

High: **0.65**

Low: **0.425**

This map will determine what parts of the buildings map will show through.

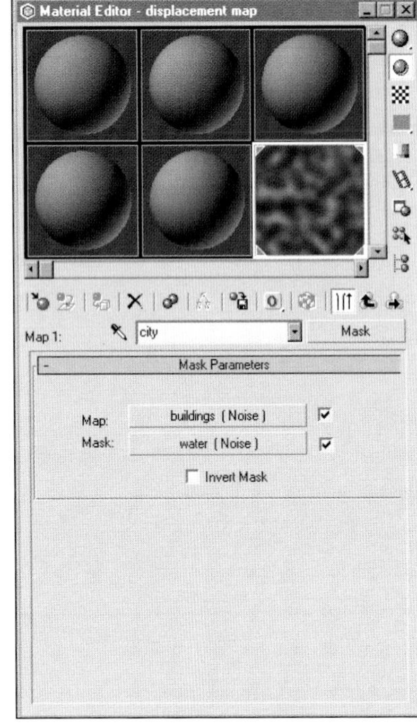

Create a Noise map for the Map and Mask slots of the city Mask map.

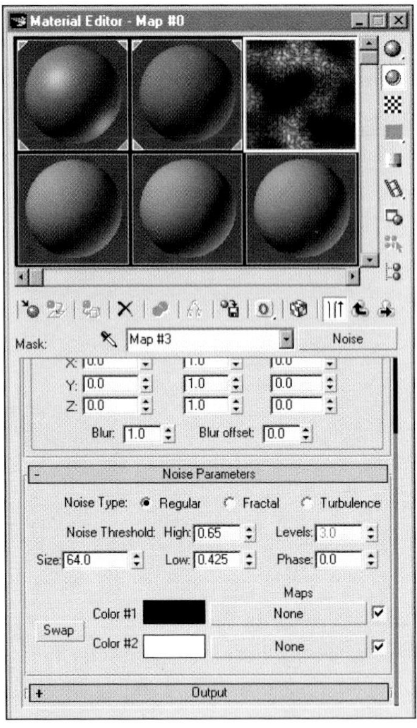

Noise Parameters for the Water map.

7 At the composite map level, create another Mask map. Name this map **wave**.

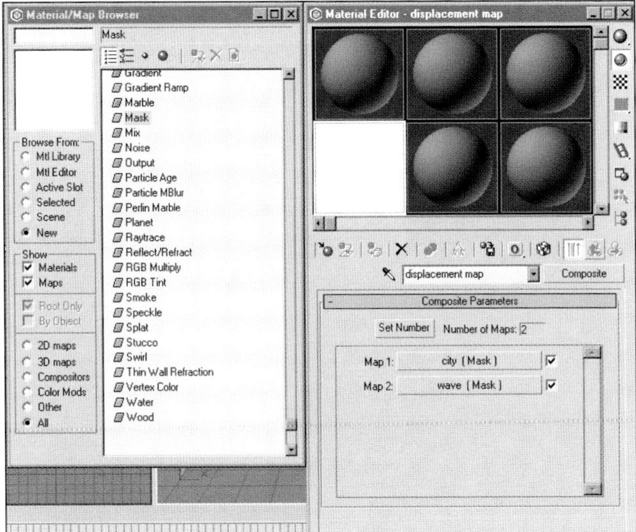

Create a second Mask map.

8 Create a Gradient map in the Map slot and set all colors to white. Name this map **wave_white**.

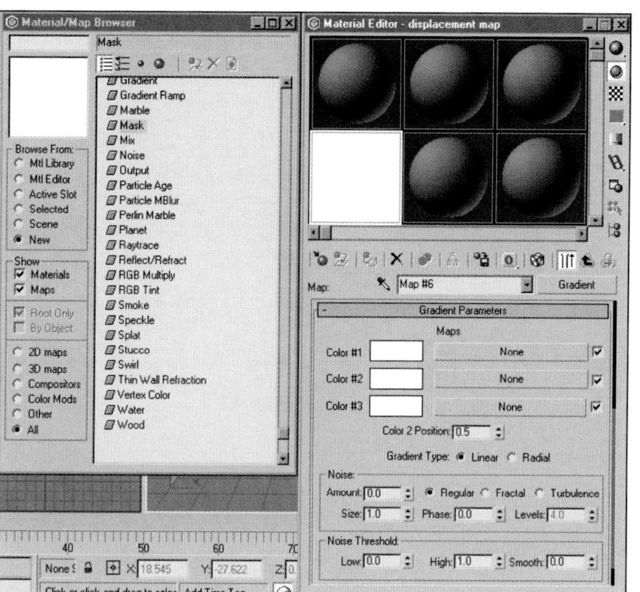

Create a Gradient map and set all colors to white.

9 Create a Gradient Ramp in the Mask slot. Name this map **wave_mask**. Set the start and end flags to black and set the Gradient Type to Radial. Check the Noise option and set the noise to these settings:

Amount: **0.15**

Type: **Fractal**

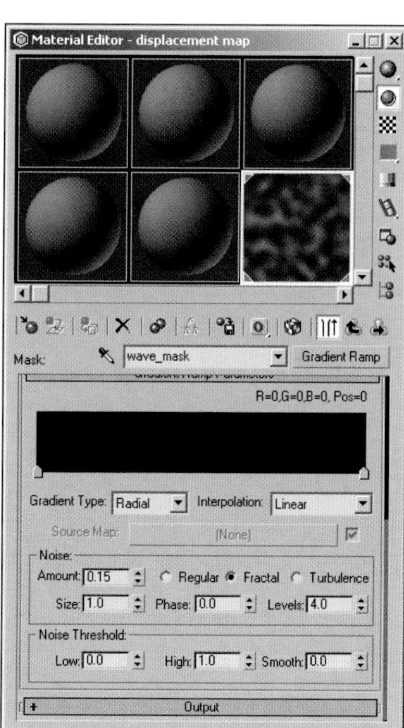

Gradient Ramp Noise parameters.

10 In the Material Editor, in the Gradient Ramp you created, create three flags. Label them **Flag One**, **Flag Two**, and **Flag Three**. Make sure all five flags are set to pure black.

Flag properties dialog. Use this to set the colors of all five flags to black.

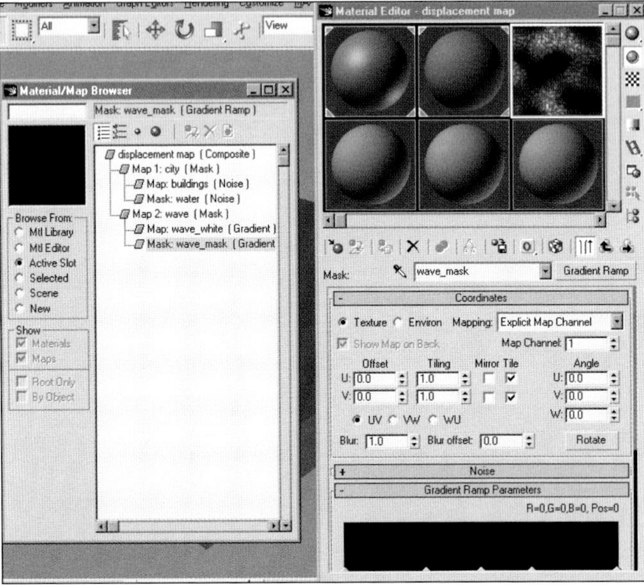

This is what the map hierarchy should look like.

11 Click and drag the composite map from either the Material Editor or the Material/Map Browser to the Map slot of the Displace modifier you applied to the plane as an instance. Set the Displace modifier's Strength to **15**.

Drag the composite map to the Map slot of the Displace modifier on the plane.

ANIMATE THE RAMP

Now that you've created the Displacement map, you will need to animate the flags in the Gradient Ramp wave_mask.

1 Press the Animate button. Set the active time segment from frames 0 to 100.

2 Go to frame 40. In the Material Editor, in the Gradient Ramp Parameters rollout, slide each of the flags slightly to the right. This will create keyframes for them at frame 0 and at frame 40. Set the color of Flag Two to white. Set the Noise Amount to **0**.

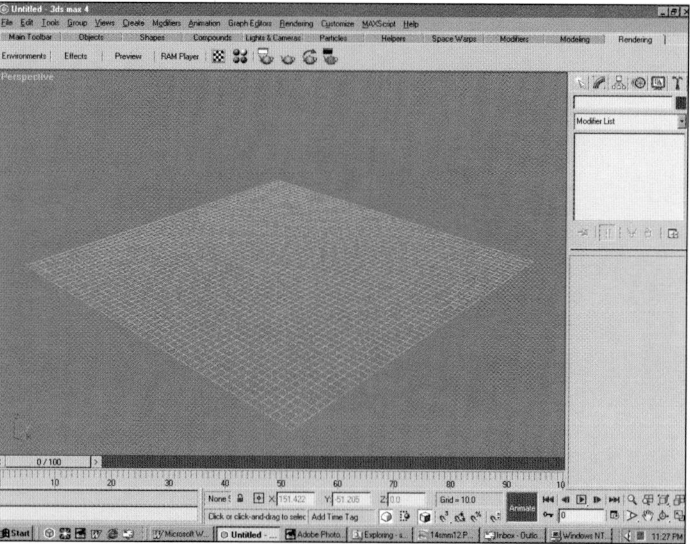

Activate 3ds max 4's Animate mode.

3 Open Track View, right-click the Filters button and turn on Animated Tracks Only, Materials/Maps, and Materials/Parameters. Right-click Objects and select Expand All. The flags you just animated should become the focus.

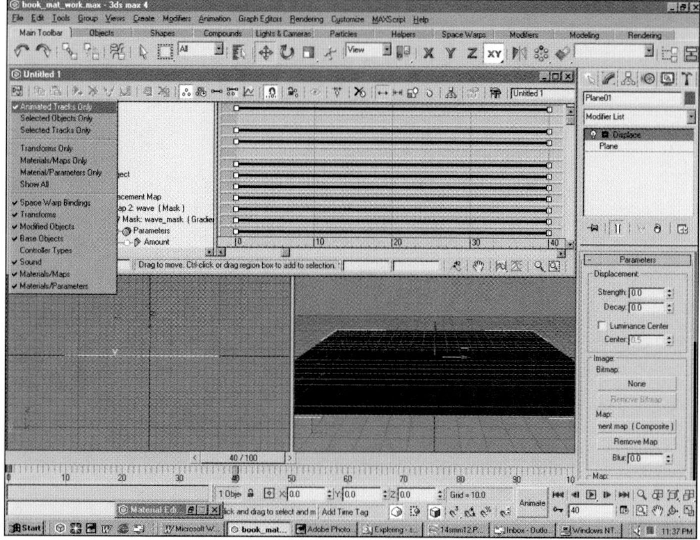

Use the Animated Tracks Only filter in Track View to focus on the keys you created.

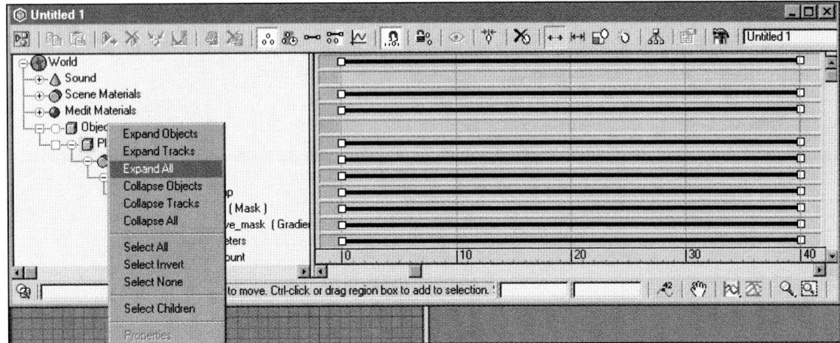

Expanding the object hierarchy.

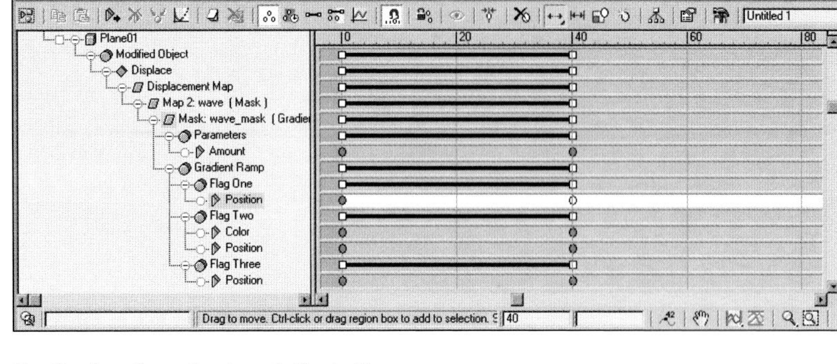

The Gradient Ramp flag keys in Track View.

4 Arrange the keys for Flag One so that the first one is on frame 0 and the second one is on frame 75. Right-click the keys to open the Key Info dialog. Set the first key's value to **0** and the second key's value to **100**.

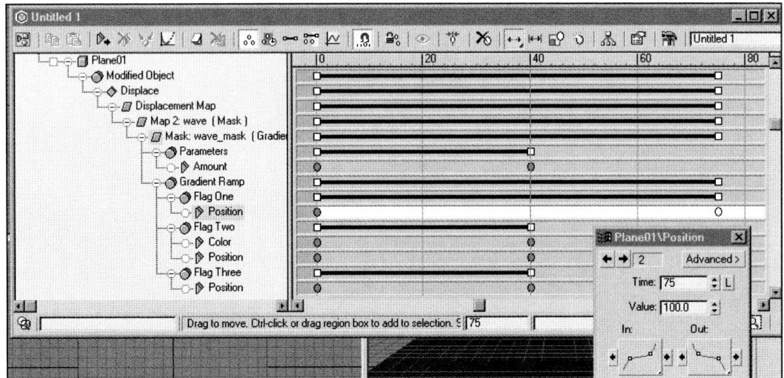

Arranging the keys for Flag One. Use the Key Info dialog to set the keys' values.

5 Set up Flag Two's Position keys so that the first one is on frame 5 and the second one is on frame 80. Set their values to **0** and **100** like you did for Flag One.

6 Set up Flag Two's Color track. The first key is black; the second one is white. Copy the first key to frame 80 so that the flag will animate from black to white and then back to black.

Note: Here's a hint to do this faster: Shift+drag the key at frame 0 to frame 80 to duplicate it.

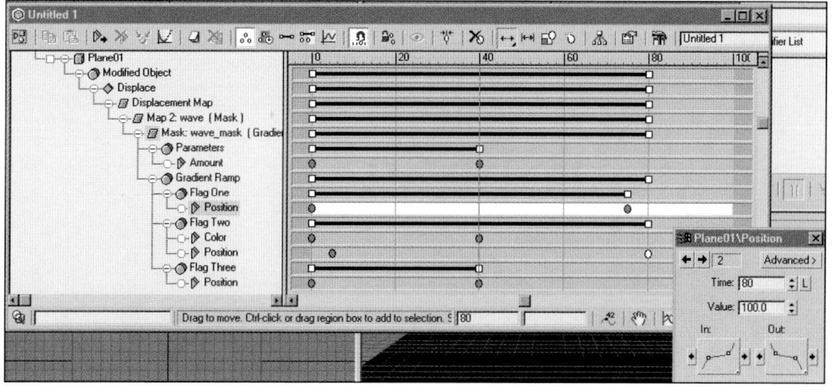

Arranging the Position keys for Flag Two. Use the Key Info dialog to set the keys' values.

7 Set up Flag Three's Position track. Move the first key to frame 15 and the second key to frame 100. Set the value of the first key to **0** and the second key to **100**.

8 Arrange the keys in the Amount track under Parameters to adjust the fading out of the noise. Move the key at frame 40 to frame 70. Shift+copy the key on frame 0 to frame 50. Change the out curve of the key at frame 0 to linear. Change the in curve of the key at frame 50 to linear. The Amount track should have a function curve that looks like the accompanying figure.

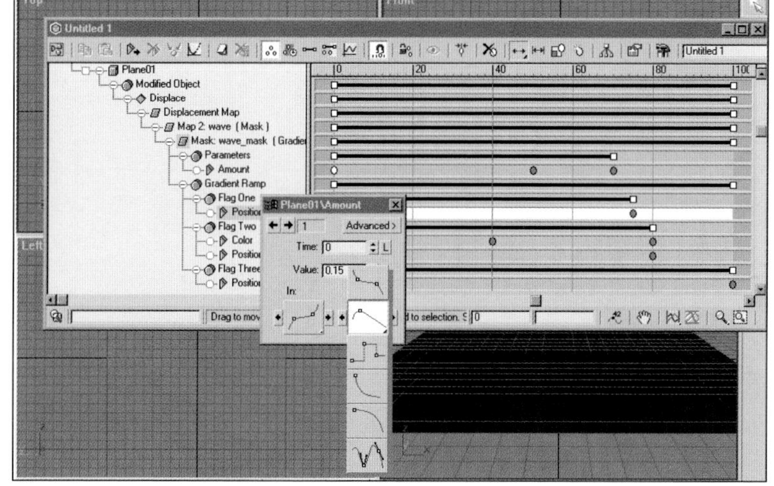

Use the Key Info dialog to set the in and out animation curves for the Amount keys.

The finished Track View layout of the animation should look like the accompanying figure.

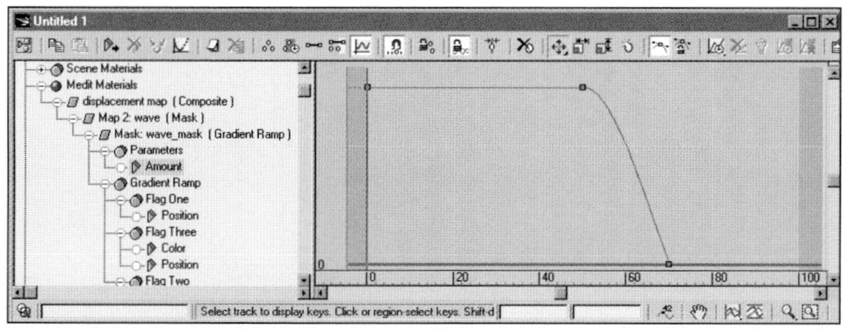

The function curve for the Amount track.

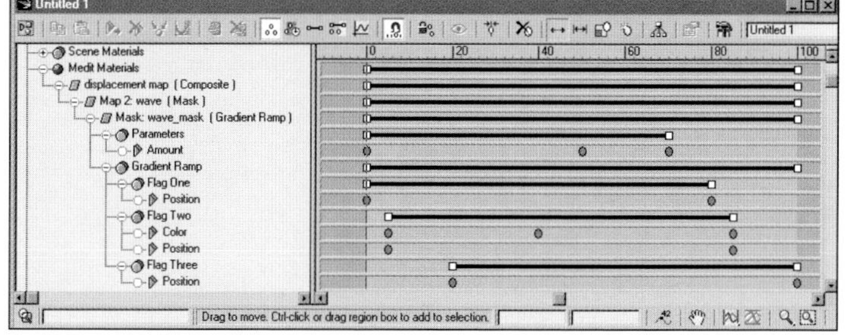

The finished key arrangement in Track View.

CREATE THE SCRIPT

MaxScript is a powerful tool. It has tremendous depth, but it is easy to learn the basics. If I run into a situation in which I want to do something in 3ds max 4 that I can't do in the standard user interface (or that would be too slow to do in the interface), I usually investigate using MaxScript to help me accomplish my goal.

There are several ways you interact with completed scripts. Scripts can expose their own interface elements in the Utility panel, in a modeless floater window, as a Macroscript button in the Tab menu, and now in 3ds max 4 as a modal floater window and in a quad menu. MaxScript can also exist in places where it is automatically evaluated without any user interaction, like in a scripted animation controller. This project will make use of a scripted utility and a scripted position controller.

Note: Unfortunately, there aren't many resources out there for learning MaxScript. There is very little published material on the MaxScript language, and only a few Web sites offer a handful of tutorials. In my opinion, the best source for learning MaxScript is to find some scripts already written and take them apart a line at a time to see what each command does. The MaxScript listener is great for testing single lines of script. The best reference available is 3ds max 4's Online MaxScript Reference right in the 3ds max 4 Help menu. I keep it open out of habit most of the time, and I use it regularly.

1 In the MaxScript panel, define the script as a *utility*.

This tells 3ds max 4 to place the interface in the Utility panel.

```
utility nailsurface "Automated Hammer"
(

)
```

Note: For more information, see the section "Scripted Utility Panels" in the MaxScript Reference.

2 Define the interface elements.

You will need two **pickbutton** elements for selecting the plane and the nail. You need a third **button** to be pressed to begin the processing and a **progressbar** element to display the progression of the script creating the nails.

```
pickbutton picksurf "Pick Surface"
pickbutton picknail "Pick Nail"
button nailit "Nail it!"
progressbar pb
```

Note: For more information on **pickbutton**, **button**, and **progressbar**, see the section "Rollout User-Interface Control Types" in the MaxScript Reference.

3 Create event handler expressions for the interface elements.

When **picksurf** and **picknail** are pressed, you will display the picked objects on the button to show that they have been picked.

```
on picksurf picked ps do
(
 picksurf.text = ps.name
)

on picknail picked ps do
(
 picknail.text = ps.name
)
```

4 This is the event handler for the button **nailit**.

At the core of the handler for **nailit** is the *for loop* that duplicates the nail, assigns a position script controller, and writes a script that tells each nail to follow a specific vertex on the plane.

The lines starting with **t.position.controller.script = ** are assembled from a set of variables and drive each copy of the nail object **t** based on the position of the vertex **j** that it's linked to.

The expression being assigned to the **progressbar** value **pb.value** needs a little explanation. Since **j** and **maxvert** are integers, the result of their division is an integer. You need a fractional value to find the percentage that **pb.value** wants. So with MaxScript's easy typecasting, you force them to be floats when you divide so that their result should be a value between 0 and 1. You multiply that number by 100 to find the percentage that has been completed.

The loop collects an array of the nail objects into **settmp**. After the loop is finished, **settmp** is made into a named selection set called **nailset**.

```
on nailit pressed do
(
  maxvert = picksurf.object.numverts
  u = picksurf.object
  settmp = #()
  for j = 1 to maxvert do
  (
    t = copy picknail.object
    append settmp t
    t.position.controller = position_script()
    t.position.controller.script = \
    ("(in coordsys world (getvert $" + u.name + " " + (j as string) + "))")
    pb.value = ((100*((j as float)/(maxvert as float))) as integer)
  )
  selectionsets["nailset"] = settmp
  settmp = undefined
  messagebox "Script Finished."
)
```

Note: For more information, see the sections "For Loop," "Script Controllers," and "SelectionSet Values" in the MaxScript Reference.

5 You will extend the functionality of the script with a few lines that make sure you remember to select the nail and the plane.

```
if (picksurf == undefined) then (messagebox "Pick a surface!")
else if (picknail == undefined) then (messagebox "pick a nail!")
else
(
    .
    .
    .
)
```

6 Keep the nails hidden until rendered.

This optimization to the script will keep the nails hidden until rendered. When hidden, the position scripts aren't evaluated constantly. These four lines set up a system that automatically unhides the nails only during rendering, and the user is never even aware that they get unhidden.

```
callbacks.removescripts id:#nailcb
hide t
callbacks.addscript #prerender ("unhide selectionsets[#nailset]") id:#nailcb
➥persistent:TRUE
callbacks.addscript #postrender ("hide selectionsets[#nailset]") id:#nailcb
➥persistent:TRUE
```

Note: For more information, see the section "General Event Callback Mechanism" in the MaxScript Reference.

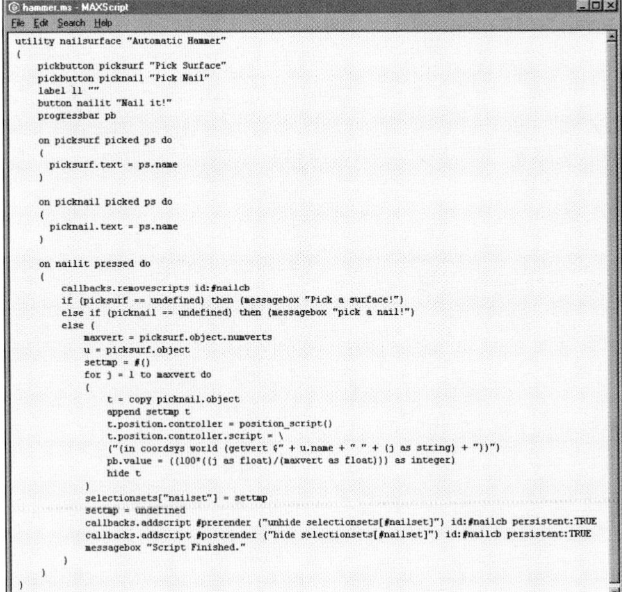


```
utility nailsurface "Automatic Hammer"
(
    pickbutton picksurf "Pick Surface"
    pickbutton picknail "Pick Nail"
    label l1 ""
    button nailit "Nail it!"
    progressbar pb

    on picksurf picked ps do
    (
      picksurf.text = ps.name
    )

    on picknail picked ps do
    (
      picknail.text = ps.name
    )

    on nailit pressed do
    (
        callbacks.removescripts id:#nailcb
        if (picksurf == undefined) then (messagebox "Pick a surface!")
        else if (picknail == undefined) then (messagebox "pick a nail!")
        else (
            maxvert = picksurf.object.numverts
            u = picksurf.object
            settmp = #()
            for j = 1 to maxvert do
            (
                t = copy picknail.object
                append settmp t
                t.position.controller = position_script()
                t.position.controller.script = \
                ("(in coordsys world (getvert $" + u.name + " " + (j as string) + "))")
                pb.value = ((100*((j as float)/(maxvert as float))) as integer)
                hide t
            )
            selectionsets["nailset"] = settmp
            settmp = undefined
            callbacks.addscript #prerender ("unhide selectionsets[#nailset]") id:#nailcb persistent:TRUE
            callbacks.addscript #postrender ("hide selectionsets[#nailset]") id:#nailcb persistent:TRUE
            messagebox "Script Finished."
        )
    )
)
```

The finished Automatic Hammer script.

7 Save your script as **hammer.ms**. Evaluate the script. It should produce a utility that looks like the accompanying figure.

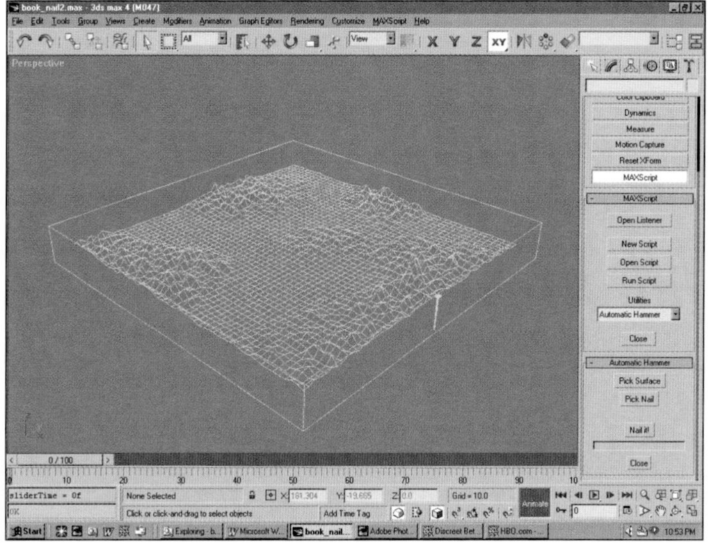

The Automatic Hammer scripted Utility panel.

Note: You can find the complete script, hammer.ms, on the accompanying CD-ROM.

8 In the Automated Hammer Utility Script, pick the plane, pick the nail, then press the "Nail it!" button and watch the progress bar grow.

When the progress bar is full, a *message box* will let you know that the script has finished. At this point, the nails have been placed but are hidden and will not automatically display.

9 Hide the original nail object.

SET UP THE LIGHTING AND RENDER

The objects have been built, the textures have been created and applied, and the script has been written and run. To see the results of your labor, you need to set up simple lighting and a camera before you render.

1 Create a target spot at X = –100, Y = –200, Z = 200. In the General Parameters rollout, turn on Cast Shadows. In the Spotlight Parameters rollout, set the hotspot to **55**. In Attenuation Parameters, turn on Use Far Attenuation and set the Start distance to **125** and the End distance to **1000**. Move the spot's target to XYZ 0,0,0.

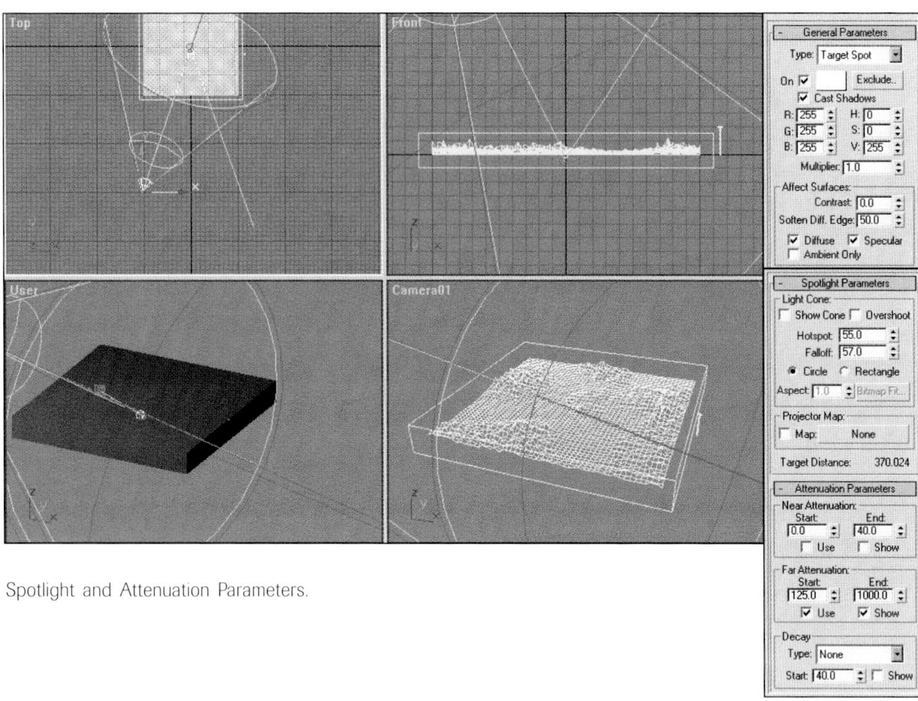

Spotlight and Attenuation Parameters.

2 Create a target camera at X = 150, Y = –300, Z = 180. Move the camera's target to X = –15, Y = 0, Z= –20. Adjust if necessary to find a good view of the nails.

3 Render and save your results as **Nailtable.avi**.

Watch the explosive wave break over the islands!

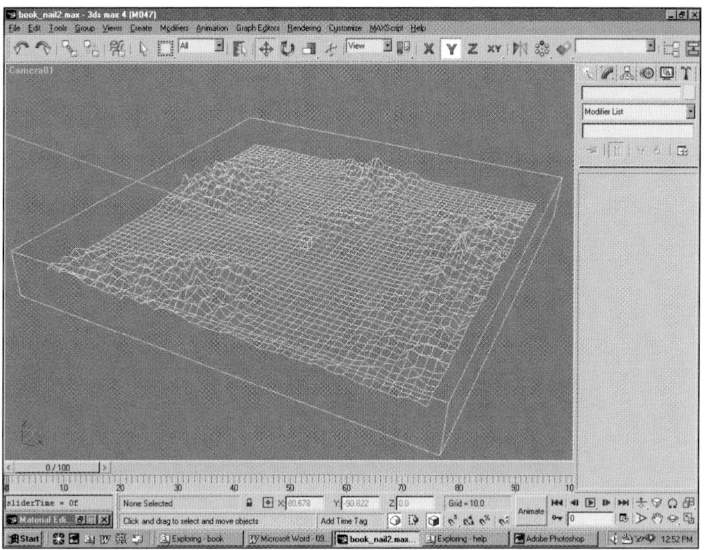

Find a flattering view with the camera.

Modifications

The inspiration for this tutorial is the small toy people keep on their desks that they press their faces or hands into and leave an impression. It was the inspiration for the nail table effect in the movie *X-Men* as well, which was my inspiration for writing this chapter. People always seem to like to imprint their hands and sometimes their face in those little things, and the full extension of this tool could be assigning an Animated Relief map of a human face to the Displace modifier. In fact, you can create any prerendered or procedural animation and play it back as a Displacement map, driving the motion of the nails.

You could get a map or satellite image and create a relief map of a real place rather than a procedurally created noise landscape.

What other ways can you optimize or append the script? What cool effects can you create when MaxScript automates the tedious details for you? MaxScript provides many ways to link objects and tools within max in nearly infinite combinations.

I agree that MaxScript is a powerful tool.

NON-PHOTOREALISTIC RENDERING

"Beauty (n.): The power by which a woman charms a lover and terrifies a husband."

—AMBROSE BIERCE

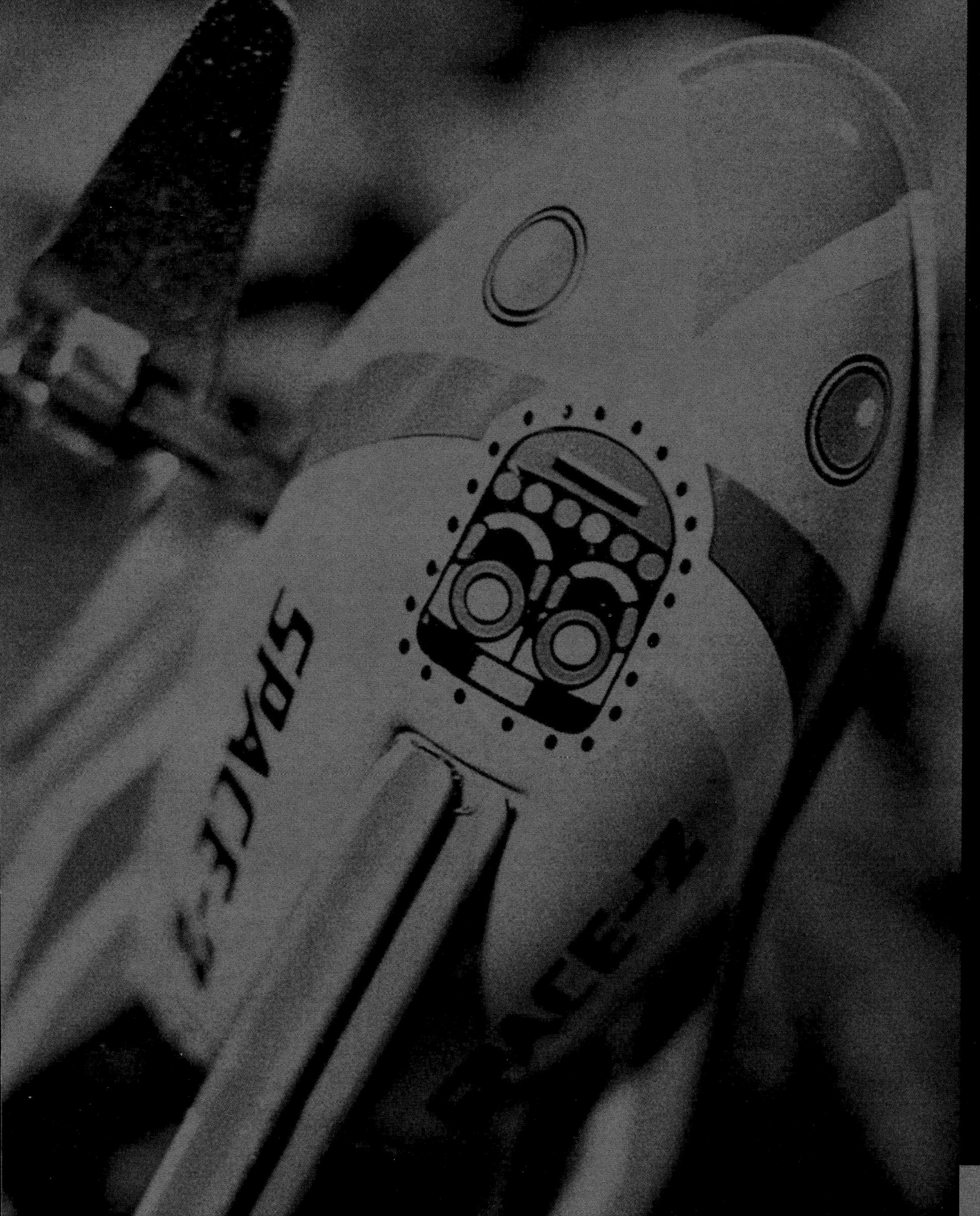

Creating Simulated Natural Media Looks

Non-photorealistic rendering (NPR) is the technique of applying abstract, stylized, or simulated natural media looks to a rendered 3D animation. There are lots of different NPR looks; perhaps the most popular one is the 3D-cel look, in which 3D graphics are rendered to look like traditional inked and painted 2D cartoons (similar to most cel-animated cartoons). This project shows you how to create both a cel look and a sketch look using 3ds max 4, Adobe Photoshop 5.0 or later, Falloff materials, and a few filters.

Project 12

Non-Photorealistic Rendering

by Laurent M. Abecassis

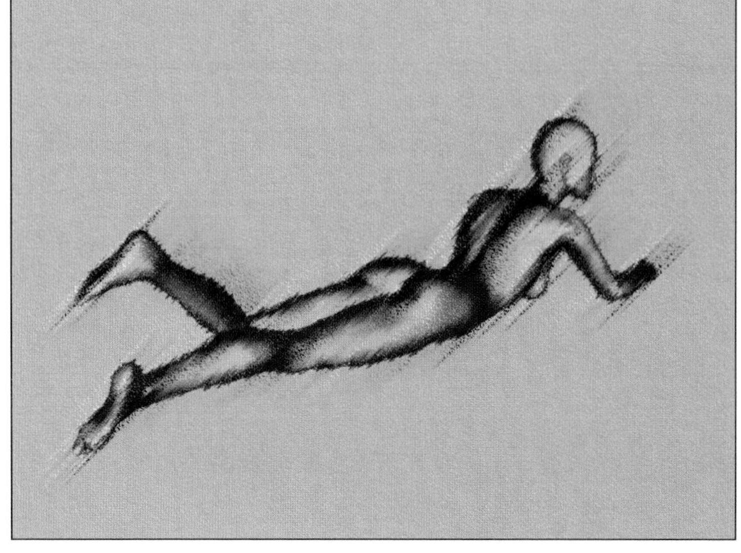

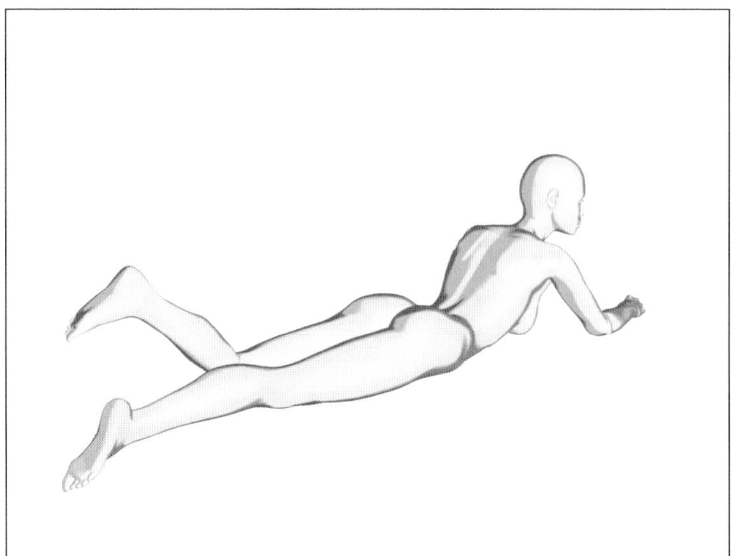

Note: This chapter, including text, imagery, and all associated files on the accompanying CD-ROM ©2001 by Laurent M. Abecassis. All rights reserved.

Getting Started

For this tutorial, you'll start with a simple scene consisting of an imported Zygote character and a camera. Open the scene **woman.max** from the accompanying CD-ROM.

For reference, you can also open the scene **woman_npr.max** from the accompanying CD-ROM. It is the final scene with all the correct settings.

> **Note:** The model "woman" used for this effect is copyrighted and used with permission from Zygote Media Group, which specializes in human figure modeling. They offer models for sale individually or in collections at **www.zygote.com**.

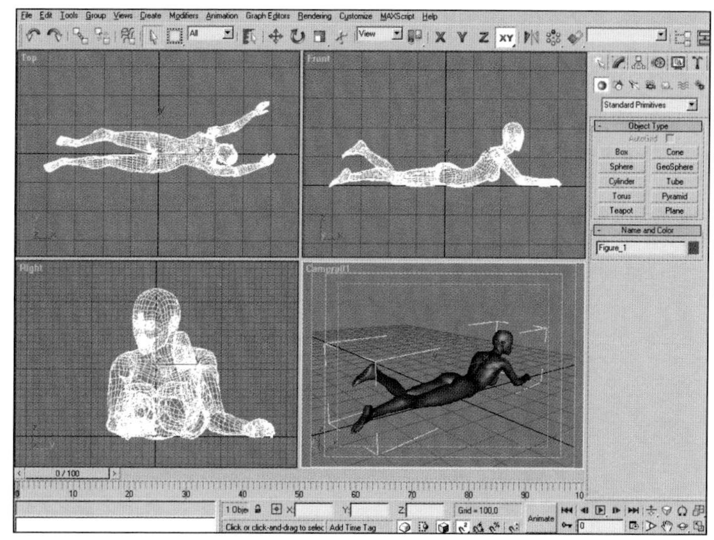

Start with this simple scene.

Set Up the Basic Material

Start by creating the material that will help you produce a traditional sketched look.

1 In Rendering/Environment, adjust the Background Color to a light gold such as R 210, G 190, B 120.

Changing the background color will match the hue of the figure that will be drawn later in the chapter.

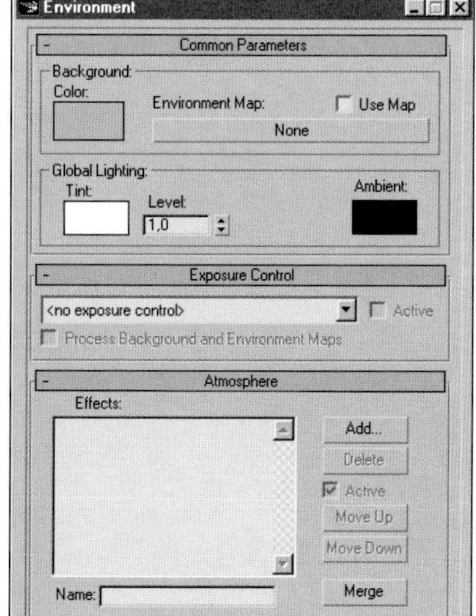

Set the Background Color to a light gold.

2 Go to the Material Editor, select the Woman material, and make your Ambient, Diffuse, and Specular colors the same as your background color.

All of the colors will be similar to achieve the effect you are trying to create.

3 Set Specular Level and Glossiness both to **0** and apply the parameters to the Woman object.

By changing these settings, you will avoid a white shine to the model, which would cause the rendering to lose its "traditional" look and feel.

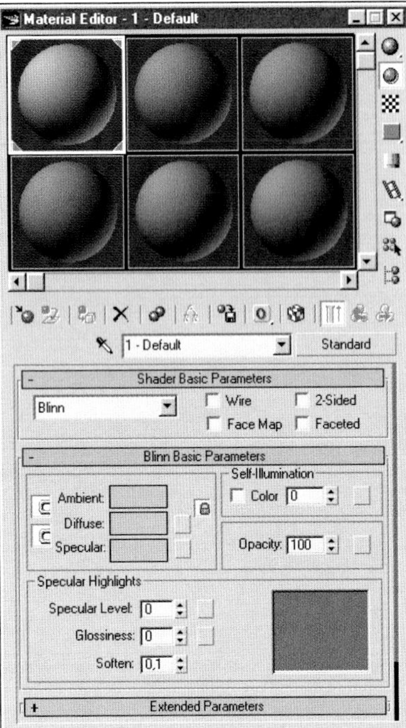

Make the Ambient, Diffuse, and Specular colors the same as the background.

4 Go to the Camera01 window and render the image.

This is a good example of a quick, stylized look you can apply to your renderings. Using 3ds max 4's material tools, it is fairly simple to apply creative, non-realistic materials and backgrounds to a scene.

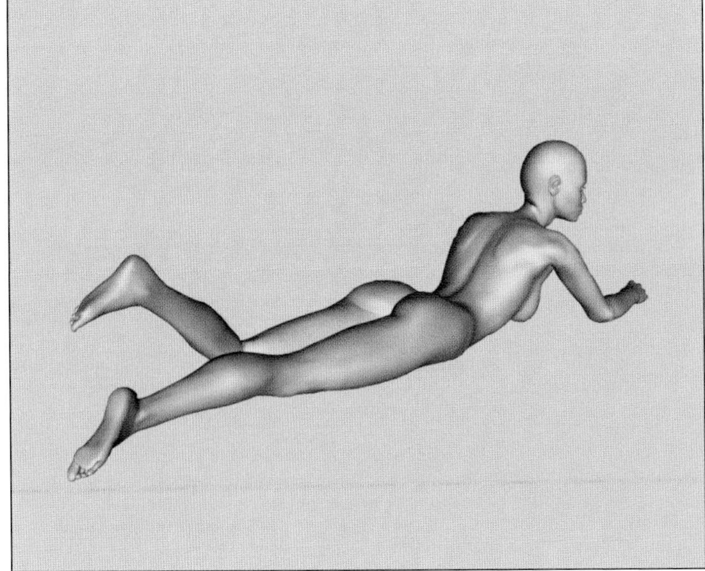

Render the Woman image with the new settings to achieve a smoother effect.

Set Up the Falloff Material

The Falloff material will help you achieve the effect that the rendered woman model is actually a hand drawing.

Note: When determining what effects to apply to an image, try doing some real artwork using traditional media to create your mood and then reproducing it digitally.

1 In the Material Editor, apply a Falloff map to the Diffuse Color slot.

   Applying the Falloff map to the Diffuse Color slot will cause the areas of the model with this material to have a highlight on their outer edges, making it look as if they were lit with Rim Lighting, a common lighting effect used by photographers.

2 Render the scene to preview the effect that Falloff creates using default settings.

3 Change Falloff Type to **Shadow/Light**.

   This reverses the effect of the light on the model.

Note: You might want to review the max help files for Falloff material. Many combinations can be used to create some really artistic effects.

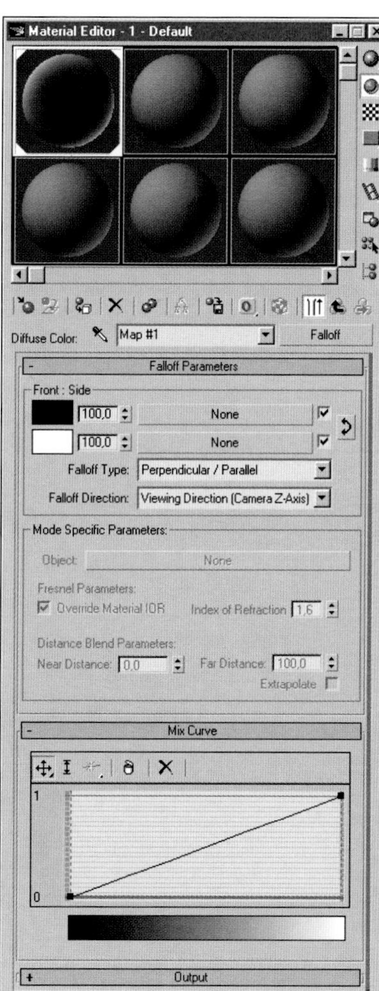

The default Falloff Parameters.

4 Change the white to the same color as the background (R 210, G 190, B 120). Change the black to a darker version of the background color (R 100, G 90, B 30).

   These settings will allow the model to blend in the background to make it look as if it were "drawn" on the background.

5 Change the Mix Curve to match that in the figure shown here. This will make the Falloff simulate an outline on the shading.

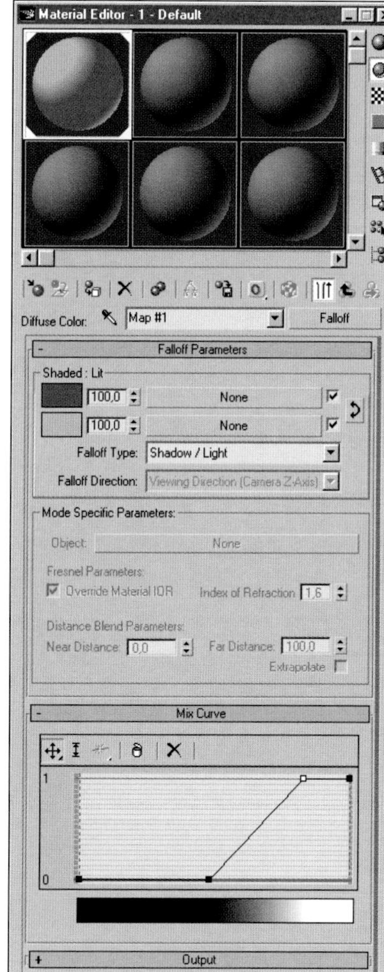

Change the default Falloff Type, color, and Mix Curve settings in the Material Editor.

6 Render a still image and save it as **sketchwoman.tif**.

Your image should now look similar to the one shown here.

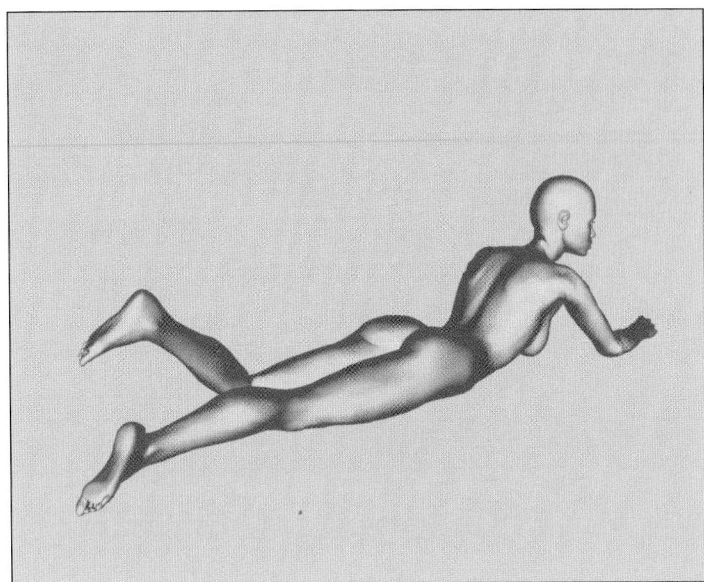

Render the Woman image with your new Material Editor settings.

Set Up the Photoshop Process

In this next section, you'll use Adobe Photoshop to apply filters to the image you just created in the preceding steps. These image manipulation filters will make your illustration look more like a sketch.

1. Start Photoshop and open **sketchwoman.tif**.
2. Right-click the Background layer in the Layers window, select Duplicate Layer, and name the duplicate layer **Pastels**.

Note: It is important that you apply the Pastel layer before the Strokes layer to get an appropriate amount of smudging under the drawing lines.

3 Create another duplicate of the Background layer, naming this one **Strokes**.

You should now have three layers. Using these multiple layers makes it easier to adjust and mix the filters to achieve the "sketched" look.

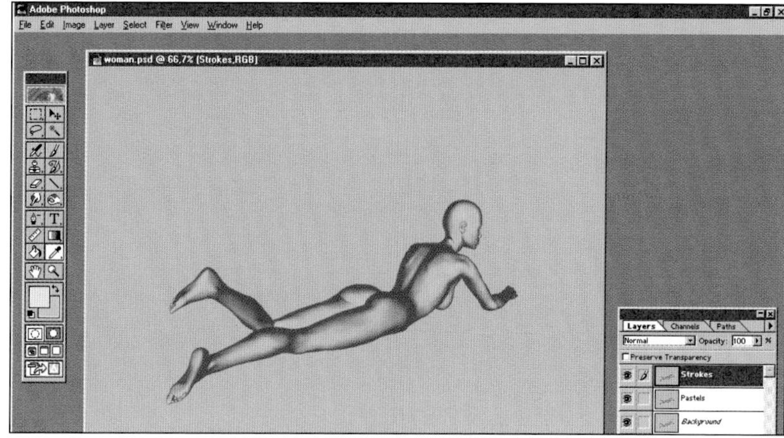

Create three duplicates of your image's Background layer in Photoshop.

4 Select the Pastels layer and add the Rough Pastels filter, located under Filter/Artistic/Rough Pastels. Use the following settings:

Stroke Length: **40**
Stroke Detail: **20**
Texture: **Sandstone**
Scaling: **100**
Relief: **10**
Light Direction: **Top Right**

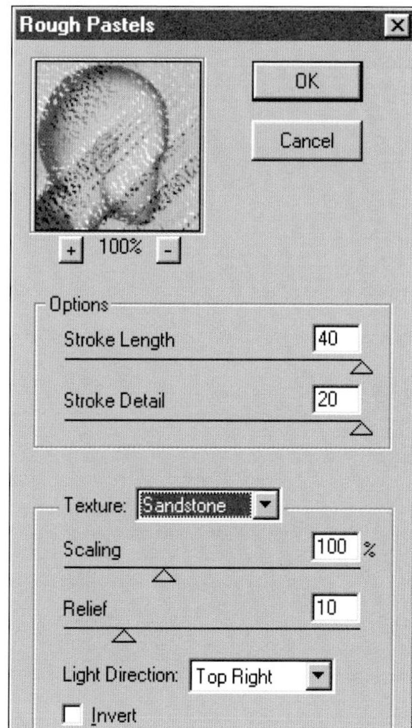

The Rough Pastels filter.

Note: When you use Photoshop filters, try different combinations to get your effect. Try to use more layers and add more effects to push the envelope in design. Art is based on imagination and constantly bending the rules to achieve something that makes us look twice and ask why or how.

Note: You should always save multiple copies of your images when you get to an effect or look that you like. You can always go back to that particular image and work from that file without trying to remember all of the steps it took you to get that effect.

5 Select the Strokes layer and add a Sprayed Strokes filter, located under Filter/Brush Strokes/Sprayed Strokes. Use the following settings:

Stroke Length: **20**
Spray Radius: **15**
Stroke Direction: **Right Diag**.

Note: Another way to apply filters in Photoshop is to create an action. This enables you to apply your effect to a folder where you have rendered your animation as a sequence of numbered files. With Photoshop 6, you can also create and save layer styles.

The Sprayed Strokes filter.

6 Set the Strokes layer to Multiply instead of Normal in the Layers window and flatten your image layers.

The image is a bit too dark and the colors appear burned, so you should apply some color correction.

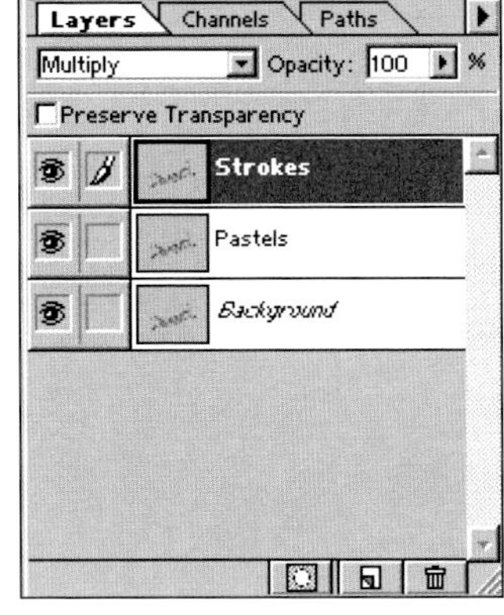

Set the Strokes layer to Multiply.

7 Go to Image/Adjust/Brightness/Contrast and set the Brightness to **40** and the Contrast to **25**.

This removes the dark look of the image.

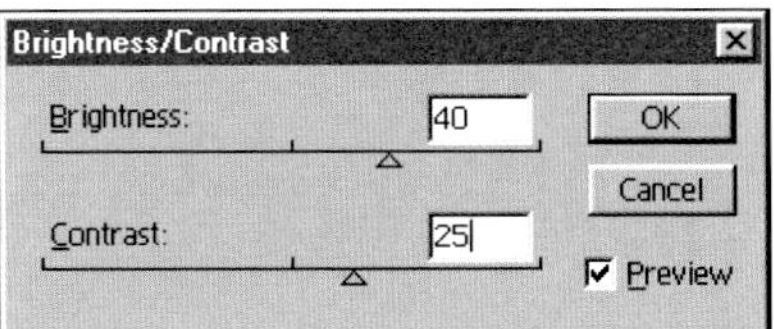

Adjust the Brightness and Contrast.

8 Go to Image/Adjust/Hue/Saturation and set the Hue to **–10** and the Saturation to **–30**.

This removes the color-burned effect and adds some variation to the hue.

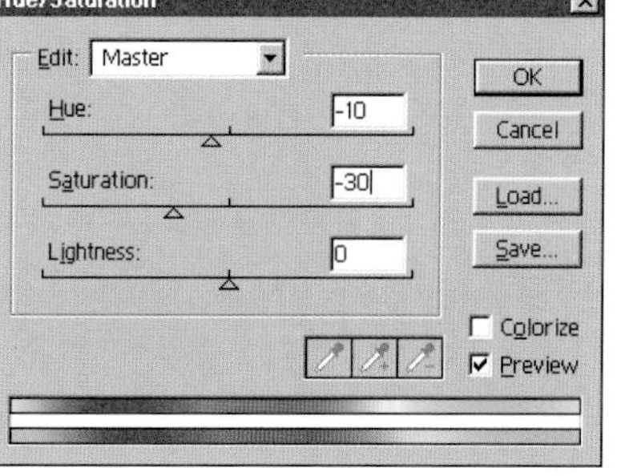

Adjust the Hue and Saturation.

9 Your final result should resemble the accompanying image. Before going on to the next section, you might want to save your file.

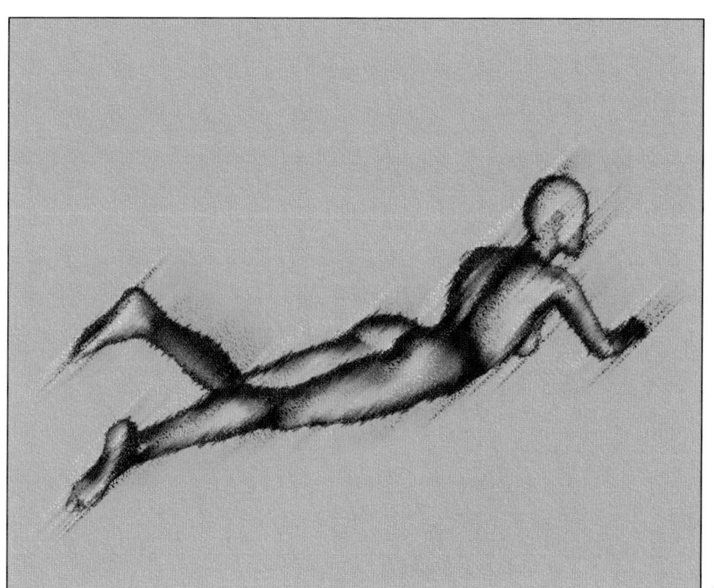

The final, color-corrected image.

The 3D-Cel Look

The next step in your study of non-photorealistic rendering is to achieve a more well-known look: the 3D-cel look. You will accomplish this directly in 3ds max 4 without commercial plug-ins or other external applications, using many of the Falloff materials from the preceding sections but with a different approach. For the 3D-cel look, you use the same scene you used to create the sketch look.

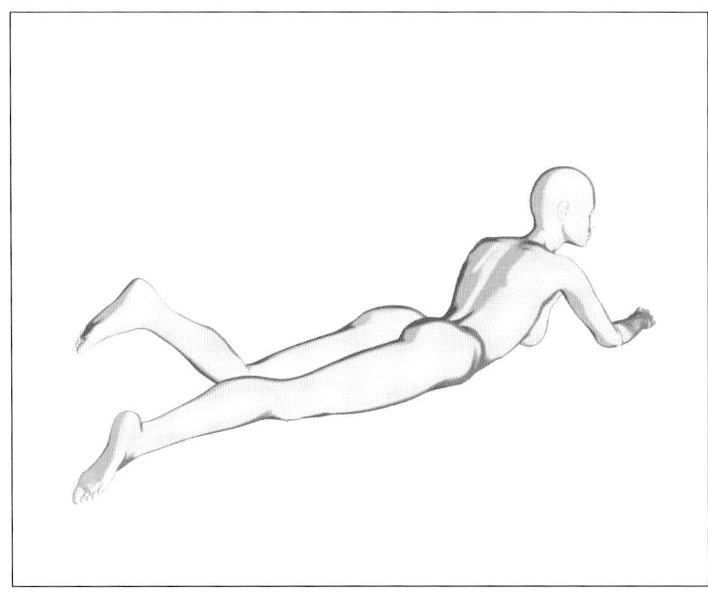
The 3D-cel look.

1 Open scene **woman.max** from the accompanying CD-ROM.

You can also open the scene **woman_cel.max** from the accompanying CD-ROM. This is the final scene with all the correct settings.

2 Set your Background Color in Rendering/ Environment to pure white.

Set Up the Outline Material

This section details the steps for setting up the Outline material for your 3D-cel effect. The first material you need to create is the Outline material, which simulates the ink and paint look.

1 Adjust the Woman material to match the accompanying figure:

Self-Illumination: **100**
Specular Level: **10**
Glossiness: **10**

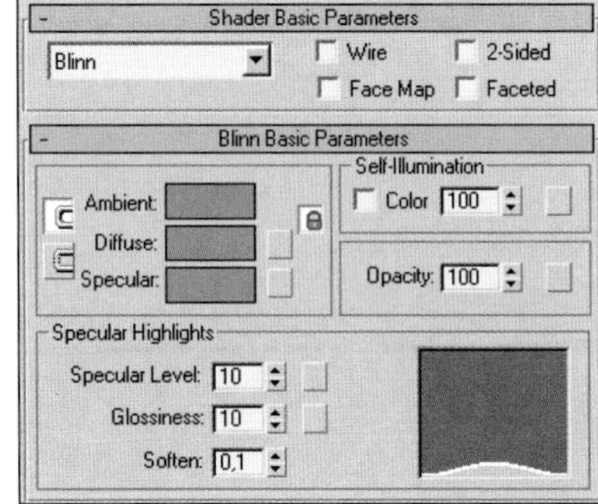

Adjust the Parameters of the Woman material.

2 In the Diffuse slot, add a Falloff material and change its name to **Outline**. Set its Type to **Towards/Away**.

The Towards/Away option sets the angular Falloff ranges between face normals that face toward (parallel to) the Falloff direction and normals that face away from the Falloff direction. The Falloff range is based on a 180-degree change in face normal direction.

Note: There are unlimited possibilities that can be created by adding multiple materials such as the Mix and Blend materials. Try to use multiple combinations to come up with your own techniques.

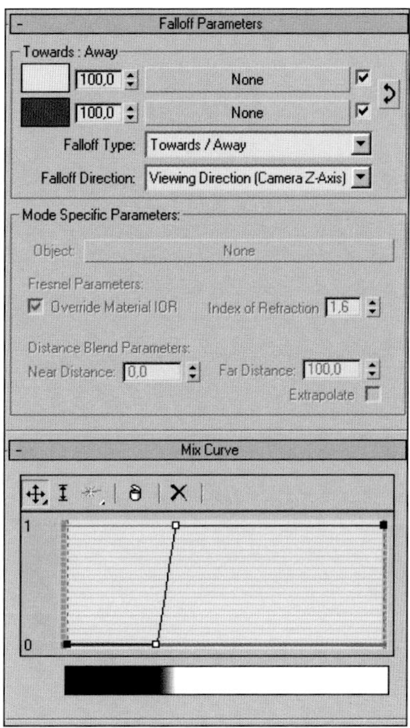

Adjust the Falloff Parameters.

3 Change the black to a flesh-like color (R 250, G 220, B 200). Change the white to a darker version of the flesh color (R 150, G 30, B 0).

These settings create a darker outline on the model's edges.

4 Change the Mix Curve to match the figure shown previously. Render your file.

Your image should show an almost flat cartoon drawing like the one shown here.

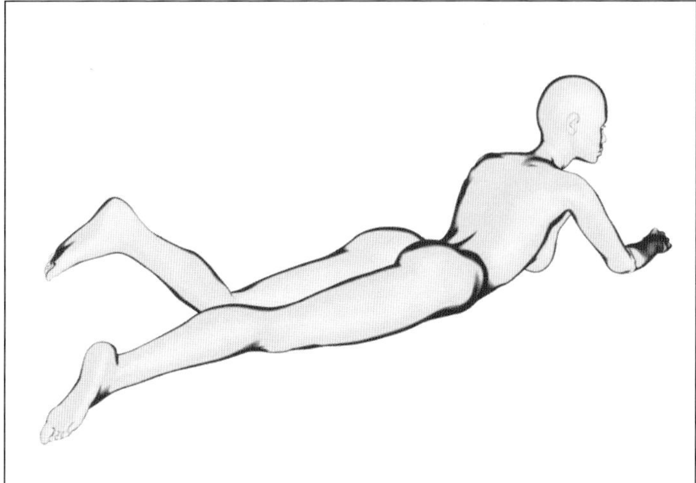

Render the cartoon-like image.

Set Up the Shaded Material

This section details the steps necessary to create the shaded material of your 3D-cel effect. In the same Diffuse channel used in the preceding section, you'll add a Falloff that is controlled by the lighting to create shadows.

1 Press the Falloff button and choose a Mix. The Replace Map dialog will ask you to keep or discard the current material. Because you still need it, choose Keep old map as sub-map.

You are actually applying a mix of Falloff materials in the diffuse channel—the first one we created is still used, but by adding the Mix we can add another Falloff material and have even greater control over the final image with multiple Falloff Effects.

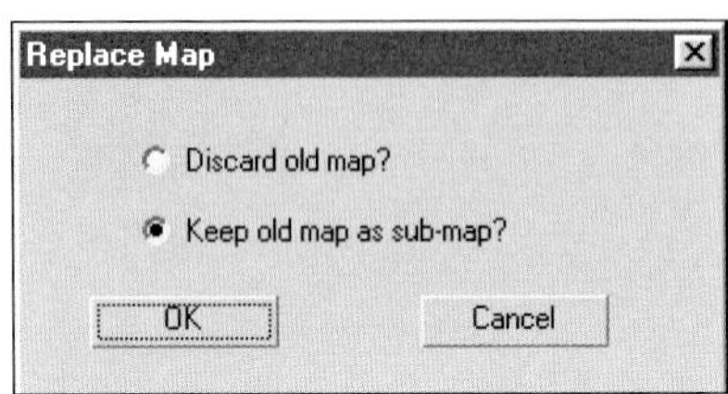

Keep your old material as a sub-map.

2 In the Color #2 slot, add another Falloff and change its name to **Shadows**.

Be sure to add this Falloff to the slot next to Color #2 and not into the Mix Amount slot.

You use this slot to create the shadowed area on the object.

3 Set its Type to **Shadow/Light**. Change the black to R 220, G 120, B 80. Change the white to R 250, G 220, B 200.

4 Change the Mix Curve to match the figure shown here.

You might want to compare the before and after images to see exactly how these new settings create the shadow on the woman's body.

5 Set your Mix Amount to **50** so that both of the Falloff materials will be used at 50%.

Because you just created a material that is affected by the lighting of the scene, you need to create a light.

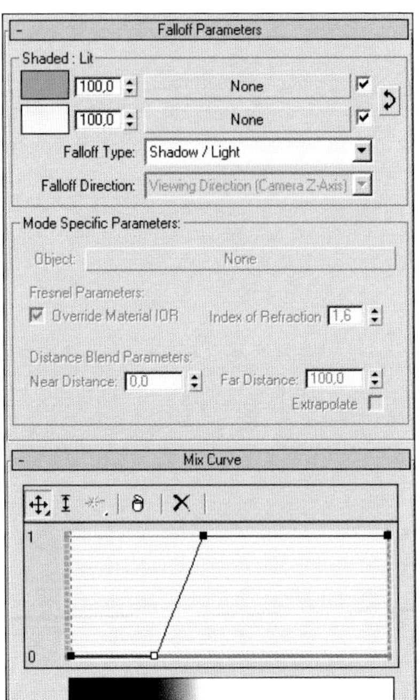

Adjust the Falloff Parameters of your Shadow material.

6 Place an Omni light just on top of the Woman mesh and then render the image.

Using simple Falloff materials and Mix, you just created a 3D-cel look.

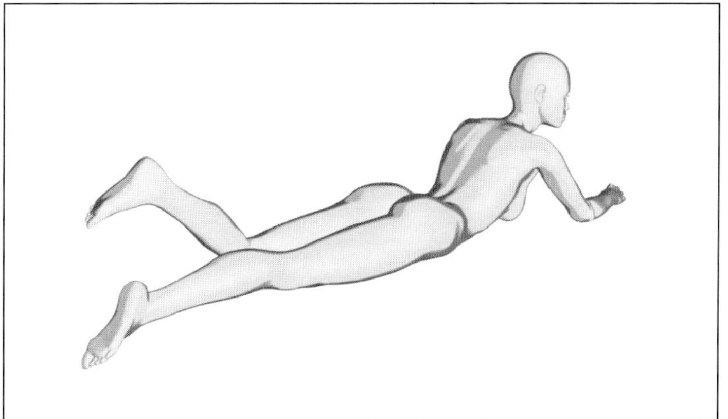

Render your finished 3D-cel effect.

Modifications

You can use this project's techniques to add never-before-seen looks to your 3D scenes. Experiment by using different values with your filters or trying out the various commercial Photoshop plug-ins such as Picture Man-Hand Drawing and Halftone Pattern. You should also consider loading your rendered sequence in Discreet Combustion and applying filters to sequential animation frames.

You can also use the Video Post directly in 3ds max 4, but using external software gives you more control over preview.

Note: Another way to achieve a 3D-cel look is to use Illustrate!, which is available from Digimation. Illustrate! is a powerful toon shader with features no other plug-in can offer. It can even render animation in Flash format. On the accompanying CD-ROM, you will find a 30-day evaluation version of Illustrate! 5.1 for 3ds max 4.

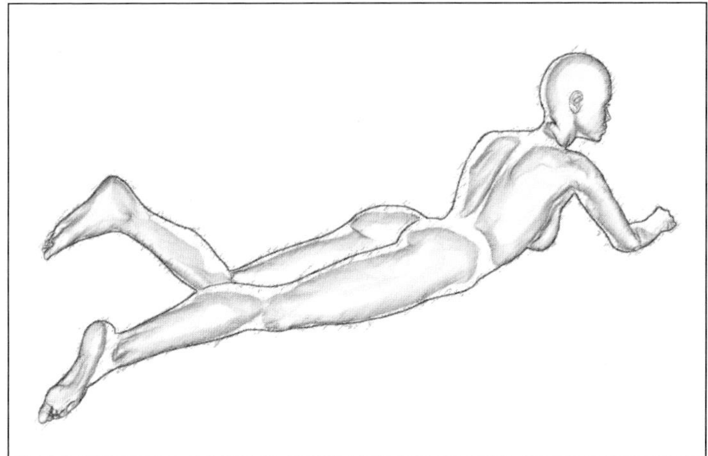

Experiment with new plug-ins such as Picture Man-Hand Drawing and Halftone Pattern.

CAMERA MATCHING

"If you want to be successful in a particular field of endeavor, I think perseverance is one of the key qualities. I haven't met anyone (who is successful) who hasn't been able to describe years and years of very, very difficult struggle through the whole process of achieving anything whatsoever. There's no way to get around that."

—GEORGE LUCAS

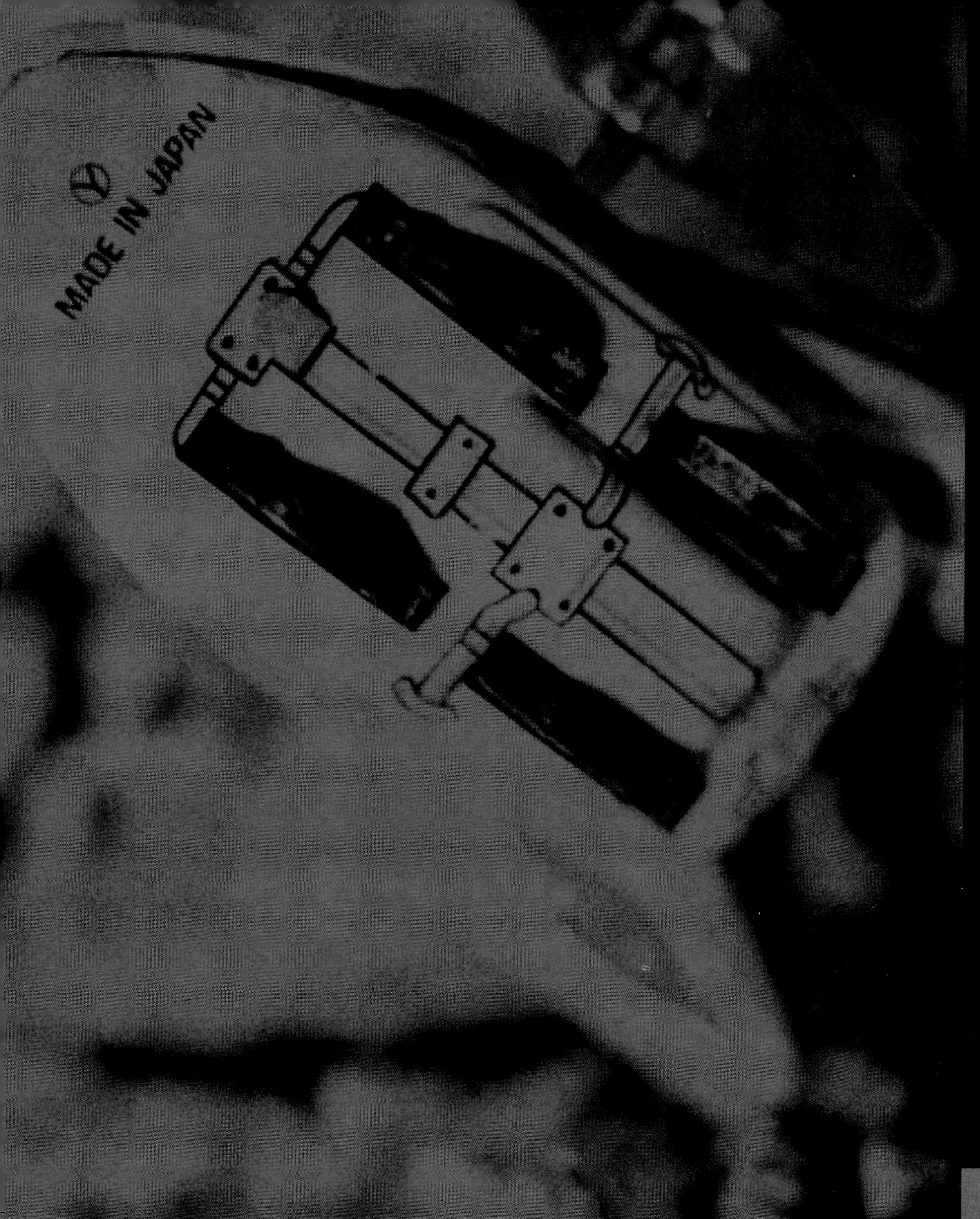

Realistically Insert a 3D Model into a Piece of Digital Video

In today's industry of special-effects-loaded movies and the pursuit of lifelike computer graphics, you would be hard pressed to find a movie that does not have some sort of 3D aspect to it. Taking a piece of video and successfully inserting 3D characters and models into it is what has made movies like *Star Wars: Episode I*, *The Matrix*, and *X-Men* the brilliant visual-effect masterpieces that they are. 3ds max 4 has the tools to give you the power of a multimillion-dollar effects studio. In this tutorial, you will learn how to use a section of digitally shot video, simple geometry, and lighting to create an environment for your 3D models and animations to exist in. You will see how easy 3ds max 4 makes it for you to create your own professional-looking animations and video!

Project 13

Camera Matching

by Marcus Richardson

How It Works

In this tutorial, you will be using a simple probe droid–looking model. This will enable you to concentrate more on the lighting, camera angles, and reflections rather than having to worry about complex animation. Keep in mind, though, that after you have set up the scene properly, you will be able to import your own models and animation into the scene. This particular tutorial will be using still video to get you used to max's tools. Using moving video requires precise measurements, led tracking points, and a lot of extra steps that would make it impossible to teach in one tutorial. As the background for the scene, you will be using a digital video segment of a dark, rainy alley shot on a tripod to reduce camera movement. Its resolution is 720×480, which is standard for digital video. This means that after you are done with this tutorial and have put your own characters into the scene, you can put it on videotape and marvel with your friends at how cool you are!

Getting Started

To get started, load **CameraMatch01.max** from this project's folder on the accompanying CD-ROM. You will see the probe droid and nothing else in the scene. (We have added arms and a simple bone structure to enable you to animate it later.) The droid was made out of a simple sphere, extruding polygons out of it and mapping it with the Space Metal material in the 3ds max 4 Space Material library. You can view the complete file by opening **CameraMatch02.max**.

Setting Up the Camera

This is the meat of this tutorial. You will be creating a free camera and inserting the background.avi. The first thing you need to do is group and hide the droid to get it out of the way.

1. In the Front viewport, drag and select all of the droid. In the top toolbar, click Group and group the droid. Name it **Droid**. Click the Display icon in the right toolbar and click Hide Selected.

   You will unhide the droid later for the animation.

Note: Another way to select the droid is to click the Select by Name arrow in the top toolbar and click All.

2. Click in the Front viewport to make it active. In the object creation toolbar to the right, click the Camera icon and create a free camera in the Front viewport. You can set its position to X = 0, Y = 0, Z = 0 if you want, but it does not matter because you will be moving the camera anyway.

3. Right-click in the Perspective viewport and press "C" on the keyboard.

   This will set the viewport to the view of the camera you just created.

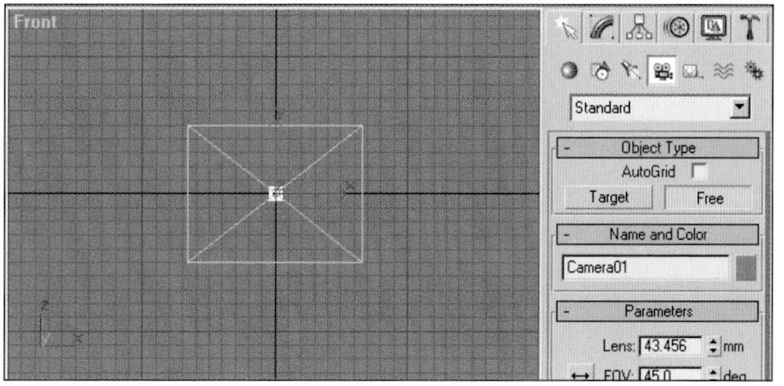

Create a free camera in the Front viewport and use the default settings.

4 Now you need to insert the background AVI into the environment background. In the top menu, click Rendering and navigate down to Environment. Under Common Parameters in the environment pop-up box, click the None button under Environment Map.

This will open the Material/Map Browser.

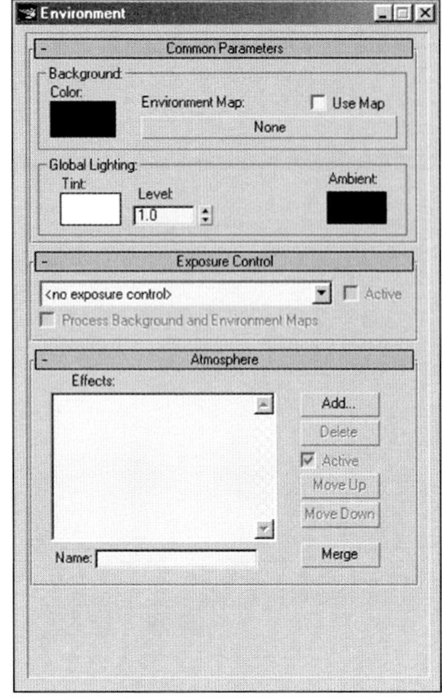

Click the None button to open the Material/Map Browser.

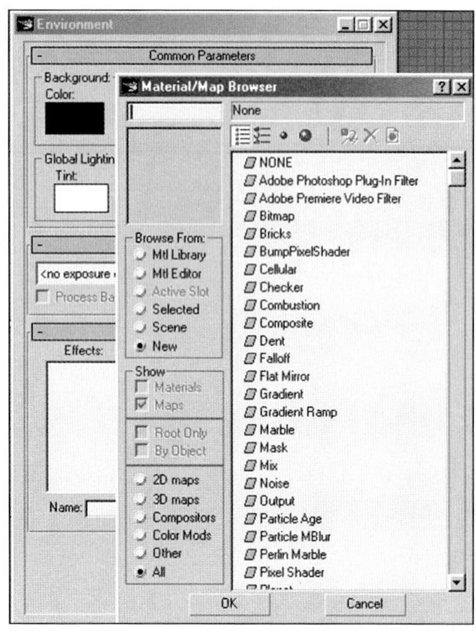

The Material/Map Browser will enable you to insert the background video.

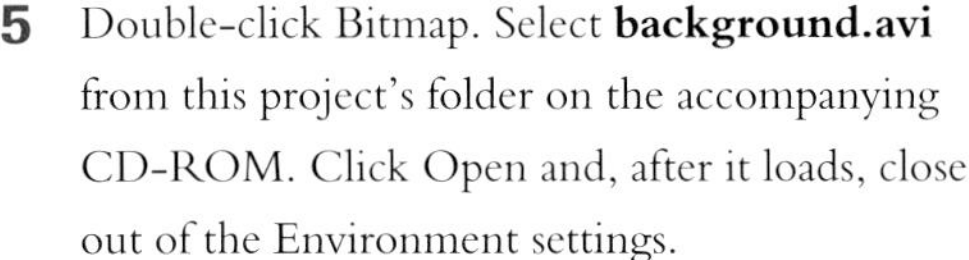

5 Double-click Bitmap. Select **background.avi** from this project's folder on the accompanying CD-ROM. Click Open and, after it loads, close out of the Environment settings.

Now you need to get the background.avi to show up in the viewport.

6 At the top of the screen, select Views and select Viewport Background. Under Background Source, click Use Environment Background. At the bottom of the menu, click Display Background and then click OK.

You will see the movie clip appear in the Camera viewport. You need to set the animation length to that of the footage.

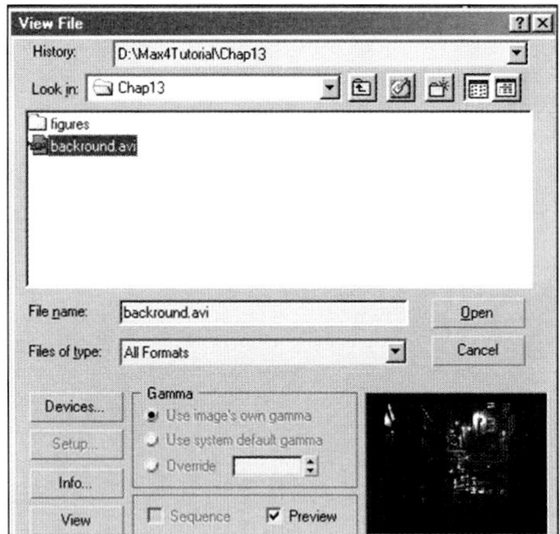

Select background.avi from this project's folder on the accompanying CD-ROM.

7 Select File at the top of the screen, and then select View Image File. In the View File dialog, select background.avi from the accompanying CD-ROM and click the Info button.

You will see the statistics of the video clip. It says 720×480, Undefined, 129 frames. You might also notice that there is a bit of blurred video after that.

8 In the Animation Control area at the bottom right of the screen, click the Time Configuration icon. Under the Animation heading, set the Length to **120** to coincide with the number of frames in the movie clip and to edit out the blurred video.

Creating the Ground Plane

Before you continue, I would like to reiterate that you are not using exact measurements. So from here on out, a lot of the work you do will be based on test screen renders and visual interpretation. I prefer this method because it is faster and yields the same results. You will also be typing specific coordinate sets into the new Absolute Transform Type-In boxes at the bottom of the screen. First, however, you need to make sure to set up your units correctly.

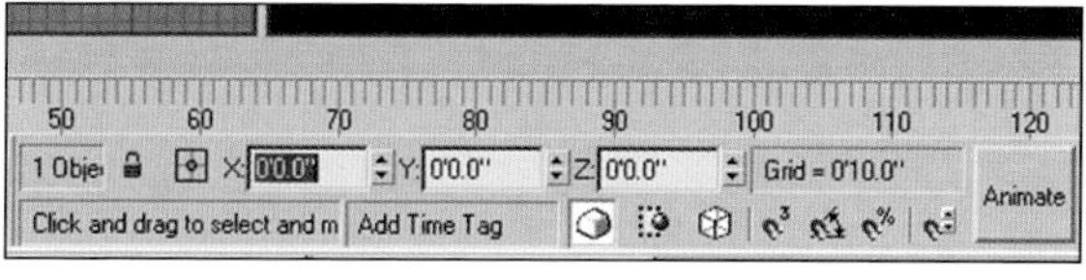

The new Absolute Transform Type-In boxes at the bottom of the screen.

1 Click Customize at the top of the screen and then Units Setup. Click US Standard and select Feet w/Decimal Inches.

I stepped off this alley from the camera to the end, and it measured roughly 100 yards. There are 3 feet in a yard, so in the Top viewport, you need to create a box that is 300 feet long.

2 Type in the dimensions of **300'0.0"×1'0.0"**. Name the plane **Ground**.

Now you will be visually adjusting the camera to place the Ground plane in the proper position.

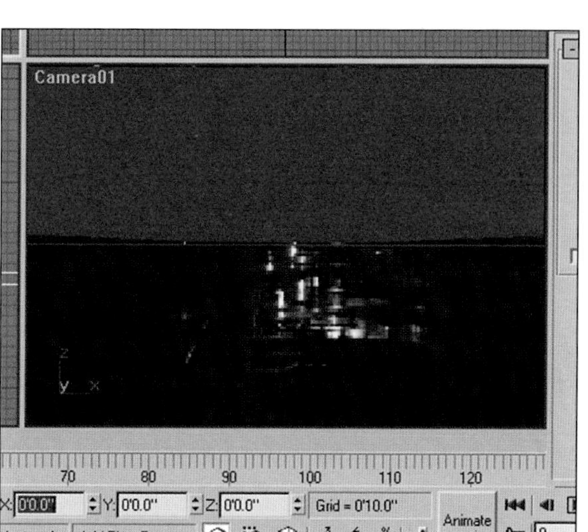

Camera view of the Ground plane when created.

Note: If you created the plane at X=0, Y=0, Z=0 world coordinates, you'd see the box being clipped by the camera. This is okay because you will be moving the camera.

3 In the Top viewport, select the camera, click the Move tool, and type in the transform coordinates of X = –19'6.0", Y = –248'0.0", Z = 83'0.0".

You will see that the box no longer is being clipped, but it is still at the wrong angle.

4 To adjust the plane angle, you need to rotate the camera. With the camera still selected, click the Rotate tool and type in the rotation coordinates of X = 84.5, Y = –0.017, Z = –0.017.

Now you will notice that the angle is starting to look correct, but the ground is still too short. Like I said, you don't have exact measurements.

5 Select the Ground box and type in the Length **4200'0.0"**. You will now apply a Matte/Shadow material to the object.

Note: You can change between Wireframe mode and Shaded mode by pressing the F3 key. This will become very handy when you start adding more objects to the scene.

6 Press "M" on the keyboard. This will open the Material Editor dialog. Select one of the empty spheres. Click Standard/Matte/Shadow. This will open the Matte/Shadow dialog. Make sure you click Receive Shadows. Apply the Matte/Shadow material to the Ground object. You will now do a quick test render to see what you have done.

7 Select the Camera viewport and click the Quick Render Teapot in the Top-sliding menu. See what happened? Nothing! Don't panic, that is exactly what you wanted to do. Create a sphere in the Front viewport and move it down, touching the Ground plane.

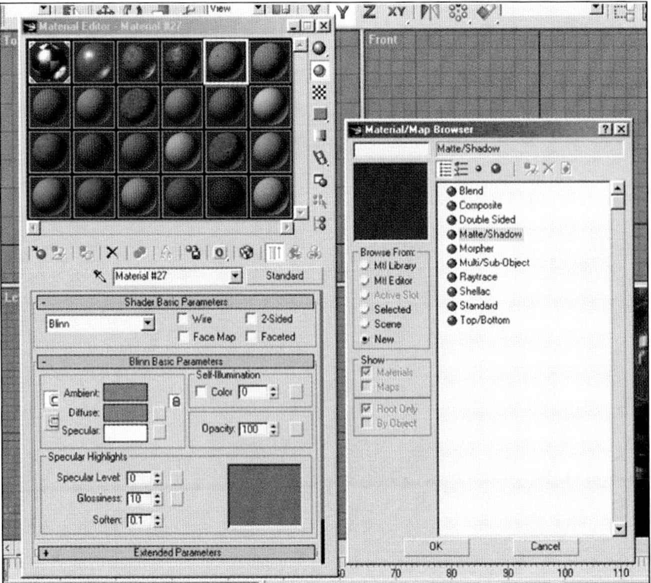

Select the Matte/Shadow material.

Note: Now would be a good time to set up a Quick Render key. You will be doing a lot of test rendering, and having a hotkey saves tons of time. Go to the top of the screen to the Customize/Customize user Interface/Keyboard tab. In the left column, you will notice an alphabetical list of all the commands that can utilize hotkeys. Click anywhere in that column and press the Q key. This should scroll down the list to the Q selections. Select the Quick Render option. In the right column, place your cursor in the Assign Key area. Press the key that you want to use and select Assign Key. I use Q, but it is already assigned. I suggest I or J.

8 Press the Quick Render button again or your hotkey. You can see that the sphere still looks out of place, but it is resting on the ground.

A quick render of the sphere.

SETTING UP THE BASIC SCENE LIGHTING

Okay, now that you have some geometry in the scene, you need to set up the lighting. This step is, I feel, the most important in any camera-matching scenario. Getting the correct lighting is the key to making your objects look like they are part of the scene.

1 Take the sphere you just made and, in the Top viewport, move it back along the Z-axis until it looks like it is in the area of the light shining into the alley. Use X = 0'6.0", Y = 988'0.0", Z = 53'0.0". Go to the Create panel, select the Lights tab, and select Omni.

   You are now going to set up a three-point lighting system with omni lights. I have found that this is a great way to give the objects a realistic look.

2 In the Top viewport, create an omni at X = –800'0.0", Y = 0, Z = 0. Make sure Cast Shadows is not checked! Name this light **Backfill**. Click the light you just created, hold down the Shift key, and drag the light to the right. When the Clone dialog appears, select Instance.

   This should clone the omni. This is important because it will enable you to adjust all the lights at the same time. You can use the coordinates X = 800'0.0", Y = 0.0", Z = 813'0.0" and name it **Sidefill**.

3 Select the new light, again hold down the Shift key, but this time drag back along the Y-axis. Again, click on Instance. Use X = 3'10.0", Y = 1700'0.0", Z = 1500'0.0". It should already be named Sidefill02. The lights should form a triangle.

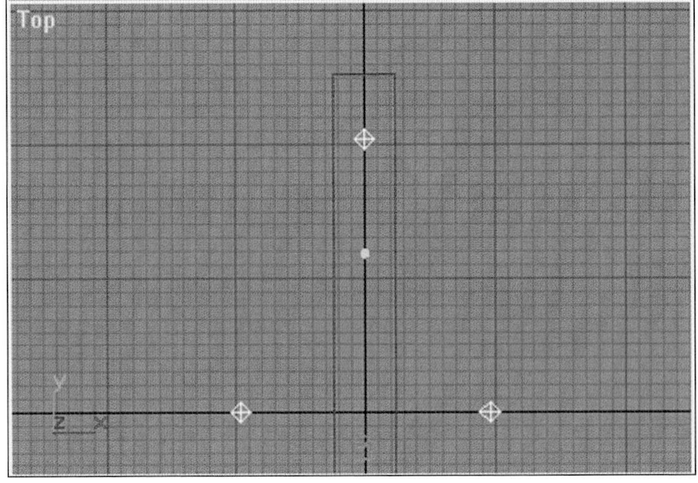

How to arrange the omni lights in the Top view.

4 Go to the Create panel, click Lights/Target Spot, and check Cast Shadows. In the Top viewport, start at the left of the screen and drag the target to the sphere. You can use X = –670'0.0", Y = 1243'10.0", Z = 1168'00.00" for the light and X = 200'0.0", Y = 1200'0.0", Z = 0'0"0.0 for the target. Select the Camera viewport and press your Quick Render key.

You'll notice that you have some depth to the sphere now with a shadow being cast on the ground plane. However, the light is much too bright for this scene.

5 Click one of the omni lights, adjust the V value of it to **140**, and press your Quick Render key again.

Notice how the sphere looks more like the scene.

6 Click the Spot Light, set its V value to **150**, and Quick Render again.

Note: You might not see a shadow yet, which is fine. You might need to adjust the value of the lights yourself to get the best look for your monitor.

Note: Because you instanced the omni lights, all of their values are adjusted to 100.

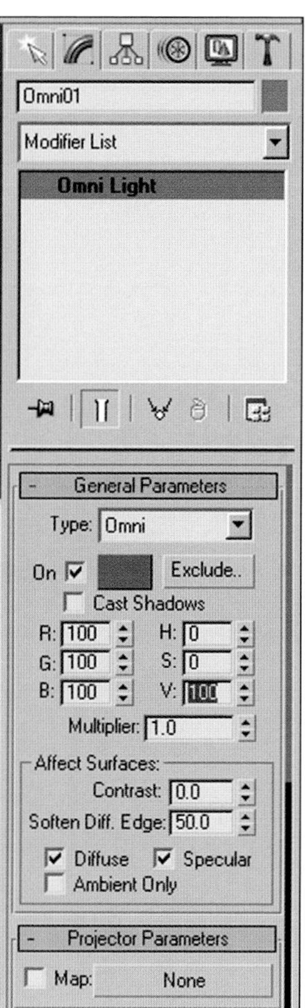

Set the omni light V value to 140.

Creating Scene Objects

Now that you have your lighting set up, you can create masking geometry for objects like the dumpster, the telephone pole, and walls. Before you start, I would like to restate that because we do not have exact scene measurements, a lot of this will be done by eye. I will give you exact sizes and coordinates for this tutorial, but when you try your own pictures and video, you'll have to eye it. It really is not that hard, so stick with it.

1 In the Top viewport, create a box with the dimensions of Length 96'0.0", Width 145'0.0", and Height 200'0.0". Make sure to check Generate Mapping Coordinates and name it **Dumpster1**. Move the box to X = –295'0.0", Y = 390'0.0", Z = –5'0.0". Then select the Rotate tool and rotate the dumpster to X = –2.093, Y = 7.388, Z = –3.27. In the Camera viewport, your scene should look like this.

The Camera view of Dumpster1.

Note: When doing this on your own, you might find it handy to toggle between Shaded mode and Wireframe mode by using the F3 key. When lining objects up yourself, make the object sizes relative to the scene and then move them around so that the edges match up with the objects in the scene like the dumpster!

2 Press the "M" key to bring up the Material/Map Browser and apply the Matte/Shadow material to Dumpster1. Select the sphere and move it to X = –220'0.0", Y = 470'0.0", Z = 53'0.0" in the Top viewport. It should be just partially behind the Dumpster1 object. Press your Quick Render key. You can now start to see how the object masking works.

You can see the sphere behind the dumpster.

Note: Sometimes you will find that the objects do not match up just right, and you get some double imaging. Just move the dumpster and keep pressing Quick Render to get it adjusted correctly. On more complex objects with a lot of sharp, angled edges or round surfaces, you will have to adjust the masking geometry in its Sub-object mode to align itwith the movie clip.

3 In the Top viewport, create a cylinder with the dimensions of Radius 30'0.0", Height 570'0.0". Name it **Phone pole 2**. Then, still in the Top viewport, place it at X = –287'11.0", Y = 1058'11.0", Z = –11'10.0". Apply the Matte/Shadow material to it. Then move your test sphere to X = –328'0.0", Y = 2100'0.0", Z = 180'0.0". Select the Camera viewport and press your Quick Render key.

Now the sphere appears behind the telephone pole!

The sphere appears behind the pole.

4 In the Top viewport, create a cylinder with the dimensions of Radius 8'0.0", Height 570'0.0". Name it **Phone pole 1**. Then, still in the Top viewport, place it at X = 164'2, Y = 1706'7, Z = –3, assuming you want the pole with the light on it. Apply the Matte/Shadow material to it as with the dumpster. Move your test sphere to X = 152'0.0", Y = 2100'0.0", Z = 180'0.0". Select the Camera viewport and press your Quick Render key.

Now the sphere appears behind the other telephone pole.

5 Create a box in the Top viewport with Length as 80'0.0", Width as 145'0.0", and Height as 474'0.0" and name it **Alleywall**. Place it at X = –456'0.0", Y = 1035'0.0", Z = –5'0.0". Apply the Matte/Shadow material to it. Move your test sphere to X = –430'0.0", Y = 1300'0.0", Z = 97'0.0".

6 Select the Camera viewport and press your Quick Render key. Now the sphere appears behind the alley wall! Select the test sphere and delete it; you do not need it anymore.

Note: You can see now how easy this is! If you wanted to, you could reconstruct all the elements in the screen. But you are not going to because that will not be necessary for your animation.

Animating the Droid

Now you are going to animate the Droid object flying around in the scene. You can follow the animation, or you can make him do whatever you want. Keep in mind that if you make him go behind something that hasn't been created yet, you will have to create those elements on your own using the preceding steps.

1 Under the Create panel, click Display/Unhide By Name. This will bring up the Unhide dialog.

2 Select the Droid Group and click OK. Select the droid, go up to Group at the top of the screen, and click Ungroup. The arms and bones are linked to the main body sphere, so that is the only thing you need to animate.

Note: It is very, very important that, before animating the droid, you ungroup it. If it is not ungrouped prior to animation, the droid's arms will move off its body!

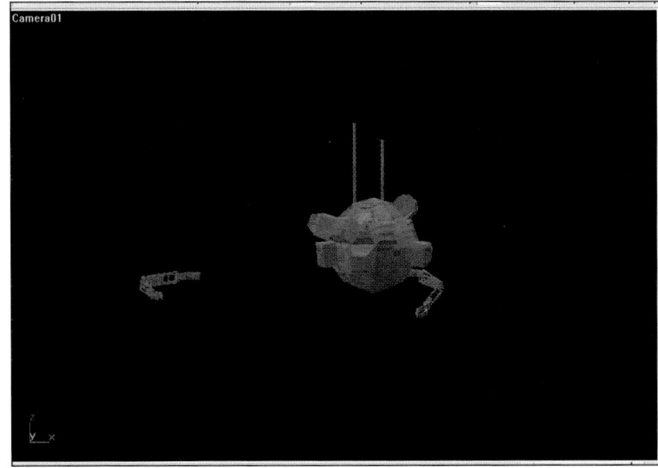

Make sure to ungroup; otherwise, the arms will move away from the body.

3 Click the Droid body sphere and move it to X = 100'0.0", Y = 2400'0.0", Z = 14'0.0" at the far end of the alley behind the wall. Turn on the Animate button and move the slider to frame 30. In the Top viewport, move the droid to X = –90'0.0", Y = 2130'0.0", Z = 70'0.0".

4 Move the slider to frame 60 and move the droid to X = 170'0.0", Y = 2080'0.0", Z = 250'0.0" so that it moves up and behind the telephone pole. Select that last key frame in the time bar, hold down the Shift key, and drag to frame 70. This should have created a copy of the last key frame at frame 70.

This will make the droid pause for 10 frames.

The droid is behind the pole.

5 With the Animate button still on, drag the slider to frame 100 and move the droid to X = –130'0.0", Y = 1200'0.0", Z = 75'0.0" back behind the dumpster. Drag the slider to frame 120 and move the droid to X = –5'00.0", Y = 162'0.0", Z = 35'0.0".

Notice that it is above the puddle, but the puddle does not reflect it. In the next section, you will learn how to add the finishing scene effects.

There is no reflection of the droid in the puddle.

Making the Puddles Reflect the Droid

To add the last bit of reality to the scene, you want to make a reflection in the rain puddles when the droid flies over. To do this, you are going to create another Matte/Shadow material with a raytraced mask on it. This will enable the droid to reflect in the puddles only.

1 Open the Material Editor and select an empty sphere. Click the Standard button and select Matte/Shadow when the Material/Map Browser pops up.

2 Under the Matte/Shadow properties, make sure that both Opaque Alpha and Receive Shadows are checked. Set the Shadow Brightness to **1.0**. Under Reflection, click the Map button and select Mask. The Replace Map dialog will appear. Select Keep Old Map as Sub-map and click OK.

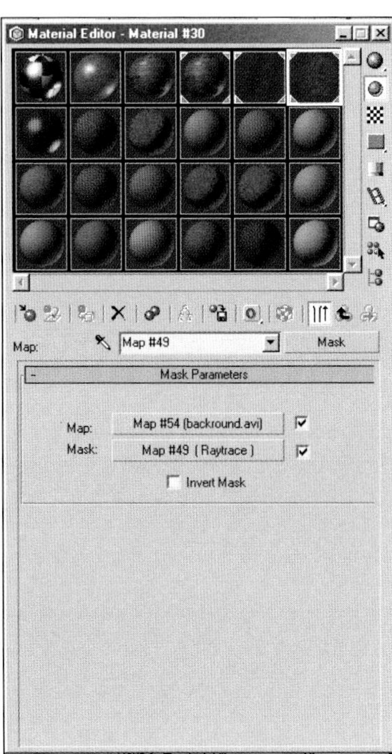

The mask material properties should look like this.

3 Click the Map button (it will say Map # bitmap). Under Bitmap Parameters, click the None button next to bitmap. Navigate to the Chapter 13 folder on the accompanying CD and select background.avi. This will give you a masking layer for the reflection. Click the None button next to the Mask, select Raytrace, and leave all the parameters as default.

4 Select the Ground plane and apply to it the material you just made. If you hit Render now, you should be able to see the reflection of the droid just barely. Remember that this is a dark scene, so that's why the reflection is not popping out. The next section will show you how to really help the visibility of the reflection and the droid!

The Finishing Touches

You might have noticed that it is still difficult to see the droid reflected in the puddles. To put the final touches on this scene, you are going to add a simple glow in video post to the droid's antennas. This not only will make the droid show up better in the puddles, but will also illuminate it in the dark alley better. And, of course, all probe droids have lights on their antennae anyway, right?

1. Press "M" to open the Material Editor. Select the Red metal-looking sphere. To save time, this has already been applied to the top parts of the droid's antennae. Click the Material Effects Channel and set it to **1**.

2. Close the material and, in the top menu bar, select Rendering/Video Post. Click the little render teapot with the arrow to Add a Scene event. Camera 1 should already be highlighted; click OK at the bottom.

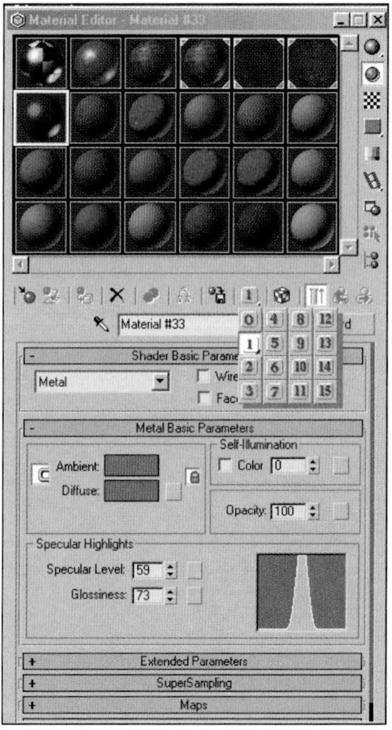

Set the Material Effects Channel to 1.

3. Click the yellow box with the wavy line that pops up to add an Image Filter event. Select Lens Effects Glow from the drop-down menu and select OK.

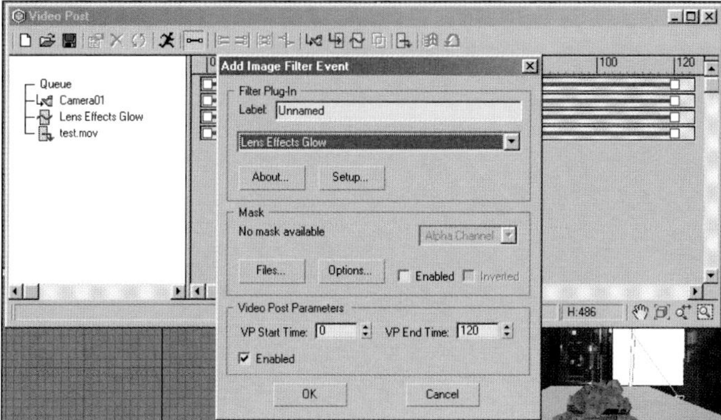

Select Lens Effect Glow from the drop-down list.

4 Click the yellow box with the down arrow. This will open the Add Image Output Event. Click Files and navigate to somewhere on your hard drive where you want to save the render. Select the format. I recommend a QuickTime movie, but you can use whatever you like. Click Save and then OK on the Image Output Event.

5 Now you will set up the glow. Double-click the Lens Effects Glow and click Setup in the pop-up box. This will bring up the Lens Effects Glow setup box. Before you do anything here, make sure your animation time slider is set to frame 105 so that the droid is in view and over a puddle. Click VP Queue and then click Preview. This will render the scene in the window.

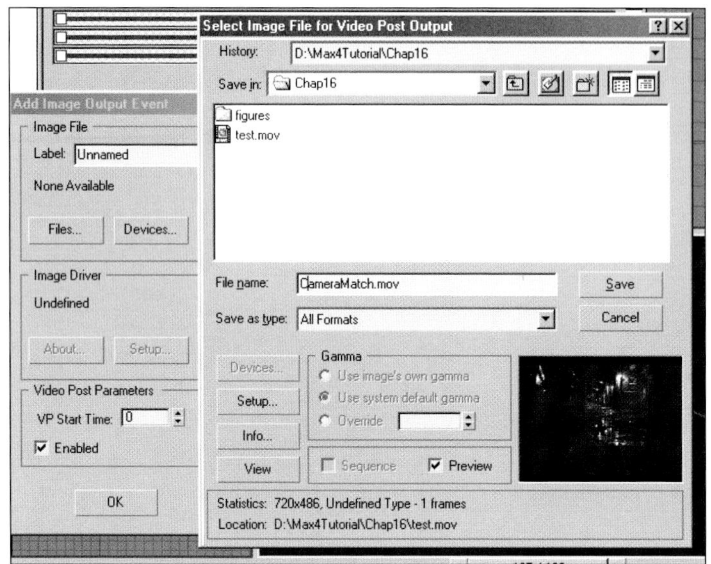

Specify in what format and where you want to save your render.

6 Under the Properties tab/Source, deselect Object ID and select Effects ID. It is already set to **1**, which is what you set the Red Metal material to in the Material/Map Browser. You should see the scene rerender, but nothing looks different. Click the Preferences tab and set Effect/Size to **1.2.** Under Color, select User and set the Intensity to **60.0**.

7 After the scene rerenders, you should see a nice glow on the droid's antennas and in the puddle reflection. Click OK and you are ready to render the scene. Click the little running man at the top of the screen. In the Execute Video Post pop-up, select Range 0 to 120 and select your size under Output Size. Click Render and watch it go! (This is a perfect time for one of those Render Wonders that all of us computer animators are so familiar with.)

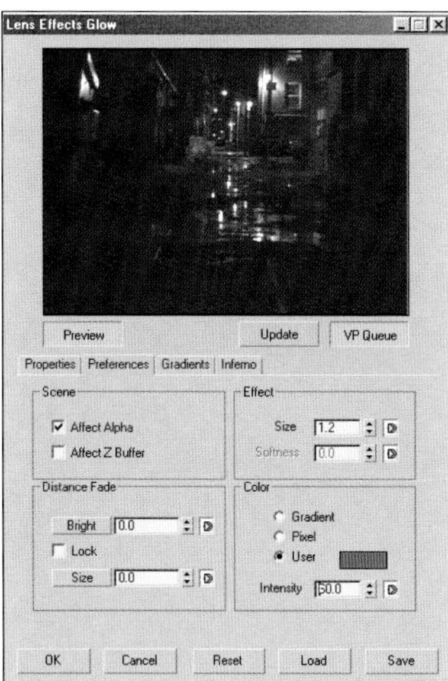

Set these parameters to achieve the proper glow.

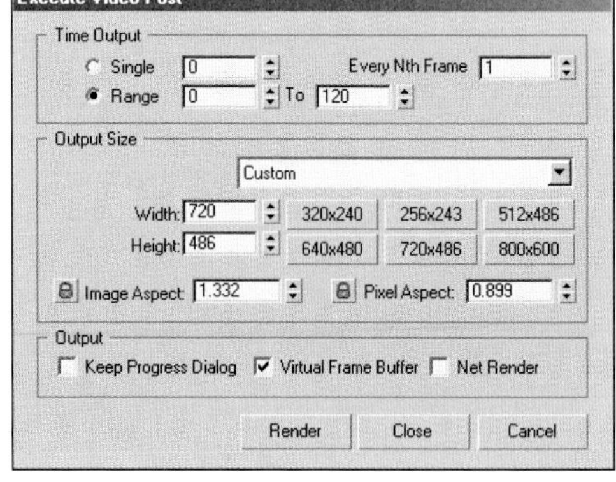

Select your Output Size and render that sucker!

Note: For this first render, I recommend 320×240 so you can get a feel for what the scene looks like. When using your own models (or if you want to put this scene to tape), render 720×4865 for NTSC video. If you are sending it to a DV Tape, render at 720×480.

Note: To animate the arms, all you need to do is select a bone and move it up or down with the Animate button on. You can do that yourself if you want to. You can also make the droid rotate upside down and do all sorts of things. Be creative!

Modifications

Using your own models is the best way to customize this scene. You could add some more realism to this scene by adding spotlights to the droid. You might also want to try to create a particle system that acts like rain and bounces off the droid.

In this project's folder on the accompanying CD are a few other examples of other camera matching scenes I have done with still pictures. They are called Ship.avi and Swamp.avi. Have a look—maybe they will spark some ideas!

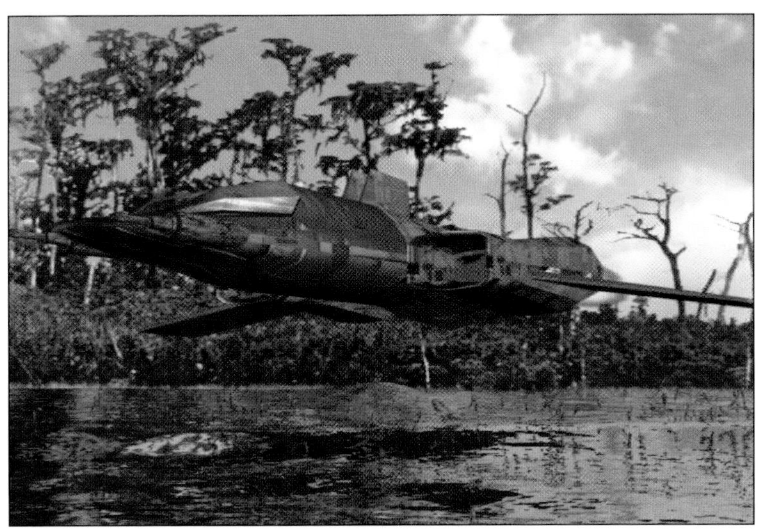

A spaceship landing in a flat picture of a swamp.

A character I created walking through a flat picture.

APPENDIX

"Drama is life with the dull bits cut out."

—ALFRED HITCHCOCK

What's on the CD-ROM

The accompanying CD-ROM is packed with all sorts of exercise files and products to help you work with this book and with 3ds max 4. The following sections contain detailed descriptions of the CD's contents.

For more information about the use of this CD, please review the ReadMe.txt file in the root directory. This file includes important disclaimer information as well as information about installation, system requirements, troubleshooting, and technical support.

System Requirements

This CD-ROM was configured for use on systems running Windows NT Workstation, Windows 95, Windows 98, and Windows 2000. The following minimum requirements are recommended for running the CD; system requirements for the included software will vary.

Processor: 486DX or higher
Memory (RAM): 24MB
Monitor: VGA, 640×480, 256 colors or higher
Storage Space: 10MB minimum
Other: Mouse or compatible pointing device
Optional: Internet connection and Web browser

Loading the CD Files

To load the files from the CD, insert the disc into your CD-ROM drive. If autoplay is enabled on your machine, the CD-ROM setup program starts automatically the first time you insert the disc. You may copy the files to your hard drive or use them right off the disc.

Note: This CD-ROM uses long and mixed-case filenames, requiring the use of a protected mode CD-ROM driver.

Exercise Files

This CD contains all the files you'll need to complete the exercises in *3ds max 4 Magic*. These files can be found in the root directory's Examples folder.

Third-Party Programs

This CD also contains several third-party programs and demos from leading industry companies. These programs have been carefully selected to help you strengthen your professional skills in 3ds max.

Please note that some of the programs included on this CD-ROM are shareware—"try-before-you-buy"—software. Please support these independent vendors by purchasing or registering any shareware software that you use for more than 30 days. Check with the documentation provided with the software on where and how to register the product.

- **Adobe Acrobat Reader.** This program allows you to view and print Adobe PDF files. PDF files are reliable and easy to read.
- **Blob Mod.** Blob Mod is a simple metaball modifier. It will place a metaball at every vertex of a mesh.
  Directory: 3rdParty\peterwajte\blobmod\BlobMod.dlm
- **Chase.** Chase Gravity is a Particle space warp that causes particles to chase the space warp or a designated object. It is useful for creating flocking-type animations or using particles to outline an object.
  Directory: 3rdParty\peterwajte\chasemod\sticky.dlm
- **Forrest Pack Lite.** Forest Pack is a package of eight plug-ins for 3ds max and 3D Studio Viz designed to give a complete solution for the creation of large surfaces of trees and plants.
  Directory: 3rdParty\forestpacklt\setup.exe

- **Hair.** Hair is particle that simulates hair. Mainly intended for creating long head hair, it can also be used for short body hair.
  Directory: 3rdParty\peterwajte\hair\pw_hair.dlo
- **Illustrate! 5.1.** A technical illustration renderer for the 3ds max and 3D Studio VIZ environments. It takes your 3D scenes and renders them as hand drawn images. Illustrate! supports a wide variety of drawing styles.
- **Key_Shifter.** This MaxScript from Stefan Didak (animagic) offsets Path Constraint objects along a path.
- **Particle Paint.** This material turns a particle system into a spray paint can. Any time a particle comes near an object with a Particle Paint material on it, the materials are blended.
  Directory: 3rdParty\peterwajte\ppaint\ppaint.dlt
- **Particle Displace.** This plug-in is a simple particle displacement modifier. It works the same way as the regular Displace modifier, except a particle system is used to displace the object instead of a gizmo. This plug-in makes it simple to create an object and particle system.
  Directory: 3rdParty\peterwajte\pdisplace\pdisplace.dlt
- **Solidify**. Solidify is a modifer plug-in that takes your surfaces and makes them solid.
  Directory: 3rdParty\solidify\solidify.dlm
- **Texporter**. This is a utility plug-in for 3ds max. Its main purpose is simple mesh painting.
  Directory: 3rdParty\texporter\plugins\Texporter3.dlu
- **Ultimate MAX Internet Guide.** This guide contains a searchable database of over 450 Internet sites. You can search by simple built-in functions like listing all sites that have free tutorials, or use a more specific keyword search engine.
  Directory: 3rdParty\appliedideas\setup.exe

Bonus Projects

In the Bonus Projects folder, you will find five extra projects, including completely new projects and expanded material for existing projects. We have included them (in PDF format) as a bonus to you.

Bonus Project 1: Smoke and Wind by Sean Bonney

Realistic smoke effects require special consideration in the areas of collisions, momentum, and volume. In many cases, smoke will collide with scene objects in a vague, approximated manner and will vary in momentum and volume according to the expected wind and thermal properties of a scene. In this project, you will consider wind and smoke together because the movement of the smoke will be determined by the perceived motion of air masses in the scene.

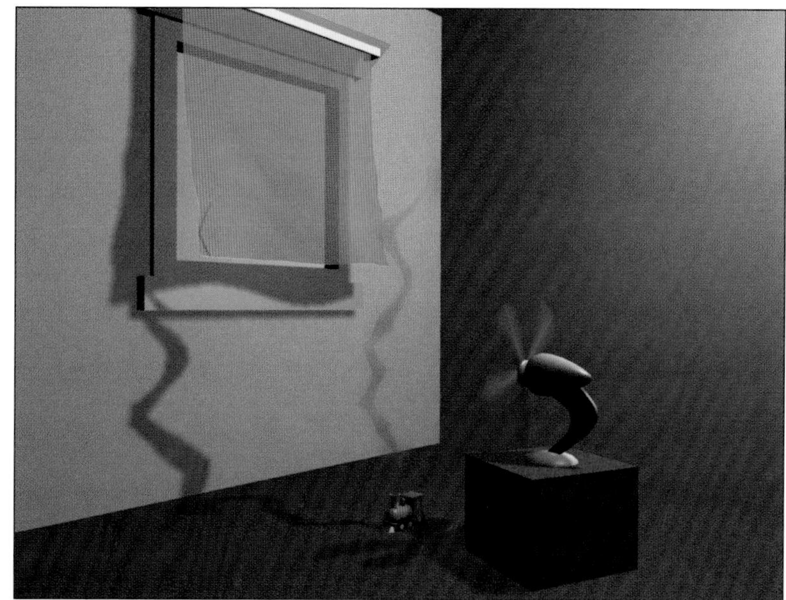

Bonus Project 2: Modeling and Mapping a Head by Laurent M. Abecassis

Because we are accustomed to seeing heads and faces from the moment we are born, we can detect any irregularities in the look of a modeled head without even understanding what the problem is. This project teaches you to model a realistic head using the NurMs technique and the TLUnwrap freeware plug-in. NurMs is a subdivision of modeling techniques that enables you to work on a low-resolution mesh that you subdivide at render time. TLUnwrap is a freeware modifier created by Mankua (**www.mankua.com**) that enables you to unwrap your UVW map directly in the viewport. This helps you generate the image maps needed to achieve a realistic look.

Bonus Project 3: Facial Expressions and Lipsynch by Laurent M. Abecassis

This project is all about expressions and lipsynch. It explains to how to set up the various parts of a face and suggests ways to animate them using 3ds max 4. This project explores which morph targets are needed, how to use morph targets to mimic facial expressions, how to use bones and skin to create head motion, and how to use a LookAT constraint to animate the viewport of the character.

Bonus Project 4: Expanded Project 3 Content by Daniel Manahan

This project teaches advanced users how to model the intricate ground and archway used in Project 3, "Underwater Scene."

Bonus Project 4: Expanded Project 8 Content by Sue Blackman

This project teaches users to articulate the complicated motion of the grabber claw assembly used in Project 8, "Mechanical Machine."

Read This Before Opening the Software

By opening the CD package, you agree to be bound by the following agreement:

You may not copy or redistribute the entire CD-ROM as a whole. Copying and redistribution of individual software programs on the CD-ROM is governed by terms set by individual copyright holders.

The installer, code, images, and files from the author(s) are copyrighted by the publisher and the authors.

This software is sold as-is, without warranty of any kind, either expressed or implied, including but not limited to the implied warranties of merchantability and fitness for a particular purpose. Neither the publisher nor its dealers or distributors assumes any liability for any alleged or actual damages arising from the use of this program. (Some states do not allow for the exclusion of implied warranties, so the exclusion may not apply to you.)

INDEX

Symbols

B

C

D

E

F

G

H

P

Q-R

S

THE NEW RIDERS

3D Studio MAX 3 Fundamentals
Michael Todd Peterson
0-7357-0049-4

3D Studio MAX 3 Magic
Jeff Abouaf, et al.
0-7357-0867-3

3D Studio MAX 3 Media Animation
John Chismar
0-7357-0050-8

3D Studio MAX 3 Professional Animation
Angela Jones, et al.
0-7357-0945-9

Adobe Photoshop 5.5 Fundamentals with ImageReady 2
Gary Bouton
0-7357-0928-9

Bert Monroy: Photorealistic Techniques with Photoshop & Illustrator
Bert Monroy
0-7357-0969-6

CG 101: A Computer Graphics Industry Reference
Terrence Masson
0-7357-0046-X

Click Here
Raymond Pirouz and Lynda Weinman
1-56205-792-8

<coloring web graphics.2>
Lynda Weinman and Bruce Heavin
1-56205-818-5

Creating Killer Web Sites, Second Edition
David Siegel
1-56830-433-1

<creative html design>
Lynda Weinman and William Weinman
1-56205-704-9

<creative html design.2>
Lynda Weinman and William Weinman
0-7357-0972-6

<designing web graphics.3>
Lynda Weinman
1-56205-949-1

Designing Web Usability
Jakob Nielsen
1-56205-810-X

[digital] Character Animation 2 Volume 1: Essential Techniques
George Maestri
1-56205-930-0

[digital] Lighting & Rendering
Jeremy Birn
1-56205-954-8

Essentials of Digital Photography
Akari Kasai and Russell Sparkman
1-56205-762-6

E-Volve-or-Die.com
Mitchell Levy
0-7357-1028-7

Fine Art Photoshop
Michael J. Nolan and Renee LeWinter
1-56205-829-0

Flash 4 Magic
David Emberton and J. Scott Hamlin
0-7357-0949-1

PROFESSIONAL LIBRARY

Flash 5 Magic with ActionScript
David Emberton and J. Scott Hamlin
0-7357-1023-6

Flash Web Design
Hillman Curtis
0-7357-0896-7

Flash Web Design: the v5 remix
Hillman Curtis
0-7357-1098-8

HTML Artistry: More than Code
Ardith Ibañez and Natalie Zee
1-56830-454-4

HTML Web Magic
Raymond Pirouz
1-56830-475-7

Illustrator 8 Magic
Raymond Pirouz
1-56205-952-1

Inside 3D Studio MAX 3
Phil Miller, et al.
0-7357-0905-X

Inside 3D Studio MAX 3: Modeling, Materials, and Rendering
Ted Boardman and Jeremy Hubbell
0-7357-0085-0

Inside 3D Studio VIZ 3
Ted Boardman and Jeremy Hubbell
0-7357-1002-3

Inside Adobe Photoshop 5.5
Gary David Bouton and Barbara Bouton
0-7357-1000-7

Inside Adobe Photoshop 5, Limited Edition
Gary David Bouton and Barbara Bouton
1-56205-951-3

Inside Adobe Photoshop 6
Gary David Bouton, et. al
0-7357-1038-4

Inside AutoCAD 2000
David Pitzer and Bill Burchard
0-7357-0851-7

Inside LightWave 3D
Dan Ablan
1-56205-799-5

Inside LightWave 6
Dan Ablan
0-7357-0919-X

Inside trueSpace 4
Frank Rivera
1-56205-957-2

Inside SoftImage 3D
Anthony Rossano
1-56205-885-1

LightWave 6.5 Magic
Dan Ablan, et. al
0-7357-0996-3

Maya 2 Character Animation
Nathan Vogel, Sherri Sheridan, and Tim Coleman
0-7357-0866-5

Net Results 2: Best Practices for Web Marketing
Rick Bruner
0-7357-1024-4

Photoshop 5 & 5.5 Artistry
Barry Haynes and Wendy Crumpler
0-7457-0994-7

THE NEW RIDERS PROFESSIONAL LIBRARY

continued

Photoshop 5 Type Magic
Greg Simsic
1-56830-465-X

Photoshop 5 Web Magic
Michael Ninness
1-56205-913-0

Photoshop 6 Effects Magic
Rhoda Grossman, et. al
0-7357-1035-X

Photoshop 6 Web Magic
Jeff Foster
0-7357-1036-8

Photoshop Channel Chops
David Biedny, Bert Monroy, and Nathan Moody
1-56205-723-5

<preparing web graphics>
Lynda Weinman
1-56205-686-7

Rhino NURBS 3D Modeling
Margaret Becker
0-7357-0925-4

Secrets of Successful Web Sites
David Siegel
1-56830-382-3

Web Concept & Design
Crystal Waters
1-56205-648-4

Web Design Templates Sourcebook
Lisa Schmeiser
1-56205-754-5

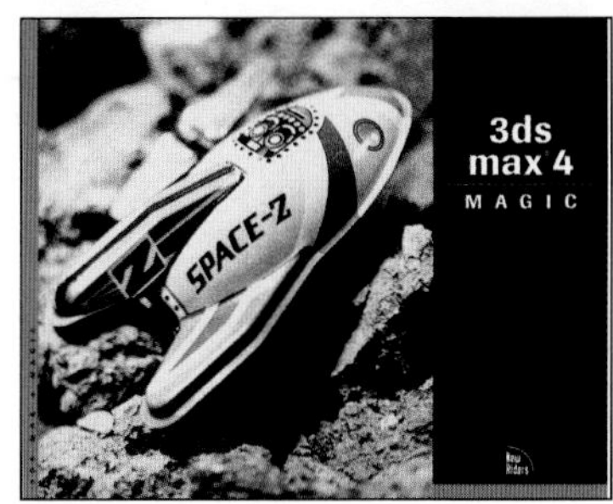

ds max 4 Magic

ach New Riders book has been created with you, the omputer graphics professional, in mind. Complete effects, daptable solutions, time-saving techniques, and ractical applications. Buy your favorite LightWave, ds max, or Maya book online today.

ds max 3D Workstation with Accelerated Graphics

Build and purchase online your own customized 3ds max 3D workstation, and choose from a wide selection of hot 3D OpenGL graphics cards luding Nvidia, Intense 3D, ELSA, and IBM FireGL2 plus ug-ins and monitors.

ds max 4

ds max™ for Windows® is the orld's best-selling professional 3D odeling, animation, and rendering ftware for creating visual effects, aracter animation, and games evelopment.

ggested List Price *** **$3,495**

ds max Plug-ins & Real-Time Animation Systems

We carry every 3ds max plug-in made, as well as TYPHOON—which is a versatile real-time imation solution fully integrated with 3ds max for "live air" and "live to tape" productions. Call for special icing and FREE demo tape.

*** Call us today, mention this ad, and get scount prices on ALL discreet products.**

Intellistations.com

The Ultimate Internet Resource for Video, Film, 3D, and Creative Graphics Professionals.

Buy Online via our Secure Ordering system for VISA, MC, and AMEX

Build your Video/3D Dream Machine with our **Online Configurator**

IntelliStations.com is your source for Digital Content Creation tools that will allow your projects to be done on time, every time. The one you really want for video editing, 3D animation, Web design/graphics, and more.

Our knowledgeable technical production engineers will also ASSIST you with INTEGRATION of your IntelliStations.com system with your professional production equipment.

If you have questions while building your dream system, you can call us 24x7x365 at 1-800-501-0184 for assistance from one of our IntelliStations.com DCC specialists. Ask about our no money down and creative financing programs.

Check out CGchannel.com, our content provider for 3D reviews, demos, and more!

discreet™

SONY Authorized Professional Reseller

IntelliStation® is a registered trademark of International Business Machines Corporation. Intellistations.com is a division of WSI | Multimedia. IntelliStations.com is an Authorized IBM Business partner and is in no other way associated with International Business Machines Corporation. Windows, Window 95, Windows NT, the Windows NT logo, NetMeeting, and Internet Explorer are trademarks or registered trademarks of Microsoft Corporation. Intel, Pentium, LANDesk and MMX are trademarks or registered trademarks of Intel Corporation. Other company, product, and service names may be trademarks, registered trademarks, or service trademarks of their respective owners. PCs shown here, excluding servers, ship with an operating system unless otherwise indicated.

Publishing the
Voices that Matter
in a World of
3D Technology

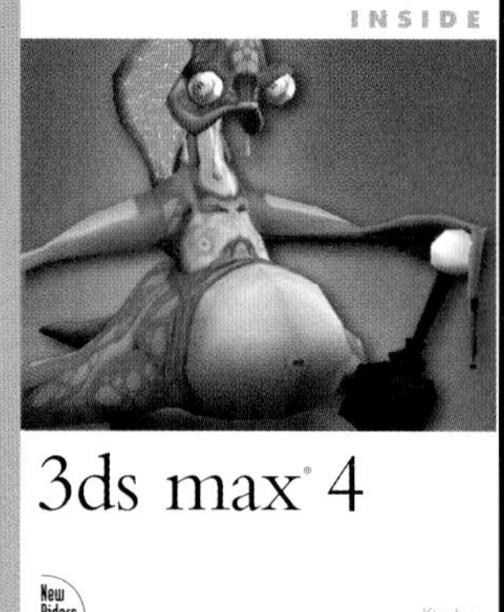

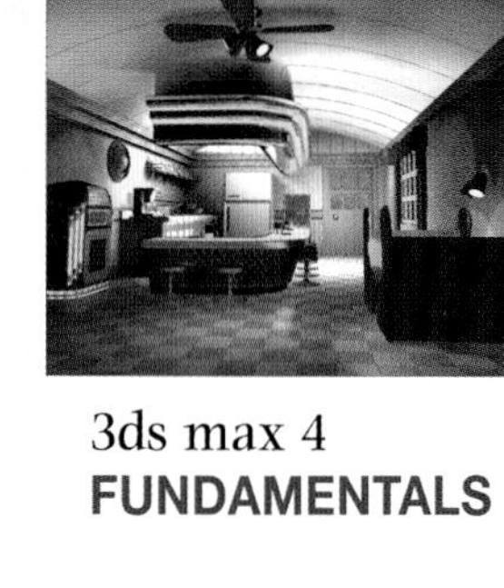

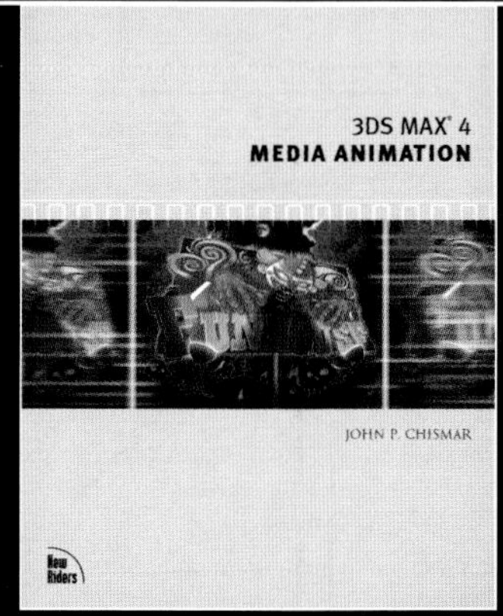

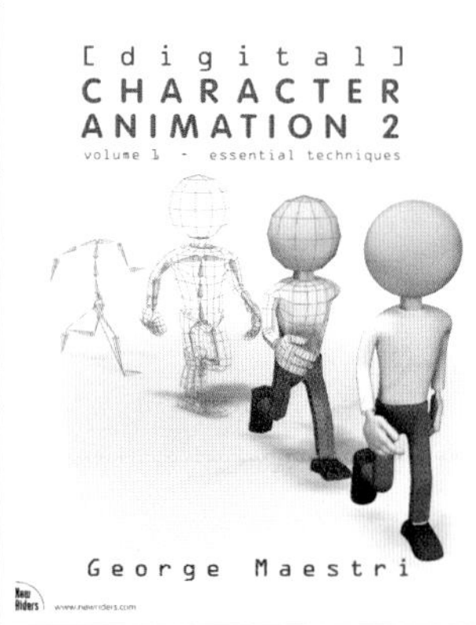

Inside 3ds max 4
Kim Lee
ISBN: 0735710945
$49.99

3ds max 4 Magic
Sean Bonney
ISBN: 0735710937
$45.00

3ds max 4 Media Animation
John Chismar
ISBN: 0735710597
$49.99

3ds max 4 Fundamentals
Ted Boardman
ISBN: 073571066X
$39.99

[digital] Lighting & Rendering
Jeremy Birn
ISBN: 1562059548
$50.00

[digital] Texturing & Painting
Owen Demers
ISBN: 0735709181
$50.00

[digital] Character Animation 2
George Maestri
ISBN: 1562059300
$50.00

www.newriders.com

Solutions from experts you know and trust.

www.informit.com

OPERATING SYSTEMS

WEB DEVELOPMENT

PROGRAMMING

NETWORKING

CERTIFICATION

AND MORE...

Expert Access.
Free Content.

New Riders has partnered with **InformIT.com** to bring technical information to your desktop. Drawing on New Riders authors and reviewers to provide additional information on topics you're interested in, **InformIT.com** has free, in-depth information you won't find anywhere else.

- Master the skills you need, when you need them
- Call on resources from some of the best minds in the industry
- Get answers when you need them, using InformIT's comprehensive library or live experts online
- Go above and beyond what you find in New Riders books, extending your knowledge

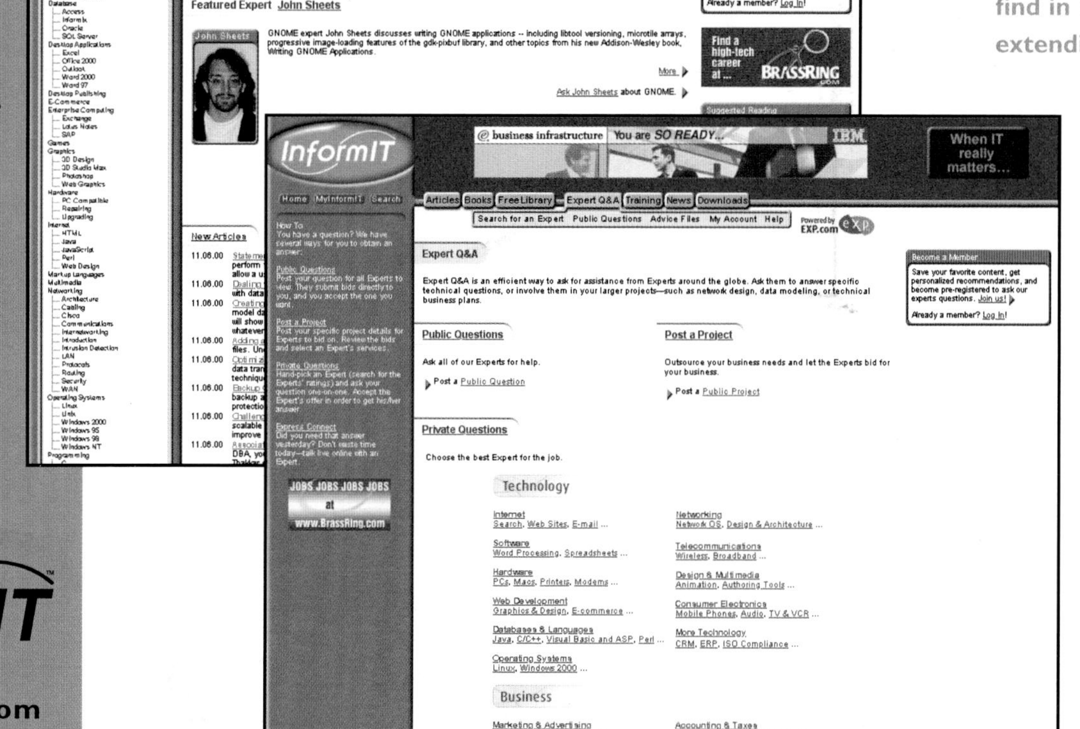

As an **InformIT** partner, **New Riders** has shared the wisdom and knowledge of our authors with you online. Visit **InformIT.com** to see what you're missing.

www.informit.com

www.newriders.com

The 3ds max 4 Magic CD

The CD that accompanies this book contains valuable resources for anyone using 3ds max 4, not the least of which are:

- **Project files:** The starting project files and completed example files provided by the authors enable you to work through the step-by-step projects.
- **3ds max 4-related third-party software:** Many valuable plug-ins and programs are included, such as Ultimate MAX Internet Guide, Forrest Pack Lite, Solidify, and Texporter. (For a full list of the included third-party software, please see Appendix A, "What's on the CD-ROM.")
- **Bonus chapters:** Five bonus projects, ranging from complete projects to expanded material for existing projects, are included on the CD.

Note: For a complete list of the CD-ROM contents, please see the Appendix, "What's on the CD-ROM."

Accessing the Project Files from the CD

The majority of projects in this book use pre-built 3ds max 4 files that contain preset parameters, artwork, audio, or other important information you need to work through and build the final project.

All the project files are conveniently located in the CD's Examples directory. To access the project files for the "Rope Swing" project (Project 5), for example, locate the following directory on the accompanying CD: Examples\Chap05.

We recommend that you copy the project files to your hard drive, but this is not absolutely necessary if you don't intend to save the project files.

Colophon

3ds max 4 Magic was laid out and produced with the help of Microsoft Word, Adobe Acrobat, Adobe Photoshop, Collage Complete, and QuarkXpress on a variety of systems, including a Macintosh G4. With the exception of pages that were printed out for proofreading, all files—text, images, and project files—were transferred via email or FTP and edited onscreen.

All body text was set in the Bergamo family. All headings, figure captions, and cover text were set in the Imago family. The Symbol and Sean's Symbol typefaces were used throughout for special symbols and bullets.

3ds max 4 Magic was printed on 60# Mead Web Dull paper at GAC (Graphic Arts Center) in Indianapolis, IN. Prepress consisted of PostScript computer-to-plate technology (filmless process). The cover was printed on 12-pt. Carolina, coated on one side.